THE HOGGS OF TEXAS

THE HOGGS
OF TEXAS

Letters and Memoirs of an Extraordinary Family,
1887–1906

Edited by

VIRGINIA BERNHARD

Texas State Historical Association
Denton

Library of Congress Cataloging-in-Publication Data
Bernhard, Virginia, 1937–
The Hoggs of Texas: letters and memoirs of an extraordinary family 1887–1906 /
Virginia Bernhard.
  Includes bibliographical references.
  ISBN 978-1-62511-001-5
1. Hogg family. 2. Hogg family—Correspondence. 3. Hogg, James
Stephen, 1851–1906—Family. 4. Texas--Biography. 5. Texas—Politics and
government—1865–1950. I. Title.
F385.B458 2013
929.20973—dc23
                                        2013036570

Contents

Acknowledgments

A S A HISTORIAN who specializes in seventeenth-century Virginia and Bermuda, I never imagined I would spend so much time with Ima Hogg in nineteenth- and twentieth-century Texas. My interest in her grew after I took my students to visit Bayou Bend, the house she filled with early American antiques and gave to the Museum of Fine Arts, Houston. My *Ima Hogg: The Governor's Daughter* (1984, 3rd ed., Denton: Texas State Historical Association, 2011) was the inspiration for this book. Ima herself selected and edited some Hogg family letters as a present for her brothers, and these letters whetted my appetite for more. I proposed this project to two friends who also happened to be distinguished Texas historians, Cary Wintz and the late Archie McDonald. They were enthusiastic, and my first thanks goes to them.

I also thank Kate Kirkland, who took time from her own research to answer my Hogg questions, and Margaret Lawler, who supplied me with some Hogg family stories. Lee Pryor lent me a photograph and his enthusiastic support. Carl Cunningham served as graphics advisor. Friends too numerous to name listened to endless anecdotes about the Hoggs. My Austin friends Pat Heard, Rosi and Harrison Wagner, and Pat Kruppa and Jimmie Savage provided encouragement, ideas, and hospitality. And thanks to Gambrill Wagner for deciphering a word that puzzled us all.

At Rice University's Woodson Research Center, Lee Pecht, Philip Montgomery, and the center's staff were most helpful. My profound thanks to Brenda Gunn, Margaret Schlankey, Roy Hinojosa, Arne Glazier, Kathryn Kenefick, Isaac Benavidez, Sarah Traugott, Zack Vowell, and the rest of the staff at the Dolph Briscoe Center for American History at the University of Texas at Austin and to Lorraine Stuart, Amy Mobley, and others at the archives of the Museum of Fine Arts, Houston. I am grateful to the staffs of the Houston Metropolitan Research Center and the Clayton Library Center for Genealogical Research. Thanks also to my University of Saint Thomas colleagues in the History Department, to Jim Piccininni and the Reverend George Hosko and the staff at Doherty Library, and to the Reverend Ted Baenziger, Brooke Deely, and UST's Women, Culture and Society program. Thanks also to Megan Cooney at the Texas State Library and Archives.

At the Texas State Historical Association, my special thanks to Ryan Schumacher, Mike Campbell, to the readers of my manuscript, and to my copyeditor, Bonnie Lovell.

My husband, Jim Bernhard, my research assistant, advisor, and editor, now knows more about the Hoggs than he cares to know. He also knows that I could not have done this without him.

Introduction

ALL THAT MOST PEOPLE KNOW about the Hogg family of Texas is that they had a daughter named Ima. But there is much more to their story. The Hoggs—the larger-than-life James Stephen (he stood six feet three inches and weighed nearly three hundred pounds), governor of Texas from 1890 to 1894; his petite wife, Sarah (Sallie) Stinson Hogg, who died tragically of tuberculosis in 1895; his children, Will, Ima, Mike, and Tom—were a picturesque and legendary family.

The Hoggs' public history and their remarkable dedication to public service can be found in a handful of books, but their private history, for the most part, has remained as they left it—unpublished—in letters and a memoir that Ima Hogg was working on at the time of her death in 1975.

In many ways the Hogg family's history reflects the larger history of families in late nineteenth- and early twentieth-century America. The Hoggs lived in a time when butter was churned by hand and babies were born at home. Most drinking water came from wells, and indoor plumbing was rare. Lamps burned kerosene, or "coal oil," which was dangerously flammable. Bacteria were a newfangled notion, and the origins of diseases such as diphtheria, typhoid, and tuberculosis were still mysterious. Children attended school only a few months a year, and universities were for an elite few. The Civil War and the end of slavery were fresh memories. Racial segregation was the norm, and the N-word was in common usage. People traveled by horse and buggy, and paved streets were few. General stores sold "dry goods," flour came in cloth sacks, and lard in barrels. Ready-to-wear clothing was a novelty, and people who could afford it had their clothes made by seamstresses and tailors—if they could not, they made their clothes at home. Most Texans lived in rural areas and made their living by farming, and many of those who had moved to towns could still remember how to milk a cow and birth a foal. But momentous changes in everyday lives were on the way.

In the 1880s, railroad tracks were spreading like a giant steel web across the land, and by the 1900s, a forest of oil derricks had sprung up in East Texas. Both of these changes affected the Hoggs. Steam-powered trains carried goods and people, including politicians like Jim Hogg, from town to town, city to city, faster than anyone had ever imagined. Railroads were America's first giant corporations, with the oil industry close behind. For the first time, government had to weigh the interests of ordinary people against the powers of big business. Jim Hogg made his political career challenging railroads, and his family made a fortune in oil after his death. Family letters tell the story.

When Sallie and the children visited her parents in East Texas and Jim Hogg worked in Austin, newsy letters and childish notes kept them close. When Will, the eldest, went away to boarding school, his father was often too busy to write, but Sallie did her best to answer Will's pleas for a letter from home "once a week." After Sallie's death, Will reminded Ima: "Dear Sis: Please do not neglect your duty of writing them [Mike and Tom] a joint letter once a week. Don't forget to write me once in a while and your dear Daddy every day."[1] If Ima did indeed write to her father every day, many of those letters have not survived—but a treasure trove of others did. With two-cent stamps (postage rates in those days were two cents per ounce; postcards, a penny), the members of this Texas family wove a close network of affection and advice.

James Stephen Hogg also wrote to his siblings, especially his sister Martha Frances Davis. Old enough to be his mother, she was his best friend, political confidante, and frequent houseguest. He wrote to John, who was always distant, and perhaps a bit envious of his brother's success. Another sister, Julia, died the year after Sallie. There was a gaggle of nephews and nieces, some in need of money, and all in need (their uncle thought) of advice. Hogg attended to them all, making loans when he could, inviting them to board with his family in Austin, and writing lectures on industry and frugality that would make Benjamin Franklin blush.

Jim Hogg also wrote letters explaining his daughter's name: Ima Hogg. No middle name.

By the time Ima was ten years old, newspapers around the nation carried stories that Governor Hogg of Texas had daughters named Ima, Ura, and Shesa, and sons variously named Hesa, Harry, or

Moore. In 1896, a year after his wife's death, the former governor replied to an inquiry by a Chicago newspaper editor about his children's names: "I beg to advise you that the names of my children are William, Ima, Mike and Tom—three boys and one girl—whose ages are, respectively, 21, 14, 11, and 9 years. . . . The names of Ura, Hesa, Shesa, Harry, and Moore Hogg are the mythical creatures of campaigners who failed to beat me for office." Hogg went on to explain that "the name 'Ima' was given to my daughter a few days after her birth and the singular application of it to the old, well-established, name of her paternal ancestors did not occur to any one until I had entered political life."[2] But the name stories would not go away. A few years later, in 1899, Hogg told a journalist, "The truth of the matter is, that she was named by her mother. Her mother was reading a book somewhere in which one of the characters which interested her exceptionally was named Ima. About that time the little girl came along, and she was named Ima. We never noticed the play of her name until it was called to our attention."[3]

That was not true. The name "Hogg" itself had long elicited jokes—as Jim Hogg well knew: His father, the stern, no-nonsense Joseph Lewis Hogg, had always been sensitive about the family surname. Riding his mule down a road in Wood County one day, he greeted a stranger approaching him on horseback and, as was the custom in those days, introduced himself: "My name is Hogg." "And my name is *Pigues*," said the other. As the story goes, Joseph Lewis Hogg dismounted from his mule in a fury and challenged the man to a fistfight. But the stranger was not making a joke: his family name was Pigues, and he lived in nearby Mineola.[4]

When young Jim Hogg worked on a newspaper in Tyler in 1870, he was "sensitive about his name and shape." Horace Chilton, one of Hogg's closest friends, remembered one afternoon when Hogg, setting type near open window, heard a man in the street outside calling "Piggie—Piggie, Sooey—Sooey" in derision of his name. Hogg responded "with such language and gesture of his burly right arm that the mimicry was not repeated at his expense."[5]

When Jim Hogg's eldest son, Will, began his schooling, he "had many fights at school because the older boys teased him about his name," so said Rose Merriman, who remembered the Hogg family from her East Texas childhood. "I have always thought," Mrs. Merriman said, "Jim Hogg named his only daughter Ima just to show he was not bothered in the least about his unusual name."[6]

But that daughter herself had another explanation: In 1969, when a folk history scholar wrote to Ima Hogg to ask about her name, she answered in a gracious letter, explaining that her father had named her for the heroine of a Civil War poem written by his beloved eldest brother.[7]

Fiercely protective of her father's reputation, Ima Hogg wanted others to think of him as highly as she did. She saw to it that his letters (some carefully censored) were transcribed and bound. The result was 150 volumes of correspondence covering his terms as attorney general and governor, through his death in 1906. In 1951 she oversaw the publication of a volume of her father's speeches and state papers, and she worked closely with historian Robert C. Cotner on his 1959 biography of Hogg.[8] And Ima Hogg herself edited a collection of family letters. At Christmas 1935, she gave Mike and Tom (Will had died in 1930) each a bound volume, "Family Letters," with their initials in gold on the cover. A selection of these letters is published here for the first time. With them are other family letters culled from the Ima Hogg papers in Austin and Houston. Connecting the letters are parts of Ima Hogg's memoirs: her recollections of life in the Governor's Mansion, visits to her grandparents' country home in East Texas, student days at the University of Texas, and the history of her family. She was working on this project when she died in 1975.[9]

In 1974, at age ninety-two, reading family letters, Ima Hogg wrote: "Reading the letters opened a floodgate of memories long dormant while my attention had been devoted to other matters. Now the same compulsion which had led me into various fields of endeavor has been irresistible. The past haunts me. I feel as if I were entering upon a dangerous expedition leading me into unexplored paths not without pitfalls."[10]

In the memoirs, as in the letters Ima Hogg chose and edited, there is an idealized portrait of the family as she wished it to be—but perhaps not as it was. The Hogg family, like all families, was far from perfect. Hogg's frequent travels were hard on his wife. Sallie's years of illness cast a pall over the household. Will and his father were not close. Mike and Tom did poorly in school. Hogg's sister, Martha Frances, "Aunt Fannie," was a domestic tyrant. The letters in this volume, poignant and funny, wise and loving, show the Hoggs as a real family. Their tensions and disappointments, as well their achievements, were shaped by the rapid changes in their world as Texas and the nation entered the twentieth century.

Note on Sources

Of the letters in this volume, most are typescript copies of originals. Some of the manuscript letters are in the Ima Hogg Papers and the James Stephen Hogg Papers at the Dolph Briscoe Center for American History at the University of Texas at Austin and in the Hogg collections in the archives of the Museum of Fine Arts, Houston. The original letterpress volumes of J. S. Hogg's correspondence as attorney general and governor are in the Texas State Library in Austin. Beginning in the 1930s, Ima Hogg had photostatic copies made, resulting in 150 bound volumes of materials dating from 1836 to Hogg's death in 1906. She donated sets of these to various Texas libraries, including the Woodson Research Center at Rice University.

In this book, the adults' letters, spelling, and punctuation have been corrected for clarity. Ellipses indicate omitted passages with extraneous materials—names and obscure references, for example, that do not advance the narrative of the family's history. Brackets and italics indicate passages deleted from typescripts. Ima Hogg was a careful censor. To save her brothers' feelings, and to protect her father's political reputation, she chose to exclude some parts of the family letters when she had them transcribed. In many cases, the original letters have not been located. The children's letters are presented as their authors wrote them, with no corrections.

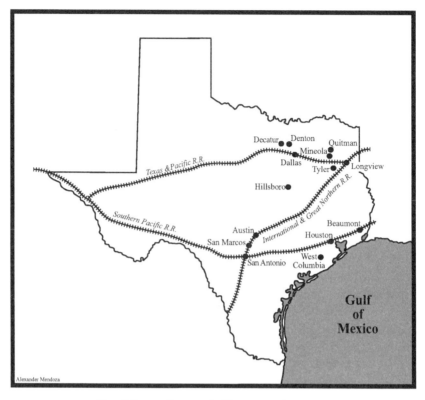

THE HOGG FAMILY'S TEXAS, 1887–1906

The Hogg Family: Three Generations

JOSEPH LEWIS HOGG (1806–1862) m. LUCANDA McMATH HOGG
(1806–1863)

MARTHA FRANCES HOGG (1834–1920)
m. William Brownlee Davis
Children   Daniel Davis*
             William Brownlee Davis Jr.

* Infant, deceased.

JULIA ANN HOGG (1839–1896)
m. William Wallace McDugald
Children   Joseph Lewis McDugald
                 James McDugald
m. Henry Clay Ferguson
Children   William Brownlee Ferguson
                 Bismarck Ferguson

THOMAS ELISHA HOGG (1842–1880)
m. Anna Eliza McMath
Children   Lucanda Hogg
                 Hermilla Hogg
                 Francis Baylor Hogg
                 Ethel Hogg
                 Annie Hogg

JOSEPH LEWIS HOGG, JR. (1845–1848)

JOHN WASHINGTON HOGG (1848–1912)
m. Eva Dorinda Renshaw
Children   Joseph Lewis Hogg*
                 Velma Hogg
                 Maud Hogg
                 Eugenia Hogg

JAMES STEPHEN HOGG (1851–1906)
m. Sarah Ann Stinson (1854–1895)
Children   William Clifford Hogg (1875–1930)
                 Ima Hogg (1882–1975)
                 Michael Hogg (1885–1941)
                 Thomas Elisha Hogg (1887–1949)

JOSEPH LEWIS HOGG JR. (1854-1872)

RICHARD HOGG (1856–1863)

---

* Infant, deceased.

List of Illustrations

Following page 134

1. Sarah (Sallie) Stinson Hogg and James Stephen Hogg, ca. 1875. *The Ima Hogg Papers, di_08340, the Dolph Briscoe Center for American History, the University of Texas at Austin.*
2. James Stephen Hogg and Ima Hogg, ca. 1883. *The Ima Hogg Papers, di_08341, the Dolph Briscoe Center for American History, the University of Texas at Austin.*
3. The Governor's Mansion, ca. 1890. *Courtesy of Texas State Library & Archives Commission.*
4. Ima Hogg, 1892. *The Ima Hogg Papers, di_08339, the Dolph Briscoe Center for American History, the University of Texas at Austin.*
5. Governor J. S. Hogg and Family, 1894. *Courtesy The Museum of Fine Arts, Houston.*
6. Tom, Will, and Mike Hogg, ca. 1896. *The Ima Hogg Papers, di_08337, the Dolph Briscoe Center for American History, the University of Texas at Austin.*
7. Tom, Ima, and Mike, 1903. *The Ima Hogg Papers, di_05908, the Dolph Briscoe Center for American History, the University of Texas at Austin.*
8. The Varner-Hogg Plantation, 1907. *The Ima Hogg Papers, di_08338, the Dolph Briscoe Center for American History, the University of Texas at Austin.*

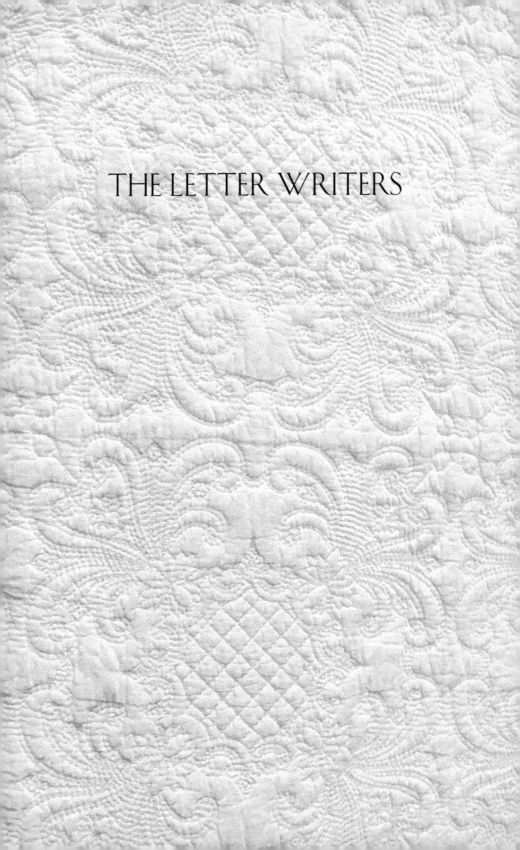

THE LETTER WRITERS

The Governor and His Family

JAMES STEPHEN HOGG (1851–1906)

Born and raised on a 2,500-acre plantation called Mountain Home, James Stephen Hogg learned how to cope with sorrow and poverty before he was twenty. His father, General Joseph Lewis Hogg Sr., left Mountain Home, in Cherokee County, Texas, to fight in the Civil War and died in Mississippi in 1862. Jim Hogg's mother, Lucanda McMath Hogg, and his youngest brother, Richard, age six, both died a year later. Left behind were six siblings: Martha Frances, a young widow of twenty-eight; Julia Ann, twenty-four; Thomas Elisha, twenty-one, away at war, John Washington, age fifteen; James Stephen, twelve; and Joseph Lewis Jr., nine. Like many a Southern family after the Civil War, the Hoggs found themselves with no slaves and no money. (Part of their old plantation is now a park called the Jim Hogg Historic Site.)

In 1867, at age sixteen, with little formal schooling, Jim Hogg found work as a typesetter on the *Texas Observer* in Rusk, Texas, two miles from his home. The next year he took a job on the *Quitman Clipper* in the small town of Quitman, more than seventy miles away in Wood County. After working briefly for the *Palestine Advocate* and the *Cleburne Chronicle,* he tried sharecropping, but received only ten dollars for six months' work. He used that money to attend a private school in Quitman for a term. (A petite, brown-haired girl named Sallie Stinson at that school would one day become his wife.) In 1869, Jim Hogg and his brother John leased a patch of farmland in Wood County, but that venture did not last long: Jim was shot in the back by a vengeful outlaw whom he had crossed. He nearly died.

While he recuperated, Jim Hogg thought about what he wanted to do with his life. In the 1870s Texas was still part of the "Wild West," where outlaws prowled and Indians raided, but it was also a land where dreams might come true with hard work. Jim Hogg dreamed of becoming a lawyer. In those days young men read law, usually under the tutelage of a seasoned lawyer, until they felt ready to pass the state bar exam. Hogg moved to Tyler, a thriving East Texas town, found work on the *Tyler Democrat-Reporter*, and studied borrowed law books. In 1871, when the Southern Pacific Railroad laid out a town called Longview in nearby Gregg County, young Jim Hogg quickly moved there and started his own newspaper, the *Longview News*. He was twenty years old. In the 1870s as Reconstruction ended, there was plenty of news for a newspaper to print: Heady talk of railroads and business opportunities and the political future of Texas could be heard on every corner. But Longview was a rough, saloon-filled railroad town, and in 1872 Hogg moved his newspaper to Quitman and named it the *Quitman News.*

At age twenty-two, Jim Hogg won his first election: justice of the peace in Wood County—whose county seat is Quitman.

At age twenty-three, he married Sarah Ann (Sallie) Stinson.

At age twenty-four, he passed the bar exam and was admitted to practice law in the state of Texas.

At age twenty-five, he entered the race to represent the Twenty-Second District (Kaufman, Rains, Van Zandt, and Wood Counties) in the Texas legislature—but he did not win. It was the only political race he ever lost.

At age twenty-seven, he was elected county attorney of Wood County.

At age twenty-nine, he was elected district attorney for the old Texas Seventh District, with headquarters in Tyler.

In 1886, at age thirty-five, he was elected attorney general of the state of Texas.

In 1890, after two terms as attorney general, Jim Hogg, age thirty-nine, was elected governor of Texas. By then Jim and Sallie had four children: Will, age fifteen, Ima, eight, Mike, five, and Tom, three.

Jim Hogg, the first Texas-born governor of his state, served two terms with a dedication to reform and a determination to succeed as large as his portly frame. He set out to harness the railroads and corporations that were operating in Texas and make them subject to state regulations. The Railroad Commission, established in 1891, was his proudest achievement. A masterly politician and a charismatic speaker, he became a force to reckon with in state and national politics. One historian called him the "last people's governor of Texas— perhaps the only one."[1]

In 1901, former governor Hogg got in on the first Texas oil boom at Spindletop, near Beaumont. He became one of the founders of the Texas Company, later known as Texaco. Always occupied with business and politics, Hogg was never too busy to attend to his family: his children, his siblings, his nieces and nephews. Until his death from heart failure at age fifty-five in 1906, Jim Hogg was a family man. He is buried, along with his wife and their four children, in Austin's Oakwood Cemetery.[2]

Sarah Ann (Sallie) Stinson Hogg (1854–1895)

Born in Georgia in 1854, Sallie came to Texas in 1868 with her two brothers, John and James, and their widowed father, a former Confederate colonel named James Alexander Stinson. He soon married again and prospered as the owner of a large plantation with a gristmill and sawmill at a little settlement called Speer, about eleven miles from Quitman in Wood County. He sent his daughter to a private school in Quitman in 1869. There, at age fourteen, she met an impecunious but well-spoken eighteen-year-old named Jim Hogg. He was taking a "short course" at the school with the money he had made from sharecropping. After that the two young people parted ways, as Sallie continued her schooling and Jim went off to seek his fortune.[3]

Five years later, as an ambitious young justice of the peace in Wood County, Jim Hogg began courting Sallie Stinson. She was then nineteen; he was twenty-three. Colonel Stinson did not look with favor on this courtship. He wanted Sallie to finish her education, and perhaps to find a more prosperous suitor. But Sallie persuaded her father otherwise, and a wedding date was set. She and her stepmother hurriedly sewed her trousseau on a neighbor's new sewing machine, the only one in Wood County.[4] Sarah Ann Stinson and James Stephen Hogg were married in the Stinson parlor on April 22, 1874. (In 1974, Ima Hogg had the Stinson house moved to Quitman, to what is now a park called the Governor Hogg Shrine Historic Site.[5]) The newlyweds set up housekeeping in a small four-room house on the Gilmer road near Quitman.

On January 31, 1875, the Hoggs' first child, a boy named William Clifford (both names were in Sallie's family), was born.

On July 10, 1882, Sallie gave birth to a daughter named Ima (a name chosen by James Stephen Hogg).

On October 28, 1885, Michael Hogg was born. Like his sister, he had no middle name.

On August 20, 1887, the Hoggs' fourth child, Thomas Elisha (named for Jim Hogg's late brother, Thomas Elisha) was born.

On January 20, 1891, Sallie, along with Will and Ima, saw Jim Hogg sworn in as governor of Texas.

In the summer of 1895, Sallie was diagnosed with what was then a dreaded disease: tuberculosis. She died on September 21, 1895, her husband and children at her bedside. She was forty-one years old. She is buried in Austin.[6]

WILLIAM CLIFFORD (WILL) HOGG (1875–1930)

Born in the small town of Quitman, the eldest son of Jim and Sallie Hogg spent his adolescent years in the Governor's Mansion in Austin and at a private school in Omen, Texas. His letters are those of a studious, serious-minded young man. Much closer to his mother than he was to his father, Will briefly attended Southwestern University in Georgetown (1892–1893). He took a year off from his studies to work at the Southwestern Insane Asylum in San Antonio, a new state institution that had opened its doors in 1892. In 1894 he entered the University of Texas, where he earned his law degree in 1897. That year he moved to San Antonio, where he practiced law somewhat unsuccessfully until 1902. He then joined his father's Austin law firm, but in 1905 he moved to St. Louis to take a position with the Mercantile Trust Company.

After his father's death in 1906, Will returned to Houston to practice law and manage the family finances. Mercurially hot-tempered, he could be dictatorial and overbearing. Will worried about money: Jim Hogg had sold his interest in the Texas Oil and Fuel Company (later Texaco) and he was not a rich man when he died. But he believed that his beloved Varner plantation had oil under it, and he told Ima, "Don't ever let Will sell this plantation. We have oil here."[7] He left instructions not to sell the Varner land in Brazoria County for at least fifteen years after his death. In 1917—eleven years after Hogg's death—the first big oil well came in at Varner. Other wells soon followed, and the family's financial worries were over. By 1921 their land was producing millions of barrels a year.

Governor Hogg's eldest son chose business over politics as a career (although he played a large role in the impeachment of Texas Governor Jim Ferguson in 1916), and when oil made him and his siblings independently wealthy, Will Hogg devoted much of his time and money to philanthropic causes. The University of Texas, his alma mater, was high on his list, as were the Museum of Fine Arts, Houston; the Girl Scouts; the YWCA; the Boy Scouts; and various civic projects for Houston, including Memorial Park and the development of River Oaks, where in 1929 he and Ima built a mansion called Bayou Bend, now part of the Museum of Fine Arts, Houston.

Will never married, but he enjoyed living well, with a Park Avenue apartment in Manhattan and a ranch in Mexico to amuse him when he tired of Texas. He collected the paintings and sculpture of the western artist Frederick Remington, and it was Will who interested Ima

in the collection of early American art and antiques. Vacationing in
Europe in 1930, Will suffered a gall bladder attack and died after
surgery in Baden-Baden, Germany, on September 12, 1930. Ima was
by his side. He was fifty-five years old—the same age as his father at
his death. He is buried in Austin.[8]

IMA HOGG (1882–1975)

M iss Ima, as she came to be known, was born in Mineola, Texas,
in 1882. Jim and Sallie Hogg's only daughter was given a name
that would lend itself to legend, humor, and on at least one occasion,
a crossword puzzle clue in *The New York Times*. Ima grew up as
the petted daughter of a public figure who idolized her, and the feeling was mutual. She became her father's best friend and companion
after Sallie Hogg's death, but he did not dictate her life. After she
attended the University of Texas from 1899 to 1901, she went off
to study music in New York. She planned to become a concert pianist. Ima's photographs at the turn of the century (she was eighteen
in 1900) show a slender, pretty young woman, sometimes with an
impish smile, sometimes with a pensive look. She loved horses and
dogs and hunting and fishing as well as dances and parties. More than
one young man was in love with her.[9]

When Jim Hogg was injured in a train accident in 1905, Ima aban-
doned her music studies to care for him. On the morning of March 3,
1906, when she went to his room to wake him, she found her father
dead of heart failure. For many months afterward she was not herself. Modern mental health experts would say she was suffering from
depression. By the time she was twenty-three, Ima Hogg had stood at
the deathbeds of both parents. But she found solace in her music, and
in June 1907 she sailed for Europe to travel and study piano in Berlin.
She stayed abroad for almost two years.

She attended concerts and operas; she went sleigh riding. Ima
Hogg never married (perhaps because her Aunt Fannie told her that
she would be a carrier of tuberculosis) but she may have had a serious romance in Germany.[10] Her brother Tom wrote to her there in
the spring of 1908, begging her for the "secret" she promised to tell
him "one of these days." Whatever the secret was, in 1909 she came
home to Houston and taught piano to a select group of pupils. In
1910 she and her brother Mike sailed to Europe, traveling in England
and Germany. On Ima's return, she decided that Houston needed a
symphony orchestra, and she began a project that created the Houston Symphony in 1913.[11]

In the summer of 1914 she returned to Germany, arriving just in time for the outbreak of World War I in August. She did not come back to Houston until October. In the summer of 1918, when Germany was losing the war, Ima Hogg's depression returned. Had she lost someone she loved? No one knows. But it would be three years before she was well again. For much of that time she was under the care of physicians in Philadelphia and New York. Her brother Will encouraged her to find a new interest, and with his encouragement Ima began to collect American antiques. She had given up the idea of becoming a concert pianist, and collecting furniture and art soon became her passion.

In 1966 her River Oaks mansion, Bayou Bend, at 2940 Lazy Lane, became the American decorative arts wing of the Museum of Fine Arts, Houston. Along the way, she had founded the Houston Child Guidance Center (1929), established the Hogg Foundation for Mental Health (1940), served a term on the Houston School Board (1943), and won national awards for her historic preservation projects in Texas. Among these were her grandfather Stinson's house, the Varner-Hogg plantation house in West Columbia, and several antebellum structures at Round Top. She also continued her support of the Houston Symphony, serving as its president from 1946 to 1956.

In later years she kept a pace that would have daunted a person half her age. Always elegantly dressed, she graced Houston's social and artistic scene like the grande dame she was. Her father would have been proud.

Ima Hogg died on August 19, 1975, from complications after a taxi accident in London. She was ninety-three years old. She is buried in Austin.

MICHAEL (MIKE) HOGG (1885–1941)

Closest in age to Ima was Mike, three years her junior. He was born in Tyler, but spent much of his boyhood in Austin. After their mother's death in 1895, Mike and Tom attended boarding schools in Texas and New Jersey. Like Will, Mike chose the University of Texas and its law school, finally earning his law degree in 1911. Will once described him as "not particularly studious," but "fairly aggressive and industrious."[12] After their father's death in 1906, Mike helped Will manage the family finances, and when World War I came, Mike served his country, was commissioned as a lieutenant, and rose to a captain's rank. He saw action at Saint-Mihiel and the Meuse-Argonne Forest. Wounded in the fall of 1918, he wrote to Will: "My wound was nothing at all. I got a slight clip in the neck. Hardly a sign of it."[13] Mike returned home to Houston in April 1919. He and his brother Will shared the sumptuous offices of "Hogg Brothers, Inc." atop the eight-story Hogg Building at 401 Louisiana Street in downtown Houston.

In the spring of 1927, when he was forty-two years old, Mike decided to follow his father's footsteps into politics. When a seat on the Texas legislature became vacant, he ran in the special election and won. Many people still remembered Jim Hogg and readily voted for his son. Mike Hogg served two terms in the legislature and won a reputation as the foe of big business interests and the defender of the "little people" his father always championed. Mike often punctuated his speeches with "By golly!" just as his father had used "By gatlins!" Jim Hogg would have been proud.

Mike lived with Will and Ima at Bayou Bend until, at age forty-four, Mike Hogg married a woman no one in his family knew. Much to the surprise of his siblings, Mike Hogg and an attractive Dallas divorcee, Alice Nicholson Fraser, were wed in Galveston on July 20, 1929.[14] By 1931 the couple was living in Houston's River Oaks, in an elegant mansion next door to Bayou Bend. Alice and Ima, sisters-in-law, became good friends, and worked together on various civic projects, especially the River Oaks Garden Club. But Mike became ill with cancer in 1938, and after a two-year struggle, he died at his Houston home on October 10, 1941, just short of his fifty-sixth birthday. He is buried in Austin.[15]

Thomas Elisha (Tom) Hogg (1887–1949)

The youngest of the four Hogg children, Tom was the only one born in Austin. He was eight when his mother died, and he did not do well at boarding school. But his father described him as "that thoughtful, big-hearted, letter-writing boy."[16] Tom left the Lawrenceville School in Lawrenceville, New Jersey, in December 1904, after a severe case of pneumonia. He later worked as a ranch hand on a ranch near Kerrville, and in 1905 spent some time at Colorado College in Colorado Springs, Colorado.

Tom evidently suffered from periodic depressions and wrestled with a drinking problem. In July of 1906, the summer after Jim Hogg's death, Will wrote to Ima, "I do not know what to suggest with reference to Tom." Their youngest brother was then under a doctor's care in Mineral Wells, Texas. A year later he joined the U.S. Marines and wrote to Will that he "had not drawn so much as a glass of beer" since he left home. But trouble with his eyes forced him to leave the military in 1909.[17] For a time he lived in Houston with Will and Ima.

On July 10, 1912, when Tom was twenty-five, he and Marie Willett, age twenty-one, were married in Tyler. The couple lived for a time at Varner, the Hoggs' country home in Brazoria County. Then they moved to Colorado, where Tom worked in the advertising department of the *Denver Post*. In 1917 he registered for the draft in World War I, but was not eligible because of eye problems. He and Marie moved back to Tyler by 1920, and then to San Antonio by 1921. There they built a lavish house, and Tom began raising registered saddle horses on a farm he named Varner Hills. Will advised him to curb his "Rolls Royce vanities." Tom enjoyed spending his share of the family's oil money, but he also wanted to care for others: he wrote to Will of the need to provide for their aging Aunt Lillie, as "the only surviving relative of our mother."[18]

In the 1930s Tom and Marie moved to a ranch near Kerrville, Texas, and later to Tucson, Arizona. A worried Mike Hogg wrote to Ima about Tom and Marie: "I don't know which of them is the worst problem." By 1938 the couple was living apart. Tom was ill and in Baltimore, Maryland, and Marie was living the life of a socialite in San Antonio.[19] In 1939 the couple was divorced. In 1940 Tom was in Colorado, recovering from an unnamed illness. On May 21, 1942, Tom married Margaret Wells. The couple settled in Yuma, Arizona. Margaret wrote to Ima that Tom was "really a different person and I am going to try to keep him that way." From the summer of 1942 until Tom's death in 1949, Ima and Margaret and Tom exchanged letters and visits.[20]

Thomas Elisha Hogg died of heart failure at age sixty-one in Yuma on March 8, 1949. He is buried in Austin.[21]

Jim Hogg's Brothers and Sisters

MARTHA FRANCES HOGG DAVIS (1834–1920)

Born in 1834 at Mountain Home, Martha Frances was the eldest of the seven children of Joseph and Lucanda Hogg. In 1850, at age fifteen, Martha Frances married William Brownlee Davis, eighteen years older than she. Davis and her father had practiced law together. Their first child, a son, Daniel, was born in 1850 and died at birth. Another son, William Brownlee Davis Jr., was born in 1852—the year that William Davis Sr. died of tuberculosis. Widowed at seventeen, Martha Frances had more grief to bear: In 1862 her father, General Joseph Lewis Hogg Sr., and Major James Barker, the man she had hoped to marry, both died in the Civil War. The next year brought more sadness with the deaths of her youngest brother, Richard, and her mother, Lucanda Hogg.

At age twenty-nine, "Sister Frank," as they called her, comforted the orphaned siblings still at Mountain Home—Julia, John, Jim, and Joseph. Martha Frances would live out her life as a widow, and she was always a devoted sister—especially to Jim Hogg. Old enough to be his mother, she would always be his best friend and confidante.

Intelligent, strong-willed, and opinionated, Martha Frances Hogg Davis divided her visiting time among her siblings and their families: John in Decatur, Julia in Denton, and Jim in Austin. When her son William married in 1879 and began his medical practice, she visited him and his wife, Sara Frances (Fannie), their daughter, Pearl, and their son, Marion, in Grapevine, Texas, and then in Pueblo, Colorado. Sallie Hogg went to Pueblo hoping to find a cure for her tuberculosis in 1895, but it was too late. After Sallie's death, Martha Frances moved to Austin to help care for the motherless Hogg children. But the sixty-one-year-old "Aunt Fannie," as the children called her, found the constant commotion in the Hogg household (three children, ages thirteen, ten, and eight and a menagerie of pets) unnerving. Will, twenty, was busy with his studies at the University of Texas, and Jim Hogg decided to send his younger children off to boarding school.

Aunt Fannie continued to visit Jim and the children in Austin and to live with them from time to time. When she was not with them, she wrote them long, effusive letters. In her last years she lived with her son William in San Diego.

Martha Frances Hogg Davis died in 1920, at age eighty-five.[22]

Julia Ann Hogg McDugald Ferguson (1839–1896)

Jim Hogg's other sister, Julia Ann, was born at Mountain Home in 1839. Twelve years older than Jim, Julia lived at home until the end of the Civil War, helping her sister Martha Frances care for the younger children and waiting for her fiancé, William Wallace McDugald, to come home from the war. In 1865 he and Julia married, and he set up his medical practice in Rusk, Texas. It was Dr. McDugald who treated Jim Hogg's gunshot wound in 1869. Julia and William had two sons, Joseph Lewis, born in 1865, and James, born in 1870. William McDugald died not long after that, and in 1873 Julia married

Henry Clay Ferguson, an attorney seven years younger than she. The couple lived for a time in Decatur, where Julia's brother John and his family lived on a ranch outside the town. Julia and her second husband had two sons, William Brownlee, born in 1874, and Bismarck, born in 1876. Later the family, which also included Julia's two older sons, moved to Denton, where Julia's eldest brother, Thomas Elisha, and his family lived. In 1888 Julia's eldest son, Joseph Lewis McDugald, age twenty-three, was killed in Tyler, Texas.[23]

Julia and her youngest brother, James Stephen Hogg, corresponded faithfully, and her husband, H. C. Ferguson, helped Hogg in his political campaigns. Sallie and the Hogg children visited Julia and her family in Denton, and Julia's children spent time in Austin.

When Sallie died in the summer of 1895, Jim Hogg poured out his grief in a mournful letter to Julia. Julia herself died a few months later, on February 22, 1896.[24]

Jim Hogg remained close to Julia's family, writing regularly to her husband and to her sons as they grew to adulthood.

THOMAS ELISHA HOGG (1842–1880)

The eldest son of Joseph and Lucanda Hogg, Thomas Elisha was born at Mountain Home in 1842. He was nineteen when the Civil War broke out, and he left Weatherford College to enlist in the Confederate Army. In 1862, when his father died in the war, Tom took up his role as head of the Hogg family. He mustered out of the army as a captain in Lane's Brigade, Texas Division, C.S.A. On July 16, 1866, he married his Mississippi cousin, Anna Eliza McMath. The newlyweds settled at Mountain Home, a plantation much diminished by the war. Tom was now the guardian of his two younger brothers, James Stephen, fifteen, and Joseph Lewis, twelve. He began to study law, and to earn money in the meantime he started a small school at Rusk. By 1870 he and Anna had two young daughters, Lucanda and Hermilla. Young Jim Hogg, living with them, was learning the printer's trade at the *Texas Observer* in Rusk. His brother Tom soon joined him in the newspaper business, buying another Rusk newspaper, the *Cherokee Advertiser*.

There was sadness in the Hogg family in 1872 when the youngest surviving brother, Joseph Lewis, died at age eighteen, In 1873 Tom Hogg wrote "The Fate of Marvin," an epic Civil War poem with a heroine named "Ima." (That is one of several stories about how Ima Hogg got her name.) In 1875 there was celebration when Tom Hogg and his brother Jim were both admitted to practice law before the

Texas bar. Tom moved his family to Denton, Texas, where he soon had a thriving law practice and by 1876 was a county judge. In 1880 Tom Hogg contracted typhoid fever on a business trip to Dallas, and died on September 29, 1880. He was only thirty-seven years old. He left his widow, Anna, and five young children: Lucanda, twelve; Hermilla, eleven; Baylor, eight; Ethel, six; and Annie, three.[25]

As the years passed Jim Hogg helped to look after Tom's wife and children. Anna died in 1892. She had already lost two daughters: Ethel, who died in 1889, and Lucanda, who died in 1891. Annie, the youngest, died in 1900. Jim Hogg was an attentive uncle to the surviving children, Hermilla and Baylor, as they grew up and had families of their own.

JOHN WASHINGTON HOGG (1848–1912)

Jim Hogg's other older brother was born four years before him, at Mountain Home. John shared a hardscrabble life with young Jim after the Civil War, but in 1870, as Jim decided to go into the newspaper business, John decided to leave East Texas. He moved to Wise County, at the edge of the Texas frontier. Indians still threatened pioneer settlements in northern Texas, and in July 1870 John joined the U.S. Cavalry in a battle against the Kiowa Indians at the Little Wichita River. He fought with distinction and was later recognized by the Texas legislature for his service.

In 1872 John married Eva Dorinda Renshaw, the daughter of a prominent physician in Decatur. With land inherited from Eva's family, the couple established a ranch, where they lived for nearly twenty years. The town of Decatur grew from 579 in 1880 to 1,746 in 1890, and in 1891 John moved his family into town. In 1892 he was appointed postmaster there. The couple had four children: Joseph Lewis, born in 1875, died that year; their three daughters—Velma, born in 1877; Maud, born in 1882; and Eugenia, born in 1884—lived to adulthood.

Like his brother Jim, John Hogg took an interest in politics. He was elected tax assessor of Wise County in 1876, sheriff in 1878, and county clerk in 1880. A history of Wise County described him thus: "Personally, Mr. Hogg is a man of heavy stature; he is a man of strong intellect and decided view; he has served three terms as an alderman of Decatur and had taken a patriotic interest in the material affairs of the town. His mental qualities are commanding, much above the average, and had his environment been different [he] would doubtless have adorned places of eminence in emulation of the career of his distinguished lamented brother, Governor James S. Hogg, whom he pronouncedly resembles in the forceful qualities of his intellect and character."[26]

Jim Hogg often wrote to John, begging him to come and visit, or go fishing, or join a vacation trip, offering to pay all expenses. John almost always refused. But Jim's children—Ima and her brothers— and John's older children—Velma and Maud—often traveled by train between Decatur and Austin.

John Washington Hogg died in 1912 at age sixty-four.

PART I
THE HAPPY FAMILY
1887–1892

IN 1890, AFTER TWO TERMS AS ATTORNEY GENERAL, Jim Hogg, age thirty-nine, was elected governor of Texas. By then Jim and Sallie had four children—Will, age fifteen; Ima, eight; Mike, five; and Tom, three—to move into the Governor's Mansion. It would be their home for the next four years. They filled the grand antebellum house with music and laughter, sing-alongs, and stately receptions, entertaining an endless procession of relatives and visitors. As one guest recalled, "I don't think any family ever lived in the Mansion who had as much fun as Governor Hogg and his family."[1] The good times, however, were clouded by Sallie Hogg's delicate health. She would die of tuberculosis in 1895.

When Attorney General Hogg and his family first moved to Austin in 1887, they found a bustling town with a population of nearly 15,000. State politics was its main business. Dallas, with 38,000 people by 1890, was Texas's largest city, but to Jim and Sallie and their children, who had grown up in rural East Texas, Austin was impressive. The city had thirty mule-drawn streetcars clacking along on ten miles of track. Streets were not paved, but many were lit by gas lamps. By the time the Hoggs left the Governor's Mansion in 1895, Austin was replete with urban amenities: electric streetcars since 1891, and an underground sewage system, waterworks, and electric lights. It was still a small city in those days, with its grid of streets laid out between Shoal Creek and Waller Creek, bounded by the Colorado River to the south and Fifteenth Street to the north. There were gentle hills and an abundance of trees—live oak and cottonwood, pecan and walnut. (Before his death in 1906, Hogg requested that a pecan tree and a walnut tree be planted on his grave.)[2]

The first railroad, the Houston and Texas Central Railway, had come to Austin in 1871, and the International-Great Northern came in 1876. Since then two other railroads, the Austin and Northwestern Railroad and the Missouri Pacific Railway, connected Texas to cities in the Midwest and Northeast. Austin passengers could go by train (at speeds of thirty miles an hour) to St. Louis, Chicago, Philadelphia, New York, and Boston, with journeys eased by Pullman sleeper cars and dining car buffets. "Two Days Between Texas and New York," as one railroad advertised.[3] As governor, Jim Hogg harnessed the power of the railroads operating in Texas, but as a passenger he enjoyed their convenience. So did the rest of his family.

The Hoggs also enjoyed Austin's cultural life. There was the Millett Opera House, where touring companies performed everything from *Macbeth* to *Il Trovatore*. There were music teachers who gave a precocious Ima Hogg piano lessons. And there was the University of Texas (UT). It had opened its doors on September 15, 1883, with 13 faculty members and 218 students, and graduated its first class of 32 seniors on June 15, 1887. Three of the Hogg children—Will, Ima, and Mike—would one day call UT their alma mater.

Before he moved his family to Austin, Attorney General Hogg stayed for a time at the Avenue Hotel at 717 Congress Avenue, three blocks from the Capitol grounds. A few blocks away on Sixth Street, a cattle baron named Jesse Lincoln Driskill had just built a grand sixty-room hotel. (Years later former governor Hogg would occupy a suite there, and one day the Driskill would have a suite named for him.) Hogg settled at Mrs. M. L. Andrews's boarding house at 1010 Lavaca, just across the street from the white-columned Governor's Mansion. He could watch the construction of the new state Capitol, second in size only to the national Capitol. Built of Texas red granite, towering more than three hundred feet in height, it would not be finished until the spring of 1888. Meanwhile, Hogg worked in the old Land Office Building, which had stood since 1857 at the edge of the Capitol grounds near Eleventh and Brazos. There he may have encountered a draftsman named William Sydney Porter who worked in the Land Office from 1887 to 1891 and was better known after 1899 as a writer named O. Henry.[4]

Jim Hogg was also a writer—of letters. In the midst of his work to establish the Railroad Commission and his hard-fought campaigns for governor in 1890 and 1892, he wrote regularly and frequently to Sallie and the children when they were apart, to his two sisters and his brother, to his eldest brother's widow, and to various nieces and nephews. To James Stephen Hogg, orphaned at age twelve, family ties were almost—but not quite—as important as political connections.

It was in the winter of 1887, while Sallie and the children were still in Tyler, that J. S. Hogg (as he usually signed himself) began writing to them. This letter to twelve-year-old Will, like many letters to follow, is a mixture of fatherly praise and advice seasoned with political news and familial affection.

January 29, 1887
Master W. C. Hogg,
Tyler, Texas.

My Dear Son:
  I was greatly pleased with your letter. Your very noble purpose
for not visiting Austin with your mother was very gratifying to me
and no doubt raised you high in the estimation of your teacher. . . .
Your strict adherence to such principles will be certain to make you
a great and good man.
  I should like to have you see the Legislature while it is in session. As it will not adjourn until April no doubt you will get to see
it. Austin is in many respects a nice and pleasant place, but I much
prefer Tyler to it. The Senatorial race is up and is creating intense
interest. Yesterday the vote stood: Maxey—30; Reagan—54; Ireland
33 votes. As it takes 89 votes to elect, neither of the Candidates are
likely to get the requisite number for a long time. So the Legislature is
"dead-locked" so called. They began voting last Tuesday and today
is Saturday with no immediate prospects of election. The current
opinion is that a "Dark Horse" will be elected.* Your Ma can tell
you what this kind of a being is in politics. I shall try to visit home
next Saturday. Give kisses and love to Mama, Auntie and Sister and
Mike; and tell Hettie and little Ima "howdy." Be a good boy.
                                            Your Papa
                                            J. S. Hogg[5]

"Auntie" was Martha Frances Hogg Davis, Hogg's widowed
eldest sister, fifty-three, who divided her time among various relatives. Hettie was the Hogg family cook; little Ima was her daughter.
The other Ima, Jim Hogg's daughter, remembered them years later:
"Father thought she [Hettie] was the greatest cook anywhere. She
was devoted to the family and her first and only child, a little girl, was
named after me. Little colored Ima was born in Tyler shortly after we
moved there and was a privileged character in our family."[6]

---

* Until an amendment to the U.S. Constitution in 1913, state legislators, not voters,
elected U.S. senators. The winner of the 1887 race for the U.S. Senate in Texas was
not a dark horse, as Hogg predicted, but the candidate he favored: John H. Reagan,
then a U.S. congressman. He defeated Samuel Bell Maxey, the two-term incumbent,
and John Ireland, a former Texas governor. Reagan served in the Senate until 1891,
when Governor Hogg persuaded him to head the new Texas Railroad Commission.

As Attorney General Hogg took up the duties of his new office, Sallie and the children left Tyler in February 1887 for a visit with her father, former Confederate Colonel James Alexander Stinson, and his family on their plantation near Speer, a small community (now no longer in existence) near Mineola in East Texas. Will left school to go along with Ima, then age five, and Mike, age two, for the visit to their grandparents. It was winter, but children's schooling in the nineteenth century was somewhat erratic. Texas law required only four months of mandatory school attendance, because many families needed their children as farmhands. (Governor Hogg would see this law changed to six months.)

From Austin, on February 17, the busy attorney general wrote to his wife, two hundred miles away:

> Dear Sallie:
>   This morning I got up early, got my breakfast at 8 o'clock and now "have time" to write to you and "the babes." We are all quite well, and hard at work. . . . I would give anything to see you all. Tell the children I think of them every day, and as often wish to see Mike in his prattling, toddling ways; Ima in her dancing and antics and Willie in his manly demeanor and "book investigations"—and Sister admiring Mike's growth and beauty.
>   You did well in your arrangements at Tyler, and everything is satisfactory.
>   Enjoy yourself in every way possible; make your stay at your Pa's to suit yourself, and write me often. Love to all.
>   Your Affectionate Husband
>   J. S. Hogg.[7]

Attorney General Hogg was indeed hard at work. His position furnished him with two assistants and one clerk, but he wrote most of his documents and letters by hand. As his daughter, Ima, remembered, "There was no carbon paper for duplication. The many copies were made by a long outmoded letter press."[8]

Sallie, though she may not yet have been certain and probably had not told her husband, was then a month pregnant. Later that spring she and the children would move to their new home in Austin. The house at 500 West Fourteenth Street was in a neighborhood of spacious residences on the west side of the city. Like other Austin homes in those days, it had no running water, but its grounds had room for horses, milk cows, and other livestock. Ima later remembered that

Austin in those days looked "like a little farming village" because "nearly everyone owned cows as well as horses." At the house on Fourteenth Street, the Hogg family "always had a cow and a horse and carriage and a little goat and some dogs."[9]

In the Hoggs' case the livestock included (so the story goes) the cow that came with them from Tyler: "Mr. Hogg had a very beautiful Jersey heifer that through some mishap, had lost a horn. When he was selected Attorney General in 1886 and the family was preparing to move to Austin, his friends urged him to sell the cow. Mr. Hogg, however, could not stand the idea of selling her to the butcher, and when the family moved to Austin the cow went along, too."[10]

For Sallie, there was daunting work to be done: settling into a new house, two active young children to look after, and the arrival of a new baby to prepare for. Years later, Ima recorded her memories of her mother as she coped with the pressures and pleasures of being the wife of a public official:

> Mother was quite small, about five feet, two inches tall, and never weighed over 108 pounds. Her distinguishing feature, everyone said, was her tiny, beautifully formed hands. Her little feet never gave her enough support for I remember her complaining of them after standing any time. She had dark brown hair, gray eyes, and fair skin with little color. Without being a beauty, her even features gave her a sweet and refined appearance.
>
> I do not know what all the things were which influenced my mother's taste but she was well prepared to be the wife of any public man except that she was very reticent and modest and, also, physically not strong. She was of a very artistic temperament, exceedingly fastidious, well read and accomplished in all the arts of homemaking. She must have had some executive ability for our house ran smoothly and rather lavishly for our means. We seemed to have everything that we could desire though we knew that we should not ask for much spending money.
>
> I can look back upon many small economies which she practiced. . . . Buttons on our clothes were always taken off to be used on the next garments; even hooks and eyes and bones were removed from old dresses.
>
> Somewhere mother learned to be an exquisite needlewoman. She always had ready a piece of embroidery, or hand work, which she could take up while talking with visitors. It was the style when I was a child for little girls to wear white aprons over gingham and woolen

dresses and my aprons were the most exquisite hand-made creations
made of finest muslin, dimity or swiss with rolled and hand-whipped
ruffles edged with real lace trimming or eyelet embroidery. She did
not always make these herself but she would have felt disgraced if I
had worn anything made on a machine. . . .

I often wonder now how she managed on my father's small
salary.* There were no extravagances outside of the household but
my mother always had a few very fine gowns made each year. . . .
Mother would have been happy to make her own dresses had she
had the time but, of course, she did not. She spent much time over-
seeing the work of a seamstress who came into the house to make
the boys' shirts, my clothes, and perhaps some of her housedresses.

I have been trying to remember what Mother's first reception
dress was like. . . . I remember we thought it was very beautiful
and I am still confused as to whether it was black taffeta with large
orchid brocaded figures outlined with some kind of tinsel and beads
or whether it was orchid color with orchid brocade on it. I know we
all went into ecstasies over her appearance, especially brother Will.[11]

It was Will, the eldest of the Hogg children, who no doubt helped
his mother with some of the difficulties of moving into a house in
Austin that hot summer. Attorney General Hogg, consumed by the
demands of his office, spent long hours at work. He did find time to
compose a long letter to his fifteen-year-old nephew, Baylor Hogg,
in Denton. The boy was the only son of Jim Hogg's late brother,
Thomas Elisha, who had died in 1880. Thomas's widow, Anna, lived
in Denton with Baylor and her four daughters, Lucanda, nineteen;
Hermilla, eighteen; Ethel, thirteen; and Annie, ten. Jim Hogg did his
best to be a father figure to these children, especially Baylor, who
had written to him hoping for a position in Austin. Unfortunately
there was no job available. His Uncle Jim wrote kindly, if bookishly:
"Upon the subject of your inquiry of the 14h inst., you are advised,
that the Legislature will not again meet for two years, except in case
the Govr. calls special session; in which event I will notify you in
ample time so as to give you an opportunity to strike for the place you
desire. . . . Impatience is always to be avoided as productive of unrest
and instability; while a well guarded desire and ambition to improve
your opportunities and situation is in every respect commendable,

* The attorney general of Texas made $2,000 per year; the governor, $4,000. A
dollar then was worth about twenty of today's dollars.

and without which no man can succeed."[12] Jim Hogg was ever the dispenser of how-to-succeed advice.

On August 20, 1887, Sallie gave birth to the Hoggs' fourth child, Thomas Elisha. It was apparently a difficult birth, and there were complications. Children were born at home in those days, and the nature of Sallie's condition is not recorded. The birth may have left her with pelvic injuries (Tom was a large baby), or she may have had childbed fever, a malady still prevalent in the late nineteenth century, when sanitation was primitive and the role of bacteria in infections was not widely known.

As Ima recalled Tom's arrival: "Mother was very ill after he came and it was not long before he began to pine. For a long time nothing could be found to agree with him. Finally the doctor recommended a negro wet nurse and it was necessary for a time to keep him most of the time in her house. She was a remarkable negro woman. Her little house was clean as a pin and she also had a strong baby boy who nursed along with Tom."[13] Tom was breastfed until he was a year old.

Sallie's frail condition, the care of the new baby, and the burdens of the attorney general's office kept Jim Hogg and his family close to Austin, and family letters and travels were few the year after Tom's birth. They began again in the summer of 1888. That was the summer that Jim Hogg's nephew, Joseph Lewis McDugald, age twenty-three, the eldest son of Hogg's sister Julia, was shot and killed in Tyler. The shooting occurred on Saturday, August 4. On August 9, Jim Hogg wrote a letter of condolence to Julia:

Dear Sister—
In your sad moments of distress over the tragic death of Lewis, I feel that it is impossible for me to do more than to express my grief in common with yours. As I left Tyler Saturday night, perhaps an hour before the fatal occurrence I met Lewis and talked with him. He appeared in good spirits and was certainly acting the part of an upright gentleman. During the day before I met him a time or two and most favorably impressed with his gentlemanly bearing. Enroute to Austin I heard of his murder, too late to return. On getting here I wrote Dr. Hicks and sent him a mite for Lewis's relief if such should be possible. He wrote me the particulars, which taken with what Mr. Gus Taylor wrote me leads me to the unquestionable belief that he was killed without cause. I should have gone to his side but from the news I received I knew it could only be to attend his funeral. To do this in the condition that the trip had left me

really was a peril I felt that prudence as well as yourself would not demand or expect of me. I am now feeling clear of the threatened bilious attack and shall visit you at my earliest opportunity—perhaps sometime next week. Tell Mr. Ferguson to take no action towards prosecuting Lewis's assassin until I see or write to him. I wish to look into the matter with him.

We are all well and join in love and condolence to you.

On that same day Hogg wrote his son, Will, who was spending the summer with the Stinsons in Speer.

> My Dear Son—
> By to-day's Express we had "Bill" to send your saddle in care of Mr. Bruce. Your mama could hardly understand what a boy wants with such a thing as a saddle when his breeches have no patches in them, and again she was somewhat afraid you would soil it or wear it out. This I knew better about for I was a boy once myself—she was not! So on a family conference we all agreed to risk you with it, even if you did have good "pants." We trust you and feel sure all things will be safe. Bring it back with you. We are all well, but lonesome without you. Tom is walking—running—around generally.
> Love to all the folks.
> Your Father,
> J. S. Hogg[14]

The "Express" was the train from Austin to Mineola, where S. R. Bruce, a family friend, would then deliver Will's obviously expensive saddle to him at Speer, fifteen miles away. Three days later thirteen-year-old Will received what seemed to him alarming news about his baby brother, and he wrote at once to Sallie in Austin:

> August 12, 1888
> Dear Mother:
> Do please write and tell me all about Tom getting hurt and how he got hurt and who hurt him and what limb is broken and is there much danger of it being fatal. I am so distressed about it, and I feel like I could make it hot for the niger that hurt him . . . . Give me a whole letter on Toms getting hurt if you dont I am coming home and see him. When I got your letter I felt like I could kill a few nigers for Tom. I guess Papa kicked about it and I dont blame him one bit. For all you know he may be injured for life. Tell Papa to have

Dr. Wooten* to look into the matter and examine it, and if Tom is injured for life it wont be good for those nigers if they are to blame, and I advise you to take Tom away from them.

Kiss Tom 1000 times for me, and all consider yourself kissed. Mike Ima and Papa have my love. Tell Papa to write and also you and Mr. Oliver† and that very soon.

Aff'

Your Son

W. C. H.[15]

Young Will used the N-word freely in this letter—a usage repugnant to modern sensibilities but common in his own day, as was the use of the lower case in "negro." In the late 1880s slavery was barely a generation gone, and racial segregation ruled. In her memoir, Ima recalled that "Texas between then and the early nineties was still restless after the Civil War—with some remnants of lawlessness. There was tension between the races. . . . the scars remained a long time."[16] In Texas, African Americans made up nearly one-fourth of the population.

Tom's injury was evidently not serious. At the time it happened, his father was preoccupied with the state Democratic Party convention in Dallas, where he was nominated by acclamation for another term as attorney general on August 15.[17] He did not mention Tom's injury when he wrote to his sister Martha Frances a few weeks later. In this same letter he glossed over Sallie's serious illness after Tom's birth, claiming that she had "been sick but little" since they moved to Austin. Jim Hogg was always optimistic, even to Martha Frances.

Sept. 16, 1888

Dear Sister—

We are all in good health. For more than a month Willie has been at his grandfather's—Mr. Stinson's in Wood County—where he begs to stay during the winter to study the "stock business" as he expects to embark in that enterprise when he gets grown, <u>as he says</u>. The probability is that we will send him two years to the Omen High School in Smith County. He is quite well advanced now, but hardly

---

* Dr. Thomas D. Wooten was the Hoggs' family physician and was later president of the Board of Regents of the University of Texas.

† Henry Oliver was Jim Hogg's stenographer and confidential clerk.

enough to quit school for any special training even in the business it
seems he has his heart set on. It is possible his inclination to become
a "Knight of the Range" or "Boss of the Herd" has been the result
of his profound admiration for his two Uncle Johns. That he has
distaste for the "professions" is hardly to be doubted. This has been
produced by his witnessing the struggles to which I have been driven
for success. It is not my intention to try to change his natural inclination, but shall only give him a fine education so that he may push
nature to its highest degree of success in its line of growth.

Sallie has been sick but little since we came here, and looks like an
eighteen year old girl. She has many friends among all classes here—
especially with her neighbors. Ima is going to school and is learning rapidly. As a natural born musician she has but few equals. Her
eyes are entirely well, and she has a constitution like her "daddy."
Mike has not been sick since you left, but is the same delicate, pale
faced, white-headed, "tube rose" that marched around practicing
the instincts of a gentleman last year. Without doubt he is a natural born gentleman, without a single dirty spot in his nature. Every
one loves him immediately on seeing him. Tom is a "blunderbuss"
on John's style. He is larger than Mike, and is very much affected
by "negro ways." His black mammy still nurses him, though he is
running around and jabbering. Since she took him he has not had a
moment's sickness. All in all he is a fine boy. . . . Sallie has been wanting to wean him, but has not done so on my account. In October she
will take him with the other children to her father's where she will
remain a month, during which time it is probable I shall be in Washington attending the U.S. Supreme Court. . . .[18]

By force of circumstances over which it seems I had no control
I was renominated [for attorney general] and perhaps will have to
remain here two years more. I am indeed sick of public life, but it
looks as if I will either have to stay now in harness for the next term
or go out "under fire," which is out of the question. Am more than
gratified, really, at the situation, as it is only the will of the people in
endorsement of my official course. Truly the endorsement is flattering and gratifying, but I crave the quiet and independence of private
life, which I am going to enjoy at the end of my next term in spite of
all Combinations that may take place to prevent it. . . .

I would be highly flattered to have John and his family visit us
while we are in Austin. I know he would enjoy it and have no cause
ever to regret it. If you can do so persuade him into coming down
this Winter. If you tell him I am anxious he will then <u>certainly</u> not

come. Velma and Maud are said to be fine girls, and I am anxious to see them. Love to Eva and the family.

Your Bro.[19]

Jim Hogg's oldest sister Martha Frances was his best friend, but his older brother, John, was never close to him. Jim never gave up inviting him to visit, but he never came. John and his wife had had three daughters, Velma, eleven; Maud, eight; and Eugenia, four. John preferred to stay on his ranch outside Decatur, with his family. As his brother wrote to a cousin, he "rarely ever leaves there even for the nearest town."[20]

From her proud father's letter, it appears that Ima, age five, was already showing her talent at the piano. Her study of music had begun under her mother's tutelage: "Mother had some musical training and, I believe, some talent. Her hands were very small and flexible. Later she did not play so much but my earliest recollection is of her nimble fingers playing from the classical sonatas and semi-popular works of the day. She guided my early musical training and, looking back upon it I realize that she had had some very sound training herself."[21]

"Sister Frank" was always frank—whether about family or politics. She was quick to answer her brother's letter of September 16, writing him on September 22. (See the Note on Sources, p. xiii, for meaning of italicized material.)

Dear James:

I proceed this morning, bright & early, before I get off on some other tangent, to do what I had proposed to do soon, when I received yours. First and foremost—I am delighted to learn of the final cure of Ima's eyes, though I had expected her to grow out of it sooner or later.

Don't tell me a word about gentleman Mike. I know him to be as perfect as inborn manhood can make a boy. Naturally refined from babyhood he must be innately a gentleman always.

Flattering? I should say it was, for a man who has knocked the bottom out of things right and left. But I was sorry you had to accept [the nomination for a second term as attorney general] for you'll now go on and on: and finally settle down a poor man I fear. I don't believe you'll ever get out of it. It looks like, it, I am sure; and I know you'll have no mouth for refusing the United States Senate. That's about where you'll land. I shouldn't be surprised at anything—even President (when the South is allowed one). I'm not joking. . . .

John laughed his lazy laugh when he read your invitation to come to Austin on a visit. He is a queer boy,—cock of the walk here, but out of his sphere it seems to me.

Eva is a noble woman, a lady from instinct, good as gold always. They have another girl—a beautiful girl too. John's children are all nice, smart girls—No sardines, rest assured, and he and Eva mean to educate them well. Velma is at Denton at school. She and Maud are well advanced. Maud is seven years and reads like a woman in any book. She is rather a prodigy, and very beautiful.

Will Sallie take Tom with her or leave him with his black-mammy? Poor little Sallie. I grieved for her in the death of bright, rosy, healthy looking Cliff. It was a sad disappointment to them all I know.

Take care of your health and write occasionally to—
"Frank"[22]

Sallie's half-sister, Clifford "Cliffie" Stinson, had died suddenly of "black jaundice," as it was called then. It is known now as leptospirosis, a bacterial infection of the liver carried by rats.

Will Hogg was still with the Stinsons at the time, and his father wrote to him on September 27:

> My Dear Son—
> The distress inflicted on us by the news of Cliffie's death has been deep and heavy. I was at Tyler this week when I first heard it, and wrote to your Mama. She has been in bed ever since but is now improving. I got home this morning and think she will soon be up. Poor Cliffie. No better girl ever lived, but her place in heaven is in every way above any here. We are also pained to hear of Uncle John's death, but his health had been so bad that we were more prepared to hear of it.—Do your full duty by our afflicted kin, my boy, and lend as much comfort to them as possible—All others here are well. . . .[23]

The "Uncle John" in this letter was Sallie's brother, not Jim Hogg's. Cliffie's death made an impression on six-year-old Ima. As she recalled: "The earliest tragedy in our family that I can remember was when Aunt Clifford died of black jaundice. We were not there when she died. She was reported as being very beautiful and a gifted musician, and was cherished by the whole family."[24]

Sallie Hogg had evidently taken to her bed at the news of Cliffie's death. She was very attached to Cliffie, and had given her eldest son the middle name, "Clifford," for her half-sister.

The Stinson household was a large one. As Ima remembered:

> Grandfather had five children, my mother and two sons by his first marriage: John the oldest, Mother, and James. Mother was five years old when her mother died. Grandfather's second wife was a widow with children. . . . Grandfather's second wife died young and his third marriage was to the grandmother we loved and knew so well. By her he had two daughters, Lillie and Clifford.[25]

Ima had fond memories of Lillie, her mother's surviving half-sister:

> Aunt Lillie made a great companion of me and she used to love to ride on her horse with me behind her. Sometimes I was permitted to ride on a very gentle horse along with her. She paid many calls this way and took me to see people who lived in much the same fashion that Grandfather did. Aunt Lillie was a fair musician and I believe, taught piano. I do not know where she had been trained but she seemed to know a great deal about the theory of music. She and I would play duets on the piano and we were always learning something new.[26]

Ima, who had celebrated her sixth birthday in July 1888, was now old enough to write letters—a habit her doting father encouraged. In November she wrote to Hogg's sister Julia in Denton, and her father enclosed it with a note:

> Dear Sister—
> Ima's letter herein enclosed to you is a sample of her recent progress at school. It is her own work throughout, and is naturally to you. For fear you would not receive it if it went alone, I take occasion also to write you. She has been remarkably well up to yesterday when she was taken with cold, but promises to get up soon. All others are in good health. Tom is by odds the finest, largest boy of his age in the City. Sister Frances promises to come down this winter and I trust you will be here at the same time. I am so pressed with work that I cannot write often.
> Your Bro.,
> J. S. Hogg[27]

Ima's letter to Julia has not been located. Her cold, like her eye problems mentioned in letters two months earlier, may have been the result of diphtheria. As she remembered:

> Before we moved to Austin I had diphtheria which left me a very frail child for quite a long time, and I was susceptible to bad head colds and ear troubles. I had some trouble with my eyes after this illness, also.[28]

Ima was fortunate in her recovery. Diphtheria could be a killer. The bacteria that cause this infectious childhood disease were not identified until the 1880s, and there was no vaccine until the 1920s.

Ima's father soon wrote another letter to Denton, this one to Julia's son, Bismarck Ferguson, age twelve, a year younger than Will:

My Dear Nephew—

During my absence in Washington last October [on the Supreme Court case mentioned earlier] and since, my private letters have accumulated fast, and have been necessarily laid aside in order that pressing work of a public nature should receive attention. While holding office I reverse a common rule and attend to "public duties first." So your nice and very welcome letter found place along with many others of a personal character.

I was really surprised that you could write and compose so well. Really you have improved splendidly, and will in a short time be up with grown boys in an educational way. Willie has improved very well, but I fear he is going to let you distance him. If you do so I shall feel prouder of you than otherwise. I am almost confident that you can beat Brownlee [Bismarck's brother, two years older] now, although he is a very smart boy. Tell him he will have to "hump himself."

Herein find $1 postal note with which you will please me to subscribe for yourself a nice story paper.

Give my love to all.

Your Uncle Affectionately
Jas. S. Hogg[29]

Early in January 1889, Jim Hogg wrote to his brother Tom's widow, Anna:

Jany. 3d

Dear Sister Anna—

I was glad to hear such good report of all the children. . . . You have certainly done the work of an untiring, skillful, magnificent manager for your whole family. It is unparalleled in the whole State, and some day you will even say so yourself. I have an eye on the boys [Baylor and his Denton cousins, James, Brownlee, and Bismarck] and keep posted about them. They can and will make magnificent men, and go high in life's way. Ethel must be educated in music, and I trust to have the privilege of paying her tuition, on the terms of her and my agreement. If she complies with it, I certainly shall. You did exactly as I wish by sending the first bill, and I cheerfully hand you a p.o. order for $6.65 payable to her, to cover the amount. Continue to send them to me as they are due. I wish you to send her and all the children down in the spring and at a leisure time come yourself. With love to yourself, family and all others,

I am Your Bro.

James[30]

That January Jim Hogg also sent family news to Sallie's father, Colonel Stinson: "We are all up and quite well except Mike. He is thin, delicate and disposed to be feverish, but toddles around. Tom is especially tough and healthy. Sallie, Willie and Ima are in their usual good health. It's not my fault they do not visit you. Sallie just dreads the long trip alone, and I cannot leave."[31]

In early March, Sallie and Ima and the two younger boys finally made the trip from Austin to Speer. Will was then attending school in Austin. Speer was also known as Stinson's Mill, for the large sawmill that Sallie's father owned. He had built his spacious two-story house there in 1869 from pine and oak grown on the place. The Hogg children always looked forward with great anticipation to their visits to Sallie's family home. The journey itself was a treat, at least as Ima remembered it, and the visit, with its idyllic pleasures of country life, even better:

We would start out early in the morning on the train from Austin with a big basket lunch and go as far as Troup, Texas, where I think, we changed trains for Mineola. This seemed to take a very long time. We would spend the night in Mineola with some friends, either at the home of the Bruces or the Gileses. If the weather permitted, Grandfather sent a hack drawn by the "clay bank," now called "palomino" horses to town and early in the morning we set forth for his farm, which was fifteen miles from Mineola. We crossed many creeks and sloughs and the water was apt to be high. . . . Many times the rivers or creeks were so swollen the water would be over the shaky board bridges. It was frightening because it seemed impassable, unless the driver was familiar with the location. It took until four o'clock in the afternoon after an early start to arrive at Grandfather's home.[32]

Grandfather's home was a little paradise to us. It was on the slope of a hillside which went gently down to a swift, flowing shallow creek. The house was commodious and was a lovely cool place in the summer. The premises provided for a vegetable garden filled with every variety of vegetable, an orchard which never seemed wanting of the most luscious fruits, large juicy peaches, plums and even apples and pears. There was always a large melon patch with watermelon and cantaloupe. . . . Anyone was welcome to gather the fruit. It fell to the ground and the pigs were turned in to eat what could not be gathered. Nothing delighted Grandfather more than peeling peaches and apples and splitting melons for the children to eat. He would rise in the morning at daylight at whatever hour that was, and in melon time he always had on the back porch half a watermelon split ready for each child to enjoy.

After a hearty breakfast with beaten biscuits, ham, grits, and eggs. . . . Grandfather would start to the mill with the boys at his heels. This did not seem to trouble him, but of course the boys were not long in the mill before they were out wading in the creek or running along the millrace or playing with the lambs or kids. Every year we would choose a kid or lamb as pets and probably annoyed the animal to death but it amused Grandfather to let us indulge ourselves in this way.[33]

The mill was a lumber mill, but Ima's grandfather also ran a cotton gin and a "flour and corn meal mill," as Ima described the gristmill in her memoir:

A lake a mile or so above the mills furnished the water . . . There was a race like one sees in Holland where gates were opened to make the water flow swiftly enough to run the mills.[34]

There was a great deal of life around the mill. The farmers from all the countryside would bring their wheat and corn to be ground and their cotton to be ginned. Grandfather took his pay in toil. Wagons were unloaded with oak and pine logs which were to be sawed into lumber at the lumber mill and if I am not mistaken, shingles were also made at this same place. He had also, a cane mill for making syrup and sugar. . . .

Grandfather was a man of far above medium size, about five feet, eleven inches, with white hair and white beard, and brown eyes. His skin was fair with rosy cheeks, He never seemed tired and supervised everything on his farm. He had a great many acres of farm land and had some of them tilled for himself and rented numerous other small farms out. He was always sweet-tempered and gentle and merry, and loved the children and of course, we loved him. He seemed to be a very important man because besides receiving all the products of the farmers, he seemed to be their advisor. He was also the Postmaster. Several times a week, I don't know if it was every day, the postman would arrive on horseback with bags of mail. Grandfather would unlock the little Post Office at the corner of his yard and all the country people would come in for mail.*

Grandmother Stinson seemed the next most important person on the place. She always had rheumatism but was very active in her house-keeping. . . .[35]

And she loved gardening, as Ima remembered years later.

[There were] all sorts of every variety of rose bushes, the old fashioned flower beds outlined with bricks on edge. I think some rose bushes were 6 feet high. There were moss roses and black and green roses. . . . There were bulbs, too, yellow jonquils, so fragrant. The yard was kept almost polished with brushing. There was no grass. . . .

Under the roof of one of the porches was a wonderful water well with cold spring water which was drawn up by oaken buckets. While one was being drawn up full of delicious water, the other went down. Another porch above this one had long benches where the milk crocks were full of fresh milk, mornings and evenings. Cheese cloth covered the crocks. The cream was over an inch thick and after twelve hours could be rolled off. This went into delicious biscuits and gingerbread. Of course there was a large smoke house where the rafters all hung with bacon and ham. When smoked ham was sliced and fried, the gravy was red. This was good on lye hominy and grits. . . .

---

* The Speer post office was short-lived. It opened in 1886, and by 1890 Colonel Stinson was its postmaster. The post office closed in 1896.

The ell where the dining room and kitchen were was built high off the ground. Under this was a big cellar storeroom where corn, wheat, and potatoes were stored in barrels for the winter.[36]

There were very few people in that part of the country who would take domestic employment so everyone in the household had some chores. It was always my task to sweep the porches early in the morning, and somehow this was made to seem very attractive to me, and I was encouraged to sweep thoroughly and without complaint. By nine o'clock the house was in complete order and all were ready to begin their knitting or piecing of quilts or embroidery or any other handwork. There was a quilt frame in one of the bedrooms which was easily rolled in the ceiling when not in use. Visitors often came in the afternoons and would sit around the quilt frame where there was always a quilt in the process of being quilted. I was permitted to quilt but I imagine my childish stitches later were ripped. Grandmother knitted all Grandfather's socks. I think much of the yarn was hand spun. The wool that was sheared from the sheep was cleansed and carded to be sent somewhere to be spun. Grandmother either cooked or supervised her cooking and Father thought she made the best biscuits in the world. Grandmother was of a gentle, sweet temperament and jolly. She was large so her rheumatism gave her more than usual trouble. The table was always set with extra places so that travelers could stop by and be welcome at any meal. There were usually guests. Grandfather was a pious Methodist, an elder in the church, and he brought up his children in the same way. He had come from a long line of Methodists. No meal was ever taken without his blessing. . . .[37]

While Sallie, Ima, Mike, and Tom enjoyed themselves at the Stinsons,' work and school kept Jim and Will in Austin. Jim found time to dash off a short note to his daughter:

March 7, 1889
My Dear Ima—

When I got up this morning I saw "Patti Rosa" on the little bed with her hands up, her head reclining on the pillow and her eyes set on me as if she was about to say: "Papa where are my little brothers and Sister?" Poor thing, she looked so lonesome and made me feel so! Willie has a whining "puppie" for Mike. It, the donkey, and the little negro keep up some racket, but are very quiet compared to Tom and Mike. Be a good girl.

Your Papa[38]

Ima's doll was named for Patti Rosa, a popular young singer-comedienne who toured the United States in the 1880s and 1890s. Ima remembered her well: "One of my first recollections in Tyler [where Ima lived from age two to age four] was of going . . . to hear a light opera singer named Patti Rosa."[39] Patti Rosa also played the banjo, which Ima learned to play by the time she was ten. The "little negro" was probably the child of Tom's former wet nurse, who may have worked in the Hogg household.

Sallie and the younger children spent part of the winter at Speer that year, and Ima cherished fond memories of winter as well as summer visits:

> I remember bitter weather at Grandfather's when we felt the need for warm clothes and heat. Every room had an open fireplace and depended on wood for heat. It seems to me that it was very comfortable after the fires had had time to blaze and burn. Grandfather's furniture may or may not have been beautiful, but it seemed so to me. The parlor was a very special place with an old rosewood square piano which I now have, by the way, and Victorian furniture of an earlier time. It was the style then to hook rugs and I remember the magazines which came with enticing patterns for hooked rugs. Aunt Lillie [Sallie's half sister] used to send away for these patterns and yarns with all the necessary implements to make them. People also tore up all old clothes and made strips which were sewed together into balls and which were sent out to some neighboring farmer's wife to be woven into rag carpets. The better country houses had these rag carpets woven into strips which were sewed together for their halls and other rooms with an occasional hooked rug on top. A good deal of ingenuity was used in making bright carpets with these rags. Many vegetable dyes were prepared on the kitchen stove. Elderberries were used and barks of many trees were boiled down until they were a desirable shade or color. The rags were then dipped to the color desired.[40]

With the eye of the decorative arts expert she would one day become, the young Ima noticed the Stinsons' interior decorations:

> There were many other ornaments which today, would seem hideous to us. Antimacassars [crocheted doilies] were used on the mantel pieces and the backs and arms of chairs. Grandfather and Grandmother's bedroom was where we gathered, however. There

were rocking chairs, a very beautiful mantel clock, a four-poster bed, bureau, etc. There was a guest bedroom downstairs behind the parlor and two bedrooms upstairs over the parlor and guest bedroom. The attic, which was over the grandparents' and Aunt Lizzie's* bedroom, had stacks of magazines and some kind of spinning wheel or loom and then there were some old trunks. This was a grand place on rainy days to pore over old magazines.[41]

In that winter of 1889, Jim Hogg's niece Hermilla, the eldest daughter of his late brother Tom, had a new baby, born January 8. The new baby was named Anna, after her grandmother, Anna Hogg. Hermilla also had a two-year-old daughter, Ethel, who was named for Hermilla's younger sister, Ethel.

Hermilla's husband, Robert Kelso, wrote to Hogg: "Hermilla & baby both well. Hermilla very uneasy for fear she will be as large as her Uncle James. She now tips the beam at 140 lbs."[42]

Uncle James, at nearly three hundred pounds, was indeed large: "Fat" as he called himself in the following letter.

April 13, 1889
Mess. Mills & Averill,
St. Louis, Mo.
Dear Sirs—

Please send me a variety of your best samples of Summer suits—including gray and black and wool and silk finish styles. The last you sent me for Spring are too heavy for a fat man in this hot climate. I want your <u>coolest</u> goods.

Truly,
J. S. Hogg

P.S.

It also looks like the 20% per cent you allow agents ought to be deducted from a regular customer like myself.[43]

Later that April there was sudden, tragic news from Denton: Anna Hogg's daughter, Ethel, age fifteen, had burned to death at home in a terrible accident: she had tried to light a stove with a can of kerosene. (Accidents involving the use of highly flammable kerosene to kindle fires in wood- or coal-burning stoves were common in those days.)

Ethel was musically talented, and her uncle Jim had been paying for her piano lessons.

---

* "Aunt Lizzie" Phillips was Colonel Stinson's widowed sister.

On April 24, he wrote to Martha Frances, who was in Denton at the time:

> The shock of Ethel's awful death grows worse with me as I think over the sad affair. I am whipped out. Poor Anna.
>
> When it suits you return to remain with us. You are certainly more than welcome and always make yourself 'worth your way.' Enclosed find $25—When you need more, <u>no odds when, draw on me for it</u>."
>
> I am getting well. Had a hard contest over the E.L. RR Case. The Judge has it under advisement.[44] All well.—Give love to Anna, Sis Julia and all the folks.
>
> Your Bro.,
J. S. Hogg[45]

As the summer of 1889 approached, supporters urged Hogg to run for another term, but he claimed he was not interested.

On June 1 he wrote to Martha Frances:

> My mind is quite well made up that at the end of next year my official tenure will end for many years to come. I feel that I have served the public long enough and without any undue selfishness can retire to a more pleasant, less arduous, and certainly more lucrative place in private life, and, unrestrained follow my professional pursuits.[46]

The rest of this letter is full of domestic news:

> Our cook got sick two or three weeks ago since which time we have had some trouble in that respect. Sallie as usual undertook the job and has fagged under it. She has a long, lean, water-jointed Swede woman swinging the kettles and pots about in the kitchen. She manages to mix the [biscuit] dough so it sticks well in the middle and affords a pretty fair crust on the outside. So now we get along tolerably well.[47]

Ima remembered the Swedish woman as an excellent cook:

> We lost her soon after she came for she married William Palmquist, the white gardener. They settled down to bring up a family. William was a valued servant. Then followed a colored woman cook who

had lived in New York. She was a real character and loved to impress us with her knowledge of the great city so that Broadway, Macy's big store on Fourteenth Street, Delmonico's Restaurant, and the Fifth Avenue Hotel were like places in a fairy tale.[48]

When Ima was twelve, she would live the fairy tale, visiting New York City on a tour with her father in 1894.

In the rest of his June 1 letter to Martha Frances, Jim Hogg urged her to come to Austin: At all times we should be glad to have you with us to remain at your pleasure. Any hour that you wish to light in here will be pleasant to us. I have been trying to get Sallie, and I think she is now about in the notion, to spend a few weeks or a month at different health resorts in the State. If she does this I am likely to 'batch' or swing around the circle for my own health, which is never bad. We are all well. We shall look for you right away. Tom's a 'buster,' Mike's a 'duster,' Will's a 'guster' and Ima's a whale— when it comes to sleeping late and playing the piano at odd times.[49]

Martha Frances accepted her brother's invitation and came to Austin sometime in early June. Sallie and Ima then departed for Wooten Wells, a popular resort in Central Texas, outside the small town of Bremond, about forty miles north of Bryan. Thousands of people went there to drink and bathe in the mineral waters. But for Sallie, already in frail health, getting there must have been arduous. They traveled 130 miles from Austin to Bremond by train (a trip of at least four or five hours) and then climbed aboard a mule-drawn car on a narrow-gauge railway for the three-mile run to Wooten Wells. In the heat of a Texas summer it would not have been a pleasant journey.

Back in Austin, the Hogg household was, as Jim wrote to Sallie "doing well. Tom [who would be two years old in August] is fattening very fast and is about as happy as if he had a dozen 'mammies' and sisters around him. He and Mary* and his 'Aunt Fannie' are great chums."[50]

Two days later the fond father, in the midst of preparing to argue another railroad case before the state supreme court, wrote to Sallie again:

---

* Mary was probably a servant in the Hogg household, perhaps the mother of the "little negro" mentioned earlier.

On tomorrow I shall present the I.&G.N. Case in the Sup. Court, and can then get off a few days for the Wells. Will leave to-morrow evening or next day, probably. We are all well. Tom is fattening very fast, and is the best child I ever saw—"present company" excepted. (This is for Ima, of course.)

Your Husband Affectionately

J. S. Hogg[51]

Attorney General Hogg's suit against the International-Great Northern Railroad argued that I&GN, controlled by the New York railroad tycoon Jay Gould, should move its Texas offices to Palestine, Texas. Hogg won the case.

The summer of 1889 brought demands on Hogg to enter the gubernatorial race. In August he received a rare letter from his brother John:

Aug. 3rd, 1889

Dear James:

I have been repeatedly asked by your friends lately whether you expected to be before the people for Gov. & not Knowing could not tell them. What about it? If you have any inclination in that direction let me Know, so that we can put in some hedgework. This is thought to be one of Gov. T[hrockmorton]'s strongholds. Of course what you say or write shall be Kept private. All well,

John W. Hogg

Jim Hogg's response to this letter was somewhat chilly: "The public press seem to regard me as a candidate for Governor, and it is common for my friends to write to me as such, though it is not so."[52]

James Webb Throckmorton had been governor for one year (1866–1867) during Reconstruction, and had later served in Congress. For Hogg, Throckmorton was on the wrong side, being for big business and railroad interests. Attorney General Hogg was still holding himself neutral in this contest. In August he took a brief seaside holiday and may have discussed his position with his close friends, John McCall and J. M. Robertson, while the three enjoyed a stay at the Corpus Christi Beach House, taking "daily baths in the briny deep."[53]

Although public duties, mainly his campaign against the powerful Texas Traffic Association, a conglomerate of railroad interests, consumed him, Jim Hogg kept up his family correspondence. He wrote a long letter to his sister-in-law Anna about her son Baylor's desire to attend Texas A&M:

> It has a fine reputation in all respects, and Baylor would do well there. . . . From recent reports of his industry, exemplary habits and kindly treatment of his mother and sisters, I am much cheered over the prospects of his making a most worthy, honorable and successful man. Put him on his honor in this matter. . . . At all events keep me informed as to your disposition of him, what he does, how he progresses, and what his ambition is.
>
> We have some afflictions at our house. Sallie and Sister are yet somewhat disabled but are improving from the "smash up" while out carriage riding some weeks since. Others all well.[54]

Sallie had gone carriage-riding in Austin with Martha Frances, with unfortunate results. On August 13 she sent a telegram to her traveling husband: "HORSE RAN AWAY SMASHED BUGGY WE ARE NOT HURT DO NOT NOTICE PRESS ACCOUNT." Sallie always tried to spare her husband any anxiety, but she was still feeling the effects of the accident nearly two weeks later. No doubt she welcomed the peace and quiet at home when fall came and the children started back to school. Attorney General Hogg was immersed in his work that fall and still considering the governor's race.

As late as November 1889, Jim Hogg had not yet made up his mind to run for governor. On November 9 he answered a letter from a cousin in Hillsboro whom he had not heard from in years, reporting family news and remarking about his own career: "My home is at Tyler, but I am temporarily residing here." On November 30 Hogg wrote to his brother John, "I am yet undecided about making the race for Governor next year."[55]

That day he also wrote to Lillie Stinson, Sallie's half-sister, who was about to be married on December 15:

Dear Lillie—
    Your letter of the 25th has reached me. Its announcement that you are to be married on the 15th prox. conveyed me old news in a new form, and that is what so deeply impressed me. Fifteen years ago when Sallie and I married, you were only a prattling toddler. Soon you will enter life's way under the full responsibilities of womanhood. From all reports your choice is a good one, and I for one shall most cordially welcome him into the family. Sober, honest, industrious, and endowed well by nature with splendid faculties, carefully

developed, the young man to whom you have plighted your faith and in whose hands you have committed your future, promises to go to the front along with our best men. No doubt you will do your part by him, and happiness will ever accompany the prosperity that awaits you both.

If possible, and I shall try and make it so, I shall attend your wedding.

Your brother,

J. S. Hogg[56]

He did attend the December 15 wedding, but his confidence in the marriage's success was misplaced. Lillie and her new husband were soon divorced, and Lillie remarried. Her second husband, David Burkett, was, as Ima remembered him, "a very substantial man who loved children and spoiled all of us. They came to live at Grandfather's house and Uncle Dave was a great help to Grandfather in all his many activities."[57]

Meanwhile, Sallie had already taken the younger children to Speer, possibly to help prepare for Lillie's wedding. Seven-year-old Ima wrote one of her first letters to her father:

Dec. 5, 1889
Dear papa;
    last morning we had to hav a light it was so dark. I scribele on the other side of the paper. Don't look on the other side papa. Come to Aunts wedding the 15. Ant Jennie is reading a book tonight. I went to Effie and I picked 4 pounds of cotton.* I weigh 51 pounds today. Mike weighed 33 pounds to day,
    something is a matter with Aunt Lizzies heart.
    Mamma is working on a craz work.†
    I wood like to know what you and Brother are doing.

Write soon.

your Daughter

Ima Hogg[58]

What Jim Hogg was doing in December 1889 was resisting pressure on him to run for governor. He wanted to continue his work for

---

* Ima's Aunt Jennie was a Stinson relative. Effie was most likely one of Colonel Stinson's tenants. He had fourteen houses of sharecrop workers on his 4,000-acre spread.

† Sallie was doing crazy work, the needlecraft of sewing odd bits of fabric together and then attaching them to a backing to make a crazy quilt.

railroad regulation in the state, and besides that, he said he did not want to call attention to his "threads of poverty. The honest truth is," he said, "I am too poor to hold such an office."[59]

Ima remembered her Aunt Lizzie as "quite thin and old, though I remember her also as being merry. I usually stayed in the room with her but I cannot remember much of anything she ever told me except that the bureau we both used had belonged to my great Grandmother and that some day it would be mine."[60] It may have been Aunt Lizzie who first sparked Ima's interest in antiques and historic preservation. The bureau is now in the antebellum house at Varner-Hogg Plantation Historical Site in West Columbia, Texas, which Ima Hogg restored in the 1950s.

Something else in her visits to the Stinson place left an indelible impression on young Ima:

> All around Grandfather's house were little farms and I was per-mitted to go to the little houses where there were children to play with. Even in those days I wondered at the lack of comfort and ambition among them. They were meagerly furnished and the chil-dren seemed very ignorant. While Grandfather's garden was filled with every variety of vegetable and fruit, their gardens had almost nothing more than cabbages and potatoes and if you would eat at their table you would have, without change, salt pork, corn bread and molasses and sometimes black eyed peas and sweet potatoes. I can remember wondering about the contrast. Some of the children in the families had hare-lips and I am quite sure most of them had hook worm. The mothers dragged around in an anemic way in mother hubbards [shapeless, smock-like dresses], barefooted, usually with a baby and seemed utterly without ambition. They did not even have preserves which could easily have been made had they wanted to gather the fruit. There were few chickens around their houses while Grandfather and Grandmother had a great variety of poultry—chickens, turkeys, ducks and geese. It puzzled me as to why they did not do likewise.[61]

The likely reason for the children's harelips and the mothers' anemia was poor nutrition. Hookworm, not uncommon in those days in the rural South, also causes anemia. Evidently Ima's grandfather Stinson not did not concern himself with the health of his tenant farm families.

Ima's father wrote to her on December 8:

My Dear Ima—

I have received your two nice letters, and felt so proud of them. Willie is now writing to his Mama and I undertake the task to you. He and I have <u>dressed up</u> and will go to church directly. He has a new hat and looks very nice in his new suit. I think I will go to your Aunt Lillie's wedding. Kiss Mama, Mike and Tom, and all the kinfolks for me. All well.

Your Papa[62]

Kisses were abundant in the Hogg family. Ima remembered that "each morning when we awoke and every evening when we went to bed, Father gave us a warm kiss on the cheek. This habit lasted all our lives."[63]

With Lillie's wedding on December 15, the Hogg family began a festive holiday season. But as soon as Christmas and New Year's celebrations were over, Attorney General Hogg was once more hard at work, and often traveling on state business. When her father was away, Ima missed him. She scratched out a note to him one February day while she was at school, using his official attorney general stationery: "Where are you at now? Write soon."[64]

In the winter of 1890, Will, then age fifteen, was not enrolled in school. He was spending time with the Stinsons, as he had done in 1888. He kept his parents up to date on the news from Speer:

March 14th 1890

Dear Mama & Papa:

I have the pleasure of announcing to you that I have finished those 500 rails, and can call on you for a saddle and bridle. I want a regular cowboy saddle one with side-pockets on it and a good one too—one that will last me always. Mama please have it sent at once for grand-pa is going to town next week and I can get it. Can you send my <u>target rifle</u> with it by express. Write me at once to let me know you sent it.

We are all well but Aunt Lizzie she has been sick a week. I left the rifle at Evan Easton's*before I left home. Are you going to send me some shirts? <u>colored.</u>

---

* Evan Easton was a neighbor friend of Will's, probably the son of Lucy Easton, a widowed dressmaker who lived at 611 West Fourteenth Street, just a block from the Hogg residence.

<u>Write often</u>
Your Affec't.
Son W. C. Hogg

Please send me $2.00 to get me some boots with. these I have got are worn out. can I raise a crop next year?[65]

Will's wardrobe needs were probably not high on his parents' priority list that spring: Jim Hogg had at last been persuaded to run for governor. He was busy planning his campaign, and Sallie was suffering from severe headaches. They did not answer Will's letter for nearly two weeks.

On March 14, the date of Will's letter to his parents, Jim Hogg wrote to his brother-in-law H. C. Ferguson (Julia's husband) in Denton, "I am now hard worked." He also wrote that day to his brother John in Decatur: "As soon as I can get off I shall run up to see you and confer on a plan of campaign."[66]

On March 26, the busy politician found time to answer his eldest son's letter:

My Dear Son:

I am glad to have such good reports of your excellent behavior and industrious services at your grandfather's for the past few months. Your working to split the five hundred rails is a matter of much pride to your mother, your sister and myself. We all know that a boy of fifteen who will split rails and work industriously, as your grand father reports that you have, will make a first class man some day. Your honesty, sobriety, independence and industry pursued into manhood will lead you to great success. I am indeed proud of you.

Enclosed you will find an order for ten dollars and one for five dollars, out of which to buy you a saddle, bridle and such wearing apparel as you may need. Any merchant there at Mineola will take it at cash price and collect it from me through the bank. Don't be extravagant with your saddle, but get such an one as will serve you well.

Your mother and the children, as well as myself, are all well. We hope you will make a fine crop, have good health and a happy time. Write to me once in a while and to your mother and sister at least once a week.

Your Father, Affectionately—
Jas. S. Hogg[67]

Attorney General Hogg opened his campaign for governor on the afternoon of April 19, 1890, with a speech on his old home ground in Rusk. Not far from Mountain Home, the plantation where he was born, the candidate spoke to a crowd of more than 3,000, some of whom climbed trees for a better view. His speech, which lasted almost three hours, was widely praised—even by the opposition.[68] The contest was on.

Hogg's brother John, who was active in Wise County politics and precinct convention plans, wrote to him from Decatur three days later: "Your chances are indeed flattering & should no changes be made, I am perfectly sanguine as to the result." In Houston on a speaking engagement in late April, candidate Hogg sent a note to his married niece there, Lucanda Hogg Owen, who was Hermilla's elder sister. He regretted not calling on her: "All day Saturday my callers continued until after dark, and it rained the next morning." But he added: "When you hear of my being in Houston again send me your residence number and I shall surely see you."[69]

That same day he wrote to Lucanda's mother Anna in Denton: "I got to see Lou at the 'speaking' last Saturday night. She looked better than I ever saw her. In fact Owen and Lou make a fine pair and are indeed happy. . . . [Lucanda had recently married William Henry Harrison Owen, a railway mail clerk in Houston.] My work is very hard, but I shall stay with it. Will try to be at Denton soon. Send me Jimmie and Baylor's address[es]. I wish to write them."[70]

No matter how busy he was, Jim Hogg kept up his family correspondence, and his family helped his campaign. His brother John wrote enthusiastically about an upcoming speaking trip to Decatur. In Denton his niece Hermilla's husband, Robert Kelso, and his sister Julia's husband, H. C. Ferguson, were enthusiastic supporters, excited about a projected July 4 audience of 10,000 for Hogg's speech.[71]

While Jim Hogg was making speeches around the state, Sallie was ailing again, this time with an unnamed malady. She wrote to her husband from Austin on May 24: "Dr. Wooten says I am improving some. I am still very weak. . . . The children are quite well, and happy as big sunflowers."[72]

While her husband campaigned, Sallie must have taken comfort in having Dr. Wooten close at hand. His home and office were in an imposing Victorian structure at 107–109 East Tenth Street, about nine blocks from the Hoggs' residence. Sallie could easily send for him, and like most physicians in those days, he made house calls.

In her father's absence, Ima paid a visit to his office in the Capitol building and wrote him a letter:

Austin, Texas
May the 30 1890

Dear Papa,
     I thought I would write to you. Bill is bussy sending off your speeches.*
     We are going to sell Billy if we can.† I do wish I could see you! Papa. Tom is getting so he will play dolls with me. I hope he will lern to play with Mike and Brother Willie and my self[.]
     Papa I must go home now. So Good by. I will give you a 1000 kisses.
          Write to me soon,
          Ima Hogg
          Austin, Texas[73]

On the same day that Ima wrote to J. S. Hogg, Sallie wrote to him again with her usual fortitude and good cheer:

Austin, May 30th 1890
My darling Papa—
     The time is beginning to seem interminably long since you left, and yet it will be some time before you get home. Will you be home after you speak at Greenville?
     I am afraid you will be completely worn out on this trip as it will be such a long one.
     We are all getting along nicely. The children are very well. They sold their goat this morning for 60 cts, which they will invest in each of them a football. I have had only one spell of my headache since you left, and it only lasted me an evening and night.
     I have no news of political importance. From all I can gather from the papers things are getting "hot" all over the State.
     I will have to draw Jane's and George's salaries before you get home. They say they want to fix up for emancipation day in big

---

* Bill Boulding was the Capitol porter.

† Billy was the Hogg children's pet goat, which they sold that very day.

style.* I will close for this time. Mike waked up this morning talking to papa. Write as often as you can to us.

> Yours affectionately,
> Sallie[74]

Ima would be eight years old in July 1890. Mike was five, and Tom was not yet three. As the eldest of this trio, it was no doubt Ima who negotiated the sale of the goat.

With Jim Hogg constantly traveling, that summer, Sallie's Aunt Lizzie came to Austin to help look after the younger Hogg boys while Sallie and Ima went off once again in search of a cure for what ailed Sallie. Ima remembered:

> Mother's health was poor and I believe this is the only thing which cast a shadow in our home. Father sent her to whatever doctors he thought could help and would urge her to go away to some of the resorts where they hoped her health would be improved. The source of her trouble they thought was her stomach. So she went to watering places . . . to drink the waters and take the baths.[75]

This time they went to the town of Sour Lake, near Beaumont. The lake there was famous for its mineral waters. It had been a health resort since the 1850s. In the 1880s, Sour Lake had two general stores, two hotels, and a population of 150. Ima did not enjoy her time there:

> Sour Lake had a terrible old hotel but after two weeks there my mother was always greatly improved. She drank the water and took the baths. We were greatly impressed by the stories of the miraculous cures there. A good many ladies went there for the famous mud baths to improve their beauty. There were several wells close to each other, all with different mineral content. Somebody prescribed which one would best suit the patient. No one seemed to know what was the root of my Mother's great physical disability.[76]

Jim Hogg, briefly back in Austin, penned a quick note to Sallie at Sour Lake on July 3:

---

* Jane and George were the Hoggs' African American servants, and Emancipation Day was June 19, marking the day in 1865 Texas slaves learned that they were free. "Juneteenth" in Texas was (and remains) a day of celebration.

Dear Sallie—

In response to your call find enclosed ten dollars. As you need means freely write for what you want. I got home yesterday in good health and find the little ones happy, fat and on good terms with Aunt Lizzie. I want you to feel perfectly easy for everything will go on well under her management. When you get tired go where you please for health recreation and fun. Tell dear Ima to write to me regularly. Will leave for New Braunfels tomorrow.

Yours

J. S. Hogg[77]

The long, hot summer of gubernatorial campaigning was drawing to a close, and Jim Hogg wrote a long letter to Martha Frances. She was visiting in Pueblo, Colorado, with her physician son, William, his wife Sarah F. (Fannie), and their children, Pearl, ten, and Marion, seven. Jim Hogg wrote to his eldest sister as he always did after every political triumph:

July 5, 1890

Dear Sister—

Last Saturday night I closed a three months' campaign at San Antonio for the Governorship. Most of that time I have been from home. I may start again tomorrow. At the outset I intended to win if an upright, clean, canvass would do so. Prospects are good, though the contest has been quite warm. My friends everywhere have been faithful and enthusiastic. At each of the forty-five appointments that I have filled a fine crowd has greeted me. Houses cannot hold my audiences and as a consequence I have been forced to speak in open air. To my surprise I have not failed in voice or physical strength, and as you know I would never strain my mind. So in every way I am all right. Tell William he has missed lots of fun this year by being out of Texas. I wish I could see him.—Sallie has just got back from Sour Lake, a little improved. Her health has been bad all the year.

The children are all in fine health. Willie has finished his crop, and returned home. He has worked well and is now at school preparing to enter the A&M College in the fall. I was at Denton last week and found them all well. My four nephews there are fine, promising young fellows and I am proud of them.

I trust you will find time and pleasure to write once in a while, and come down and see us. Love to William and family.

Your Bro.,

J. S. Hogg[78]

Though he told his sister he was "all right," he was near exhaustion. Four days later he opted out of a speech in Abilene, saying that he was "bilious, fatigued, fat, and to some extent collapsed."[79]

Martha Frances answered her brother's letter with unbounded enthusiasm:

Pueblo, July 16th 1890
Dear James:

It did me a world of good to get a letter from you. I have felt ever since like something very pleasant had happened, or was about to transpire. It is the first line since I left Austin. I had a notion to get up a correspondence between the children.—should, if we did not get Dailys [sic] from there, and so keep well posted. The "Political pot" has boiled with William and I, ever since your grand opening at Rusk, morning, noon, and night. But aren't you getting sorry for the other fellows? All is so very monotonous—and to take their own counties is just too cruel. I was sorry when Wheeler besmearched [sic] himself by the Wichita performance—Wait, there is the postman's whistle—I must read the news. Hurra for Hurray! G-e-C-k heads a Hogg delegation to the county convention. It's too funny! Don't you suppose that was done for fun? Poor Randall!—"Having been defeated by the Democracy of my own County!" Now that makes me sorry. I'm sorry for Cook and Wheeler, but could wring Hall's old red head off with his total of "1." I'm glad that's his total, and do hope it will remain so to the end—the old cat's paw. But poor Pendleton!—He's been sliding along on the rail of that cyclone, side by side with Culberson, in the wake of the electric wave on which you ride so nicely. Why couldn't his brother have waited yet a little while! Well that Fort Worth Gazette is a whale. I was sitting near a lady, looking over the returns, and she was near enough to see. "Well," she says, "I see Hogg all over that paper."

[Portion omitted from typescript.]

I should have enjoyed the ovation tendered you at Denton. I think Cook lost his grip and got mad—couldn't be blamed much either. Well, Texas has honored you throughout, and shouted in unmistakable thunder tones: —"Well done, good and faithful servant." Matlock is dead as Hector. That's right, too. He's mean anyway—was mean to his poor sick brother.

Well, I'm sorry you offered for Governor, and believe it would be best for you to be beaten, but—well, I'd a <u>leetle</u> rather you were victor as you've commenced it. But William says you are a goner into politics—that it is too fascinating for a man to pull out easily. He says you'll be in Congress next, because you are a born politician. I believe that the tide is in and swishing for captains whose crafts are filled with the rare cargo of sterling integrity.

If you get Pendleton, Culberson, McGahee [McGaughey], and old laughing John McCall—and Miss Brewster—you'll enjoy it. Uncle Henry McCulloc [McCulloch] stands a pretty good chance, too. [Portion omitted from typescript.]

Frank[80]

Martha Frances Hogg Davis was her brother's most adoring fan. The "grand opening at Rusk" was Hogg's speech on April 19, announcing his candidacy. The field was crowded at first, and Martha Frances had nothing good to say about her brother's opponents: Thomas Benton Wheeler, Lieutenant Governor of Texas, ran against Hogg in his campaign for the gubernatorial nomination. George Clark, a lawyer from Waco, had supported Hogg as Attorney General, but opposed his proposal to establish a state railroad commission. Clark would be Hogg's opponent for governor in the bitterly fought election of 1892. Judge Gustave Cook, a Confederate veteran from Houston, also ran against Hogg for the nomination, as did Land Commissioner Richard M. Hall. Avery L. Matlock, a West Texas politician, had feuded with Hogg since 1882, spreading rumors about Hogg's alleged deal-making with the builders of the new state Capitol, which Hogg emphatically denied. Martha Frances was enthusiastic about her brother's running mates: George C. Pendleton, former speaker of the house and one of Hogg's close friends, would be elected lieutenant governor; Charles A. Culberson would be elected attorney general and would succeed Hogg as governor in 1894. "McGahee" (W. L. McGaughey) would be land commissioner, and John McCall would be state comptroller. Miss B. B. Brewster had worked for Hogg while he was attorney general. Henry E. McCulloch, a former Texas Ranger and Confederate general, was a staunch Hogg supporter.[81]

After their return from Sour Lake, Sallie and Ima were off again, visiting Hogg's sister Julia and her family in Denton, arriving there July 19 on the evening train. Ima, tired of traveling, wrote to her father:

July 23, 1890

Dear papa,

I want to see you so bad. I am home sick to see you all. How are you all. Are you all well? Tom I guess is bat [bad] as ever. I have 15

c. of my money.

You must write soon.

I must cose [close]

So good by

Give love to all

Your daughter

Ima Hogg

This letter was enclosed with the following:

July 26, 1890

Dear papa,

I wrote to you and I forgot to male it. How is Mike and Tom? I love to here [hear] they are all well.

I gess you kno Miss Dasy. She is [illegible] me some new pieces and paper rosies and lots of pretty things.

Brownie is sick with slow fever Doctor Blunt says.

Give love to all and give a 1000 kisses to all in the family.

Good by

Your Daughter

Ima Hogg[82]

Ima's cousin Brownlee's "slow fever" was a nineteenth-century name for typhoid fever. In an era when livestock and humans lived in close proximity, and water for drinking and washing usually came from earthen wells, typhoid was a familiar disease, always debilitating and sometimes fatal. Caused by bacteria contained in fecal matter, it typically lasted for four weeks. Jim Hogg's brother Thomas Elisha had died of typhoid in 1880. By the early 1900s, better sanitation and a vaccine helped to curb the disease.

Ima's father wrote to Sallie from Austin:

July 26th, 1890

Dear Sallie—

We are all well but have the "heat." Raw-rubbing, sly-scratching, grim grunting is the earnest exertion of your "brats" and their "pop" this shining, scorching season. Willie, Mike and Tom are indeed affectionate and inseparable. Aunt Lizzie is as mild and pleasant as ever, and our cook seems happy. So we are consuming the time of your absence in a "suitable manner."

Political news comes flowing in all the time in the most happy

way—that is to our side. My vote in the [Democratic] Convention
here to-day stood 83 for to 52 against me. The "boys" are happy.—
It's doubtful if I leave home until the [state] Convention as it's too
hot. Love to all. Tell Ima I miss her letters.

Your Husband[83]

A few days later, perhaps because of Brownlee's typhoid fever,
Sallie and Ima moved on to visit the John Hogg family in Decatur.
Jim Hogg sent a note to his wife there on August 1:

> Dear Sallie—
> After a few days' absence I returned yesterday from Tyler. Our
> boys and Aunt Lizzie are all well. Mike and Tom are _trying_ to learn
> their ABC's from Aunt Lizzie, as Willie gave up the job in his usual
> impatient disgust. Some day I hope they will get through with their
> lesson.—We have a good cook and, though lonesome are getting
> along well. Be sure to bring John and Velma with you, and Eva also
> if she'll come.
>   Affectionately, in haste, Yours,
>   J. S. H.[84]

As always, Jim urged his brother and his family to visit him in
Austin, but they rarely did. This time Sallie and Ima brought thirteen-
year-old Velma back to Austin with them.

On August 3 Jim wrote triumphantly to Martha Frances of his
successful gubernatorial campaign: "In the 'land slide' most all Texas
has fallen on my side. The convention work now will be a matter of
form."[85]

The "convention work," which began in San Antonio on August
12, ran true to Jim Hogg's prediction. His one opponent (the others
had dropped out of the contest) Lieutenant Governor Wheeler,
had 18¾ votes; Hogg, 836 . Then the vote was made unanimous.
James Stephen Hogg was the Democratic Party's nominee for governor (which in those days was tantamount to election). His win was
assured, but the nominee still had more speeches to make, hoping
to get legislators elected who would support his cherished Railroad
Commission.

Politics and ongoing work on his still-pending railroad cases before
the U.S. Supreme Court in October engulfed him, but the candidate
found time to attend to various domestic matters. He paid Sallie's bill
($9.90) at Sanger's department store in Dallas and started a search for

a family cook. The erstwhile "good cook" had departed, and Hogg wrote to a friend in Brenham in search of a replacement.

Sept. 2, 1890
B. Bryan, Esq.
Brenham, Texas.
Dear Sir and Friend—
    We want a good negro woman to do our cooking and washing. Can't you get us one, about forty years old without a family, whom your good wife can recommend? We have six in family and will pay from $10 to $15 pr. mo. and furnish comfortable house to a good woman. Let me hear from you.
Your F'd,
J. S. Hogg

A few days later, Hogg wrote to the friend that he had found a cook himself, one that had lived with his family several years in East Texas.[86]

Another more pressing family matter demanded Jim Hogg's attention that fall. He had discovered that fifteen-year-old Will, who had been "at school" in Austin that summer preparing to attend Texas A&M, was not yet college material. On September 18, Will's father took him by train to enroll, not at Texas A&M, as planned in July, but in a private school in Omen, Texas. Will's grandfather Stinson, who had been an enthusiastic supporter of the founding of Texas Agricultural and Mechanical College in 1876, must have been disappointed. But A&M was not right for Will.

    Ima wrote of her brother:

My brother Will seemed so very much older than us. He was nearly nine years older than I and always seemed a young man to me. He was a great help to my mother and in the years before I was able to go with her he had been the one to accompany her on her shopping expeditions and I think this accounted for his later very fastidious taste. He knew as much as any woman about materials and appropriate dressing.

It was while we were living at the mansion that Father decided that Brother should go to a country boarding school near Tyler. At this school he lived with Professor Orr and was given a great respect for scholarship. For many years Brother was a serious student, due, I imagine, largely to this very fine training at Professor Orr's School.

Here he also learned something about agriculture. Among the family letters will be found some references to this period of his schooling as well as a summer he spent at my Grandfather's farm in East Texas, where he learned many useful things about farm life. This my mother and father agreed, would be a wholesome experience for him. I think, up until this time, Brother's schooling had been entirely in the public schools of Tyler and Austin, possibly beginning in Mineola.[87]

The Summer Hill Select School, founded by Dr. A. W. Orr in 1876, was a thriving institution with more than 300 students by the time Will attended it. Omen itself was a small East Texas town with a population of only 550 in 1892. It was 249 miles from Austin. Will would be a long way from home.

Jim Hogg also found time to counsel his eighteen-year-old job-seeking nephew, Baylor Hogg, in Denton:

> My advice to you is, to get some good endorsements from the business men of Denton and go to the banking houses of Fort Worth and Dallas. . . . Let them know that you are willing to do any kind of honest work, and that you are not too clean to dirty your hands nor too tender to work from sun-up to midnight. Keep in mind the lesson that was taught you in your early readers: 'If at first you don't succeed, try, try again.[88]

Sallie, despite her summer travels, continued in poor health, and the presence of John Hogg's eldest daughter, thirteen-year-old Velma, must have been a welcome diversion in the Austin household. At her Uncle Jim's request, Velma would live in Austin with the Hoggs for nearly two years, attending school and taking music lessons along with Ima.

As her father continued his travels around the state in his gubernatorial campaign, Ima missed him desperately.

October 3, 1890
Dear Papa
    I wish you [could] come home the 5 of Oct I cant do without you. Please come home. I haven't much to say. Mama has been very sick. But is better. I hope she will get well.
            I hope you are well.
                            Write soon
                            Your daughter
                            Ima Hogg[89]

With Sallie ailing and their father about to leave for Washington to argue a Supreme Court case in a few days, the younger Hogg children were sent for a visit to the Stinsons. At least one of the children— Tom—had whooping cough. This childhood disease, which causes severe coughing spells, lasts for several weeks and is highly contagious. Ima and Mike seem to have had it, too. Not until the 1920s was an effective vaccine for it discovered. The 1940s saw a combination vaccine called DPT, for diphtheria, whooping cough (pertussis), and tetanus.

As Ima wrote to her father:

Oct 8, 1890
Dear Papa,
I am glad to get here at Grandpas.
Tom ant over the hoping caf [whooping cough]. Mike is well. It has been raining here.
We eat sugar cane every day. I love it.* I wrote to write a few lines.
I must close.
Write soon.
Your Daughter
Ima Hogg[90]

On October 10, a somewhat harried Jim Hogg wrote to his brother:
Dear John—

   In the haste of my preparation to leave for Washington to-night I write to say that Velma is in good health, is doing well at school and in her music lessons, and is a splendid girl. We are all proud of her, and she seems satisfied. With the permission of Eva and yourself we shall be more than glad to keep her in our family a few years—until she is educated anyway. She and Ima are good cousins and seem to be devoted—Sallie is not in good health but is getting along smoothly in her usual good tempered and happy way. She thinks a great deal of Velma and finds her good company, during my absence especially.

   My work is excessive and seems to grow without prospect of abatement. I have had no rest for many years, but my health seems good. Will remain several weeks on the present trip and wind up my cases before the U.S. Sup. Court. With love to all.
                                   Your Bro
                                   J. S. Hogg[91]

---

* Sugar cane was a popular remedy for whooping cough.

Before he left for Washington, Jim Hogg also wrote hurriedly to his sister Julia about their brother John and his future.

Oct. 10th 90
Ms. Julia Ferguson,
Denton Texas.

Dear Sir [sic—this was indeed a hurried letter.]—

I appreciate deeply what you say by your last letter in behalf of Bro. John. For a long time I have desired to see his talents devoted to pursuits more suitable to them. Possibly I can yet help him in some way, though it is doubtful if he would accept an appointment if I could with any propriety tender him one. I trust to see him succeed in other ways.—My work is excessive. Will leave for U.S. Sup. Ct. tonight. In haste, All well and send love—
Your Bro.,
J. S. Hogg[92]

The October days in Washington and his court cases, plus the November 4 state election, made a killing workload for Hogg. He did not win his case before the U.S. Supreme Court, but he won the election.

James Stephen Hogg, who would celebrate his fortieth birthday in March 1891, would be the youngest, as well as the first native-born governor of Texas. He had much to accomplish. He was so consumed by work that he nearly forgot to pay Will's boarding school bills.

Nov. 12, 1890
Master W. C. Hogg
Omen, Texas

My Dear Son—
Not from negligence but from over-work since the election I have omitted to send you amount due for your last months tuition, board, &c. until now. Enclosed find P.O. order for $17 covering it, and leaving a penny or two for other purposes. We are all very well. Write often and take pains with your letters. We are proud of [them] and shall keep them.
Your Father,
J. S. Hogg[93]

Hogg had another request from a relative for a job that fall. Hermilla's husband, Robert Kelso, wrote to him in early November asking for a job, such as "Private Secretary," but his uncle-in-law could find no position for him. In his answer, Hogg wrote, "I trust this will not too deeply disappoint you for I have for you great affection and hope yet in some way to contribute to your pleasure and success." Kelso's answering letter on November 14 registered his disappointment and contained a sad postscript: "Our little One, does not seem to grow any better." Anna Elizabeth, the baby daughter born to the Kelsos in January, had fallen ill. She died on December 5, 1890.[94]

Meanwhile, the peripatetic Martha Frances had left her son and his family in Colorado and was now visiting her sister Julia and her family in Denton. On November 15, Hogg wrote to Julia's husband, H. C. Ferguson, "Come down and bring Sister with you. We are all well, but my work worries me some."[95] The governor's work was for one of his major legislative goals: a Railroad Commission for Texas. The November election not only put him in the governor's office, it had won the passage of an amendment to the Texas Constitution to provide for the Railroad Commission. This long-debated amendment stated that the "Legislature . . . may provide and establish all requisite means and agencies invested with such powers as may be deemed adequate and advisable (to regulate Railroads)."[96] An official proclamation of December 19, 1890, confirmed it. Now the legislature would have to craft a bill to create the commission. That would occupy much of the new governor's time in the spring of his first term. But he worried about Sallie's health. She was seldom well. He confessed that fact to Martha Frances on December 7. "We are all well except Sallie. She has been feeble all year, but heroically stands all her ailments."[97]

Nevertheless, the governor-elect and his family spent a happy Christmas season, anticipating his January inauguration. Answering a letter from a young Hogg cousin who was attending school in Massachusetts, he wrote that "Sallie and the children are well, and have, together with myself, spent a pleasant holiday." In typical Jim Hogg fashion, he added, "Come to see us as soon as you are out of school."[98]

That winter James Stephen Hogg and his family would move from their Fourteenth Street house into the antebellum Governor's Mansion, which was built in 1856. On January 20, 1891, Sallie sat in a place of honor in the House chamber at the Capitol, along with an excited Will and Ima, to see James Stephen Hogg sworn in as governor of Texas.

Ima had vivid memories of this occasion:

> Father took the oath of office in the Senate Chamber of the great,
> new pink granite Capitol.
>
> The Inaugural Ball was given in the Chamber of the House of
> Representatives. Mother wore an exquisite lavender brocade gown
> with deep lavender metallic orchids outlined with silver thread.
> Brother Will came running to me when he first saw her dressed,
> crying, "Sister, Sister, come see how beautiful Mother looks." People
> came from all over the State to attend the Inauguration.
>
> I was eight years old and remember the crowded chamber, the
> square dances with quadrille. . . .[99]

If her parents danced, Ima did not mention it. But she had other
memories of them:

> She and Father were both very young when he was first inaugu-
> rated, but a woman of thirty-six in those days was supposed to be
> very sedate and dignified in her dressing. Mother did not often wear
> bright colors. She was perhaps influenced in her choice by my father
> who liked soft, quiet colors like gray, buff, blue and lilac. He disliked
> any of his family in any shade of red. . . .[100]

Sallie dressed to please her husband, and he sought her advice on
other matters:

> Mother was Father's confidante and advisor in all questions. He
> trusted her intuition and judgment about people and they always
> seemed to like the same people. He told me later that he always
> discussed everything with her, even his business and felt that a wife
> should be in every way a complete partner.[101]

As the governor's wife, Sallie Hogg was far more than her husband's confidante: Even though she was in frail health, she oversaw
the details of endless gatherings and receptions at the Governor's
Mansion and supervised the activities of four children. Will was
often away at school, demanding frequent letters from home. Sallie's
first task as the governor's partner was to refurbish his residence: the
white-columned Greek Revival mansion had eighteen rooms and nine
fireplaces. By 1891 when the Hoggs moved in, it was in need of major
repairs, As Ima recalled:

We were prepared for a most hospitable home but I shall never forget our consternation on first seeing the interior. It was in dreadful disrepair. The white calcimine walls were badly cracked and shabby and the dark woodwork was worse. Our family did not attempt to live in it without trying to freshen and redecorate it in, I am sure, a modest way. It was entirely papered and painted immediately at my Father's expense. Mother was always very fastidious and she would never have dreamed of living in it as it was. Later, Father was reimbursed for all he had spent. . . .

Before we moved into the mansion, many days were spent scraping hardened chewing gum from under the tables and chair arms. There were literally buckets of old chewing gum scraped, even from the door moldings. . . .[102]

Ima's memoir contains a detailed description of the mansion as it was when her family lived there:

The Southeast room was our general sitting room. Behind it was the dining room and in between, a very small wash room with basin which, I think, had running water. You entered the house across the wide columned porch into the wide central hall which ran through the house. On the northeast were the large double parlors with wide opening. Upstairs were five bedrooms in the main body of the house, two over the library and dining room, a large one over the front parlor and two small ones with [a] narrow hall over the back parlor. This was a passage-way from the front bedrooms upstairs to the ell. Stepping down from this narrow hallway two or three steps, you entered the ell and crossed another narrow hall to a large bathroom in which was an enormous tin tub, said to have been made for Sam Houston. This was the only bath. None of the bedrooms had running water, only bowls and pitchers were available. One may imagine the popularity of the old bathtub. Behind the bath were two small servant's rooms with narrow hallway from which ran the back stairs down to the kitchen. On the first floor of the ell were the kitchen and two smaller rooms, one used for the servant's hall and ironing room, the other for a store house. There was a covered porch running the full length of the ell and across the back of the dining room. The only heat the house had was from fireplaces, except in the bathroom which had a good wood stove. I think the kitchen had a sink with running water. The house was lighted by gas but there was no gas cooking stove, only a very large range which burned wood.

It was, as today, a noble old building on the exterior, and on the interior, beautiful high ceilings with the same interesting door and window moldings. . . .

The Southwest bedroom had the famous Sam Houston four-poster bed and another one without the tester [canopy]. The Southeast bedroom, which was Father's and Mother's room, had very attractive, late Victorian walnut furniture. It seems to me that this furniture was moved in by us—our own, but there was also an extra bed. The Northeast bedroom, a guest room, also was furnished in this late Victorian period. There were two other small bedrooms on the North side, one of which was used by the white maid and the back one by my brother, Will.[103]

Oddly, Ima neglected to say where she and Mike and Tom slept.

In the long hall and to the right of the front door, on the wall, was a telephone with a large box containing batteries. You rang Central by cranking the handle. No one used the phone during a storm.

The block of ground surrounding the mansion was fenced in with a white painted picket fence except at the back where there was a board fence at least seven feet high. In those days the block was divided up into spaces for various and sundry uses. There was the usual front lawn and croquet lawn, a little pond or pool, and flower beds, then on the kitchen side, space for a vegetable garden and fruit trees with wonderful big figs, peaches plums, and a fine bearing quince tree from which beautiful preserves were made, and a place for the cows and horses in the stable and a large lot for the horses to run in and for the children to play in. Near the back porches was a large wash shed. I believe it had a cistern in the center or nearby. Here, of course, the family washing was done every Monday and perhaps Tuesday. The vegetable garden was Father's great pride and it always had nearly every vegetable in season besides a patch for experimentation. . . . Mother was a very ardent flower gardener. She specialized in coleus, begonias, and geraniums and what else I do not remember. We kept a nice Victoria [two-seated carriage] and a pair of beautiful horses. These were a matched pair of black horses, presented to Father by Uncle John Hogg. He had gotten them from W. T. Waggoner of Decatur. We also had a three-seated hack or car-ryall which was used for picnics and country driving, and a small trap with a Shetland pony for the children. This little pony all of us rode and . . . were frequently pitched to the ground, but no one was ever injured. . . . This pony was supposed to be mine, but most of the time the boys were riding her. Dainty, as we called her, lived a great many years . . . . [Six years later, in 1902, they would give Dainty to their cousin Hermilla.] She had many pranks, a very mischievous and harmless beast. She seemed to have a real sense of humor and nothing delighted her more than to take a crowd of youngsters in the trap and whirl around fast so that she would turn it over. Then she would look back, perfectly still, with her nose turned up as if she were laughing. We would brush ourselves off, get back in the trap and start merrily on as if nothing had happened. Whenever we stayed still too long, perhaps eating ice cream in the trap or having a picnic lunch, she would get bored and vary this monotony by upsetting us. She was small and the trap was small and no harm was ever done.[104]

Rough-and-tumble play was part of the children's life in the Governor's Mansion:

Our grounds were a neighborhood playground. Contests for running and jumping and vigorous outdoor games were always going on in good weather. I was allowed to compete with the boys. My two brothers and I were so nearly the same age; although I was older, and they seemed very much younger to me, we were great playmates. . . .[105]

They tried to show me how to wrestle, play marbles and enter into all of their games. It made of me a real Tom-boy.[106]

I am afraid visitors to the mansion must have thought we were a pretty rowdy trio, Mike, Tom, and myself. Of course, Brother was dignified and not often conspicuous. We three would start at the top of the steps and slide down one after the other with a great thud into the center hall. Nothing seemed to cure us of this until Tom fell off midway and hung by his chin from a corner of one of the steps. He bled considerably and frightened all of us. Father took tacks and hammered them all the way down the railing of the stairs.

I do not know what theories my father and mother had about disciplining children but I never saw Father administer any corporal punishment. I don't think he believed in it. We were not very disciplined, at any rate, but Mother had a little switch which she would use on our legs sometimes. I am sure we needed it more often than we got it. . . .[107]

Elsewhere, Ima wrote: "Of course we screamed bloody murder and she told us it hurt her more than it hurt us."[108]

Ima's father had other ways of disciplining his children, as Ima remembered,

He was a devoted family man. It had been his observation that many men who were in public life failed as parents. So he took time to teach us right from wrong in his own thoughtful way. . . . Our baby brother Tom, somewhere learned a vocabulary of curse words. Father, himself, never used a stronger word than "By Gatlins." Tom's smart-aleck language distressed Father. At last he decided to deal with Tom's swearing, so he put soot in his mouth to let him look at himself. I can't say Tom was cured. All of us learned not to follow the example of many other children who passed the fruit stand and snitched an apple . . . One day I asked for a quarter to go to the skating rink. Father having nothing smaller than a fifty cent piece gave that to me. He waited two or three days for the change, than asked me for it. Of course I had spent it. He said, "Now Sissy, you asked for a quarter." I saved up and repaid him. Somehow he found out most of the children who went to Sunday School kept out a nickel to get a milk shake at Lamme's after church. So we were given an extra nickel to spend for the customary milk shake. These are only examples of how vigilant he was of our behavior. . . .[109]

Sometimes the Governor's patience wore thin:

The paling fence around the mansion grounds was a nuisance to us children, and we were always knocking a paling off through which our neighbors could crawl in. This annoyed Father a great deal because he was always having to have the fence repaired. . .[110]

Years later, Ima reminisced about good times in the Governor's Mansion:

At the mansion, young people came almost every Saturday night to dance. There was impromptu music which they sometimes furnished themselves and I remember seeing them dance the Schottische and the Polka. Father and Mother did not dance. I think Mother would not dance without Father and it had been a long time since he had tried, but he loved to watch the young people having a good time as did Mother.

Our house was the center of social life. While many men came to talk over affairs in the evening there were many evenings when Father would play six-handed Euchre with neighbors or house-guests. Mother played when she felt like it but I think when the day was done she was perhaps too tired to join in, besides, she was often ill. . . .

Sunday evenings were always spent around the piano singing favorite hymns or old songs such as "Home Sweet Home," "Old Kentucky Home" and "Swanee River," "Little Nellie Gray," "Annie Laurie," etc. Anyone who could play the piano or any instrument or sing was always a favorite with Father. There were several young ladies and girls in the neighborhood who were starred as musical and dancing entertainers. My childish efforts on the piano and banjo were in frequent demand, too. Some of the girls in the neighborhood could recite and they were frequently invited over to entertain.

One of our most welcome visitors was old Uncle Bob, an ex-slave who had followed Grandfather and Uncle Tom in the Civil War and had been the younger boys' body servant. He was a grand old character, very black with kinky gray hair and he had the proud look of a Rameses. Uncle Bob could have boasted of noble blood for it was said his father was an African chieftain whom Grandfather Hogg had purchased in New Orleans. Uncle Bob loved to play the fiddle and his annual trip to Austin was a release as his wife, Aunt Easter, did not permit him to fiddle at home. She was a very pious Baptist and believed the fiddle was the devil's own instrument. Uncle Bob, of course, did not share this belief. He would sit in the corner at our receptions with a cutaway coat and striped trousers in great elegance with his fiddle and he was usually the center of attention. . . . His father had been Grandfather's coachman. I had always heard that it was the only thing his royal highness would condescend to do, so when Uncle Bob came, Father would love to have him drive his carriage. . . .[111]

In Austin, the Hogg children's cultural enrichment was not neglected, either. Sallie and Jim were theatergoers, and often took Will and Ima to performances. Ima's lifelong love of the performing arts began here:

When we first moved to Austin, the excitement of Edwin Booth's coming to play in Hamlet was so great that even I, little as I was, thought I should go to hear him too. Needless to say, I was not taken, but my brother Will was. Booth died shortly after this performance.*

Austin's principal and perhaps only theater was the Millett Opera House where traveling companies performed almost every day of the week in the season. Father and Mother had a box for the season and frequently attended. Brother and I were permitted to go on a great many occasions. Shakespearean companies came for extended engagements. Ward, James, and Kidder headed one of the favorite Shakespeare companies. Ward was an accomplished English actor who had been touring Texas for many years. He and Father had become friends while he was sojourning in Mineola or Tyler. They would always pass greetings when he came to Austin though of course, he was too busy to visit us, usually with two performances a day. Keene, who was famous for his portrayal of Richard the Third, and Madam Modjeska, the great Polish actress, were also friends of Father's from earlier times. . . .

Small opera companies visited Austin for protracted periods also each year. The Grau Opera Company, which I presume had nothing to do with the great Grau in New York, presented delightful operas such as "Bells of Normandy," "William Tell," "Il Trovatore," and "Norma." At any rate, people became familiar with many of the lesser French and Italian operas.[112]

Ima, who later aspired to become a concert pianist, recalled her musical training in Austin:

> When we first moved to the mansion, Professor Ludwig . . . came to live in Austin. He was from Russia and had studied piano with a brother of Anton Rubenstein, though I think the impression was he had studied with Anton himself. Professor Ludwig made a real sensation in Austin by his talk and his performances, and Austin was very proud of having him. Pupils flocked to him for study. Mother had early begun my piano lessons herself because I was a little too small and young to be sent to a teacher. Later there was a Miss Brown in Austin who gave me lessons, but when Professor Ludwig came I was sent to him. Each year he gave students' recitals and I always played at these. There is no doubt that Professor Ludwig

---

* Booth played Hamlet until 1891 and died in 1893.

gave a great impetus to piano music in Austin. His taste and verdict on all things musical were taken as final. . . .[113]

Ima began taking piano from Professor Edmund Ludwig at age eight. By the time she was ten, she also played the banjo. Professor Ludwig taught music at his home, at 302 East Seventeenth Street, about nine blocks—walking distance—from the Governor's Mansion. Ima's musical gifts were already evident:

> He quickly saw it was easier for me to play by ear than to read music so he taught me by playing first and letting me follow. It took me a long time afterwards to overcome such a handicap. Several times a year his pupils appeared in concert. I played too, in recital, Chopin, mazurkas and waltzes far beyond my comprehension but imitating Prof. Ludwig. He was quite a prima-donna.[114]

There was lighter entertainment in Austin as well:

> Those were days when the advent of a circus to town was really of prime importance. Father always found time to take us and all the neighbors' children. The owner of the circus always saw that he and his party had most advantageous seats. We went early to enjoy the clowns. Some of these fellows gave Father the greatest amusement. One thing that was always a disappointment to us was he never took us to the side shows. He had a distaste for anything that was deformed or abnormal. We later learned this was his reason for not taking us to the side shows. For days after the circus we children went through all sorts of contortions, trying to practice some of the acts of the acrobats and Father would look on and applaud. We attempted the most dangerous things to Mother's horror, but Father always seemed to know we would not get hurt. . . .
>
> One time when Father went to San Antonio, they were breaking up the menagerie over there and he brought back to the mansion all different kinds of exotic birds. He built a large cage on the north side of the house for them. They were all kinds of cockatoos and other beautiful plumed birds, some lovely songsters. Before Father went to the office in the morning, he always had a little visit with the animals and birds. . . .
>
> At the same time, there was a little parrot which never stayed in this cage, but was free to roam. Father had bought her from a Mexican out on the river. This little bird with the red head was Father's

constant companion. She lived with us for a great many years and was as human as is possible for anything to be. She would wait every day at noon at the front door of the mansion, and when Father would come up the walk she would begin screaming and flapping her wings, calling "Papa, Papa" as she ran toward him. He would take her up and she would get on his shoulder and begin nibbling at his ear, her way of demonstrating her affection. In the house, she would crawl up on the back of his chair and listen intently to the conversation. If anyone said anything funny, especially Father, she would throw back her head and give forth peals of musical laughter. There was a young neighbor of ours, Miss Annie McCoy, a lovely young pianist and great favorite in our family. She had taught Jane, our parrot, to laugh. Father had a great attachment for this bird and when she died years later at the 19th Street house, he was truly grieved.[115]

In the mansion, the governor kept a regular work schedule:

The hours of office work before 1900 were from daylight to dark. Father was a very early riser and was at his office at work much earlier than men dream of now. There were no restaurants so Father came home at the middle of the day for a hearty meal. Dinner was usually at that time. He always found time to relax after this meal, no matter how pressing affairs might be. He seemed to feel that a fifteen minute nap restored him completely. Except for the time when we went away in the summer, we had a good warm supper at dusk and in the evening if there were more conferences or anything else the people came to our house. . . .[116]

Such a household required a staff:

We did not have many servants regularly. There were the cook and the customary housemaid in the house and one white man to take care of the gardens, horses and cows and do the driving. My brother Tom recalls a negro man "George" who attended the horse and cows and did the milking. I do not remember him. It is my impression that the State gave no appropriation for these servants and I remember they were paid by the month, a little bit more than was the custom which as I recall it, was about $15.00 per month for the maids with perhaps a raise later. I do not remember what the man received.[117]

Sallie Hogg had not been long in the mansion before she began a search for a housemaid. As Ima remembered:

It was difficult to find a maid who was accomplished and equal to the tasks. My Mother went to a very substantial German family—the man was a cigar maker in Austin—and asked their advice about getting a good German girl. At that time they had a visitor from Germany, a sister of the man's wife. Her name was Grace Bauer. She was not of the service class, but they offered her to Mother until she could find someone. Grace was a very beautiful girl, fairly well educated, and before long she was so devoted to my Mother and my Mother to her that she stayed on with us as long as we were in the mansion and told my Mother she would never leave her as long as she needed her.[118]

Even with servants in the mansion, it was Sallie Hogg who supervised everything:

After the laundress came on Monday, Grace, the maid, ironed on Tuesday. Father's shirts and collars were sent to the Chinese Laundry nearby.

There were certain days for baking salt rising bread, beaten biscuits, cakes of all kinds and cookies to fill the cookie jars for the children and their playmates. Springtime was an ordeal. The carpets were taken up, put on a stiff line and beaten. For some strange reason . . . the furniture went outdoors too to be scrubbed and perhaps varnished. Housekeeping was a rugged occupation.[119]

Sallie also kept accounts of the mansion's enormous quantities of foodstuffs:

Things were purchased wholesale—barrels of sugar and flour, one hundred pound cans of lard, cases of canned vegetables when there were none to be had from the garden, etc. Chickens were purchased by the dozen on foot, turkeys as well. When chickens were $2.00 a dozen hardly anyone could afford them. Bacon was bought by the side and I think was five or ten cents a pound. . . . Each week were baked quantities of bread, cakes and pies with wholesale preserving and canning of fruits in season. Our store room was a delight. Mother went about with a great bunch of keys and nothing came out of the store room that she did not check. . . .

Of course, there were no great formalities in serving at the table. There were always hearty meals but they were simple and wholesome. . . .From the upstairs back hall steps which led down into the kitchen was a favorite place for the children to sit so we heard kitchen talk while we watched the preparations which went on for regular meals and for many parties. The negroes related gruesome ghost stories tales of people buried alive, and every sort of superstition.[120]

Ima recalled lavish menus for the parties:

Chicken salad, baked turkey and baked ham, and beaten biscuits, of course, were the main dishes for receptions. Green olives were just being introduced, that is, as far as I remember. Celery was a scarcity but was served and lettuce was very different from what we have now. Salted nuts, especially almonds, were always used. There were many varieties of cakes—marble cake was beautiful and delicious. Spice cake seemed to be another favorite. In season, fruit cakes were made. But I recall Lady Baltimore Cake as being very frequently made with lemon layer cake as second best. Pies were ever ready and I imagine they were never allowed to become stale. The cookie jar was never empty and beaten biscuits were a necessity. I can remember hearing the beating of the biscuit dough and used to take a great delight in taking my turn with the wooden mallet. The Saratoga potatoes fascinated me more than almost anything because our cook took the greatest pains with them cutting them large and very thin then letting them soak in water for a long time, then carefully draining them and dropping them into a deep iron pot of hot grease.* There was another thing which was very difficult to make and I do not know where they can be found anymore—a very delicate crisp sweetened waffle made on a kind of lacy waffle iron. This we often had for parties and it took a long time to make them. Father was very fond of salt rising bread and we always had this as well as light bread and hot rolls. Then there was a bread which he enjoyed, called Steam Boat bread, not a yeast bread, something similar to that which is now called Sally Lunn, I think.[121]

---

* Saratoga potatoes became better known as potato chips. They were first served in the 1880s at Moon Lake House, a well-known resort in Saratoga, New York.

Jim Hogg loved a good meal. He could never forget going hungry in his youth (when he was sixteen and traveling across Texas, he once went without food for three days). When he was a young county attorney in Wood County in 1878, he was "thin and muscular," but he soon began to put on weight. As one Wood County resident remembered, when he ate at the boarding house in Tyler he always ate dessert first, so as not to be too full for it at the end of his meal. By the time he was governor in 1890 he weighed nearly three hundred pounds. He was an imposing figure. "Governor Hogg was a very large and powerful man, requiring four large napkins to cover him while he was eating, sitting well back from the table; he was always very jolly, very affable, and ate with a great deal of gusto."[122]

New Year's Day was a day for a grand reception at the Governor's Mansion:

> These called for great preparations. Men came in to cover the carpets with white canvas and everything was elaborately decorated. It was the day when people festooned the windows and pictures and door openings with smilax. The large crystal chandeliers in the two parlors were also delicately outlined with smilax which could not be put too near the lights because they were gas and as I recall it, did not have any shades over the flames. The mantels were always banked with flowers. Table decorations were entirely different from those now. They were usually quite low with forms made of tin and filled with wet sand. In these, flowers were packed very closely together to give a clear outline with a special motif and color. I cannot remember how the tables were covered, but I believe, having seen my Mother's interest in qualities of damask, that the damask of fine Irish linen was used. Young men in Austin who were interested in social functions came in to assist with the decorations. Neighbors arrived to do what they could to help in the kitchen and dining room. There was a colored porter at the Capitol named Bill Boulding who always came to stand at the door and announce the guests as they entered the parlor.[123]

These grand occasions, as her daughter recalled, were a trial to Sallie Hogg:

> She was very delicate and frequently gave her orders from her bed. The maid, Grace, was thoroughly capable of carrying out everything and could supervise almost as well as Mother. I always remem-

ber how difficult it was for Mother to stand at receptions and finally Father got her a high stool which she sat on or leaned against so that she could get through receptions without being too fatigued. She was entirely too conscientious and should have delegated a great deal more than she did to the servants. The winters were cold and the mansion quite drafty and I am sure the receptions were an ordeal, but she enjoyed performing what she thought was her duty.[124]

Besides her frequent headaches and bad colds, Sallie Hogg had pneumonia every winter that the family lived in the drafty Governor's Mansion, where the only heat came from fireplaces and a coal grate. Before the days of antibiotics, pneumonia was often a life-threatening illness, and although the family had Dr. Wooten and Dr. Swearingen, Ima remembered that it was Jim Hogg himself who acted as head nurse when Sallie had pneumonia, using a home remedy: hot packs on her chest, sides, and back around the clock. These poultices, as Ima recalled, were soft cotton bags full of cornmeal soaked in kerosene and turpentine. Jim Hogg used this same treatment years later when Tom came down with pneumonia at boarding school. Apparently it worked.[125]

In May of 1891, Sallie and Ima left Austin for Hot Springs, Arkansas. Hot Springs was literally that: forty-seven natural thermal springs, with temperatures of 143 degrees, flowed from Hot Springs Mountain into the historic town. There were luxurious hotels for guests who came to bathe in the waters, but nine-year-old Ima did not think they did much for Sallie: "I was not greatly impressed with the benefits of Hot Springs although it was a very beautiful place. Mother did not seem to gain anything there."[126]

Meanwhile, Will, age sixteen, was finishing his first year at school at Omen. He was anxious to get home. Above all, he missed his mother. With Sallie at Hot Springs, he wrote to his father:

May 28, 1891
Dear Father,—

I wrote you about 2 or 3 days ago for my bill. I have received a letter from mama saying that she was at Hot Springs Ark. I will be ready to come home in 2 weeks from today. I want to come home first and then wait until mama comes back, and she can get me some clothes.

I can then go visiting if I want to. If you are not boarding I can come home and read a good many books 'till mama comes back.

If you are boarding I guess it will be cheaper for me to stay here 'till mama comes.

If I had some clothes I could go to Tyler and stay until mama comes. But I guess its best for me to come home. I wanted to visit Mrs. Marsh and all of them. They are such good friends to me.

School will be out on the 11th of June, and then you can look for me home, if I get my bill. If you have not already received my bill, here it is for 1½ months, $33.00; counting in enough to bring me home. If mama was at home and could send me what clothes I need then I could go to Tyler.

I hope soon to be home a <u>changed boy</u>.[127]

Though he was obviously anxious to see his mother, Will may have taken comfort from his father's answer:

June 1st, 1891
Dear Willie—
I got home last Thursday from a trip to Tyler and to your Grand Pa's. Will leave for Huntsville to-night to attend the S.H. [Sam Houston] Normal Commencement, but will return in a day or so. I spent the day yesterday with Mike and Tom at Mr. McCall's. They are fat, fine and happy. Your mama and Ima report that they are doing well at Hot Springs. When your school closes I want you to come on home as I am lonesome and need you for company and to read to me as well. I am really proud of the good reports of your course and conduct at school. With your high sense of honor, self-respect and industrious habits, I feel perfectly assured of your success in life. When I look at Mike and Tom and think of the good example you are setting for them I feel happy in the assurance that none of my sons will ever blacken a name that I have so jealously guarded from poverty in boyhood until now. Find the $33. p.o. order.
                                Your father,
                                J. S. Hogg[128]

Then he wrote to Sallie:

June 1st 1891
Dear Sallie
Find p.o. order for $30 in obedience to your <u>hint</u>. If you need money and it is not forthcoming draw on me. I spent yesterday with Mike and Tom at McCall's. They are indeed happy and ought to be.

Mrs. B. and the others out there are the best people with children I ever saw. For a fine dinner the one I got there took the premium. Will and they are all well. Kiss darling Ima for me. No news.

Yours,

J. S. Hogg[129]

With Will at school, Sallie and Ima away, and Governor Hogg traveling, Mike and Tom were staying with Hogg's state comptroller and close friend, John McCall, and his family in Austin.

Hogg was working hard that summer. In April, after a long struggle, the Texas legislature had passed the act creating the Railroad Commission, providing for oversight of railroad rates and the operation of "railroads, terminals, wharves and express companies" within the state. But it was the governor who had the power to appoint the commission's three members. On June 10, 1891, the first Texas Railroad Commission came into being, with Railroad Commissioners John H. Reagan (he resigned his U.S. Senate seat to chair the commission), former Texas District Judge William Pinckney McLean, and Lafayette Lumpkin Foster, a former speaker of the Texas House of Representatives.

Fall came and the children went back to school, and another round of social life in the mansion began. At Christmas there was at least one relative in attendance for the 1891 holiday: Brownlee Ferguson, Julia's fifteen-year-old son, was visiting. Jim Hogg wrote to H. C. Ferguson the day after Christmas: "We are glad to have Brownlee with us. He is a nice boy and is having a good time."[130]

On January 1, 1892, there was the traditional New Year's Day reception at the mansion. An undated letter to Will written in early 1892 shows Sallie bravely doing her duty as both mother and governor's wife:

My dear boy—

Don't think your Mother has forgotten her boy you know I have been <u>very busy</u> ever since you were here getting ready for another reception, and oh! I am so glad it is over. The flowers you sent Mama were so pretty. Many thanks for them, I sent you a small box [of treats from the reception] it was the only size I had. I could have sent you other things but they would not keep long enough to get to you. Everything passed off very nicely (so everybody says) I hope you are quite well. I am not feeling at all well, so Mama will say goodbye. . . .[131]

Sallie wrote often to her eldest son. Some of what she wrote has been excised in the typescript of the following letter. The original has not been located.

January 18th, 1892
My dear boy
[Portion omitted from typescript.]
Don't study too hard yet make good use of your time. Your economy down there at school will enable papa to do a better part by you. He says he will <u>finish you up</u> in any profession you desire to follow. Tom & Mike are frozen up and in the house. So I will quit for this time. Goodbye. God bless you.
Your devoted
Mother[132]

Sallie's poor health worried her. She wrote to Will on January 25: "The New Year is fast passing away; Time is so fleeting, Mama and Papa are growing old. Every year seems shorter as we grow older."[133]
Sallie Hogg was only thirty-seven.
She kept up her letters to Will at school.

Austin, Texas, Feb. 15 1892
My precious boy—
I received your letter yesterday, it is needless to say I was delighted. It found us all well. I have had a very severe cold that has made me feel quite unwell. The weather is much colder this morning. I sent your bible last Friday. Bill [the Capitol porter] I reckon has sent your pants he said he was going to send them last Thursday. The City is full of witnesses in the Allee case [a sensational murder trial], of which you have heard. Dr. White the new Superintendent at the Lunatic Asylum is in charge. I have never been out to see them. I have such a feeling of sadness that I do not feel as though I could go out there soon.
Sister is practicing so sweetly now I wish you could hear her. I am teaching Mike and Tom their a.b.c.'s, it is quite a task. Well it is Monday morning and I will have to help about dinner, so excuse Mama this time, just so you hear from us.
Do not study too hard Willie it will, I fear, injure your health. Take care of your health if you lose that you will be set back more

than your hard study will accomplish. Good bye. God bless you. All join in love.

Your Affectionate
Mother[134]

In a few days, Sallie was feeling better, and she wrote cheerfully to Will:

Austin, Texas, March 6th 1892
My dear boy

I know I will be busy tomorrow, as it will be Monday, and is always a busy day with all housekeepers. I went to church today. The day is perfectly beautiful. Mr. Brock Robertson is spending the day, Guy's father. I hope Guy is doing well now, do all you can to help him to be a good boy, but don't allow yourself to be led off by anybody. If you say so I will send you a coat and vest from here or you can go to Tyler and get you one. Papa says you can go to Tyler and get you one if you like. I expect I can do better here. Write me back immediately about it, exactly what you would like to have. We are all quite well. Papa is very busy. I am so sorry for him he has to work so hard. I hope this will be the last campaign he will ever enter personally. I want him always to work for his friends of course. We had lettuce out of our garden today for dinner. You will have to wait until I get our bible home before I send you the births of us all.

I will send your account as soon as I can. I can't bother Papa often. I will have Bill to attend to it for me. I will wait for the next month and send all together. So goodby for this time.

Your affectionate Mother
Sallie H.[135]

Sallie had good reason not to "bother Papa." Not only was he planning another campaign for governor, his Railroad Commission was under fire: The first lawsuit against the commission came in April, and it involved his good friend Tom Campbell, the state-appointed receiver for the I&GN. Other cases by other railroad interests would soon follow, and the constitutionality of the commission was repeatedly questioned. The controversy would not be settled until 1894, when a U.S. Supreme Court case, *Reagan v. Farmer's Loan and Trust Company*, ruled that the Texas Railroad Commission was constitutional.[136]

Hogg's first term as governor had been full of controversy, and his efforts to regulate railroads operating in Texas had made many enemies. With these in mind, he wrote a long, thoughtful letter to Will on April 19 as he began his next political battle:

My Dear Son:

On tomorrow I leave home to begin a second campaign the next day at Wills Point for Governor. The guiding star of my life has been Duty and fidelity to Trust. In following it many bitter antagonisms have been aroused against me but I hope they will temper and melt away in the light of Truth. You may at times feel annoyed by newspaper filings but looking over a life of forty one years, in every way searching earnestly for something on which to base a charge my enemies have been unable to find and they can never find a single dishonorable act connected with my private or public career. In this respect I am fortified and feel strong in the cause of justice to stand for the people's rights. No[w] my son there is nothing that affords me more pleasure than to say to you as I leave on a long, hot campaign in which my name will not be spared, that I have in all respects led an honorable life. Your course at school has been so manly and thoughtful of my feelings and interests that I have no burdens added to an already heavy load from your actions. Year by year my confidence in you has increased until now I am led to confidently believe that I shall be spared the humiliation of most public men for my son has never committed an act unworthy [of] his name.

With an abiding faith in God Almighty and that in all respects the guiding Star of Duty will lead to h[appi]ness in the life hereafter, if not in temporal affairs, I remain,

> Affectionately
> Your Father,
> J. S. Hogg[137]

With her husband again on the campaign trail, Sallie took the children for a stay at the Stinsons'. Jim Hogg was entering what would be a bitter, hard-fought race for the governorship.

On May 3, Hogg and his opponent, George C. Clark, met at Cameron, Texas, in a joint debate, speaking for several hours before a large crowd. They did the same thing the next day at Cleburne. The governor had not had time to write to Sallie, and she was growing weary of managing by herself.

Dear papa,

This is the 6th of May and not a word or letter have I received from you. You are certainly and surely carrying out your word as to my having to paddle my own canoe during the canvass. You must remember I have several in my canoe and without a loving word or cheer from papa my boat might sink.

We are all up, Ma has been very dangerously ill but is able to [get] out again. We went fishing and caught a nice lot of fish. Mike caught one, Sister several. Grace is not at all well, looks very frail.

Be sure to have Neals to water the garden thoroughly. And tell him to take Mrs. Swearingen some beans when they bear and anything else that is in the garden.

Pa is looking for Bob Bruce and Judge McCord out today to take a fish.* How I wish you were with them. Send me news every Sunday.

I will say goodbye for this time. All the babes send love and kisses with Mama.

> Yours affectionately and devotedly,
> Sarah Hogg[138]

Jim Hogg had no time for fishing that summer. He was constantly campaigning, constantly traveling. And the candidate did not like to travel by himself. As Ima recalled:

> During the years that he had to campaign he always seemed to want one of the children with him. Before I was old enough and Mother was not well enough, brother Will went with him. Then I frequently accompanied him on his campaigns. . . .[139]

There is nothing in the family letters about Will's father taking him on the campaign trail in 1890. Will spent that spring and summer at the Stinsons'. In the gubernatorial campaign of 1892, it was Ima who went with Hogg on the hustings. The *Dallas Morning News* noted on June 14 that "the Governor and his little daughter" were using Hogg's railroad pass to good advantage.[140] In June they went to Denton for a major speech. Denton, about forty miles north of Dallas, was a fast-growing town: From 1880 to 1890 its population more than doubled, to 2,558—a growth spurred by the completion of

---

* Bob Bruce and Judge McCord were friends of the Hoggs' from Mineola.

railroads that connected Denton with the rest of the country. In 1890 the North Texas Normal College (now the University of North Texas) had opened its doors. Besides that, Denton was the home of Hogg's sister, Julia Ferguson, and his widowed sister-in-law, Anna Hogg, and a gaggle of nieces and nephews.

A brass band met the train that brought Ima and the governor, who spoke to a large and enthusiastic crowd. After the speech the *Denton County News* reported that "Miss Ima Hogg gave a reception at the H. C. Ferguson home that was something of a social event."[141]

But, as Ima remembered, the trips with her father were not always easy:

> We experienced the greatest inconveniences making train connections, laying off for hours at junctions at midnight and arriving at any hour at some destination. It seemed to me there was a great deal of rain and I remember often being pulled out of the mud in order to make some scheduled appointment. Father had a way of letting you feel in the background which was what he knew I would like. Often we visited friends at these times and I would enjoy the children of the family while he spoke, but many times all of us would go and inconspicuously be among those in the audience.[142]

The story of Governor Hogg having children named Ima, Ura, and Hesa entered Texas lore soon after he was elected, and it made national news. In May 1891 a Kansas newspaper reported that "Governor Hogg of Texas has three bright children, two girls and a boy, whose names respectively are said to be Ima Hogg, Ura Hogg, and Moore Hogg. These names were bestowed by Governor Hogg himself."[143] Hogg was a masterly politician who knew how to please his audience when he made speeches. If he pointed to his daughter and her little friends and joked that "This is my daughter Ima, and this is Ura, and that is Moore . . . ," one can imagine the crowd's amusement. Ima always denied it, but the story took on a life of its own. In the summer of 1892, a story circulated around Texas that when Hogg appeared, Ima and a little friend of hers sat on the platform "at more than one of his speakings. And on each occasion the big East Texan playfully introduced them as 'my daughters, Ima and Ura Hogg.'"[144]

The story was widely circulated. After the election was over (Hogg won), he received a letter from James P. Owens, a Texan then living in Denver, Colorado:

Hon. Jas S. Hogg
Austin, Tex
Dear Sir:

I trust you will pardon me for being so inquisitive, but as I have had a dispute over it I appeal to you for a decision. Please tell me if you have three children named Ura, Ima, & Hesa? were they so christened?

This all came about by a party knowing I was a Texan asking me if it were really true that the Governor's children were named as above. I said no, but he was quite sure of it—So I trust you will be kind enough to help me out of it.

Very Truly Yours
Jas. P. Owens
213 Ernest & Cranmer Bldg
Denver Colo[145]

The governor's reply to this letter has not been located.

Hogg had waged a vigorous campaign, making eighty-nine speeches in three months. But he was never too busy to think of his family. His sister-in-law Anna had become seriously ill, perhaps with cancer, in Denton, and on July 9, the day after he ended his round of campaign speeches, he wrote letters to Anna and to H. C. Ferguson, recommending that Dr. Swearingen in Austin see Anna, as he said to Ferguson, "to save her life or alleviate her suffering."[146]

Dr. Swearingen had been close to the Hogg family ever since they moved to Austin. Ima remembered him: "We had a wonderful family physician at the Mansion, Dr. Swearingen, and he, like everyone else who knew Mother, was devoted to her. He came immediately on call and did not mind how long he stayed or at what hour it was necessary to call him."[147] But Dr. Swearingen could do little for Anna Hogg. She had only a few months to live.

Meanwhile, Anna's brother-in-law had an election to win. As governor, Hogg had made a name for himself as the champion of the "little people" over big business, and had waged war against railroads and corporate interests operating in the state of Texas. Hogg's opponent, George C. Clark, argued that Hogg's regulatory measures were driving investment capital out of the state and accused Hogg of demagoguery. Neither side could resist cartoons and slogans based on the image of a candidate named Hogg who weighed nearly three hundred pounds: "We love Hogg for his Grit." "Hogg has rooted in the public pastures long enough, turn him out!"[148] The gubernatorial campaign of 1892 was one of the most vitriolic campaigns in the history of the state.

When the hot summer campaign of 1892 was over, James Stephen Hogg had won the Democratic Party's nomination for a second term as governor.

PART II
AT HOME AND AWAY
1892–1895

Politics was meat and drink to Jim Hogg, and his appetite was as large as his person. He relished the crowds he attracted and the speeches he gave, in Texas and elsewhere. In his second term as governor and the year after he left office, he traveled constantly, and his family missed him. When he was at home, receptions and dinners, Sunday evening songfests, and visiting nieces and nephews made the Governor's Mansion a lively place, with a doting paterfamilias presiding.

That is how it was in Ima's memoirs, composed many years later. But there were shadows in this glowing family portrait. In the fall of 1892, Will began his freshman year at Southwestern University, but for reasons that remain unclear did not return there for the spring term. Anna Hogg, mother of five and widow of Hogg's eldest brother, died. Sallie Hogg's health continued to decline. From September 1893 to February 1894, no family letters have been located. Tom contracted typhoid fever in the spring of 1894. Will left Austin to work for a time at the Southwestern Insane Asylum in San Antonio.

In June 1894, Governor Hogg took Ima with him and twenty-three prominent Texans on a tour of major U.S. cities to promote investments in Texas. Ima, age twelve, was the only female on the tour.[1] An ailing Sallie reminded her husband not to forget about his eldest son, then nineteen. Hogg, caught up in politics and business ventures, wrote dutiful letters when he traveled, but often seemed oblivious to family concerns.

In March 1895, Hogg left Austin on an extended business trip to New York and Boston. In April, Sallie was diagnosed with tuberculosis. In May, she and Ima left Texas to seek a cure in Colorado. Mike and Tom went to stay with the Stinsons, and Will stayed in Austin, studying for a law degree at the University of Texas. Jim Hogg did not return to Texas until June. He did not see Sallie and Ima until August, when he took Will, Mike, and Tom with him to Colorado to be at her bedside. All of the family was reunited at last in the late summer of 1895, but Sallie was very, very ill.

• • •

In August 1892, the Democratic Party had nominated Jim Hogg again for governor, but he could not count on an automatic win in November. George Clark had formed his own party, the Jeffersonian Democrats, and Thomas Nugent was running on the Populist Party ticket. Hogg would have to keep on campaigning until election day. He was already exhausted from months of traveling and speaking. In August, when the Democratic convention in Houston was over, he came home to Austin and was confined to his bed for about ten days with what he called "something like a bilious attack."[2] But he was soon able to write to his sister Julia's son, James McDugald, about attending the University of Texas.

Sept. 6, 1892

Dear Jimmie:
    While my finances are low and necessarily must so remain while I am in office, I shall nevertheless take pleasure in doing what I can to aid you in completing your education through the University here, in obedience to your expressed wish by favor of the lst inst. I can at least furnish you board, books and stationery for the next year, by which, on proper application eschewing theatres, balls and frolics of all kinds, you can graduate in the law department with distinguished honors. You possess fine abilities, good character, a splendid constitution and elements of greatness, which if cultivated will lead you to success. I am proud of you and will be glad to render you such assistance as my limited financial condition will permit.
    So, you can pack your trunk and come to my house at any time before the beginning of the fall session and buckle yourself down to work.
                                    Your Uncle,
                                    J. S. Hogg[3]

Sallie wrote to Will, who was beginning his freshman year at Southwestern University in Georgetown, Texas.

Sept. 8th, 1892
My dear boy—
    Knowing you are a little "cranky" about hearing from home once a week, I will proceed to enlighten you as to our condition at this time. We are all as well as usual. Nothing unusual has occurred to change things. . . . Annie said tell you she lived at 1010 Lavaca.* However I would not take up much time in writing. Write once in a while but not so often to outsiders. The children are doing nicely at school. Sister is doing splendidly. She seems to comprehend better.
    Papa has gone to Johnson City to speak today. Poor fellow the lies that are being [told] upon him are simply appalling. Everything

---

* Annie McCoy, a close family friend, was a frequent guest at the mansion.

that can ever be heard or dreamed of is being done to beat him. Yet I know he is so pure and honest that he will beat them in the end. Justice and right will prevail in the long run. "Truth crushed to earth will rise again." Well goodbye all send love to you.

> Your affectionate
> Mother[4]

Sallie never became accustomed to criticism of her husband from his political foes, as Ima recalled: "Mother was very sensitive and suffered a great deal over campaign stories derogatory to Father. Of course, Father tried to make light of all such things no matter how he may have felt but she never could see them that way."[5]

The governor was occupied with his reelection campaign, and his opponents, Clark and Nugent—the Jeffersonian Democrat and the Populist—were giving him no quarter. He wrote a hurried note to his eldest son:

Sept. 16, 1892
Master W. C. Hogg,
Georgetown, Texas.
My Dear Sir—

Herewith I send you money order No. 19012 for fifty dollars out of which you can pay your necessary expenses until further demands are made.

We are all well. Ima, Mike and Tom are in School, each doing well, with prospects of emulating their oldest brother's good example.

> With much love,
> Your Father,
> J. S. Hogg[6]

Ima reminisced about her own school days years later:

My first school was a private kindergarten near our house on Fourteenth Street, owned by a Mrs. Ziller. She was part German and a Christian Scientist. Her school was small and had a very charming atmosphere. When Mike and Tom were old enough they first went to kindergarten at the Misses Bakers'. It was in the same block with Mrs. Hood's Seminary, which I attended. Later, these two little boys went to public school for a number of years but I continued at Mrs. Hood's and later at Miss Carrington's. One of the reasons for my going to private schools was so I would have special attention in lan-

guage and time for my piano. Mother was very intent on my learning to speak both French and German. These two schools were very
fine in English and History and Miss Carrington's was fairly good in
Mathematics, but they both were short on science.[7]

Mrs. Mary Ziller, the wife of August Ziller, the deputy state and
county tax collector, held classes at her house 506 West Fourteenth
Street, just a few doors away from the Hoggs' residence at 500 West
Fourteenth. When the Hoggs moved into the Governor's Mansion in
1891, schools for the younger children were still close by. The Misses
Mary and Emily Baker had a small private school on the corner of
Colorado and West Tenth Street, less than a block from the Governor's Mansion. Mrs. Hood's Seminary at 202 West Eighth Street was
about a block further. Mike and Tom and Ima were only a hop, skip,
and a jump from school.

Miss Carrington's University Preparatory School, which Ima
attended later, was also close to the mansion, on the southeast corner
of Tenth and Guadalupe. The Misses Mignonette and Lillian Carrington were the principals, and Mignonette became a good friend of
Sallie Hogg's.

Jimmie McDugald arrived at the mansion on September 26. Sallie,
who had been ill, wrote to Will: "I am gradually improving. . . .
Jimmie came last Monday. He got in the University by a scratch."[8]

In Denton, Anna Hogg's long illness was drawing to a close. On
November 2, a mournful Sallie wrote to Will, "We are sure of but one
thing in life, and that is death."[9] On November 4, 1892, Anna Hogg
died at age forty-six. She was buried in Denton the next day on a
family plot near her husband and their eldest daughter, Lucanda, who
had died in 1891, and their younger daughter, Ethel, who had burned
to death in 1889. The family plot also contained the grave of Anna's
infant granddaughter, Anna Elizabeth Kelso, who had died in 1890.

Four days after Anna's death, the November 8 election put Governor James Stephen Hogg back in office for a second term. When
the votes were counted, Hogg had 170,486 to Clark's 133,395. The
Houston Daily Post carried a cartoon of a giant hog labeled "J. S. H."
swallowing a body labeled "Clark," with the caption, "The Last of
Clark."[10]

Jim Hogg's brother John, still seeking the success that seemed to
elude him, may have felt a pang of jealousy when he wrote shortly
after the election:

Nov. 25th, 1892
Dear Jim:
I will be an applicant for the position of Post Master at this
place [Decatur] and write asking your advice in the matter. It is
worth, I am told, from $2500.00 to $3000.00 per year. In case
I make the application, can or will you be in a situation that
you can assist me in getting Coke's & Mills's influence.* I have
bought property and am now moving to town in order that I
may be convenient to School. Taking the stand I did for Judge
Smith for Congress, against Cockrell may work against me in
getting his (Cockrell's) endorsement.† No news. All well Love
to all—let me hear from you

Your Bro.
John W Hogg[11]

This letter was written on the letterhead of the New York Life
Insurance Company in Decatur. Its president was Jim Hogg's friend
John McCall. John Hogg, now forty-four, had been sheriff of Wise
County from 1878 to 1880 and had served a term as county clerk in
1882. For a man with a family, the postmaster's job was a lucrative
one. At $3,000 a year, it would be worth over $70,000 in present-day
dollars. John and Eva were moving from their ranch into Decatur so
that their daughters, Velma, fifteen; Maud, ten; and Eugenia, eight,
could attend school there.

In Austin that winter the Governor's Mansion was a lively place,
with twenty-two-year-old Jimmie McDugald added to the Hogg
household and preparations underway not only for Christmas but
also for the New Year's reception and Jim Hogg's second inauguration in January. In December, Sallie was feeling well enough to order
clothes, including a pair of "boy's pants age five" for Tom, from "Ed.
Kiam, Mammoth Clothier, Houston, Main St. at Congress Ave."[12]

Ima recalled festive times at the mansion, often with houseguests
for the formal balls.

> Dinners and receptions were very formal, and the Mansion was
> the center of life with many parties going on. . . . So many daughters

---

* Richard Coke and Roger Q. Mills were the two U.S. senators from Texas.

† Jeremiah V. Cockrell was a district judge in Texas's Thirty-Ninth District who
had run against Smith for Congress in 1892.

of Father's friends around the State visited us . . . As there was no one else at the Mansion the young lady visitors allowed me to assist them in their toilettes. This was to me a special privilege. The young ladies loved to have me brush their long tresses and to pull their silk strings in their corsets. It was the style to have little waists, eighteen or even twenty inches around. No one used any cosmetics, perhaps a little prepared chalk or rice powder, all of which did not adhere. . . .

Many of the young ladies were talented. I remember an exquisite blonde played the violin; another was a fine pianist. Anyone in town who could perform on an instrument was welcome and invited to entertain friends in the evenings. . . . Father's beautiful voice blended in as falsetto, baritone or bass as needed. Mother could play the piano, but usually I was called on to lead at the piano.[13]

That winter the governor, recovered from the rigors of the fall campaign and election, went back to long days at the Capitol, every day but Sunday. As Ima remembered:

Sunday was a Sabbath in our house—though a busy one in its way. Father, of course, never went to the office under any circumstances, nor worked on Sunday. He stayed at home with Mother, probably both of them thinking this was good for their souls. We children were hustled off to the Methodist Church on East 10th Street for Sunday School regularly every Sunday morning, and as long as we lived in Austin my two younger brothers and I attended. Mother was a very pious Christian but seldom felt equal to expending the extra energy it took to go to Church. It had been Mother's heart's desire for my brother Will to be a Methodist minister and . . . he seriously considered preparing himself for the ministry. Mother came from a long line of strict Methodists and I understood there had always been Methodist ministers in the family. . . .

Father was of a deeply religious nature but did not care for dogma and was physically too uncomfortable in a church pew to attend services. As long as he lived, it was the custom for him to join with us on Sunday evenings singing favorite hymns.

We usually had company for Sunday mid-day dinner. In the afternoon, if the weather was good, Father would love to fill the hack with children and drive to the country.[14]

No doubt the governor and his children saw others who were also out for a Sunday drive. Ima remembered that "it was quite the fashion for ladies and gentlemen to drive up and down Congress Avenue and over the Colorado bridge, [and] around the capitol grounds, especially on Sunday afternoons. Many Victorias [light, open carriages] drawn by fine horses with the driver on the seat above made a beautiful picture."[15] But Governor Hogg himself, as Ima recalled, "always drove on these occasions. I don't think Mother went. It was another opportunity for her to have some quiet."[16]

Peace and quiet were in short supply at the Governor's Mansion during the week, as guests came and went, and the Hogg children were usually involved:

> Life in general, around our home was an education in itself. As children we were permitted, except on rare occasions, to sit at the table with the grown people and were well instructed in listening and not being heard. The talk was always on a high plane and also was very lively. We heard a great deal about what people read and books were discussed as well as public affairs.[17]

Governor Hogg juggled family responsibilities and official business that winter, with five railroad cases in the U.S. Circuit Court at Austin. And his brother John wanted his help in procuring a postmastership in Decatur.

> Dec. 27, 1892
> Dear Jim:
> Yours of 24 last to hand and in reply will say that I am an applicant for the postmastership and would like very much that you write to Judge Cockrell at once in my behalf. I am satisfied that he has not committed himself to no one yet. There is a great pressure brot to bear in the interest of another party. I think a letter from you at once might settle the matter. If you hear from him let me hear from you.
> We are all well. Have just finished moving. Love to all
> Your Bro
> John W Hogg[18]

John Hogg did get the postmaster's job, appointed by President Grover Cleveland. Meanwhile, the New Year's Day reception and the festivities of the governor's second inauguration came and went.

In March, John Hogg wrote to his brother, asking for another political favor. He wanted to see a friend appointed to the Board of

Sanitation Commissioners, but "with a promise that it shall be my last request at your hands for a favor of this kind." But in a few weeks he wrote again to ask for another friend's appointment to the Board of Pardons.[19]

In April, Sallie and Ima visited family friends, the Finleys, in Huntsville. Ten-year-old Ima, who had traveled by herself to join her mother, wrote to her father:

April 14th, 1893

Dear Papa

I arrived here this evening safe-ly and Hancel met me at Phelps and so did Maud Whatley. I was very glad to see them both. How are Mike and Tom and brother Will? Hancel is in a concert on Monday night. I am going to it. Papa tell Grace to express my banjo just as soon as you go home to dinner. Please don't forget to do it.

I know you have lots of letters to read so I don't want to bother you. I must close. I send my best love to you and so does Mamma and all of us here [at] Mrs. Finley's. Do not bother about writing to us un-less you have time enough time.

Your loving daughter,

Ima Hogg[20]

Sallie and her daughter had consigned their menfolk to a bachelor existence in Austin. Jim Hogg wrote to Sallie on April 19, 1893:

Dear Sallie:

All three of the boys—Willie, Mike, and Tom, are well and get-ting along splendidly. Things look lonesome when I am at the house, but we manage to make out, tolerably well. The truth is our boys are gentlemen, and appear 'specially so when they have the responsibili-ties of housekeeping thrown on them. The legislature will probably adjourn sometime in June or July. Then I'll take a rest.

Ima's last letter was so sensible and nice that I want more of them.

Love to all.

Yours,

J. S. Hogg[21]

Ima kept the letters coming:

April 21st, 1893
Dear Papa
        I went to a party this evening and had a splendid time. . . . Papa I
am so glad that you sent my banjo. I was so lone-some while Hancel
was gone to school until the banjo came. Hancel is scared to write to
you because she is afraid that you won't read her letter. We are going
serenading to-night around in the neighbor-hood. How are you all?
Papa if you have time I wouldn't mind if you would write me a letter.
Has brother decided to stay home with Mike and Tom? How are
Grace and Nancy?
        Papa as I said before I know you have many letters to read so I
must close. We all send lots of love.
                                Your loving Daughter
                                Ima Hogg[22]

Ima's letter suggests that Will's plans were in flux that year. He
had celebrated his eighteenth birthday on January 31, and he had
not returned to Georgetown for the spring term at Southwestern. His
cousin Jimmie McDugald was boarding with the Hoggs and attending the University of Texas. For reasons unclear, Will was staying
at home.

After the legislature had adjourned in May, Jim Hogg wrote to
Denton to Hermilla's husband, Robert Kelso, about finding a school
for Hermilla's youngest sister, fifteen-year-old Annie, whose mother
had died the year before: "I wish you would tell her that after she
goes to school a year or so longer, I would like to have her take her
turn with us in receiving the finishing touches of a higher education.
We kept Velma about two years, and now have Jimmie. We also want
Baylor when Jimmie's time is out; and in turn the other boys and
Annie to go to school from our house."[23]

Ima noted in her reminiscences:

        Wherever we lived, members of the family were frequently visit-
    ing us. There was hardly ever a time when some niece or nephew
    was not staying at the house and going to school. Father always
    seemed to feel that he should see that some member of his family
    was being afforded a better education than they might obtain in their
    own home town.[24]

Velma, John Hogg's eldest daughter, had come to live with the
Hoggs in Austin from 1890 to 1892. The current boarder, Jimmie

McDugald, was Julia Hogg's son by her first husband. The "other boys" were Brownlee and Bismarck Ferguson, sons of Julia and H. C. Ferguson.

In June, Sallie and children set out for their summer visit with the Stinsons. But Governor Hogg, whose mind was on politics, forgot to arrange for their transportation from Mineola. Sallie let him know about it in no uncertain terms: "We came out last Saturday. You did not telegraph to Mr. Bruce, to meet us at the depot, consequently we were in quite a desolate condition on getting there. The whole town was mud, mud, and water [Mineola did not have paved streets until 1922] . . . and we waded through the mud to Mrs. Bruce's. I would have telegraphed myself but you said you would. I am tired pulling around by myself anyhow."[25]

That was as sharp a scolding as Sallie ever gave to her husband. The rest of her letter was cheerful, with news of the children. She closed the letter with

> Affectionately & lovingly
> Sallie Hogg

But "& lovingly" was inserted as a penitent afterthought.

Hogg also received a scolding from his daughter:

> June 16th, 1893
>
> Dear Papa,
>
> I arrived at Granpapa's this evening at three thirty p.m. I had a nice trip out here but a very ruff one. Please send Tom's fishing hooks and lines to Mamma. She wants them to fish with. Brother was at Mr. Jiles [Giles's] and met Mr. Jiles in Mr. Bruses [Bruce's]. Papa Mamma had to go up to Mr. Bruces all by her-self. You forgot to tellagraph to Mr. Bruce. Didn't you?
>
> We met Mr. and Mrs. Spivy at Palestine Texas and they came up to Mr. Spivey's house with us. Give my love to all my friends. How are you? I hope you are well.
>
> The trip out here seamed as if it were 50 miles long. We all got so tired but didn't let on about it to Mamma. Mamma and us are perfectly well. You can write more often. We get mail every 3 days, on Monday, Wednesday, and Friday. . . .
>
> Ima Hogg

The next day she wrote again:

Papa send us some fishing tackle we want to go a fishing. Send us poles [illegible] and all. Grandpa says that you must come down soon that fishing is finer than it has been for years and he also said that his crops were fine. We will soon have fine fruit.

Grand-pa gave us a beautiful large goat. It is an Angoler goat. It is as black as anything I ever saw. . . .

P.S. Please let Grace to hunt up my banjo books, the large one and the small one too and let Bill send it by the next mail.[26]

In Austin that summer of 1893, the governor was left with only various family pets for company. There were plenty of those, as Ima recalled:

Throughout all the years that we kept house, there were various and sundry kinds of pets for us to play with. I don't know how much responsibility we took for their care, but Father always saw that they were fed. Mike was the naturalist of the family. He gathered all sorts of little rocks and stones and baby animals and birds. If there were any wounded ones or sick ones he knew how to nurse them back to health. There were baby coons, 'possums, squirrels, kids, and all sorts of dogs and cats. Each one us would claim our own dog.[27]

On June 3, Ima's father wrote to her:

Dear Daughter:

Herewith I hand you a programme of the "University Commencement Ball." It was a splendid affair, though I did not dance. Col. S. W. P. Lanham was my guest on that night and in the absence of your Mama acted as "Belle of the Ball" with me. This programme reminds me of the frolic the boarding house people had at our house Saturday night. . . . The thing made me feel so lonesome that I cannot tolerate its repetition.—Last night the mosquitoes made a raid on me and nearly sucked a spoon full of rich blood from me. I expect they treated me about like the fleas have you since you got to the Mill. My company consists of Mike's cat, Tom's squirrel, your parrot, the fish and your Mama's duck. Poor Willie. He lost his bird, took his saddle off and I sold his horse, so that he has no living or inanimate thing here to really remind me of him except his picture on the wall. It looks at me quite naturally every time I sit at the desk. As I think of the matter, I shall vote the old hen to him. What do you say? What do Mike and Tom say? The vote of we four will be the majority of the family and so, if all agree, Will can have the hen. Now keep an eye on Mike when it comes to voting on this proposition.

Last evening I rode out to the White's. Frank met me at the door and said: "Howdy Gov. Hogg! The dogs are well!" . . . Frank is having a fine time with Mike and Tom's puppies. Crops are good here, but rain is needed. People generally report good prospects of fine crops. How are they in Wood Co.? Give love to all.

Your Papa,

J. S. Hogg[28]

Colonel Lanham was Congressman Samuel W. T. Lanham, of Weatherford. He would be elected governor in 1902.

Sallie and the children settled in at the Stinsons' for the summer. Years later, Ima remembered those visits in loving detail:

> One of the happy memories was gathering the early morning eggs or late afternoon eggs with Grandmother Stinson. She would allow us to go with her, taking a basket and gathering dozens of eggs every day. Then I was permitted to help churn in the morning. A man usually would do the milking early and someone would put the milk into the crock bowls and place them on a covered porch where cheesecloth protected the milk from insects and flies. There was a long bench with a long covered box-like affair to fit the bench and a lid which raised so that rows of milk bowls were set inside. It was a sight to see the wonderful cream which was rolled off this milk, It was as thick as butter. There were troughs in the yard for waste milk which the chickens and fowls fed from. The sour milk and clabber were sent down to the barn yard for the pigs. This part of the place was quite far from the residence and here were stalled the horses, mules, and oxen, . . .[29]

On June 6, Ima answered her father's letter:

Dear Papa:

I am more than delighted with Speer if you were only here. Papa, please fix it up some way for you to come down. . . . Papa ask the man who took your picture to give one to you and you send it to me. Mamma has been very very ill. After all the apples, peaches and plumes [plums] are ripe we have blackberries and strawberries too. You haven't got any strawberries and black[berries]. Have you? The crops are doing fine if we had more rain it would be the finest crops out. Grandpa has five mills now, two shingle mills, one flower [flour] and meal mill, and one mill to smooth lumber and a lumber mill. We all send love.

I am your daughter,

Ima H.

P.S. Papa the invitations are beautiful and I will keep them if I can as long as I can. The pencil to the ball program got broken.

Ima[30]

At an early age, Ima Hogg, the future collector of antiques, was already concerned with preserving the past.

With Sallie and the children visiting the Stinsons, the governor took his meals at the Andrews boardinghouse on Fourteenth Street. He wrote a short letter to Sallie:

June 23, 1893
Dear Sallie—

The house [the Governor's Mansion] is in good order. I am well. Spivey has not yet returned. The Commencement has closed. The weather is hot. The boarding house people [are] gay. William the gardener is faithful and is generally cleaning up. Grace puts in an appearance once in awhile but is complaining of [a] cold. Mr. Levy and Bill are happy as ever.* Col. Lanham spent one night with me. With this exception I have been alone. No news except money panic is about over, it is not so bad.

To all—

Have a nice time and enjoy yourselves. Tell the folks at home that I am very hot up here and wish I could be in the cool shade there with them. I'll be there I hope by watermelon time. Then we will all go fishing and have a big frolic. Around the house here from morning 'till night there's not a sound even of a rat, cat, or cricket. The cow, parrots, the dogs and all gone. I am like a ghost in a two story barn <u>deserted</u>. Love and affection

Your Husband and Father

J. S. Hogg[31]

Ima missed her father more and more: On June 23 she wrote to him: "Papa please write to me I get so home-sick sometimes that I

---

* R. B. Levy was Hogg's private secretary, and Bill Boulding, the Capitol porter.

don't know what to do. Papa please come down to see us in a little while."[32]

He obliged with a letter, but he was not coming to see her:

June 26, 1893

My Dear Daughter:

You cannot well appreciate how greatly I value your frequent, nicely written letters. You have improved wonderfully and I expect to see you a fine writer some of these days. In Company with General Reagan and six other friends I am to leave in a few hours for a few days "outing" up the Lake on Bull Creek. We of course expect to have plenty of fish and a nice time.—At this moment there are three little boys standing around talking to me, neither of them being as large as Tom or Mike. They are very friendly with me and remind me so much of rude boys generally. There are very few boys that behave as nicely as Mike and Tom. Don't you think so?

Well, daughter, tell your Mama that I have been boarding at Mrs. Andrews where there were 14 girls, five widows, two widowers, about six unmarried men and not one married person but myself. I can't stand it much longer. This perhaps the cause of my trip to the woods. The city looks now deserted since the schools all have closed, and the married men are collecting together in squads for comfort and pleasure.

Now write me all the news and draw on your fancy once in awhile within the confines of the poets privilege to entertain me. Give love to all.

Your papa,

J. S. Hogg[33]

In a letter she wrote to her father on June 30, Ima did her best to entice him to come to see her: "Papa my birthday is on the 10th of July and I want you to be down here on my birthday. Papa please come. We are all well. Mama was sick yesterday with sick head-ache. But is now well. . . . Grandpa's yearling is the finest animal I ever saw in my life. You must see it." If that were not tempting enough, Ima reminded her father that the watermelons and peaches and apples would all be ripe. The letter ends with a final plea: "If you can come down for my birthday let me know. We all send lots of kisses and love. Hoping you will come." She added a postscript: "Write soon."[34]

Hogg and his cronies had enjoyed their fishing trip, as he wrote to Sallie:

June 30, 1893
Dear Sallie:

After an absence since Monday evening out fishing returned last night brown and healthy, full of vigor and spirit of labor, ready to stand the summer's work. Nothing could have refreshed me more. Our party was made up of General Reagan, General Mabry, J. J. Faulk, J. H. Henderson, John Dowell, J. J. Tobin, R. S. Harrison, Harry Owens, four boys and Moses the bald-headed negro cook. Mr. Owens was chosen general quartermaster, financial agent and camp boss. At little expense to each of us he laid in a supply of everything necessary to make camp life pleasant. I wrote you that we would go to Gen'l Mabry's ranch ten miles above town. So we did and were not misled in the selection. During the three days we caught about five hundred fish, three coons, one squirrel and robbed a bee tree, or stump, rather.

The sun never shone on our camp for in the morning and evening the tall hills and at noon a large walnut tree protected us. Sitting in one place in the shade, I caught out of one hole (water of course) over sixty goggle-eyed perch! Ask the boys what do they think of that? It was generally conceded that I was the "perch fisherman" of the crowd. We had an abundance of the finny tribe to eat at each meal. Only one casualty occurred and that amounted to but little— I fell into the creek! Right away the rascals began to hunt for the modern enemy of the fat man—a codock [Kodak]! Well I keep my eyes open after that and gave them no chance to take an ugly picture of me.—

Well the fishing over, I now find the delayed correspondence heavy, but Spivey and Bill are on hand in good trim for the work. Mr. Levy and all the force are well. Everything at the house seems to be getting along very nicely, except at night and then lonesomeness prevails. Up to date I have seen no ghosts, but of course am like all old widowers am ready for them.—At this moment two gentlemen have called and Bill is waiting for the mail. I must therefore hurry and quit.

Tell Ima I shall write her a long letter soon. Tell Mike and Tom that they must keep out of flea beds and bull nettles so as to be in good trim to go with me fishing when I go down there soon. Tell Willie to get in good trim for the University for I expect him to win the medal there. Give all my love. In haste, Yours affectionately

J. S. Hogg[35]

Hogg's fishing companions were his close friends and colleagues: the most prominent one was John H. Reagan, the former U.S. senator, who had resigned his Senate seat in 1890 (taking a salary cut from $7,500 to $4,000) to head the first Texas Railroad Commission. Adjutant General W. H. Mabry had been appointed in 1891 in Hogg's first term as governor and would continue in that office until 1898. R. S. Harrison was assistant attorney general. J. J. Faulk, J. H. Henderson, and John Dowell were Austin attorneys; J. J. Tobin was the proprietor of the Austin Stationery and Printing Company; and Harry Owens, the camp "quartermaster," was a merchant.

A few days later Hogg wrote again to Sallie, mostly about the "money panic" he had mentioned in his letter of June 23. The entire nation felt the recession known as the "Panic of 1893." Banks collapsed; businesses closed; unemployment rose. A dollar in 1893 had the purchasing power of about twenty-four dollars at present. In the letter that follows, it is useful to know that Hogg's worrisome $8,000 debt would be the equivalent of $192,000 in today's dollars.

July 8th, 1893

Dear Sallie—

When you left home three weeks ago I expected to join you at Mr. Stinson's before this time. In fact my intention then was to remain in Austin but little for several weeks. You may recollect that I predicted that a terrible financial panic was pending and would soon shake this government from center to circumference. This led me to make an effort to put my business affairs in tangible, safe condition. . . .*

If I can get off, my stay there will be necessarily short. I am anxious to see all the people and especially Mr. Stinson and the children. I think if he and I can get out on the pond together with Mike and Tom to carry bait and Willie to hold the oars and Ima to run around on the banks in the shade and sing that famous old song about the girl hanging "her clothes on a hickory limb," we can land a dozen or so of the finest trout that ever splashed the water over that pond! Should I find that I cannot get off I shall write to you by Wednesday's mail in the hope that you may find it convenient and desirable

---

* Hogg was able to put his finances in order with the aid of the independently wealthy Texan, Edward Mandell House, who had helped him win the governorship. House was active behind the scenes in Texas politics until 1902, when he moved to New York. He later became a close advisor to President Woodrow Wilson. In Austin, J. S. Hogg and E. M. House and their families had become good friends.

to return about the end of the week. In that event bring Willie with you, if he would like to come. I know I would enjoy his company this Summer.

Your Husband, Affectionately,
J. S. Hogg[36]

Business and politics occupied the governor that summer, and he did not mention Ima's July 10 birthday in his July 8 letter to Sallie. He was not there for the big day, and a sad letter from his daughter reached him a few days later:

July 10th, 1893
My dear Papa,
 To-day is my birthday and I am eleven to-day. I am not at all glad. I don't want to get any older. I was sick yesterday evening and Ben was sick this morning, but is better now. Mamma was sick with a sick head-ache. Ben and Tom are down at the mill. Mike has a tooth grown way back in his moth [mouth] under his tongue. Mike says he wants to come home so bad. Mamma says she thinks you ought to come down here after us. We will start for Mineola Thursday and stay one day and then go on home. I went to church yesterday evening 4 miles from here. I must close as I haven't any news. . . .
Ima Hogg
P.S. . . . . Please come. Mama is coming home because she wants to see you.[37]

Ben Stinson, who lived at the Stinson's, was the children's cousin. He was the son of Sallie's brother, Jim, and his deceased first wife.[38]

Jim Hogg had told Sallie on July 8 that he would write to her "by Wednesday's mail" (July 12) if he could not come to Speer, and he hoped that if not, she could come home by the end of the week. According to Ima's July 10 letter, Sallie was already planning to return to Austin on Thursday, July 13. Since some letters are missing, it is not clear what happened. As much as he longed to frolic with his children in the country, Governor Hogg may not have made it to Speer that July. Political and financial concerns probably kept him in Austin. Overwork and hot weather sapped his strength, and as he wrote in August to his nephew Baylor Hogg, he was going to "the Coast" for a few days "to get well."

Aug. 12, 1893
Dear Nephew:

When I received your letter asking the loan of $300 to help you get on at Medical School to begin next fall, my financial condition was such that I did not feel safe in promising it. . . . I am about out of money with my salary alone to subsist on. In a whole year I have managed to save $300 out of it which I need in paying the debts referred to. Now after this explanation to you, I beg to say this: If you feel disposed to and will spend the year here at School—the University of course—your board, tuition, &c., shall not cost you anything. We will be glad to have you as a member of the family, the same as with Jim McDugald. If you have made other arrangements or if you think best to go elsewhere I shall cheerfully endorse your note bearing eight or ten per cent interest for the sum of $300 payable at some future, convenient, stated, time, to anyone who will let you have that amount.

In all respects consistent with my financial ability I am willing to aid my honorable nephew who possesses the manhood, nerve and independence to help himself. Freely write to me. I go to the Coast to get well. Will be absent a week or so.

Affectionately, Your Uncle,
J. S. Hogg[39]

Baylor did not come to Austin, but opted for medical school in Galveston instead.

Jimmie McDugald was now "James McDugald, Esq." and looking for his first job as a lawyer. His uncle wrote to him in Denton:

Aug. 23, 1893
Dear Nephew—

I have just seen the senior member of the firm of Camp & Camp of San Antonio, and am glad to say the position is yet open for you. Mr. Camp assures me that you will be able to at least make a living from the start. This means, Jim, that all the balance depends on your manhood, industry, capacity and merits. My advice is to accept. Come by here and remain a day or so for further advice, when you go down. Write to me. In haste,

Your Uncle,
J. S. Hogg[40]

Ima and her mother were in San Antonio in September, but the three boys were back in Austin, presumably in school. Ima wrote to her father on September 6 to come to San Antonio and "bring Mike, Tom, and Brother Will."[41] What Ima and Sallie were doing in San Antonio is not clear. It is possible that Sallie, who had been in poor health for much of that summer, may have gone for a medical consultation in San Antonio.

Meanwhile, Jim Hogg's second term as governor would soon be over, and he had many things yet to accomplish. He traveled constantly, making speeches, talking business and politics. When Hogg traveled, sometimes he took his daughter with him, as he had done in the campaign of 1892.

In June of 1894, father and daughter went on a tour of ten major midwestern and eastern cities organized by Texas businessmen. Governor Hogg was to publicize his reform programs and the Railroad Commission, and to attract investment capital to Texas. With the governor in special railroad cars went a company of "prominent citizens of the Lone Star State," as *The New York Times* described them.[42] They were executives, bankers, investors, journalists, and lawyers, twenty-three in all. Ima was the only female in the party. As she remembered:

> It was a very amazing and enlightening experience and Father seemed to believe that anything in which he took part was becoming for me also. The men on these trips were not restrained by my presence and used to sit around playing poker until late at night. Father gave me a chair around the table where we both looked on. They imbibed very freely of alcohol while Father drank only Apollinaris and Vichy and took no hand in the game. He never seemed to make them feel he was disapproving but explained to them he could not afford to lose even if sometime he might win. Evidently they accepted his explanation without further question. I was usually put to bed by ten o'clock. . . .[43]

At age twelve, Ima Hogg saw New York City for the first time. The nation's largest city then had a population of more than 2,000,000. By the turn of the century that figure would approach 3,500,000. Chicago was in second place with over 1,600,000, and Philadelphia was third, with 1,200,000. Governor Hogg and his party stayed at what was then New York's most luxurious hostelry, the Fifth Avenue Hotel, at 200 Fifth Avenue. Opening in 1859, its famous guests had included Abraham Lincoln, U. S. Grant, and Cornelius Vanderbilt.

It was only six stories tall, but its interior was filled with velvet and rosewood and gilt, and it boasted the first passenger elevator in an American hotel. Ima never forgot her first visit:

> We stayed at the old Fifth Avenue Hotel in New York. After all the descriptions given me by our colored cook at the Mansion, New York was a great disappointment to me! Broadway was not as wide as Congress Avenue. Macy's was not as stylish as Hatzfeld's; but the Fifth Avenue Hotel and Delmonico's were glorious enough. The elevators at the hotel were a novelty. The meals were served table d'hote—many courses, ending up with great compotes of various ice creams, strawberry, pistachio, chocolate, and vanilla flavored from the vanilla bean. The Fifth Avenue Hotel was justly famous for its cuisine. There was a great concert in Madison Square Garden with a faint memory of a great tenor, maybe Jean De Rezke. There were enormous bouquets of flowers sent to the hotels, banquets, and much attention shown at parties. We saw the first electric piano players and the first phonographs at this time. The Eden Musée [a famous New York entertainment palace, with a wax museum, concert hall, and various exhibits] was in the same block with the Fifth Avenue Hotel. I cannot remember all the places where the entertaining took place, but in Providence, Rhode Island, we were the house guests of Governor Brown of that state. He had a charming family and a daughter my own age. It was a great relief to find a little companion my own age.[44]

Ima wrote often to her mother, describing what she saw:

Fifth Avenue Hotel
Madison Square, New York
June 24, 1894
Dear Mamma:
  I stayed the evening yesterday, with Mr. and Mrs. DeFriece [DeFrece], and had a beautiful time—They showed me many lovely things; a piano that played by electricity, it could play any thing right off by the music it had to have music to play though; and I saw a kind of a box and you looked through a glass and saw many things, all moved by electricity, and in it I saw Sandow the strongest man in the world: I saw a pony do many tricks; and I saw a rooster fight, and a scene in a saloon. I went to a flower house and saw how they

kept flowers in the summer time; they had a refrigerator as large as a room and the flowers were kept in there: they had a cat as white as the snow and it had pale blue eyes, realy blue, and the wool was very long and curley, it was called an angora cat: it was the prettiest thing I ever looked at. I wish you were here with me to see all of these things: I went into one of the largest candy stores in the city and [it] was lovely. Last night I went to a show, theater, it was simply grand, one of the best plays I ever went to in my life; the principle charator was <u>Mr. Curtis</u> of Austin, Papa and every one that went thought him one of the best actors they ever saw: he gave us a box, in fact all of the party; he got some of the prettiest bouquets, and Mrs. Curtis was in one of the boxes and she sent the prettiest bouquet to me. Every-time he got a chance, he sliped a word to papa. After the play he came down and spoke with us. He got off lots of good jokes on the Austin people. He played he was a peddler and had striped stockings, and these red handkerchiefs, and the ugliest suspenders, and said "these came from Phil Hatzfelds, do you know him? He is a dry goods merchant, don't you know" and he said, "I know a man at <u>Austin</u> that keep's a big wholesale store, but I would hate to deal with him his name is John Orr!" he got off better ones than that but I cant remember them just now.

This morning I am going to stay all day with Mr. and Mrs. Fegeld [Feigl]. Mrs. Fegald is from Texas. He has something to do with the "Tammany Times."

Well I will close this letter. I think you could write me a letter and I will get it, we are going to stay here a good while longer. Give my love to all with a billion kisses.

Your Daughter
Ima Hogg.[45]

Abram Brougham DeFrece was a wealthy journalist and publisher, and evidently a New York friend of J. S. Hogg. Fred Feigl, editor of the *Tammany Times*, a New York newspaper, was a former Hogg staff member. Both men attended the theater with the Texas contingent on June 23, to see M. R. Curtis in "Sam'l of Posen" at the Standard Theatre.[46]

Ima felt uncomfortable being the only female in the touring party. She recalled her feelings years later: "I was the only girl in the party on the trip . . . I got tired of not seeing any women."[47] On June 26, she wrote to Sallie from New York: "The party had their picture taken today: papa wanted to have mine taken too but as I was the only girl along, I didn't want my picture alone with a pack of men; would you have it taken either?"[48]

On June 29, 1894, the traveling governor reported to his wife from the Oakland Beach Hotel at Warwick, Rhode Island:

Dear Sallie—

We reached this seaside Rhode Island resort at about 5 this p.m., after taking dinner in and riding over the beautiful capital city of Providence. Ima is in the other room near me playing "snap" with two little girls and a bachelor, while Governor Brown of this State looks on. In the Hall near me is the chatter of convivial Texian and Rhode Islander voices in merry social confab. We spent two days in Boston in the most pleasant way. Before the Chamber of Commerce there, by 'special invitation, I delivered an address yesterday afternoon on "Texas," which you may see published by the time this reaches you. Experienced men say they never knew such a crowded Hall of business men give anyone such attention before as they paid me. Our delegation expressed great satisfaction over the effort. So I feel very well satisfied. Yesterday morning the Governor and State Legislature received us. In the Senate Chamber before that august body I made a short speech and was accorded great courtesy indeed. Throughout the whole trip we have been royally received and entertained. From this place we will leave to-morrow and spend Monday in Philadelphia where I am to deliver an address. Thence we will go via Washington, Cincinnati and St. Louis home, remaining in each place perhaps a day. Our trip will bear great fruit for great Texas.

Well I must quit, as Ima is playing Washington Post march, and the crowd demand my attention. God bless you. Love and kisses to all.

> Affectionately
> Your Husband
> J. S. Hogg[49]

Sallie was worried about her health, and she desperately missed her daughter and her husband. Towards the end of the tour she wrote to him from the Stinsons':

July 7, 1894

My precious Husband—

I thank the good Lord for his manifold blessings, and one of which I am doubly thankful for and that is to write to you again, and to feel that you at least are near me, and in Texas. I am wild to see my child. I have never missed her so badly and sadly in my life. The days have seemed weeks, the weeks months since you all left home, This is Saturday the 7th, and no word as to when she will be in Mineola. I expected a letter yesterday telling me when to send for her. I am going to get Jimmie to go anyway Monday to see if she is there. If you ever take her again you will have to take her mamy, too. I found all able to be up at home. Ma hobbles around, just can hardly walk.

The boys are having a delightful time, eating all the melons that they can possibly hold. Tom has just eaten a half.

I have had to pull three teeth for Tom since I came out here. Negro George pulled them. The first one he walked up and let him pull out, but he yelled then. In a few days I discovered that two new teeth had come out back of his lower front teeth that must be pulled. I could not hire or persuade him to have them pulled, so Jimmie, Dave and Mr. Derrick held him while George pulled both teeth.* He cussed them black and blue and fought like a wild cat.

They say their lessons regularly and are both learning very well. Mr. Levy is so thoughtful and kind to write me twice a week, the news. Poor Judge Stayton, isn't that a calamity? Now Texas, all Texas needs him and will miss him. Boon Goode died a few days ago.† We had quite a storm this week, that extended beyond Mineola doing great damage to property, unroofing a good many homes in Mineola. Pa's fences were blown down.

You had better write to Willie and have him go up and stay with you out at the Camp, make him feel that you don't forget him. If it were not for the encampment I would meet Ima in Mineola and go home, as I have been exceedingly unwell ever since you left. I have fallen off eight—or nine lbs, and am getting thinner.

I do trust Ima will be in Mineola tomorrow when Jimmie goes over for her. If she is not I will almost die with disappointment for

---

* Jimmie was James Stinson, Sallie's brother. Of Tom's tooth-pullers, George was the Hogg family's servant; Dave (Burkett) was Sallie's brother-in-law, married to her sister, Lillie. The identity of Mr. Derrick is not known.

† Sallie was saddened by the death of Judge John W. Stayton, the Chief Justice of the Texas Supreme Court. He had administered the oath of office at Hogg's inauguration in 1891. Boon Goode was a family friend in Mineola.

him to come back without her. I would [give] anything to see you. With a world of love and kisses and God's blessings I say goodbye.

Lovingly and affectionately

Your Sallie H[50]

The ten-city tour ended, and Ima returned to her mother and younger brothers at the Stinsons'. Will was in San Antonio part of that summer, evidently working at the Southwestern Insane Asylum. His letters mention a "Mr. Jameson," who was very likely Joe Lee Jameson, who lived and worked at the asylum.

On July 9, Will wrote a stiffly formal and somewhat wistful letter to his father.

Dear Father:

Accept my congratulations on your pleasant and profitable trip—profitable to both yourself and to Texas. From the newspaper comments on yourself and party, it seems you all created quite a ripple of excitement North and East. Dr. Barker mailed Mr. Jameson copies of northern papers, so we kept posted very well throughout the whole trip.* I am indeed glad you took sister along—she learned a great deal. I received a letter from her written from Philadelphia commenting on the different cities—named Chicago as the most beautiful and of hotels said Fifth Avenue Hotel was very fine, but the Hotel Metropolis of Philadelphia was "simply" lovely and grand—owned and run by a Texas man.

I noticed in one of the papers you had several inducements offered you of partnerships in prominent firms. I wonder if you don't become a New Yorker yet (?) I want you to write me something of your plans—they will not be divulged. I would like to hear your opinion of what's best for me to do next fall—go up north to study preparatory to Law, or what? I would like to be with you to talk about your trip, but you will be "encamp" during the "Drill" and Mother will not be home, so I guess I had better stay here.

With love

Your Son

Will Hogg[51]

---

* William Louis Barker was the superintendent of the Southwestern Insane Asylum. Governor Hogg had appointed him in 1891. Barker was also one of the Texans on tour with Hogg.

Although Ima wrote to Will during her trip, J. S. Hogg evidently did not. And Will, who had been working in San Antonio that summer, was evidently uncertain of his future plans.

Will was now nineteen years old. His father had not taken him on the tour, and he had not invited him to the Encampment, as Sallie had hoped. The Encampment was a major summer event in Austin that involved young people of Will's age from all over Texas. Military volunteer units came to drill and parade, and young ladies who were the units' sponsors came to cheer them on. Ima described the Encampment in her memoir:

> General Mabry [Hogg's good friend] was head of the Texas Militia and a graduate of V.M.I., I think, and evidently had a great talent for drawing the volunteer guard from various towns all over Texas to the summer Encampment. With as little variety of amusement as was offered in those days, these companies furnished the center of local social interest. I do not know how many Encampments I saw but I remember them very well. The young men in these companies were usually from the more prominent families and it was considered quite an honor for a young lady to be sponsor for her home company.[52]

Jim Hogg finally took Sallie's advice and issued a belated invitation to Will to come to Austin for the Encampment, but Will declined:

> July 11th, 1894
> Dear Father:
>   I received your letter today. Mother not being home, I would rather not be in Austin until she comes. Did you see Dr. Barker's interview in [the San Antonio] "Express" about your trip. He got off a good joke on Mr. Wortham [the state treasurer].
>   [Portion omitted from typescript.]
>   Mother seems—in every letter she writes to me—blue and morose on account of her ill health. Write her and brace her up into a more happy mood. She said she looked like a ghoul—of course it's all imagination.
>   With love
>   Your Son
>   Will Hogg[53]

As usual, Governor Hogg's public life was at war with his private concerns. Sallie's frail health, Will's hurt feelings, and the Encampment had to compete with Governor Hogg's concern over a major national event that had begun in May of that year: the Pullman railroad workers' strike in Illinois. It was the first national strike in U.S. history. In July, President Grover Cleveland sent federal troops to Illinois—without the consent of that state's governor, John Peter Altgeld.[54] On July 18, when the Encampment ended, Governor Hogg was presented with a gold watch, and his thank-you speech turned into an oration about the strike in Illinois. As a staunch supporter of states' rights and labor's rights as well, he could not help saying a few words defending Governor Altgeld and castigating the Democratic President Cleveland for dispatching federal troops into a state for the first time since the Civil War. The speech made headlines across the nation. Hogg then defended his Encampment message in a major speech in San Antonio on August 1.[55]

On August 14, the state Democratic Party convention began in Dallas, and the outgoing Governor Hogg was much in evidence. He was not seeking another term, but he was working to assure the nomination of a gubernatorial candidate who would continue his hard-fought reforms. After days of political horse-trading, Charles Culberson, who had been Hogg's attorney general, won the nomination. After the convention, Hogg, Culberson, Reagan, House, and a few others took a celebratory fishing trip to Rockport.

Sallie and the children had returned to Austin in late July, after the Encampment. Presumably Will then joined them.

As soon as the state convention was over, Hogg, soon to be the former governor, launched himself into the fall campaign, traveling the state to make speeches for Culberson and the Texas Democratic Party. He was in his element.

On October 5, he dashed off a quick note to Sallie from the Commercial Hotel in Lufkin:

Dear Sallie:

To-night here, I made my ninth speech since leaving home. Have had large crowds, a royal time and fine success. Am quite fatigued but will get a good rest Sunday at Nacogdoches where I am to speak to-morrow.

No news. Love to the noble boys, and sweet little Ima, and to yourself the quintessence of love.

Yours

J. S. Hogg[56]

Later that month he wrote to Sallie again, this time from the Grand Windsor Hotel in Dallas, as he continued his whirlwind tour.

Oct. 21, 1894
Dear Sallie:

Yesterday I "touched the button" and opened the Fair. Today I am taking rest. Tomorrow I go to Cleburne to speak in the day and at night at Alvarado. Next day I am to speak at Hillsboro; Wednesday night at Ft. Worth and two or three other appointments will wind up my week's work so that I may reach home Saturday evening or Sunday morning. Next week following, my engagements are thick and fast, beginning at Palestine on Monday 27th. So you will be a "widow" until after the election. Hope you will have parties, dances, frolics and entertainments to pass of the time pleasantly during my absence. Keep young folks with you as much as possible for such association postpones old age to the last.—My intention was to remain here at the Fair but I cannot do so in peace. People are calling for me by letters, telegrams, and in person by committees. It is easier to speak than to apologize or render excuses. My friends seem to think I am made of iron, and their claims on me are so heavy and just that I cannot refuse so long as vitalities last. Closing my twenty-ninth speech last night I found myself much fatigued, but to-day a good rest places [me] in line all right for the week. John McCall has been with me ever since we left Austin, and you know I have not lacked for good company. We had a great time in El Paso and across the river in Mexico. From there (Mexico) I expressed to you, not the boys, a fine dog—a pup rather. It's of a large, very valuable German stock. Also I had some fine pecans shipped from Eastland to the family. The Fair is going to be fine. I hope you will spend awhile at it. If possible get Mrs. House [E. M. House's wife, Lulie] and others to come with you. Stop at the Windsor Hotel. My time is so taken up that I cannot attend the Fair but that need not prevent your attending it. Everywhere the people treat me so well that I am proud that I have gone so extensively into the campaign.

With love to the children, to the family, to the servants, and a double share to yourself.

Your Husband,
Affectionately, J. S. Hogg[57]

Hogg relished being in the political arena—especially in the limelight. Besotted by the acclaim he was receiving everywhere he went, he could not find time to escort his wife to the state fair. Not even Sallie had the power to lure him from his first love: politics.

The Houses and their two daughters, Mona and Janet, lived in a grand Austin house atop a hill at 1704 West Avenue. The two couples and their children were close friends.[58]

At the end of 1894, with his friend Charles Culberson safely elected as his successor as governor, Hogg could pause to look back over his own accomplishments and to set them down in a self-congratulatory letter to Martha Frances in Pueblo. He wrote to her just a few days before Christmas.

Dec. 20, 1894
Dear Sister:

My last message to the Legislature is about finished, Sallie and the children are all asleep and in the quiet solitude of the night I am glad to say a few words to you. After rather an eventful career of eight years at the Capitol I am on the verge of permanent retirement to private life. Recently I have reviewed the record and checked up every branch and Department of the Government. Result: Every pledge of reform I made as a candidate for Governor has been fully redeemed and now stands in the shape of accepted and acceptable law. Every institution has been operated economically, efficiently, without scandal, at reduced expense. Tonight I have the endorsement of the people and above all the support of a clear conscience. So I am willing, anxious to quit. To you I may say, I hope without the suspicion of immodesty, that the U.S. Senatorship was open to me without opposition from any source next time. Not only did I decline to become a candidate at a time when all parties wanted me to run but I promptly announced that under no circumstances would I accept the place. So my best friend Chilton became a candidate and will be elected next January without opposition. Thus my appointment of him has at last been approved (or will be) by the people, and this will finish the approval and endorsement of all my important public official acts as Governor. My period of public life is therefore "well rounded" and my cup of ambition is full. And speaking tonight in the fear of God I can say what but few men can truthfully state, that I am on friendly terms with every living creature in being that I know or ever heard of. My next start in life though in poverty will be a happy one, with prospects of success good all along the line.

The Administration to succeed me is cordial and friendly to me in every way possible. My Attorney General, Mr. Culberson, is to be the Governor. <u>My</u> Lieutenant Governor, Mr. Crane, is to be the Attorney General. <u>My</u> Treasurer, Mr. Wortham, is to succeed himself. <u>My</u> appointee as Financial Agent of the Penitentiaries—R. Watt Finley—is to be the Comptroller. <u>My</u> Appointee as Temporary Land Commissioner, Mr. Baker, is to be the Land Commissioner. <u>My</u> Appointee to fill a vacancy, Mr. Carlisle, is to succeed himself as State Supt. of Public Education. So are the Commissioner of Agriculture, &c., the Adjutant General, the State Health Officer, the Superintendent and the two assistants of the Penitentiaries, and many other officers. Under the new administration were my appointees to places and for years were associated with me intimately. Texas is my friend and I am, thank the Lord, the friend of Texas. John [Hogg], through me, was tendered either of two of the most important offices under Mr. Culberson, <u>but declined</u>. He is certainly a queer fellow. I cannot understand him except when I lay aside ambition and consider my personal comfort and pleasure.

While this letter sounds egotistical, self-laudatory, it is nevertheless permissible, I am sure to you. I am so glad that I am able to leave office honorably, and fully satisfied, that I must tell <u>somebody</u> of it—who better than yourself? Yes, yourself, My Sister, to whom I could always go for a smile, for help and encouragement in the struggling days of my blundering youth?

Well I am through, except to say that Sallie and the children are well and happy, and to send greetings to yourself, William and family.

May the Great God in whom I trust shower blessings on you all.
Your Brother,
J. S. Hogg[59]

Martha Frances Hogg Davis treasured this letter and enclosed it when she wrote to the governor's eldest son. The copy of her letter to Will is undated.

[Portion omitted from typescript.]

Willie boy, in case you're ever Governor of the Grand Old State of Texas, make this record. Yes, I know, but isn't it one to be proud of? I have kept this letter for you boys—dear boys to me—for fear you had but memory to refer to, and I knew, having the record, given by that honest hand, even tho the half is not told—would comfort you, and refresh memory even. From boyhood to manhood he was just what that honest letter proclaims him. . . .

Kiss Miss Ima on the tip of her nose for me. Why didn't you come
out, as you promised? I was quite sot up at the thought of it.

Aunt[60]

In January 1895, Jim Hogg turned over the governorship to his
successor, Charles Culberson. The Hoggs moved out of the mansion
to the Driskill Hotel, and then to Miss Mary Begley's boardinghouse
at 206 West Ninth Street, less than two blocks from the mansion. By
March, Hogg had established his law partnership with Judge James
Harvey Robertson, a Texas district judge whom Hogg had appointed
in 1891. The first office of Hogg & Robertson was at 105 West Eighth
Street, around the corner from the Begley boardinghouse. Hogg (who
could have used the exercise) did not have to walk very far to his
new job.

The winter of 1895 was a cold one in Austin. On February 15, Jim
Hogg wrote a note to his sister Julia in Denton:

Dear Sister:

My intention has been and is to visit you if I can possibly take the
time when I go to North Texas. Your letter only reminds me that I
have done about all the visiting amongst our kin-people. They have
stayed at <u>home</u> while I have done the courtesies. This is no hint, but
a broad hit at you Sister. But I am not mad. I'll surely go as often
to see you as possible, and my chances to go frequently are growing
better. Your boys all promise well. Jim is a fine fellow and will succeed. The other two will follow suit. In all their success I certainly
will take great pride. All well but frozen up. Goodbye,

Your Brother,

J. S. Hogg[61]

By March 1895, Hogg was once more on the road, this time to St.
Louis, Chicago, New York, and Boston to interest business investors
in Texas. Wearing his new attorney's hat (and also the mantle of a
popular ex-governor of Texas), he had been engaged by several companies eager to solicit investments from outside the state. In particular,
he was the agent to sell securities for the "Link Line," or Georgetown
Railroad, the connection between Georgetown and Round Rock, a
junction with the I&GN Railroad.[62] He was also working for the
Texas Sugar Refinery, the Texas Equitable Coal Company, the Oasis
Irrigation Company, and others. The Texas Promotion, Deposit and

Fidelity Company had engaged him as an advisor for $3,000 per year. Hogg had also agreed to be the legal counsel for the Texas Trunk Line railroad, for an annual fee of $5,000 (the equivalent of about $132,000 today) for ten years.[63] With this and his other enterprises, the former governor was expecting to do well financially. He also expected Sallie's health to improve now that she was free of the hectic pace of life in the Governor's Mansion. He was wrong on both counts.

Jim Hogg left Austin on March 24, his forty-fourth birthday. He would be gone until June, and he would not see his wife until August. On March 28, he sent a note to Sallie from the Southern Hotel in St. Louis.

Dear Sallie:

    I write simply to express my continued affection and to say that I shall leave for N.Y. by Chicago tonight. My trip here has been pleasant and will result well. No news.

    Give love and kisses to all the dear ones at home and this of course includes yourself.

                    Your Husband, Affectionately

                    J. S. Hogg[64]

Meanwhile, Ima wrote to her father and made him a birthday present. From the Fifth Avenue Hotel in New York, he wrote on April 6 to thank her.

Dear Ima:

    I was very proud to receive your only, but nice letter reminding me that I am 43, and that you had made me a nice cushion head rest as a birthday present. Well I had rather get a hand made present of that kind than the rarest jewel to be found in the mines of Africa. But my child I am 44! I am growing old but feel like an 18 year old boy. I will be here a week yet; probably longer. Will write you a long letter one of these days. Good bye.

                    Love to all.

                    Your Papa[65]

A week later, still in New York, he wrote to Sallie:

April 13, 1895

Dear Sallie:

    Hastily I write to express compliments. My work here is growing as my correspondence increases each day. Prospects are good, but there may be some of the Col. Sellers "visionary hope" in me.* If so I prefer it to clouds and murky forebodings that produce gloom and despair. I believe I will <u>succeed</u>. If I do then all will be well. If I do not all will be well anyway. So it goes. Your move was sensible. Take good care of yourself.

Affectionately Yours
J. S. Hogg[66]

The former governor was hoping for lucrative business deals in New York and elsewhere. The "move" he refers to was Sallie's sending the younger boys to stay with the Stinsons.

In a letter dated "Easter Morn" (April 14), Martha Frances Davis wrote to her favorite brother about his political career:

Dear James:

And it is done. The bugle notes of your Dallas speech [at the state Democratic Party convention in August] did call the clans together, and they bury the hatchet, smoke the pipe of peace, wash off the war paint and embrace. Good! Very good!! They were sick enough no doubt, But yours is the "Lion's" share, as usual. What a very fairy story your career has been. I stand in increasing wonder at your genius, "wrapped," as Napoleon, "in the solitude of its own originality," But the anomaly comes in the situation when you and George Clark out-harmonize harmony by a Clark-Hogg coalition in favor of Chilton. That <u>would</u> break the camel's back, to be sure. But Clark knows he's out of the saddle and is glad to have a mount <u>behind</u> you, as that is his only chance.†

How strange—and not so very, either,—to see you a leader of the leaders of men—such men as the Sage of Palestine**—moulding them by your own big, fat, plastic hand. I keep posted, and know intuitively. William and myself argued often about the Senatorship. He believed you were striking for it, would get it. I believed you could get it without the asking almost, but would decline. He didn't

---

* Col. Sellers was a character in *The Gilded Age: A Tale of Today* (1873) a novel by Mark Twain and Charles Dudley Warner, satirizing the business practices of the era.

† Clark was Hogg's political opponent in the gubernatorial race of 1892; Chilton was Hogg's close friend, elected to the U.S. Senate in 1894.

** The "Sage of Palestine" was John H. Reagan.

believe you or any other man would decline, and he actually looked dazed—kinder like he was disappointed, or had had his confidence in something shaken—when you declined to stoop and pick up that office, for he could see that it was at your feet. He cannot understand you, and he was so sure he did, which seems to surprise him. I think it is the surprises joined with originality that please you upon the crest of every wave. It is my principal occupation—watching your career. I've little else to do out here. I was pleased with your letter—glad to get one, as they are much like angels' visits. Hope you are all well. Love to all . . . .

Your Sister.

P.S.

Why not send Sallie out to visit us this Summer? If you cannot come too, send her and the chaps, Sallie anyway. It will do her a world of good I must believe.[67]

For the time being, Sallie and Ima and Will remained in Austin, with Mike and Tom at the Stinsons'. Once again, Ima was kept by her ailing mother's side. The younger boys wrote to Sallie from Speer:

April 17, 1895
Dear Mama
   we got your [letter] we were glad to hear from you.
We are having a fine time riding the horse in the field catching fish we had a little storm and Tom cried. Mamma let us stay all summer. I got a letter from papa and sister we run rabbits write soon

Mike

The following note was added:

Tom says they are going to clean out the [mill] race and he is going to catch some fish, he says for you to let us stay all summer. Ben has got well. Tom says Mike caught a pig in the lot. we milk the little pet cow. Grandpa has a little donkey. This is for Tom. He is standing by the fire and telling me what to write.

Mike & Tom.[68]

Jim Hogg remained hard at work in New York, as he wrote to Sallie:

April 18, 1895
Dear Sallie:
   I am well, but about as tired of New York as I ever get of any place. While I have made a great many valuable acquaintances and have done much to remove the bitter prejudice against Texas I have done nothing definite in procuring the financial aid for the railways. You know I never despair or give up hope. In this I enjoy much relief. There is always something cheerful in the prospect of to-morrow. To-morrow in my case may be a great day. It may not. Company has just come in.
   Good bye. God bless all.
                                    Yours
                                    J. S. H.
Direct letters to Youngs Hotel, Boston, after this. Make Will and Ima write me.[69]

A few days later he wrote to Ima:

                          April 19, 1895
Dear Ima:
   I was so pleased with your last letter and felt so proud that you are getting along so well with your books and music that I tore away from important business affairs to look up something for you. Nothing I could find that looked better or that I thought would suit you more than two jackets and a skirt. So by to-day's express they are forwarded to you. Now don't laugh at my taste if it is bad, for I got Miss Hollingsworth to help me. You see if you make [fun] of me you will offend her in all probability. I go to Boston to-morrow; or at least that is my intention. To-day I met little Miss Brown, of Providence, here at the hotel, with her father and Mother. She asked 'specially about you. You recollect she is the niece of Gov. Brown and took the ride with you at Providence last summer. . . .
   Your thoughtfulness of Mike and Tom on Easter was very kind. That's the way to have good brothers.
   Well, I'm getting home sick, but I must get through with my business if possible before returning. Go see Mona and give my kindest regards to Mr. House's family. With love to you, Mamma, brothers and others,
                                    Your Father,
                                    J. S. Hogg[70]

New York was not all work: Hogg managed to mix business with pleasure. On April 21, staying at the Surf Hotel on Long Island, he visited Fire Island and according to *The New York Times* leased a cottage there: "The Governor expressed himself upon his return as being greatly pleased with the island, and said he was looking forward to having a grand, good time there next season. . . . The Texas Club of which ex-Congressman Ochiltree of Texas is President, will also have its headquarters at the hotel this season."[71]

Back in New York the next day, Hogg penned a special letter to Sallie:

April 22, 1895

Dear Darling Sallie:

   Twenty two years ago to-day we were married! Do you remember? Time has dealt gently, kindly, with us both since then. We have always had plenty and have been allowed by our Great Father our share of happiness. But few days have passed without my returning thanks to Him for it all. Yesterday I spent the day (Sunday) on the Atlantic about forty miles from here at Fire Island, in company with Mr. Well, the proprietor of the Summer resort there. It is a novel, old place and enjoys the distinction of being farther out on the great Ocean than any other point of the Atlantic Coast. While out there I gathered some nice Ocean polished pebbles and common sea shells for Ima and yourself, and Willie, that I shall bring home with me, as souvenirs of the trip.

   Well, I have but little idea when I shall be at home. The Boston people have set May the first to determine whether or not they will back up the "Link Line." If they act favorably I will be alright and will soon thereafter go home. Should they not do so, I may remain somewhere "up North" all the Spring and Summer, and Fall and Winter! I must succeed! If I fail in this undertaking it will be the first, and I shall then content myself with the law practice exclusively, where really I will be happier, I believe anyway.

   Well, the company comes. Must close. God bless you. Let me know when you need money.

                              Yours Affectionately,

                              J. S. Hogg[72]

On April 29, he wrote Ima the long letter he had promised earlier:

Dear Ima:

For two weeks my room has been so crowded with callers that I have been denied the opportunity of writing you and your Mama and brothers as often as I desired. I have written one letter and am also writing this before breakfast. My business engagements are such that I have no idea when I can get off for home. Someday I will be able I hope to stay at <u>Home</u> all the time, for to me "there's no place like home." You know New York is a large place and the people are hard to get acquainted with on business matters. They have been very kind to me, and are now by their attention working me very hard.

Well I collected some nice pebbles and shells for you on the Atlantic on yesterday a week ago. They are worn smooth and are very pretty. Of course you will give Janette, Mona, Juliette, Helen and the other girls some of them. Now your letters are so nice. Can't you keep your promise? I leave for Boston to-morrow. Love to you, Mama & brothers,

Your Father.[73]

Sallie wrote to her husband on April 26, but her letter has not been located. She was obviously unwell and unhappy, and Hogg, in Boston, did his best to comfort her.

May 1, 1895

Dear Sallie:

I reached here last night from New York, and have just got your letter of the 26th. When I left there it was cold and raining and had been for a week or so. Mr. House is about always right. In his last advice to you he <u>may</u> be and I <u>think</u> he is. To make it more certain I feel that it is advisable for you to go see William [Dr. Davis] first, or consult Dr. Wooten and Dr. Swearingen fully. William can and will tell you certainly and a trip there [to Colorado] would help you anyway. <u>Wherever you go take</u> Ima <u>with you</u>. Make her your help and associate. Stop her from staying all night with other girls so that she will be constantly with you. I know if she knew how lonesome you are without her she would never leave you for anybody. Herewith I enclose to you checks for One Hundred and fifty dollars. Do with it as you please. When, or before, it gets out let me know and I will provide more. <u>If I can succeed you can go all over the earth if you wish to</u>. If I do not you can go wherever on due consideration your judgment directs for the benefit of your health. You know my

confidence in Mr. House. With it all I think it decidedly best for you
to see William before taking it.

It is only possible that I will go back there before returning home.
How long I stay here will depend on circumstances. Mr. Taylor, of
Georgetown, is here with me and feels certain that we will close out
soon for all the money necessary to complete the Link Line. If we
do then I will go home. If we do not then I may go to New York or
somewhere else to stay for an indefinite period. By all means take
care of yourself and take things easy. <u>Rest</u> is what you want—what
you need. Advise with Will. He has a bushel of sense and will do the
best by you. If I return to Texas without success you know the result.
Returning there with it you also can imagine the effect. Now do not
let anybody interrupt your needed rest. Do as you please and go
where you want to. But in going out of Texas to a cold, wet, climate,
be careful to do so on good medical advice alone. My work in N.Y.
will get results all right I think. My efforts here [in Boston] I hope
will give immediate good results.

With much love to the children I am

Affectionately, Yours, J. S. Hogg[74]

On May 4, from Young's Hotel in Boston, Ima's father wrote
another letter to her:

Dear Ima:

When I left New York last Tuesday it was cold and raining and
had been for sometime. For the last two weeks of my stay there I did
not leave my room much. Some days it is quite cold and rainy up
here. Since leaving home I have not seen many things of interest for
the reason that I have been hard at work. Some of these days when I
get able I shall take your mother and brothers with yourself all over
the Country to see all the objects of interest that either of you may
wish to see. Write me long, newsy letters, for I enjoy them.

Affectionately, Your Father[75]

The next letter from Sallie must have buoyed Jim Hogg's hopes of
having her well again.

May 8, 1895
Dear Papa

I went to see Dr. Wooten yesterday and had him examine my

lungs and chest well. He says I have bronchitis and catarrhal affection—that my lungs are all right. Now take your time, I am perfectly
satisfied, contented and not impatient at your long stay. I know you
are doing your best to succeed and I fully appreciate it all. . . . Politics
are getting hot here. I am glad you are gone. If you were here they
would say you were at the bottom of it all. The little boys are well.
Dr. Wooten says it will not hurt me to go to Col. some time in June.
Willie and Ima are well and sweet to Mama. Willie shows me the
tenderest care. Well goodbye I will write a long letter next time. With
a world of love-kisses,

> Affectionately,
> Sallie[76]

Sallie's bronchitis continued to be worrisome, and she finally
consulted Dr. Adolph Herff, a specialist in San Antonio. There the
unwelcome diagnosis came: Sallie Hogg had something far worse
than bronchitis and catarrh; she had tuberculosis. In those days, the
disease was often a death sentence. Years later, Ima Hogg recalled that
difficult time: "It was a great blow to Father," she said. "I was with
Mother all the time when she was ill, and my mind was filled with
horror."[77]

Ima and Sallie set out immediately for Pueblo, Colorado, to visit
Dr. William Davis and his family, accepting the invitation Martha
Frances had issued earlier.[78]

Will, who had stayed behind in Austin to help in his father's new
law office, wrote a letter to Sallie on May 10, the day he had said
goodbye to her as she and Ima boarded the train for the long journey
to Colorado. Mother and son were always close, and now twenty-
year-old Will felt a great sadness at Sallie's departure.

"You are gone—," he wrote, "so has the larger part of myself. . .
. When I left you at the train, it was as if I had boxed up the best of
myself and sent it I know not where—it will come back better than it
went; the remaining fragment shall improve also—to be more worthy
of it."[79]

The train ride from Austin to Pueblo was nearly seven hundred
miles, and even with Pullman sleeper cars it was a trip of three days
and two nights. It could not have been easy for the ailing Sallie Hogg.
On the final day of the trip, Sallie wrote to her husband from the
train:

May 12th, 1895
My dear papa—

I left Austin under protest for fear of your return this or next week; but Willie seemed bent on my getting off. I disliked so much to go off just as I expected you home, yet the probability was you would not be home for a month. You never said for sure you would, but that you expected to. I stayed all night with Annie [Annie McCoy, the Hoggs' former neighbor, was now Mrs. L. Milton Brown] in Ft. Worth, left there yesterday at 10 o'clock will get to William [at Pueblo] today at 12:15 so you see it is a short trip. I have not been sick since I started. My head feels a little bad this morning. I think that is from looking out on the snow and the beautiful sunshine. I want you to let me know just what you like for me to do, what the little boys are to do. I do not think it best to let them stay longer than June at home for fear they may get sick. Don't write me any thing to do that you can't financially afford for me to do. I want to see daylight ahead always. Ima has not been looking well, and I know the trip will do her good if it don't me. She is at a critical age, poor little thing. The car is so rough that it's almost impossible to write, so I will say goodbye and I will write after getting to William's. I will see them by noon.

Affectionately & devotedly yours, Sallie[80]

Soon after she reached Pueblo, Sallie wrote to her eldest son, trying to assuage his worries about her: "William has started me on a tonic that he says will soon bring me out of the woods. . . . I believe I am going to get fat and well up here." Then, a word of motherly advice: "Don't read yourself to death."[81]

Will's next letter crossed Sallie's in the mail:

May 21, 1895
Dear Mother,

I feel that you have written to me, and have said in your letter that you arrived safely and without fatigue; but I have not received it.

The office is very tastily furnished. Fine carpets, two highly polished oak tables in the two back rooms, new chairs upholstered in leather, all go to make an appearance of pleasing affluence—which is not. Every one declares "our" office to be the most elegant in town. In fact it lacks one prime attraction to me which you can no doubt guess—father. As he sent instructions to sell the horses, I hope in my next letter to be able to inform you the horses are ours no longer.

Do you know I would give anything within reason to board during this summer in the midst of some refined and intellectual family circle; so that when study hours were over, I could have the advantage of chaste and polished and instructive conversation. As it is, to reap the benefits of choice companionship, I have to strike for the city, which you know I am not prone to do.

I met and sustained another disappointment concerning the set of Blackstone Judge Denman was to send me; I went for them but they had not come. Can my patience hold out, I shall not go in for them until next Saturday.

I received a letter from Mr. Jameson inviting me to San Antonio, June 4th to the Annual Battle of Flowers. I shall not go then, but may go down some Saturday afternoon and spend Sunday with him.*

You must not expect me to write news, for I am out of the news circles. Then, you know how difficult it is to find any to write, especially in Austin. You can while away your time writing to me and your friends, for all the interest with me is at your end of the string. Tell sister to write to me for I see I am in no letter writing mood today.

With love to Aunt Fannie & Cousin Wm's family, and a thousand kisses thrown in for you and sister

Your son
Wm. Hogg.[82]

Will was feeling glum when he wrote this letter. He was worried about his mother's health and his family's finances. His father's efforts to secure eastern capital for various Texas projects had so far been unsuccessful, and the elegant new law office had little financial foundation as yet. The family residence was a boardinghouse. Jim Hogg had instructed Will to sell the horses, which were too expensive to keep in an Austin stable. Left in the city by himself, Will fretted over his law studies, wished for "chaste and polished and instructive conversation," refused his friend's invitation to the famous Battle of Flowers in San Antonio, and complained that Austin, the state capital, was devoid of news. Will was twenty years old, but the pleasures of youth seemed to have no attraction for him.

Jim Hogg, still hoping for success in his various business agreements, had returned in late May from Boston to New York and the

---

* Joe Lee Jameson was still working and living at the Southwestern Insane Asylum.

Fifth Avenue Hotel. Nine-year-old Mike, with the Stinsons at Speer, wrote to him:

> Dear papa
>
> we got letter last night telling us about the cat show you went to. I am glad you are having a good time we are too When granpa cleaned out the race we caught a tub full of fish I catch xom [some] fish every day pet cold [colt] we roap [rope] every day.
>
> Your son
> Mike Hogg.[83]

On May 27, the fond father enclosed this childish note in a letter to Sallie.

> Dear Sallie:
>
> The enclosed letter from Mike is his first to me and I hope you will keep it. I had written two letters to him in connection with Ben and Tom, but no answer came. Then I wrote them about "The Cat Show," I saw up here. This had the desired effect. Now the point in his little effort appears in these sentences: "I am glad you are having a good time. We are too!" Affection, Contentment, Independence! All expressed in so few words. That boy will win. Think of those boys catching a <u>tub full</u> of fish when their Grand Pa cleaned out the race. Think of their roping a pet colt every day! Who would deprive them of such fun? Up here the poor little millions of them look out of six story windows and skip around back alleys for their sport! I crave more to be with Mike and Tom and Ben right now than any-where else, especially if the balance of the family were there. My ambition is to have a great, big <u>Country home</u>. If the Lord spares me I am going to have it. Then we'll all have a happy time in family circles. Love to all.
>
> Affectionately, Your Husband,
> J. S. Hogg[84]

This was the end of May. The hoped-for support for the "Link Line" railroad connection he had mentioned in his April 22 letter to Sallie was not forthcoming. Unfortunately for Hogg, the country was still suffering from the depression of 1893, and investors were wary. He would return to Austin soon and seek his fortune by practicing law. Sallie wrote to Will: "Papa . . . said he would return home in a few days. He is so uncertain about it always that you need not look for him until you have proof of it."[85]

By early June, the business traveler had returned to Austin. Will was there, but Mike and Tom were still at the Stinsons', and Ima and Sallie were in Pueblo. J. S. Hogg wrote to Ima:

June 13, 1895
My Dear Daughter,
    Your sweet little letter of the 2nd has reached me from New York to which place it was directed. I left there on the first day of June and nearly suffocated during the four days travel in getting home. The weather is scorching hot here and I am rather miserable over it. The little brownies you sent me by former letter were cute and interesting and I missed the lioness your last one mentioned. Now it is too bad for you to be spending your time in writing and drawing with only bad pencils and inferior paper. Tell your Mother that I shall accept it as a great favor if she will get some nice material, for you certainly deserve it. From all I can learn you and your Mama will fatten up so we will hardly know either of you. Won't that be nice? No news. Love to all. Kiss all the family for me. Goodbye.
                                    Your Papa[86]

The next day, Hogg wrote to Sallie:

June 14, 1895
Dear Sallie:
    I am so hot that I envy the comfort of the Icelanders in their Seal Skins. Of all the scorching Summers that I have ever experienced I think this takes the lead. A fellow talked to me yesterday about two hours about the Weather and I took one of my "nervous fits" and ran off from him. So, reminded of this, I shall spare your feelings by dismissing the weather subject and getting on to the hotter one—politics. Politics you see is the hottest of all avocations—that is I have heard so. The "boil is potting" now. What the condition will be by fall no man can approximately guess.—While I am a "16 to 1-er" my intention is to keep cool and out of the fray as much as possible. Will comes in daily and is cheerful. We are both well. Crops are great. Health good. The little boys are happy. Kiss em all for me.
                                    Yours as Ever,
                                    Jim[87]

This is one of the rare letters not signed "J. S. Hogg." The politics he referred to was sometimes called "the money question," an economic issue that divided Democrats and Republicans in the 1890s. Democrats pushed for the federal government to coin silver and gold at the ratio of sixteen silver dollars to one gold dollar; Republicans held fast to a policy of tight money and the gold standard, which favored big business. In 1896, William Jennings Bryan would be the Democratic candidate for president, and his friend Jim Hogg would take to the campaign trail for him.

Jim Hogg would never stop thinking about politics, but in the summer of 1895 he was thinking often of his ailing wife. Though his letters do not dwell on her illness, he wrote to her often.

> June 17, 1895
> Dear Sallie:
>   This is Monday and we are all well. Bob Bruce wrote me that he saw the boys at Mr. Stinson's a few days ago and that they are happy. An effort is being made by the Mineola and Pittsburg people to build a railroad between those points. This would be a great thing for your Father. I am sweating out a miserable summer at the Avenue Hotel [less expensive than the Driskill]. My intention is to move out somewhere on the hill so as to get a breeze at night—I spent yesterday at San Antonio with Tom Campbell—that is I went there with him. He is fast improving and agrees to go with me to Colorado this Summer. So you may look for us at least in August. Now enjoy yourself and be stout to hold Tom down when we get there. As ever
> Yours,
> J. S. Hogg.[88]

But Sallie was neither enjoying herself nor getting "stout." She had been in the supposedly healthful air of Colorado for more than a month, and she was no better—in fact, her condition was growing worse. She confided in Will: "This is not a good climate for catarrh I have heard. My right lung has been hurting me worse for ten days. It hurts me to write . . . the use of my arm. You must not stop writing to me because papa has gotten home."[89]

While Jim Hogg stayed at the Avenue Hotel, Will continued to board—perhaps at 1010 Lavaca. Sallie's friend, Minnie Carrington, who lived at 910 Lavaca, wrote to her on June 18 that Will was "boarding in our neighborhood" and "studying very hard on his Blackstone."[90] Will and his father were not close.

On June 19, Jim Hogg wrote to Ima:

Dear Daughter:

From the good style and fine taste of your last letter I have concluded that Colorado must agree with you. It will not take long for
you to be a first class letter writer. I expect Pearl is of great assistance
to you and I hope you will help her too. Now try yourself and write
me a careful description of Pueblo and its surroundings—just about
like you would in a geography about it, You know I never saw Colorado and would like to know all about your opinion of it.

I have attended the University Commencement two or three days
and find it very interesting. I want you to graduate there some day.
As soon as the weather cools I shall go to see Mike and Tom. . . .
All well.

Your Papa[91]

The next day Sallie's husband wrote to her again.

June 20 1895

Dear Sallie:

I enclose you a letter from "Farmer" Shaw to show you his good
opinion of Ima and yourself.* Our friends ask about you daily and
are anxious to know of your speedy restoration to health and return
home. I feel confident that no lady in the State possesses a stronger
hold of friendship on her associates and neighbors than yourself.
Now take good exercise and don't take too much medicine. Be perfectly easy for everything is working smoothly with the "Texas Contingent." I doubt if we could haul Mike and Tom away from Mr.
Stinson's with a "wagon and team." They are too happy to disturb
but I shall go see them soon. Will is improving daily in every way.
He is getting thick with me and seems to enjoy life. The weather is
scorching hot. All well.

Yours,

J. S. Hogg[92]

A few days later, Jim Hogg wrote again to Sallie:

June 26, 1895

Dear Sallie:

Several gentlemen are present and each in turn has "pulled the

---

* Hogg's friend W. A. Shaw lived in Dallas and was the editor of a publication
called *The Texas Farmer*. Shaw had been a member of the 1894 junket to major cities
with Hogg and Ima.

weather on me," saying that "this is the hottest day of the season!" Well I believe it is so, and must demur to writing except to say I herewith enclose to you a draft on N.Y. for Fifty dollars, and that we are all in good health. Willie is now in the office and is "coming out" nicely.

I intend to go to see Mike and Tom in a day or so. Will stop at Tyler. On receipt of this write to me exactly what you think is best for me to do with those boys. Shall I bring them home with me or leave them down there? How would it be to carry them, let them stay awhile out at Sister Julia's or John's? When I visit Colorado in August must I bring them all the way with me? Now write candidly, and I will do what you want. Love to all.

Yours,

J. S. Hogg[93]

From the Stinsons', he wrote a long, newsy letter to Sallie:

July 7, 1895
Dear Sallie:

Leaving Austin Wednesday night last for this place I arrived at Mineola the next day at 12 noon where I got dinner and remained several hours enjoying the company of old friends. All the bridges of Lake Fork and Big Sandy had just been washed out. So I was in a dilemma. Dick McMillen was on hand though and agreed to "head the creeks" and make the trip with me. We crossed Lake Fork near Quitman in a canoe and remained at Quitman all night at the old Patten House. The brightness, newness of the old town recalled to my mind her gayest days. After spending a few hours with the good people there we made headway for Speer in a mule wagon. Getting to Big Sandy at about l o'clock P.M. we crossed on a log. Dick walked to the house for a team and your Father with Mike and Tom came to my relief in about two hours. So at last I reached here all right and found everybody well. In fact they look better than I have seen them in many a day. Rested and fresh we went up the creek fishing yesterday morning. In company with Mike, Tom, and Ben I stuck close to the shady banks to catch perch, while Dick and Mr. Stinson went on the pond trout fishing. As usual, Mike took the lead with Ben next and Tom last in catching fish. Tom baited the hooks, strung the fish and kept up the fun for the crowd. He can get in more scrapes than all the others anyway. While we were scattered along the banks in the cool shade of the jungles below the pond quietly sporting, all of a sudden Tom squalled out at the top of his voice as if a bear had him. He yelled plaintively, loudly, long, he jumped, hopped, ran over brush and briars blindly, frantically and reached my open arms in wild excitement and distress. Of course I was almost fainting by the time he reached me. I thought a snake had bit him, or that some monster had bitten him fatally somewhere. With tears in his eyes he held up the calf of his fat leg and babyishly said: "P-a-p-a—W-a-s-p stung me!" In his rambles he had found and undertook to capture a wasp nest for bait.—This furnished fun for us all, especially Mike and Ben. They found much amusement at poor Tom's expense.

Well I have enjoyed the trip and rest out here and expect to leave for Austin to-morrow. The boys? Of course they will go back with me. I cannot leave without them and they say they want to go "Just to be with Papa and the Bear!" They have gotten along finely out here but I thought best to have them near me. My intention is to board out in the Country or in the Suburbs where they can have plenty of room. Our business is increasing in Austin and I cannot leave there on account of the work we have on hand before August. Tom Campbell promises to make the trip then with me. In the meantime you and Ima had better spend awhile at Colorado Springs or at Manitou. Get Sister and Fannie to go with you if you can. When I get to Austin I will tell you about the boarding house I shall have selected for the boys. You may rest easy about them as well as Will and myself. We will manage to get along in some way until you get in good health. Willie is happy with Genl. Reagan and Judge Brown. He always was a queer boy and daily grows fonder of the company of old men and women. He visits the office every afternoon and takes much interest in its affairs.

All the family here are well. No news except your Pa and all the others have fine crops. I am proud of the way Ima and Pearl get along, and of the way Ima has improved. Pearl must be a very smart, fine girl. I know, of course, that Ima is. Give love to all.

Affectionately Your Husband,

J. S. Hogg[94]

Hogg's affection for Mike and Tom is evident in this letter, as is his distance from Will. In those days, "queer" meant "odd" or "peculiar." The old men whom Will liked were John H. Reagan, seventy-seven, and Thomas Jefferson Brown, fifty-nine. Both were Civil War veterans. Reagan was then head of the Texas Railroad Commission and Brown was an associate justice of the Texas Supreme Court. The "Bear" was the Hogg boys' pet bear cub.

Sallie's condition was growing worse, and she had not seen her husband for more than three months. Her letter begging him to come to Pueblo has not been located, but she mentioned it in her letter to Will:

July 8th 1895
Dear Willie,

I wrote to Papa Saturday that I wanted him to come up, I had been so unwell for two weeks that I felt that I could not endure it any longer. I am now getting up again. . . . My letter will reach Austin this morning that I write [wrote] to Papa to come of course I expected him to arrange his business first. I think I surpassed Job in patience in my separation from Papa, and too I did not think he was very busy now, I felt that I wanted him to help me shake off a terrible homesick melancholy feeling that seemed almost to be taking my life away. In fact I need you or Papa here all the time to be with me. I need some one to lean on, these days and cheer me up so just make up your mind to have help to nurse me back to health once more, if such a thing can be done.

You can do a great deal towards it. More than you imagine.
I am tired so I will say goodbye.
With God's blessings on you. Your mother,
Sallie[95]

July 10 was Ima's thirteenth birthday. She observed it at the Davis's home in Pueblo, with her critically ill mother. No letters describe the birthday celebration, but whatever it was, Sallie's condition cast a pall over it. J. S. Hogg wrote a solemn birthday letter to his daughter:

July 10th, 1895
My Dear Ima:

On reflection I can recall but few epochs in my life's way that present to my mind equal pleasure to this day, thirteen years ago— the date of your birth—the day when the Great God, to whom all Christians owe reverence and obedience, presented to my humble household my dear and only daughter. In all the intervening years with each recurring day I have found nothing but pleasure from this great blessing. My confidence in the purity of your nature, in your deep regard for the rectitude and refinement of your sex at all times, on all occasions, firmly supports and justifies my hope that in no act

of your life shall I ever find cause for disappointment or regret. God
bless you my worthy daughter.
Your Father,
J. S. Hogg[96]

On July 11, Hogg answered a letter from William Davis, his physician nephew:

Dear William:
    Your letter stating that Sallie is getting along well very much
relieved me. Professional obligations bind me here for several weeks
yet. My intention is now as it has been, to visit you in August. In
the meantime I hope you will see that Sallie's condition is made
known to me candidly. If she needs my attention especially I shall
quit business and go to her at anytime. Should you think it safe for
her I believe a change to Colorado Springs, to Manitou or to Denver
would be good for her. . . . keep me posted.
With love to all
                        Your Uncle
                        J. S. Hogg[97]

In her despairing July 8 letter to Will, Sallie had said that although
she was "getting up again," she had been very unwell "for two
weeks." But Dr. Davis's letter said that she was "getting along well."
Tuberculosis patients could have good days and bad days. Davis may
have suggested that Jim Hogg come sooner rather than later to visit
Sallie, and Hogg's answer reflects the difficulty he always had in bal-
ancing business and politics with family. His law practice was just
beginning, and he needed to nurture it.
    On July 11, the same day that he answered Dr. Davis, Jim Hogg
wrote a cheery note to Sallie:

Dear Sallie:
    I spent my first night in my new boarding house, out at Mrs. J.
W. Robertson's, and am in the office early much refreshed. A strong
cool breeze, no mosquitoes and good fare commend it strongly to
me. Mike and Tom are delighted. Willie may move out at the end of
this week. Mr. Owens is to bring in the young bear this morning and
then the boys will be happy. They sleep in the room with me and are
but little trouble. Mrs. R. will take good care of them. So now things

are alright until you can get strong. Our work is getting on well, and prospects are good. With love to all. In haste As Ever,

Yours,

Jim.[98]

The former governor and his two younger sons were boarding with Mrs. John W. (Sophronia) Robertson, a widow whose large white-columned house at 900 West Seventeenth and Pearl still stands on a hill not far from Shoal Creek, then the western boundary of the city. Will, taking courses at the university, was boarding with another widow, Mrs. Addie Robinson who lived on East Avenue near the edge of the campus.

As usual, Hogg did not remain in one place for long, On July 20, he described his recent travels to Sallie:

Dear Sallie:

By this morning's train in company with Gov. Culberson and others (men) I returned from the Tyler Fruit Palace where we spent Wednesday, Thursday, and Friday. Willie is yet there enjoying the company of Mrs. Marsh.* The Palace under all circumstances is very creditable. Next year it will be a great success. Mr. House and family have gone to Portland on the Bay near Rockport for the summer. Austin is hot, dry, and lonesome. I have never seen such unpleasant weather.

We are boarding at Mrs. John W. Robertson's on the hill near House's [the E. M. House residence]. She takes special care of the boys, and they seem happy with their bear and donkey. Tom is a favorite among the women—as usual—all on account of his kisses and baby ways. Mike is too sedate and strong-headed to capture new friends fast but holds fast to old ones.—The Judge and I are happy in the prospects before us.—No news. Tell Ima she has completely won Willie by her fine letters. Time for "Silver Meeting." Must go. Good bye. Love to all.

Yours as Ever,

J. S. Hogg[99]

A few days later, Hogg took the time to answer a letter from his grandnephew, Marion Davis, William Davis's son:

* Mrs. Marsh was the wife of Hogg's former law partner, H. B. Marsh, in Tyler.

July 22, 1895
My Dear Nephew:
    Your letter of the 14th was a surprise and great pleasure to me—a
surprise because I did not know you could write; a pleasure for the
reason that by it I was reminded that you, my only grand-nephew
had thought pleasantly of me. Ima and Pearl should play with you.
When your father was a small boy, like yourself, he played with the
girls almost exclusively when he got a chance. In fact he hunted them
up in preference to the boys. In that way he made me lonesome many
a day. Mike and Tom send love and will go with me in August to see
you if I can take them.
                                        Your Uncle,
                                        J. S. Hogg[100]

    In Pueblo, Sallie's tuberculosis was growing worse, as Ima wrote:

                                        July 25, 1895
Dear Papa,
    I am going to write for Mamma as she is sick and can't. The
peaches you sent Mamma were just splendid. When are you coming?
. . .
    Mamma has been sick in bed for nearly two weeks. She was
worse yesterday but is now better. . . .
Lovingly, your Daughter, Ima Hogg[101]

    William Davis wrote to Jim Hogg on July 25, the same day that
Ima wrote to him, apparently reporting on Sallie's deteriorating condition, but that letter has not been found. Dr. Davis wrote again the
next day:

                                        July 26th, 1895
Dear Jim:
    Sallie seems better than when I wrote you yesterday. Indeed
was entirely comfortable all day yesterday and up to this morning
without any medicine. Had to give her a dose of Svapniae [purified
opium] this morning.* She began to complain some.
    They [Ima and the Davis children] seem entirely happy. Ima and
Pearl are quite "chummy." They seem entirely happy with each

---

* Svapniae" was a form of opium often prescribed by physicians at the time. See *St.
Louis Clinique: A Monthly Journal of Clinical Medicine* 14 (February 1901), 85–88.

other—they are constantly together, and when they have company they treat them quite nicely. . . .

William[102]

At long last, Sallie's husband set a date to come to Pueblo:

July 27, 1895
Dear Sallie—

I will leave Texas to visit you about the 7th or 8th of August. So be in good cheer and ready to go to a cooler place. Do you want me to bring all or either of the boys with me? They are the best fellows in the State and I shall, with great pride, take them with me if you think it best. Willie has just returned from Tyler where he spent a week. Mike is in the office to do errands to-day, while Tom is keeping Mrs. Robertson company. As the bear got a little vicious I sent it on a visit to Duncan & Jones.* They have no children. You see? No news. Hot weather—Scorching! Sweat runs from me like a mountain stream. How much money do you need?

With love, Yours
J. S. Hogg[103]

At the end of July, the trip to Pueblo was imminent:

July 31, 1895
Dear Sallie:

Within a few days you may look for all of us. This includes the three boys and myself. A night or two ago baby Tom got in my lap, hugged me and said: "Papa we have not seen Mama in so long, can't you take us to see her?" Mike, standing near by chimed in and in his touching, tender voice said "Do take us!" This has been my feeling all the time and I now give way to it. So you may look for us in a few days. Willie is as anxious as the two little ones. We want to all get together and stay together. Business has run in on our firm and continues to come. Good fees on time with but little money. However we take in over $300 cash pr. month. The Judge will hold the fort until you get well. Now look out for a gay time.

Everybody admits you to be the "best woman in the World" and I think you should have us all with you for a jolly time and conse-

---

* Duncan and Jones were friends in Tyler. John M. Duncan had been Hogg's law partner in 1884.

quent fast recuperation. I feel so much indebted to Fannie, William, Sister, Pearl and Marion for their kind treatment of you and Ima. Tell them that we will try to lend joy to their household for a few days anyway. I hope you will think of some new place to which under the advice of William you can at the right time go for a change. I long for a home—permanent home—and have excellent prospects of being able to get one that will exactly suit us by or before next Winter. I want you to get well and come back to make the selection before I make up my mind. The people will have a fit almost if I do not meet them the 6th at Ft. Worth, but I feel that I should take the boys with me to see you before then. Good bye. God bless you. In haste as usual.

Yours as Ever,

J. S. Hogg[104]

Jim Hogg, ever the optimist, never seemed to grasp the seriousness of Sallie's condition. On August 1, the day after he wrote this letter he received a telegram from William in Pueblo: Sallie was now desperately ill, and her husband and sons must come at once. In the midst of preparations to leave for Pueblo, Hogg hurriedly answered a request from James McDugald, who was beginning his law practice in Belton, Texas:

August 2, 1895
Dear Jim:
    The book does not contain criminal forms nor have I a copy of Willson's. But for the fact that I am to leave to-night for Colorado and am in some what rushed [sic] I would go out and hunt Willson's forms for you. Sallie is sick in bed and I shall take the boys there by the next train,
    With full confidence that you will succeed and deserve success.

I am as Ever

Your Uncle,

J. S. Hogg[105]

An anxious father and his three sons left Austin by train on the night of August 2, bound for Pueblo. There they joined Ima for a sad vigil at Sallie's bedside. In the final stages of tuberculosis, she languished, "sick in bed," as her husband had put it, for nearly three weeks. Tom celebrated his eighth birthday on August 20, but, like Ima's thirteenth birthday, it could not have been a joyful one.

On August 21 Sallie's father wrote sadly to Jim Hogg: "Yours of the 16th inst bringing me the intelligence of daughter's precarious and dangerous condition was not altogether a surprise only that her disease had advanced more rapidly than we anticipated . . . . That her preparation has been made for a triumphant death I have no question. She was <u>always good</u>.[106]

A grieving Will wrote to Mrs. Marsh in Tyler on September 6: "Mother does not seem to improve nor to grow worse—same condition, day to day. She would suffer very much unless kept under partial influence of opiates."[107] Sallie was now heavily sedated and under the care of a trained nurse, supervised by Dr. Davis. She had only a few more days to live.

Sarah (Sallie) Stinson Hogg and James Stephen Hogg, ca. 1875. *The Ima Hogg Papers, di_08340, the Dolph Briscoe Center for American History, the University of Texas at Austin.*

James Stephen Hogg and Ima Hogg, ca. 1883. *The Ima Hogg Papers, di_08341, the Dolph Briscoe Center for American History, the University of Texas at Austin.*

The Governor's Mansion, ca. 1890. *Courtesy of Texas State Library & Archives Commission.*

Ima Hogg, 1892. *The Ima Hogg Papers, di_08339, the Dolph Briscoe Center for American History, the University of Texas at Austin.*

Governor J. S. Hogg and Family, 1894. *Courtesy The Museum of Fine Arts, Houston.*

Tom, Will, and Mike Hogg, ca. 1896. *The Ima Hogg Papers, di_08337, the Dolph Briscoe Center for American History, the University of Texas at Austin.*

Tom, Ima, and Mike, 1904. *The Ima Hogg Papers, di_05908, the Dolph Briscoe Center for American History, the University of Texas at Austin.*

The Varner-Hogg Plantation, 1907. *The Ima Hogg Papers, di_08338, the Dolph Briscoe Center for American History, the University of Texas at Austin.*

PART III
BEREAVEMENT AND
CONSOLATION
1895–1900

In Memory of My Mother
Sept. 20, 1895
S. A. Hogg died Friday night 12 o'clock[1]

SARAH ANN STINSON HOGG was only forty-one years old when she died. There must have been farewells, last words, between Sallie and her husband and children, but they were not recorded. Perhaps because her last days were such a sad time to recall, no one wrote much about them, then or afterward.

Sallie's grieving family found solace in their own ways, but ten-year-old Mike and eight-year-old Tom probably suffered more than the others. Ima took comfort in her music, Will immersed himself in his studies at the University of Texas, and Jim Hogg toiled feverishly at his law practice. Politics beckoned: the former Governor Hogg was urged to become U.S. Senator Hogg, but he refused, pleading family obligations. By the summer of 1896, he bought a house in Austin, and happily installed his children and his sister Martha Frances Hogg Davis, "Aunt Fannie," there. Domestic pleasures gave him comfort, and so did business (representing clients in New York and Mexico) and politics. Hogg and William Jennings Bryan became good friends, and Hogg campaigned for him in two unsuccessful bids for the presidency.

In 1897, Will finished his degree at the university and moved to San Antonio to open his first law practice. Jim Hogg continued to take Ima with him when he traveled: a tour of Mexico (business) and Hawaii (politics) in 1898. The next summer, Ima visited friends in Colorado, and Mike and Tom took a brief, unsuccessful turn at being ranch hands. In the fall of 1899, Ima enrolled in the University of Texas. The children were growing up.

In 1900, Hogg fought an acrimonious battle at the state Democratic convention for his constitutional amendments for railroad reforms. He shouted down his enemies and won, but he would have to wait several years for the amendments to be put before Texas voters.

As the twentieth century began, Jim Hogg was about to become a businessman with a new interest: oil.

• • •

Fifty years after Sallie Hogg's death, Ima wrote of it in her memoir. Her account is oddly brief and matter-of-fact: "Dr. Davis, we called him Uncle William, did everything he could think of for Mother, but after several months he must have notified Father that nothing more could be done to restore her health. She was young and optimistic, and I am sure no one ever dreamed that she would not recover."[2]

Tuberculosis was a mysterious, serious illness little understood until well into the twentieth century. Sallie's long history of ailments, with a dramatic weight loss in the last year of her life, was probably tuberculosis, though oddly enough, no one else in her family contracted the disease. It is possible that she had lung cancer. There were no X-rays in Sallie's day to help with diagnosis. A German physicist discovered electromagnetic radiation in 1895, and X-rays were in use by World War I. Effective treatment of tuberculosis with antibiotics did not occur until the 1940s.

A telegram carried the news of Sallie's death to Austin, and a train took her body, accompanied by her husband, children, and Aunt Fannie back to that city for burial. Early Tuesday morning, September 24, the train was met by a "committee of citizens." The funeral service for Sallie Stinson Hogg was held at the Governor's Mansion at 10 a.m., and the state offices remained closed until two o'clock that afternoon. Sallie was buried in Austin's Oakwood Cemetery.[3]

After Sallie's death, as Ima remembered, her father was "bereft." Even politics failed to comfort him: On October 8, Hogg begged to be excused from a speech he was to make at the Texas State Fair in Dallas later that month "for the reason that I cannot feel at ease or comfortable in any crowd in my present condition."[4]

On October 14, three weeks after Sallie's death, he wrote to his sister Julia. They did not correspond often, but Jim Hogg needed to put his sorrow on paper.

> Dear Sister:
>   In all the storms of an eventful life the severest shock that I ever received was the death of poor Sallie. Indeed, since Mother's death when I was twelve, I had never been called to witness the death of a relative. It is all over, except now and then—almost hourly—when memory recalls the past and with it my wife's suffering and death compared to her gentleness and virtue. Then my feelings overcome me. She never spoke an unkind word to me in her life and never had I to account to others for a word or act of hers. God knows if all men were so blessed the earth would be more like heaven. My ambition is to raise my children after her model. If I succeed the world will be much better for it.
>   Sister Frances is with us and I hope to keep her. The children all

love her and her influence over them is great and good. Some day I
will see you.

Affectionately, Your Brother,

J. S. Hogg[5]

But what Jim Hogg perceived as Aunt Fannie's "great and good"
influence in the motherless household, his children found decidedly
depressing. Ima recalled what must have been a difficult time for all
concerned:

> Our Aunt Fannie evidently was not prepared by experience or
> nature to have charge of such undisciplined children as she found us
> to be. While Father was away from home during the day, she was
> using all her strength of will and ingenuity to train the two younger
> boys and myself. She believed in giving us chores and filling every
> idle moment when out of school, with some duties. . . . Her efforts
> served mainly to make the children unhappy. She not only wanted
> to discipline us but was ambitious to see that we developed some
> scholarship. She was a constant reader and flattered herself that she
> could entertain the boys successfully with Plutarch's lives and juve-
> nile versions of the lives of heroes. So she read aloud whenever she
> was able to seize any opportunity. She had been brought up with
> brothers, I am sure, as lively as these little boys, but evidently did not
> understand their nature. . . .
>
> Brother Will was her idol. She thought he was like her and he
> really did look quite a lot like her when he was younger. For many
> years he had the same thirst for knowledge which delighted her. They
> had the same sense of humor but he grew into a more understanding
> person than she ever was. Father must have sensed the depressing
> effect she had on the children. . . . Father, though, had never heard
> any word about her and none of us ever offered a sign of complaint.[6]

Ima later recalled her younger brothers' schooling at this time:
"After my mother died, Mike and Tom, being very lively, mischievous
little boys, got along rather poorly in public school, so Father sent
them to Professor Bickler's which helped to some degree."[7]

Professor Jacob Bickler had rented the house next door to the
Hoggs' old residence on Fourteenth Street in 1893, and the family
may have known him before that. His German and English Academy:
A Day and Boarding School for Boys and Young Men, on West Elev-

enth and Blanco Streets, was operating in 1887 when Jim Hogg first came to Austin. The school was probably too academically demanding for the sporadically schooled younger Hogg boys at this point. As Ima recalled, that arrangement did not last long: "After a short period in Austin, Father felt it best to send us on to Coronal Institute in San Marcos where my two younger brothers and myself went to school. Father invited Uncle William's daughter Pearl to join us at school there. Pearl was slightly older than myself but we studied the same things, even piano, at Coronal which had a fine music department."[8]

Six weeks after Sallie Hogg's death, Ima, Mike, and Tom, escorted by Aunt Fannie, left Austin on the train for San Marcos. It must have been a traumatic experience for children who had so recently lost their mother to be suddenly placed in the unfamiliar surroundings of a boarding school.

Coronal Institute, founded in 1868, was a respected private boarding school in the Texas Hill Country. It had around three hundred students and programs of study including a "Preparatory School" for grades 1 to 6. That would have suited Mike and Tom.

Ima found consolation in her music studies after Sallie's death. She and her cousin Pearl were "advanced piano students," and when the great pianist Ignacy Jan Paderewski came to San Antonio on his American tour in 1896, Ima and Pearl were in the audience. "He was electrifying," Ima remembered. "He played one piece I was studying, an Impromptu Ballet by Schubert. It sang in my ears so long. I could try to imitate the way he played each phrase. No one, however, could ever reproduce his marvelous rich singing tone."[9]

Will was pursuing his studies at the University of Texas, where he would earn a law degree by 1897. In 1895 he was still boarding at Mrs. Robinson's, where he had lived before Sallie's death, but his father took a suite at the Driskill Hotel. The four-story Driskill, with steam heat and an elevator, was the premier hotel in the city. The former governor's law practice was doing well.

Jim Hogg wrote to Aunt Fannie on November 8, 1895.

Dear Sister:

I am glad you and the children got to the Institute safely and are well pleased.

My lonesomeness is rather painful though I am quite comfortably quartered at the Driskill Hotel.

No news. Will try to see you Saturday evening or Sunday.

With love to all. In haste,

Your Brother

J. S. Hogg[10]

Ima wrote to her brother Will about her new school and her studies, but her letter has not been found. Will answered it in a doggedly cheerful tone.

Dec. 17, 1895

Dear Sister—

I received your letter today for which let me thank you. It seemed so strange to get a letter from you, I had to rub my eyes and reread it several times for fear my senses were tricking me. Of course anybody like you and Aunt Fannie can sit down and think up some sense or nonsense to write when you have time, but a dullard like myself would be in a trance all the time thinking of something to write, were he to write often. I have not seen father in two weeks—I missed him these last two Saturdays when I went to his office.

So, you are going to take art, are you when you finish your music? That's nice—but don't you think "cooking" and "house-keeping" class would pay your bills with better results? Or, rather would not you prefer to spend your time making clothes for the boys or reading some interesting book? No—you go on and take art—but art thou ready to take art? (That's a vile pun, Aunt Fannie, but the best I can do.) I am very glad you all are happy—I am always happy, since I began to think about "being happy" etc. Outside of my horse being sick of dreadful distemper, I have nothing hanging heavy on me tonight. My only examination comes Monday—20th, of which however I have no misgivings.

Please don't expect news of me for I am one person in this wide world, about Austin that knows no "knows"—and outside of being at a loss what to write to an inquisitive and expectant sister, I care not for news. I guess you know by this time that Santa Claus is to be in Texas about the twenty-fifth; and I reckon the day before he comes you'll see a "salad-green" youth come puffing up that rocky hill where you are now—and who do you think he'll be? One that sends love to all and subscribes here

Your brother

Will[11]

The Christmas after Sallie's death was sad for everyone. Ima, Mike, and Tom were in San Marcos at school, and there was no house in Austin to come home to. Evidently the family gathered in San Marcos, where Aunt Fannie had taken up temporary residence to oversee the children's schooling. Their father no doubt joined them there. The weeks of that sorrowful winter passed slowly. Letters between family members were few, and Mike and Tom wrote not at all. But Jim Hogg visited his children at school as often as he could.

On February 20, 1896, he wrote to Aunt Fannie in San Marcos:

Dear Sister:

While with you Sunday last, I fully intended but forgot to ask you to have Ima entered in the Art Class. She has progressed so well in her music and has obeyed you so nicely that I want her to receive other advantages. Whatever she may need in this new class please get and draw on me for the expense.

If Pearl desires also to enter the art class—put her in with Ima and I will cheerfully foot all the bills. I am so much pleased with their progress that I consider any reasonable outlay for them good economy. Tell the boys I am keeping an eye on them too and am proud of their good manners and progress. With much love,

Your Bro.

J. S. Hogg[12]

Ima's early talent for drawing was evident. The art classes at the Coronal Institute produced a sketchbook with fine pencil drawings. One is titled *"Coronal" Cottage*, which was one of the buildings at the institute. The other sketch in the book is *Pearl's hand from life*. It is her cousin's hand, gracefully posed and flawlessly rendered in delicate pencil strokes.[13]

That winter there was another death in the Hogg family. On February 22, Jim Hogg's sister Julia died at her home in Denton, with her husband and two of her sons—James McDugald, by then a lawyer in Belton, and her youngest son, Bismarck, at her bedside. Brownlee, a student at Vanderbilt University, presumably could not get there in time. The funeral was the next day, and Jim Hogg was there.[14]

With the Hogg children settled in school for the spring term, Aunt Fannie evidently stayed in Denton for a while to comfort Julia's husband and sons. She then left them to spend time in Decatur with John Hogg and his family. A few days after Julia's funeral, Jim Hogg wrote to his surviving sister about their late brother Tom's youngest child, Annie:

Feby 29, 1896
Dear Sister:

The children are all well. I want you to remain in Denton and Decatur until you have made a good visit. As I came home I stopped off at Ft. Worth and saw Annie. She is at Mr. and Mrs. Robert Cook's, and by them is evidently treated well. For this one member of the family now of all others I have the most profound sympathy. Look deep down into her eyes, note her better ways and you will see Tom. Never before did I realize such resemblance of him in her. As soon as I can make arrangements for her I am going to send her to the Sam Houston Normal at Huntsville and have her well educated. When you see her let her know she has as much sense as anybody and inspire her with ambition to succeed.

> Your Bro.,
> J. S. Hogg[15]

On March 3, Hogg wrote to Annie, who was then eighteen years old:

Dear Annie—

The next quarter of the Sam Houston Normal begins at Huntsville on the 24th. instant.

The Principal, Mr. Pritchett, writes me that you can then enter and that he will take special pleasure in rendering you all the assistance he can.

Now be ready to go there and I will either go by after you or meet you in Huntsville. I know you can go to the top in Educational affairs and have great pleasure in doing so. Let me know about when you could get off and I will arrange the balance.

With kindest regards to Mrs. and Mrs. Cook and much love for yourself,

> Your Uncle
> J. S. Hogg[16]

Meanwhile, Annie's uncle wrote to her sister Hermilla's husband, Robert Kelso, who was the executor of Tom Hogg's estate, to ask if there might be twenty dollars per month for Annie's expenses at Sam Houston Normal School. If not, said Jim Hogg, "I will share an equal division of the expenses myself." A week later he received word that his friend Alvin Owsley, a Denton lawyer who knew the Hogg family, had arranged for a scholarship for Annie.[17]

A few days later, Jim Hogg wrote to Martha Frances, who was once again in San Marcos. He was busy with a jury trial, but hoped to get away in time to "run down and see you and the children tomorrow evening." He wanted to talk over Annie's future. "I want every person connected with me by affinity or consanguinity given a fair chance and make a success if possible."[18]

For the widowed Jim Hogg that spring, grief for Sallie was buried helping his family—and in work. His law practice was thriving. On March 20, he wrote to Martha Frances:

Dear Sister:

On yesterday I paid off the last debt I owe and consequently am to-day a free man! From this on I intend to remain so.

General Reagan is quite sick and I shall most likely go over to see him at Palestine this evening. In this event I will not reach San Marcos until Sunday morning.—You do not know how proud I am of the honesty of Mike and Tom as well as Ima in keeping their contract with me to the effect that they would take "jumping exercise" every morning, Tell them of this please.

Your Brother,
J. S. Hogg[19]

Sometime that spring, Will left Mrs. Robinson's boardinghouse and moved in with his father at the Driskill.

Jim Hogg was ever the devoted father, but evidently he had not been in close contact with Sallie's parents since her death in September. Not until April did he inform them that their younger grandchildren were in boarding school in San Marcos.[20]

Hogg did his best to keep in touch with his brother John that spring, On April 8 he begged John to join him and some friends on a fishing trip at a camp near Austin—at his expense. "Now don't fail," he wrote. The train tickets were already arranged, and John was to wire if he could not come. The surviving records do not indicate whether or not John came.[21]

After all the trouble Jim Hogg took to enroll Annie at Sam Houston in Huntsville with a scholarship, she refused to go. Instead, she asked if she could come and live with him in Austin. He answered her letter with a patient, renewed plea for her to attend school:

April 25, 1896

Dear Annie—

Replying to your last letter I have regretfully to say that I have no home, but am boarding at a hotel. My little ones are boarding in school at San Marcos. If I had a home I should be glad to have you come and stay with me. Some day this condition will be changed and then you shall have a first class opportunity to spend much of your time at my house, I hope.

Now Annie: If you will go to school I shall try to arrange for you to go to a boarding school here next fall, or, better still, at Huntsville. Like all girls you would prefer not to do this perhaps. But in my opinion you will receive an education rapidly and make a first class woman in a few years. Then you will be independent. If you will go I shall look after you the best I can. Be a good, reasonable girl at all times. Will you go to school?

Your Uncle,

J. S. Hogg[22]

But Annie Hogg, now nineteen years old, had other plans: she was about to be married—quite suddenly.

J. S. Hogg wrote to Annie on May 26, 1896:

Dear Annie:

While I have ever stood ready to do anything I could for you, I nevertheless feel much gratified that you have gone to Bob and Hermilla to help you out in the most important emergency in your life. From what I learn, the young man whom you are to marry is a worthy, first class gentleman and I do trust, as I feel in my soul will be the case, that you and he will get along happily together. There are no better people than Bob and Hermilla and you know old folks are sometimes hard to understand by girls. Learn them well yourself and you will love them. Let me know the exact date when you are to be married and I will try to be there. God bless you.

Your Uncle,

J. S. Hogg[23]

The "most important emergency" may have been a pregnancy.

In the late spring of 1896, there was a happier family matter to occupy Jim Hogg: a new home in Austin at last. He bought a two-and-a-half story house on a large lot on the northeast corner of Rio

Grande and West Nineteenth Streets (now Rio Grande and Martin
Luther King Boulevard). As Ima remembered this house, "There was
nothing elegant about it, but [it was] in an excellent neighborhood
and plenty of ground for a small orchard, a barn for horses and cows
and chickens and ducks and a flower garden."[24] Streets around it were
still unpaved, but a trolley car ran past it on Rio Grande Street. Just
up the hill from the University of Texas campus, the house was in
a prime Austin location. Across the street, the Hoggs could watch
the construction of an impressive Classic Revival mansion, completed
in 1899, by Dr. Goodall Wooten, the brother of their family physician, Dr. Thomas Wooten. (The Hoggs' house site is now an apartment complex, but the Wooten house is now the Hotel Ella, an Austin
boutique hotel.)* Jim Hogg bought the Nineteenth Street house, furnished, for $6,500. He did not have the cash, but his friend Tom
Campbell urged him to buy it—and loaned him the $6,500. (Hogg
paid the note in full by July 1897.)[25]

The house's new owner could hardly wait to fill it with family and
friends. On May 28, he wrote to William Davis in Pueblo.

> Dear William:
>   Come down a few days before the School at San Marcos closes
> the 7th of June, and spend the time here with me. I know you will
> enjoy it. At the right time we can go together to attend the Com-
> mencement and see the children in all their youthful glory. I should
> be exceedingly glad if you can also bring Fannie [William's wife] and
> Marion [their son] along. I have the room for them and will gladly
> give them a good time. I do not "stand in" with the Ry's [railways]
> but in a local way I can provide for your transportation after you get
> here. With love all around.
>   Yours truly,
>   J. S. Hogg[26]

He also sent an invitation to his brother John:

> Dear John:
>   Last Saturday I bought a comfortable house here and within
> about two weeks will have Sister Frances and the children in it. Send
> Velma and Maud—one or both—down about the 12th or 15th and

* Formerly the Mansion at Judges' Hill, 1900 Rio Grande.

let them spend awhile with us. Of course I should be glad to have Eva Jean and yourself also but I know it is useless to expect such a thing. Come if you can, but by all means send the girls. We are all well and join in sending you and yours much love.

Your Brother,

J. S. Hogg[27]

So elated was the former governor to have a house of his own again that he also invited his old friend and former secretary, Colonel R. B. Levy, now retired to Longview, to come and visit:

June 1, 1896

My dear Sir and Friend:—

I have just bought a very comfortable home and shall soon move my Sister and the little ones into it. So I want you and Mrs. Levy to come down and spend part or all of the summer with us. If Mrs. L. cannot leave Miss Emily, come along yourself. You shall have two rooms and a bath and Tom to wait on you*

Once more I begin to feel settled and to see ahead again some comforts of life at Home. God bless you.

Your friend,

J. S. Hogg.[28]

After the term at the Coronal Institute ended, Ima, Mike, and Tom were once again in the clutches of the redoubtable Aunt Fannie. As Ima wrote years later: "Father was so busy at his office downtown on Congress Avenue [that] he knew little of what was going on in the house." To get to his office from Nineteenth and Rio Grande, the former governor took Joe, the Tennessee walking horse, and the buggy, or he used the streetcar which ran on Rio Grande Street and made a circuit south and north going over to Lavaca. The younger Hogg children did not often ride the streetcar, as Ima recalled, because it was "a tedious trip" and they "had rather use the car fare for chili or tamales after school."[29]

Now that they had a home in Austin again, Ima, Mike, and Tom began attending school there in the fall of 1896.

As for Aunt Fannie, as Ima recalled, she "did her best to keep

---

* Tom was the servant Hogg referred to in another letter as "an old fashioned negro."

house—but that was not her forte." She moved in with "a number of canary birds to sing for her" and she "looked after them religiously." Aunt Fannie was usually "to be found reading or writing." She composed what she called "doggerel," and, as her niece observed, "It seemed to be a compulsion of hers to write."[30] But she took her housekeeping duties seriously:

> She knew how to economize—really she pinched pennies in her effort to help Father get on his feet financially. We had a hired man for all outdoors, and a cook . . . , I was assigned many tasks by Aunt Fannie. . . . She was quite a disciplinarian and expected the boys to do special chores. I was assigned the duties of making beds and caring for the cleaning of the big bathrooms and three bedrooms. She taught me to sew. So I made my own clothes. The only compensation for that was, I was free to select my own materials. Mother's example had given me a taste for pretty fabrics. I can't speak for my creations, but I studied the pictures on the old "Bon Ton" fashion magazines and did the best I could until I was ready to graduate from Miss Carrington's school. Then I protested. . . .
> I went to Father and asked him if I could have my simple white dress made by a good dressmaker for my graduation. Of course I could, so that ended my own dressmaking. Later I thanked Aunt Fannie for the experience. I learned to do the kind of fine handwork which I had seen Mother do too.[31]

Ima's opinion of her aunt can be read between the lines of the memoir:

> She had only this one son and had lived with him only part of the time. The rest of the time she was a welcome visitor in our house and in the homes of her sister Mrs. Ferguson . . . and Uncle John Hogg as well as a married niece, Mrs. Hermilla Kelso. She always commanded the situation, however in whatever home she was, but the families seemed to understand and overlooked her Spartan qualities because she was a very fascinating and charming woman despite a very severe side. We children had affection for her although we stood completely in awe of her. Underneath the whole thing we realized some way that she meant everything for our ultimate good. . . .[32]

The Hogg children made the best of it. The new house was a large, pleasant residence with spacious grounds, with plenty of room for Aunt Fannie as well as themselves, and for a menagerie of animals too.

There was always a great barnyard full of chickens, ducks, turkeys and geese at 19th Street. The ground around the house covered three-fourths of a block and like the mansion grounds, it was divided into various utilitarian sections. Father was the one who now took the most interest in the flower garden so the flower garden nearly always had something blooming in it and the vegetable garden again was his special care. He had always been in the habit of wearing a small flower of some sort in his buttonhole. Mother had always put one there and he had so much sentiment about it that he always kept the habit. The garden nearly always provided something. At the mansion, there was a small pomegranate flower when they were in bloom. On 19th Street, he had planted and successfully grown cape jasmines. These he often used, or a cornflower, daisy, garden pink, or "Johnny-Jump-Up," always something in season.

There were big fig trees and fruit trees. Near the vegetable garden was a lot for the horses and another big space where a pair of ostriches, Jack and Jill, disported themselves. Father always fed these ostriches with his own hands. They were always rather wild but came to him whenever he called.[33]

Hogg wrote to a friend, "My two ostriches have grown to be very large birds, and have afforded the people of this community, and especially my children, much amusement and pleasure." Ima had a different view of this "amusement and pleasure." As she wrote later: "No one could go near one and they were in a special lot. On rainy days they became excited enough to do a wild kind of dance. The horses and buggies that came by there were almost sure to have a bucking or runaway animal."[34]

Hogg was always partial to birds, as his daughter recalled:

Nothing amused him more than watching the barnyard fowls. He would sit on the porch and interpret their conclaves and chatter. He had a great deal of imagination about their organized life and thought he learned a lot from them. The boys were encouraged to care for the fowls and animals, but they were not systematic enough to be depended upon so a man was always kept to do the real job. The boys, at one time or another, had a pet bear and a fawn but these became troublesome and had to be sent away.

One time Father took Mike on a duck hunting trip and they shot a wild goose in the wing. She fell at Father's feet and he brought her back to Austin. She had a strange attachment for Father. Like our little parrot Jane, she listened for his voice and would run to him flapping her wings. Father was so devoted to her that when we moved to the Varner Plantation, he took "Polly" as he called her, with him and she attended him as she had at home and came to no one else. In fact, it was said that when he was not at the Plantation she would pine and go to no one. She died at the same hour that he did [March 3, 1906]. We always thought this was an interesting coincidence. Father had a rather hypnotic effect on animals and birds. I do not know if he was conscious of it or not, but he was very fond of them and they seemed to respond to him.[35]

Among the horses at the Nineteenth Street residence, Ima remembered a special one: "Father had a beautiful white horse which he sometimes rode and drove. . . . Governor [Robert L.] Taylor of Tennessee presented this horse—'Joe.' He was a gaited horse, a plantation horse, and always beautifully groomed so he was a picture under a saddle. I do not think the boys were allowed to ride him though Father gave me permission." Ima liked to take Joe for "long rides up to Mount Bonnell in West Austin."[36]

Long rides, indeed: from the house on Nineteenth Street that was a ride of about eight miles, round trip. And like all proper young ladies, Ima rode sidesaddle.

At his new home on Nineteenth Street, the former governor kept the same habits he had practiced in the mansion:

Regularly, in the evenings, if there were no guests, after supper, he would expect some music [presumably provided by his daughter at the piano] then he would begin to read. . . . His powers of concentration were astonishing. We were very noisy, undisciplined children and no amount of noisy or boisterous playing around the house ever seemed to disturb him. . . . He would sit for hours, reading, always some history or biography or work on political economy or science. He seemed completely oblivious of the outside world. He always had a big unabridged dictionary on a stand by his chair and often referred to it. He enjoyed reading the Bible and he sometimes read from some of the old poets, Tennyson, Shakespeare, Burns, Longfellow, and Edgar Allan Poe . . . .[37]

Ima never saw her father reading novels:

He said real life had more romance in it than any fiction. He expressed his interest in some of the earlier philosophers, Plato, and Aristotle, and he admired Ruskin but often said to me that he wanted to form his own philosophy and that he thought it was a mistake to be influenced by anything other than observation and contemplation and study of facts and events. He was a great nature lover and seemed to understand the heavenly bodies and all growing things. It had been his dream to become a successful agriculturalist after he retired from active business and his law practice. Whenever we traveled he enjoyed going to the geological exhibits. He seemed to have a good deal of knowledge which I did not understand, and in every city he visited factories, and spent a great deal of time hearing the methods being used. In his own way he had tried to encourage industry in the prisons of Texas. I went with him a number of times on these visits. He loved to talk with the prisoners and give them words of cheer.* I felt that he had a rather unusual attitude to what were called criminals. In fact, I believe his approach to all deviations of behavior were far ahead of his time. He visited the mental hospitals in Austin and San Antonio many times and had long discussions with the physicians in charge.†

My father's interest in politics, of course, did not end with retirement from office. The visitors to our house were many of the professors from the University of Texas and men who liked to talk about history and politics. Father liked to browse a good deal at Gammel's Book Store and was always coming home with some old volumes under his arm. He had a very good collection of Texiana which on his death, was given to the University Library. . . . In spite of the fact that he did not care for fiction, our library had all the standard novels and poets and essayists. We children were given the more popular volumes of various tales—Henty, James Fenimore Cooper, Hawthorne, books on theology, Indian lore, fairy tales and travel and all the Alcott stories.[38]

---

* In the house at Varner-Hogg Plantation in West Columbia, there is a massive oak rocking chair made for Hogg by Texas prisoners.

† In 1940, Ima Hogg established the Hogg Foundation for Mental Health at the University of Texas.

But the studious, serious Will Hogg had by this time left childhood books far behind. As his sister recalled:

I do not know about my brother Will's reading at that time. He was more inclined to read the philosophers and I used to see in his room the volumes of more profound subjects. . . .

While we lived on 19th Street, brother Will attended the University of Texas. He had two rooms on the third floor, jammed with books on a great variety of subjects. He was always at home in the evening, studying until late at night. . . .[39]

In his youth Will was not given to camaraderie. As a teenager in the Governor's Mansion, he "had a few companions, but did not mingle with our guests." As a university student, "his friends were among the younger members of the faculty, or other intellectuals. During this period he was, his sister wrote, "a hermit, burning midnight oils. . . . Aunt Fannie adored him and declared he was the image of herself, with the identical disposition. . . . I understood what she meant. No man ever lived who went through so many periods of change as Brother Will. His heart was as big as Father's and his devotion as deep. All these attributes he had in common with Aunt Fannie, plus her inflammable temper."[40] Will was "a complete introvert until after he graduated in law and moved to San Antonio. What changed him would be a conundrum. He blossomed into an outgoing extrovert. Maybe his deep attraction to Mother had accounted for his unresponsive disposition."[41] But no matter what he did, Will was always in his father's shadow.

In the summer of 1896, Jim Hogg was once again enjoying the pleasures of domestic life, but his wayward niece, Annie, was still troublesome. On June 6, he wrote to his niece Hermilla's husband, Bob.

June 6, 1896
Dear Bob:

I fully realize and do not at all underestimate the embarrassments you and Hermilla must feel over Annie's refusal to permit either of you to counsel or aid her in the preparation for her marriage. Personally and by letter I have given her advice to the contrary of her course towards you. She is young, inexperienced and perhaps out of humor. At times her temper is not of the best. It is but Christian charity to overlook her foibles. Her intended husband I learn is a gentleman.

This of itself should lead all the family to overlook Annie's whims.
. . . Act cheerfully about it. This is best. With love to Hermilla,
>Yours,
>J. S. Hogg[42]

Sometime between June 6 and July 31, Annie Hogg married a young man named Edward Magee, who apparently was not gainfully employed. The surviving letters do not indicate the details or the date of the wedding.

Meanwhile, Annie's uncle had politics to think about. By 1896, the eloquent, rotund Texas politician named Hogg had a national reputation. William Jennings Bryan had once told him, "I believe that you have all the qualifications necessary for president and there is no man whom I would rather support than yourself."[43] But James Stephen Hogg did not want to be president. Instead, he went to the national Democratic Party convention in Chicago in July and worked hard for Bryan's candidacy. When Bryan, "the Great Commoner," made his now-famous "Cross of Gold" speech against the moneyed interests who favored the gold standard as a base for the nation's economy, his nomination was assured. Bryan the Democrat would run against the Republican William McKinley, and Jim Hogg would throw himself wholeheartedly into the fall campaign. Bryan lost the 1896 race to McKinley, but he would run again in 1900, and Jim Hogg would again be a staunch supporter.

When Hogg returned to Austin after the Chicago convention, the newlyweds—Annie and her husband Edward Magee—had returned to Fort Worth, and Annie wrote to her uncle asking for help. He answered her on July 31.

>Dear Annie:
>   You ask by favor of the 25th that I assist Mr. Magee to get a temporary position. Getting positions except on merit is a very difficult undertaking. I should gladly write to some friends in Ft. Worth in his behalf if I only know what are his qualifications. Tell him to candidly write to me on this subject. Where was he educated, if at all? What experience has he had in business life? Is he sober—that is does he drink intoxicating liquors? Does he <u>know how</u> to gamble? Has he ever gambled? Does he <u>know how</u> to play poker? Does he use cigarettes or tobacco in any form? Will he work, if he gets a job, without <u>watching the Clock</u>? . . .
>>Your Uncle,
>>J. S. Hogg[44]

If Annie's husband wrote to her uncle about job qualifications, the letter has not been found. On August 3, a letter from Annie on another financial matter disturbed her uncle, and he let her know his displeasure in no uncertain terms:

Aug. 4th, 1896
Dear Annie:

I learn with much regret from your letter of yesterday that you will not let your young, and I hope, worthy husband go to work at the only job he can get. In that letter I find in reference to him the following very extraordinary expression: "We can find nothing better than driving a street car and I am entirely <u>too proud to let him do that</u>." Now, poor child, I well know the trouble ahead of you, if you should persist in this course. Really you must not understand man's sphere or the duty of a wife to her husband. What you say also reflects on him. I <u>infer</u> from other parts of your letter that neither of you have any <u>ready money</u>. This so common with young married people that I am not at all surprised at it, nor do I regard it specially unfortunate unless you should conclude to indulge too much in <u>pride</u>. If by yielding to a sense of <u>pride</u> your husband is to remain idle or to refuse to do honorable work then you commit a <u>sin</u> whose legitimate fruit will be bitter indeed.

Street car driving is an honorable employment, one which I should have accepted when I was a young man with much <u>pride</u> and greater pleasure. In this connection I must be pardoned for referring to the fact that in my youth and early manhood I split rails with <u>pride</u> . . . . that I cleared new ground and was ever proud of it; that I drove an ox team and was happy; that I was printer's devil and faced the world; that I was a ditch digger and a well cleaner and performed my work in full view of a gaping public proudly and in good cheer. <u>Pride</u> kept me from <u>idleness</u> and led me to work at any job however hard and honorable that lay before me or which I could get. By not being too particular I always kept employed, so that I was never idle a week in my life. <u>Pride</u> led me on to do better work than my associates and thus to get promotion, step by step until with <u>pride</u> I have ever looked back upon the days, hours, weeks and months when I received from $15 to $20 per month—the times when daylight never caught me in bed or away from work <u>hard work</u>—much harder . . . by far than <u>driving a street car</u>. This much I say in the kindliest spirit to you, not to rebuke but to suggest that <u>pride</u> is false indeed when it leads to idleness—Show this to your husband and tell him to ponder over it. Tell him to accept that position. Tell him to climb from it to the top though it takes hard work for years to do so. When he gets there he will reflect with <u>pride</u> on his first job.

Your Uncle,
J. S. Hogg[45]

Three weeks later, Hogg left Annie's marital and financial woes far behind as he made a business trip to the eastern seaboard. From the Oceanic Hotel, a resort on Star Island in the Isles of Shoals off Portsmouth, New Hampshire, he wrote to Mike and Tom in Austin:

Aug. 26, 1896
Dear Mike and Tom:
   Yesterday I went with four others out on the great Atlantic Ocean and fished from 7 o'clock in the morning until 1 o'clock in the afternoon. We caught 77 fish weighing in all 528 pounds. Of these I caught 14 or nearly 1/5th of the whole. I caught 1 Haddock, 3 Pollocks, 4 Rock Cods and 6 White or Ocean Cods.—What are known as and called Dog Fish bothered us very much. We must have caught a hundred or more of these but did not count them as they are worthless. Some of them are three feet long. Most of them are longer than your arm. They are nice looking fishing fish, somewhat resembling the Shark. If you will look in the big dictionary you can see the pictures and descriptions of all these fishes. Get your Auntie and Sister to help you do so. We shall leave after breakfast this morning for Mount Washington where we will spend the day tomorrow. I am the guest of Mr. Glidden of Lowell, Mass. His wife and Mr. Cummings and several other Boston and Lowell people stay most of the time with us. They are all intelligent, good, patriotic, and hospitable people. I only wish that you two nice boys could see these people as I have. Some day you must do so. Then I know you will not have <u>sectional prejudice</u>—the most inexcusable of all prejudice. When people hate each other on account of the sections in which they live they do so from ignorance. You boys must become broad and sensible enough not to be guilty of such a wrong. Good bye.

Your Father,
J. S. Hogg[46]

Mike and Tom were now eleven and nine years old. The boys would have enjoyed their father's fish stories, but at their ages, "sectional prejudice" must have been a mystery. That part of the letter was their father's effort to convince himself that the Civil War was long gone, and North and South must lay aside their enmity. Besides, J. S. Hogg was wooing northern capital.

December 1896 would be the first Christmas in the new house on Nineteenth Street, and its proud owner wanted to fill it with company. On December 9, he wrote to his brother John and his family in Decatur: "Come down and visit, send Velma, and [the] other two girls [Maud and Eugenia] and Eva [John's wife] too if you can spare them." A week later he wrote, "Am glad you will let Velma come down. Come yourself with her."[47]

Velma, age nineteen, came, but she may have been the only one. Velma stayed with the Hoggs until March, when Ima went back to Decatur with her. On March 8, 1897, Jim Hogg wrote to his brother: "Velma has been a first-class girl with us and we are all proud of her. There was no way to make her stay longer but she promises to return within two weeks."[48] Velma had endeared herself to the Hoggs when she boarded with them from 1890 to 1892. Now Velma was nearly twenty; Ima, fifteen.

A few days later, Ima's father wrote to her in Decatur:

March 13, 1897
My Dear Ima:

    I am glad to learn that you are having a pleasant time, and that your appetite is full grown. Be careful not to eat too much, as it may cause you a spell of sickness. We are all well but quite lonesome since you and Velma left.

    The carpenters are about through with the work on the gallery, and our home looks much better for it.

    Give my love to all the members of John's family and tell him that I would like for him to come back with you.

                            Affectionately
                            Your Father
                            J. S. Hogg[49]

Another, longer letter soon followed:

March 20, 1897
Dear Ima:

    Your letters very much interest me. Your description of the storm and of your Uncle John getting sleepy all of a sudden and going to bed while it raged is good. That was just like John when he was a boy. The negroes taught him to get into a feather bed when the lightening flashed to escape injury. You may not know it but I do—he was a very, very bad boy. To get some peace this trick was played on him by the negroes. Always after that when any kind of storm came he would at once crawl in bed and go to sleep. So the habit or superstition has grown on him and he keeps it up. I expect Eva is glad at times to see a storm come. I am glad you are having such a nice time, and trust you will greatly improve your time. We are all anxious to have you return as soon as you can get your visit out—sometime next week, according to your promise. Do not try to come by yourself but bring your Uncle John and Velma or one of the other girls with you. Get your Aunt Eva to come if she will. We would rather have a visit from her than anybody.

We are all well. The gallery is finished and the garden looks fine. Your little friends ask about you every time they see me.

Get your Uncle John to cash the enclosed check for you at the bank. Make out on it if you can. When shall we expect you?

Write a letter—a long one—a newsy one—to your Aunt Fannie and tell her how you practice. She will appreciate it.

Your Father,
J. S. Hogg[50]

Then another letter to Decatur, this time a long, thoughtful one to John Hogg:

March 24, 1897
Dear John:

I was glad to have your last letter and very much appreciate your compliments of dear little Ima. While we are lonesome without her we must not be too selfish. So you may keep her with you a week longer, unless I should get too anxious to see her and go after her earlier. She is the sunlight of my household and I am never satisfied with home while she is absent.

Well, to-day, I round off my 46th birth-day. Standing as I am beyond the meridian of life, in looking back I have no rebuke of conscience for any act of my life. Looking ahead I can see much of pleasure to hope for if I can only keep in my law office out of political races. My friends seem to believe that I cannot make a living out of office, or that I am of morbid ambition. In both respects they are mistaken but it is quite difficult for me to so convince them. From all directions they are now, a year in advance of the season, so to speak,

trying to get me to run for the U.S. Senate. I cannot do so. Confiden-
tially speaking I have never wanted to be a member of either branch
of Congress. I do not want to be U.S. Senator. If it was tendered to
me tomorrow I should unhesitatingly decline it.

My political ambition was completely gratified when I closed the
last term as Governor. Now I am doing well in my profession—much
better by twofold financially, than the salary of Senator would pay
me, I could do the people no good in that office. I know I can do
them much service by remaining in private life to help them guard
the laws we had so much trouble to have enacted. Again I feel that
I am entitled to the peace of private life and to the pleasure of my
family circle, both of which would be denied me in public office. At
all times during my past life I have been willing to make any sacrifice
for the great masses of the people. In the future I shall ever be ready
to do so except by holding office. Nothing distresses me more than
to have my friends on the one side appealing to me to make the race
and my little ones on the other begging me not to. This time I feel
that I should side with my children for I am due to them a double
service—that of father and mother. I am assured from satisfactory
sources that if I run there will be practically no opposition to me.
While this is gratifying and very flattering it adds no attractions to
the race. So if you hear or see a public announcement that under no
circumstances will I run for Senator, do not be surprised.—Give my
love to all the children and Eva, and come down to see me.

Affectionately
Your Brother
J. S. Hogg[51]

As the former governor told his brother, he was doing well financially. U.S. senators made $7,500 a year in those days. If Hogg was
making "better by twofold," his income was around $15,000 in
1897—over $400,000 in today's dollars. He was making five times
what he had made when he had first opened his law practice in 1895.
And he was making far, far more than his brother John.

Meanwhile, Ima's father was eager for her return home:

March 29, 1897
Dear Ima:

Enclosed you will see a photograph of our new pony and trap.
She is a "Daisy," as Mike and Tom call her. It's a fine outfit in which
you and your Aunt Fannie can go about when you get back home—

if you ever do. How long do you intend to stay? Don't try to come home by yourself nor without some lady or your Uncle John with you.

Perhaps I can get off for you in a few days. All are well. No news that I know of.

> Love to all,
> Affectionately,
> Your Father,
> J. S. Hogg.[52]

But Ima's father did not have to travel to Decatur. On April 17, he wrote to Julia's eldest son, James McDugald, that Ima "had a great time in Decatur, and brought Maud home with her." Maud, fifteen, was the same age as Ima. Young McDugald was now beginning his law practice in Belton, Texas, and as usual his uncle did what he could to help: "Send me a list of substantial friends to whom I may write letters for you."[53]

Soon there was family news of an unpleasant sort: Annie Hogg and her new husband, Edward Magee, had moved from Fort Worth to Brookhaven, Mississippi, and were in dire financial straits. Annie had written to her uncle on April 6, asking for help. He answered her on April 17:

Dear Annie:

I deeply regret the financial losses which your husband has sustained recently, and should be glad to comply with your request by delayed favor of the 6th, but in view of my own encumbrances and responsibilities, I cannot in justice to myself and family do so. Two years ago I left public office in debt, without money or a home and had my children all on hand to educate. I am not yet out of debt by several thousand dollars—much more than your husband's losses. Such is my situation. Both you and Mr. Magee are active, intelligent young people. Frugality, industry, privations, common to young married people, will lead you both to great success. God bless you!

> Affectionately,
> Your Uncle,
> J. S. Hogg[54]

Edward Magee's financial losses are not explained. Whatever they were, Jim Hogg was not willing to bear them.

On May 24, Jim Hogg sent family news to William Davis in Pueblo:

We are all well, except Mike, who is puny with cold. Sister [Martha Frances] seems to be in fair health, except her feet bother her more or less all the time. She is a fine housekeeper and appears to enjoy it very much. I wish you would write to her to take rides in open air frequently. We have a strong, gentle pony and trap with an old fashioned negro to do her bidding. Really she should go out every day and I believe she would if you were to so advise her.

My practice is very good and is growing. I am out of politics and expect to keep out.

Come down and bring Fannie and the children to see us. We have plenty of room and will give you all a fine time. In truth we will "take out" for several weeks and have a great time. Come and bring all with you.—As Sister writes the news I have nothing to add. With love to the family,

Your Uncle,

J. S. Hogg.[55]

He wanted everyone to come and see him. On June 29, he wrote to Bob Kelso to send Hermilla and their children "down to spend a while with us."[56] The Kelsos now had four children: Ethel, eight, Lucy, five, Mildred, three, and Baylor, not yet two.

The summer passed, and Will Hogg, who that spring had received his law degree from the University of Texas, had gone to work in his father's law firm—but he would not be there long. Meanwhile, his cousin Baylor had finished medical school.

On October 17, 1897, Hogg wrote to Baylor, now an M.D. who was about to set up his medical practice. His uncle advised him to think about Houston. And on the subject of career moves, he wrote, "Willie moves today to San Antonio to try his hand or tongue, at the practice of law. He goes it alone on his own responsibility."[57] For reasons unexplained, Will had chosen to leave Austin. His father did not seem overly pleased.

The senior Hogg was very busy with his own law practice and business interests, and was still trying to involve his brother John:

Oct. 21, 1897

Dear John:

Meet me at Dallas next Thursday to spend a week with me at the Fair. I'll foot all bills. For more than one reason I want you to spend this time with me, Aside from the pleasure it will afford me to have your company for the time I feel that it may lead to some pecuniary advantages to you later on. So lay aside all conventionalities and on arriving at Dallas go straight to the Windsor or the Oriental, at one of which I will be putting up, and I shall take pleasure in attending to the business.—

I am just up from a week's spell. Sister, Ima, Mike and Tom are all "down" with <u>dengue</u>. They are getting along nicely and will each be up in a day or so.*

<u>Now don't go back on me this time</u>. Love to all.

Your Bro.,
James.[58]

Jim Hogg went to Dallas in October and returned to Austin in mid-November, but planned to leave soon "for the North."[59] Before he left, he wrote to Will, who had moved to San Antonio a month ago. The letter begins with a mysterious paragraph. (The brackets appear in the typescript).

Dear Will:

Your [   ] action was manly and I appreciate the move because you had taken it before I had so advised you. I fully explained the matter [to] Judge R. and Mr. [Lassiter].[60]

"Judge R." was James Robertson, Jim Hogg's law partner. The identity of "Mr. Lassiter" is unknown. He may have been a client. What "action" the neophyte attorney Will Hogg had taken—perhaps to rectify an error he had made—is not evident.

The rest of the letter is a parental directive:

I want you to take Ima and the two boys to your grandfathers the day before Christmas to spend a week with the "Old Folks at Home." You know they will enjoy it and <u>it is right</u>. I'll pay the expenses. You can get back here New Year's Eve, take dinner—turkey—next day with "Aunt Fannie" and then go back to work in good shape. I leave tonight for Galveston and N.Y. to be gone nearly a month.

Your father[61]

Christmas plans remained undecided for several weeks. Meanwhile, Will Hogg seemed to be enjoying his independence in San

---

* Dengue fever, common in the nineteenth century, is an influenza-like, mosquito-borne disease, usually lasting six or seven days.

Antonio, and he did not go home for Thanksgiving. He wrote a cheerful letter to Ima the day after the holiday.

Nov. 27, 1897
Dear Sister:
    A painter is nearly finishing a sign on a certain bay window in
an office in San Antonio, and that sign spells: "Law Office, Will C.
Hogg." Neat simple plain and unassuming it bespeaks the qualities
looked for and wished for in everything and everybody and above
all in himself, by the owner thereof. By its simplicity and distinct
plainness it speaks to the passing throng below in louder tones than
the giant sign just above on the same street. That sign denotes all
that is beautiful in the world to me—truth, simplicity, sincerity and
modesty.
    Thanksgiving day I was the honored recipient of four invitations
to eat turkey. Do you believe it, I declined—only two, and accepted
the other two, the first two of course. I ate turkey at one o'clock,
that, glorious and beautiful, and at six repeated the performance.
At one at Mr. McNulty's; at six with Mr. Floyd McGown. The other
invitations were from Col. Gibbs and Senator Lewis.
    Last night for a wonder I went out to the Insane Asylum to the
weekly dance for the inmates.
    With love to all—say, go and kiss yourself in your new dresser
glass for
                              Your brother
                              Will.[62]

    In his teens, Will had worked at the San Antonio Insane Asylum
and made some friends in San Antonio.
    From the Fifth Avenue Hotel in New York, J. S. Hogg wrote to
Ima on December 3, still trying to work out Christmas plans:

    Dear Ima:
    Since my arrival here the weather has been bracing and fine until
at this writing, it is snowing. This "soaks in" and makes me homesick. I feel confident now that I shall reach home before Christmas
unless it is decided that Willie will carry you and the boys to Mr. Stinson's. In this event I may not get there until a few days before "New
Year's." So settle this matter by correspondence with him and write
me the result—the determination. Mike and Tom must go anyway if
they wish to [visit] with their Uncle Jim. Christmas, to me, without

them will be very dry notwithstanding the mirth and pleasure that you and your Aunt Fannie would add to home on that occasion. You know a frolic or a holiday without two such boys as those is denied many of its greatest attractions, and I should not consent to their leaving then except that we are due it to their Grandfather to do so. He will enjoy Christmas with them more than with all others. So waiving selfish considerations they must go if they want to and you know they will. As soon as you shall have settled the question of going yourself you must promptly write to me.

I have met many friends here and of course the time has been so far pleasantly spent. No news of interest.

Love to all,
Your Father, Affectionately
J. S. Hogg[63]

For reasons unrecorded, there was no visit to the Stinsons that Christmas, and J. S. Hogg planned to be in Austin after all. On December 8, he wrote to his brother John to bring his family to Austin for Christmas: "We have plenty of room and it does seem that you should strain a point, if necessary, and spend a while with us . . . ."[64]

On December 11, Will wrote to Ima about Christmas gifts:

Dear Sister:

Will you suggest something for me to bring the "boys" Christmas? Would not a nice book or two do for Aunt Fannie? How would it do to get the "boys" a watch—a real watch—a cheap one that keeps time? Or would they like books and tops or airguns or a football better? I think I'll just get them a cheap Waterbury watch apiece—watches were not so cheap when I was a boy even—you can get a good one now for one dollar. I've bought one for my own use and it keeps good time.*

Those weekly letters you so generously promised me must have been lost in the mail. I'll wager that if a large, languid, lazy lassie named Ima will look in the drawers of her dresser or in the shoe-box to the hall-rack downstairs she will find at least one letter addressed to her

brother
Will.[65]

---

* By "watches" he meant pocket watches. Wristwatches in the early 1900s were for women, and not until after World War I did men's wristwatches become popular. The Waterbury Company made clocks and, from 1880 to 1898, inexpensive watches.

Will was always the one who demanded regular letters with news from home. He did not stay in Austin for New Year's as his father suggested. He was in San Antonio on December 31, and he wrote to Ima:

Dear Sister:

Today is the last day of one more year in our lives. Tomorrow is the first day of a new year welcomed with great expectations, warm hopes and good resolutions by most every one. Let us two see if we can't live somewhat better next year. I have no new resolutions to make—only to try more resolutely to adhere to some long since made.

Hug all the family round and wish them each and every one of them, a Happy New Year for

Your
Brother
Will—[66]

With little activity in his fledgling law practice, Will had plenty of time to write to his sister. Two undated letters from San Antonio— one whimsical, one pompous—are in Ima's "Family Letters" volume.

San Antonio, Texas

Look here Sis—

Are you going to get me those photographs? Are you going to write to me sometime? If you do not get me those photographs, I'll cut you off without a cent in my last will and testament—If you do not get me those photographs I'll not let you keep house for me in mine old age. If you do not get me those photographs I'll never consent for you to have a sweetheart. If you do not get me those photographs I'll not let you come to see me oftener than "onct a month," If you do not get me those photographs, I'll hang up some other fellow's sister's photographs instead. If you do not get me those photographs, why I do not know who will get them for me.

Yours
Will
San Antonio, Texas

Dear Sis—

Probably you are correct about the biographical series—American and English men of letters. They are critical biographies, one volume to the man—so strike 'em out. Now Missey, I raise my voice in alarm—leave the <u>American Statesmen</u> series of biographies in the list. The clearest and most interesting road to a general knowledge of America's Kingdom's history goes along the lives of the men in those books. The boys will find helpful, man-making reading there.—So please leave them in. Why, James Stefinn will enjoy <u>them.</u>

Let me plead in your own behalf for another book in the list— Stevenson's Letters. There's not a more fascinating, absorbing name in latter-day letters than R.L.S. Now those letters will please and instruct you. (And just between us, I don't know but that I wuz at a min' to snatch 'em on one of my flys over to see you. Et leas it wuz temptin') His works, <u>put</u> on the shelves of that library! Now Boswell's Life of Johnson—is not <u>long</u> and will tell you of a <u>man</u>. Do as you like here—though, leaving the book in the list now will, when you come to read it, furnish ample cause for congratulation.

Before I close, let me admonish you to guard yourself from a habit of—reading that weakens, that does not instruct, that only serves to amuse in a time-killing way—a method of reading worse than no reading at all, almost. The kind of reader you must not become and which you will probably become is the butterfly-reader, the humming-bird-reader; the reader who tastes of everything within a binding and digests nothing; a flirt and coquette with good taste and thoroughness. I say you will probably become such because the larger number of readers I have seen are just such readers—I know you will become such unless you start now in the direction of thoroughness. For instance, soon you will have a complete edition of the works of Thackeray at hand; if Thackeray suits your taste, you should cultivate that taste by a careful reading of his works—a reading that will make his thought and language unconsciously a part of your own—and there is no safer standard in Eng. of this Century. Live in his works until you have sacrificed interest to familiarity which you can never do. Thackeray's novels are no mere storybooks; there is life, there is philosophy in them if you only train your mind to see it. I use Thackeray as a prominent literary party for the purpose of illustration Therefore, before you take to reading random novels that come out every day, lay the foundation of your taste with the masters that the latter-day lesser, saints of literature all more or less copy. Shakespeare, Irving, Stevenson, and others—for a young woman let her novel reading start with a thorough Thackerian training, and I say it for a number of reasons that seem good ones to me. I enclose a slip of paper with references to the standard editions of

the works of Holmes and Kipling only, because they will replace in
price the cutting out of the biographies.
                                    Yours,
                                    Will.
You might, if you desired, substitute Eliot's works for the Abbott's
histories.[67]

Ima may have read Thackeray, but she also read what she pleased
on her own. As she remembered, "If there were any current popular
novels, 'Trilby,' I believe, is about the only one I can remember, and
that was shunned.* The standard works were sufficiently interesting
and absorbing to satisfy my curiosity." Among the Ima Hogg papers
is a small composition book she kept while she lived in the house on
Nineteenth and Rio Grande. In it are her notes on Hugo's *Les Mis-
erables*, Dumas's *The Count of Monte Cristo*, and J. M. Barrie's 1896
novel, *Sentimental Tommy*.[68]
    Will had opened his San Antonio law office in November 1897,
but had not had much success. Early in the new year he was thinking
of joining an established practice with a San Antonio attorney, J. F.
Onion. On January 11, 1898, Will's father wrote to him advising him
to take the offer from Mr. Onion, who was a "good lawyer of popular
turn and varied experience." J. F. Onion had known the Hogg family
in Tyler in the 1880s.[69]
    Ima may not have had much time to take Will's advice about read-
ing in early 1898: she was preparing to tour Mexico for a month,
leaving on February 23, with her father and a party of his business
associates ("about twenty Northern people"). On February 18, her
father wrote to Will, whose new address was "Office of Onion &
Hogg, Kampmann Bldg." in San Antonio, that "Ima is busy getting
ready with her 'wardrobe' for the trip and of course expects to have
a fine time."[70]
    That same day, Ima's father wrote to Colonel Stinson, who had
evidently been ill. (That may have been the reason the Hogg children
did not visit him at Christmas.) Hogg invited the Stinsons to come to
Austin and visit Mike and Tom while he and Ima were away:

Feb'y 18, 1898
Dear Col:
    I am pleased to understand that you are getting better, and trust

* George du Maurier's 1894 gothic horror novel.

you will soon be able to come down and spend a while with us. You can leave Mineola in the morning and reach here the same afternoon. The children have a gentle pony and trap to take you about in. Nothing could please us all better than to have you come down to recuperate. The new sulphur artesian well here effects great results with sick people and I feel quite certain that they will cure you. So come down without fail. Last October Ima and I accepted an engagement to go to Mexico, and we are to start with the party next Wednesday but the boys will be here with Jim and Sister to take care of you until our return. Then we will take a turn at you. Now don't fail for any reason to come down. Bring Mrs. Stinson with you and we guarantee she will also get stout and rosy.

The children are all in fine health. Will has located in the practice of law at San Antonio. After staying by himself for several months he was offered and accepted a partnership with Mr. Onion and from all accounts is doing well. He is certainly a model young man and has made a great many friends.

Ima grows . . . more like her dear Mother. She is much larger now than Sallie ever was but has her sweet ways and fine disposition. Mike is going to be the strongest one of the family. He keeps right along with Tom who, himself, is growing fat. They are both fine boys and are learning well. <u>Now don't fail to come and bring Mrs. Stinson</u>. With love to all the family, I am yours,

J. S. Hogg[71]

The tour of Mexico, as Ima remembered it, was by a special train with its own baggage and dining cars.

Father's connections were most cordial with Mexico. During his tenure as Governor he had tried to cement friendly relationships with many Mexican states and with President Diaz, the long time dictator of Mexico. . . . Everywhere the party was received and entertained. President Diaz gave a reception at Chapultepec to which I went and a banquet where I was not included . . . I don't think we missed many places in Mexico . . . .[72]

The tourists in Mexico were missing an important event in the United States: On February 15, a few days before the Mexican tour began, the United States battleship *Maine*, on a visit to Cuba, had sunk after a mysterious explosion in Havana Harbor. Two hundred sixty-six American sailors were killed, and many Americans were calling for war against Spain. President McKinley signed a document demanding Spain's disengagement in Cuba on April 20. Spain refused, and the Spanish-American War was on.

Will Hogg, age twenty-three, hoped to get a commission to serve in the U.S. Navy, but he did not get it. His father, age forty-seven, was also eager to enlist—but he did not ask for a commission. He wrote a letter to his friend, Governor Charles Culberson:

> April 23, 1898
> Dear Governor:
> My services are at the command of my country for and during the war with Spain.
> Further discussion of the policy of the unfortunate measure is now out of place. The conflict is on and every self-respecting available man must, from impulses of pride, of honor, of patriotism, stand ready to place his business, his property, his life, at his country's disposal, to the end that our flag shall not suffer dishonor. For the want of a military education I know my unfitness in any other capacity than that of a private soldier whose duty is to obey orders from those who may have the authority to give them.
> I want no commission. I aspire to no office. With those who are to carry the muskets to do execution I stand ready to go in line, shoulder to shoulder, and to share their fate whenever and wherever you or the recruiting officer you may name shall see fit to assign me.
> At command, Your Obt. Srv't.,
> J. S. Hogg[73]

But some weeks later the portly ex-governor wrote to a friend, J. F. Banks in Kingsland, Texas, who was evidently of a similar age and girth: "Men of our sort and weight are excluded under the army rules and regulations from participating in the present war with Spain . . . . It seems that vigorous fat men over forty-five are not wanted by the government."[74]

But another Hogg, Jim Hogg's nephew Baylor, signed on as an army physician with the First Texas Volunteer Infantry, U.S.A.[75] Shortly before he enlisted, Baylor got engaged to be married, and asked his uncle for a loan. Hogg answered regretfully in the negative: "By reason of some extraordinary expenses and investments in which I have indulged this year I cannot propose to advance you the $500 loan."[76] But he invited the newlyweds to come to Austin on their honeymoon. They were to be married that November.

Colonel Stinson, whom Hogg had invited to Austin in February, did visit that spring, though the dates of his stay are not clear. In May, while Jim Hogg was away on one of his many business trips, his law partner Judge Robertson wrote to him that Stinson had "left for home" and that Aunt Fannie and the rest of the family were all well. But Aunt Fannie, as Robertson wrote, "says they have not heard from you for some time which she does not understand, and to tell you to write to her.[77]

On May 25, Hogg found time to write to Ima from the Fifth Avenue Hotel in New York: "I have gotten one good client since I came here and am about to get another. Business has kept me here longer than expected."[78]

Meanwhile, he wanted Ima to help Mike teach Tom to dive and swim. The Hogg residence was not far from Deep Eddy, a spring-fed swimming hole on the Colorado River. Perhaps Ima and her brothers practiced their aquatic skills there.

Late in June, Jim Hogg was back in Austin and tending to family. On June 25, he wrote to his brother John with another request to "come down" and visit. John's eldest daughter was already there, but evidently had been ill. "Velma is improving substantially, and I think will soon be sound and well." She and Ima had planned to go to the Beach Hotel in Galveston, a grand Victorian structure built in 1882 with "Salt Water Baths on every Floor" and "Electric Cars to and from the Hotel to all Parts of the City Every 5 Minutes." But the hotel, they discovered, was not open "on account of some kind of quarantine trouble." The quarantine had a good reason: In 1898 the Beach Hotel was found to be flushing its cesspools via pipe into the Gulf of Mexico. Galveston city officials closed the hotel until it connected to the city's sewage system. The Beach Hotel mysteriously burned down later that year.[79] Jim Hogg's letter ended with a plea to John: "If you will come down I will do the balance and see that you have a good time."[80] No extant letters testify to John's visit.

In July Hogg wrote to his nephew Baylor, in the U.S. Army, advising him to seek "the position of surgeon, not assistant surgeon . . . When you strike, strike high." He also wrote to congratulate Julia's son Brownlee, now Dr. W. B. Ferguson, who was establishing his dental practice in Waxahachie, Texas.[81]

That July, Hogg also found time for a fishing trip with his grandnephew, Marion Davis, and Mike and Tom. He wrote to Marion, who was visiting John Hogg and his family in Decatur, to bring Uncle John with him. He also invited Will, offering to pay his expenses.[82] It is not clear from the letters if either John or Will came.

Departing from tradition, Hogg did not attend the state Democratic convention that summer. He wrote to a friend J. E. Leslie, in Sherman: "I am compelled on account of my over-weight to avoid large crowds and this hot weather."[83]

He also wrote to Will, who was short of funds:

Dear Will—
    Enclosed find check on W. L. Moody & Co. for Forty Six Dollars to meet your request and note by recent favor. Hope you are healthy, active, of clear conscience, and in good spirits. . . .[84]

Meanwhile, Aunt Fannie set out by train from Austin to Pueblo. As soon as she arrived she wrote a long letter to Mike and Tom, who evidently had not been to Pueblo since Sallie's death. Aunt Fannie herself had not been there in some time.

Dear Mike & Tom:
    I intended to write you two boys on yesterday, but was not rested up enough to think. I had a lonely trip, knew no one and spoke to none but the porter and conductor. The first night I didn't sleep at all hardly, but the next night I slept <u>ten hours</u> without turning over. O but it was hot, up to Trinidad then I had to put on a thicker sack. But the last day I did have a good and amusing time watching the little cute, prairie dogs. I had forgotten all about them until I heard a little bark, like a big dog, but very little and fine. I knew at once and looked quick to see the pert little rascal, & there he sat upon his mound. Then I kept a lookout until the sun went down—watching their funny little antics—when I went to bed and slept <u>all night</u>. They were quite surprised when I drove up to the house. Your Uncle William got your papa's telegram <u>after</u> I got home.
    Everything looks very nice, the house having been repapered. The sitting room is a perfect picture gallery. And Pearl's room is worse than Ima's for pictures and trinkets. Hun [Marion] hasn't grown so very much, but he's considerable taller than I am. He and Pearl are going out to a dance at the club tonight. Pearl is taking a nap, and her mama is measuring her waist as she sleeps.
    Pueblo is not changed much. The trees in the park have grown

lots, & the park is beautiful now. Pearl has a little water Spaniel which stands at all corners, ready to slap muddy paws on any passerby. By the way, ask your papa if he sure wants a pair of "Belgian Hares" of pure breed. They sell from five to fifteen dollars a pair—according to age—and I can get a pair for two dollars from a man next door. They are very prolific, but tender—said to be more profitable than chickens, and by far more tender and sweet meat. The meat sells by the pound at fifteen cents and they weight seven and eight pounds.

The little boys that you knew are all gone from here. Tell Ima that all of Pueblo are fussing that she did not come,—the gentlemen especially. William is very disappointed. He wanted to have an excuse to turn chaperon again, I think. Pearl and Hun are learning to swim, and their pappy goes in too—at night—in the lake.

Now, I've written you a long letter and I want a long one from each of you. Have you got your clothes back in your trunk? Be sure you keep up your reading. Both of you must read "To have a Toe Hold"—and it is yours—Uncle William says so—if you will read it. Love to Ima and papa and yourselves if you are good to Sister and be good boys.

Your Aunt[85]

Aunt Fannie's granddaughter and grandson, Pearl, seventeen, and Marion ("Hun"), fifteen, were close to Ima's age. In 1898 she would be sixteen.

Will was still having financial and professional problems in San Antonio, and his father could not resist giving advice:

July 26th, 1898
Dear Will:

From what I know of the library you have, I think it would be useless—yes foolish—expenditure of money to purchase more books. Review and read over your text-books and Supreme Court decisions—let all others alone for awhile. Take care of your money, economize to the core, and build up by degrees. A hundred dollars when I was older than you are, supported me and my family at as good [a] boarding house as you can find in San Antonio, so far as the comforts of life are concerned, for a period of five months. You must excuse me for beating this idea into your head so often. Cold, rigid, and cruel economy, and a walk of two miles in the morning from your boarding house to the office, and two miles to return to supper would make a man of you, and result in more good to you in the future than any other lesson or habits that you could learn or acquire. You must not consider me as your eternal lecturer, for it is not in that spirit that I write. Keep your money: it is hard to get and should be stingily doled out by every young man who expects to succeed in any occupation in life.[86]

Leaving Will to mull over this fatherly advice, Jim Hogg set out a few days later with Ima on an ocean voyage. On July 31, 1898, father and daughter sailed for Hawaii aboard the U.S. troopship *Arizona.* The United States had annexed the Hawaiian Islands, and former governor James Stephen Hogg was among the dignitaries invited to Hawaii to witness the ceremonies. But as Ima wrote later, "The ship . . . was filled with officers and soldiers [and] was anchored at sea for a day or so when one of the rudders was out of order. This made us too late for the ceremonies." The voyage to Honolulu took eight days, and Ima, who had celebrated her sixteenth birthday on July 10, apparently had a fine time. She kept a little notebook she labeled "My Freak Book" with a record of her trip, and all of the *Arizona*'s officers signed it.[87]

She and her father were in Hawaii by August 12 and stayed at the Hawaiian Palace Hotel. Years later, Ima recalled the events of their visit in her memoir: "We were invited to Queen Liliuokalani's birthday party celebration with music and native dancing outdoors which was lovely. The palace she lived in was not elegant and she was a large unattractive woman."[88] (When Ima Hogg was in her eighties, she once startled some Hawaiian visitors in Houston by remarking "Ah, yes. I have met your queen."[89])

In October, Jim Hogg, back in Austin, heard from his ever-needy niece, Annie Hogg Magee. She and her husband were now in Hartman, Mississippi, and still short of money. Her uncle kindly but firmly refused her request for funds, reminding her that he had once offered to send her to school (she declined) but she was "now grown, with a family." All that her uncle gave her was another of his lectures on the virtues of hard work.[90] Annie's family now included an infant son, Edward Magee Jr., born the previous November.[91]

But there was some good family news: Baylor Hogg's November wedding in New Orleans. His uncle sent congratulations and regretted that he and Ima would be unable to attend: "Ima would like to go also, but as I have taken her out of school twice this year, she and her teacher have both become quite sensitive about it." But he changed his plans. On November 12, he wrote to Baylor that he would be present at the wedding.[92]

The devoted uncle wrote to another nephew, James McDugald, then practicing law in Cleburne, about James's half-brother, Bismarck Ferguson: "It may be a first class plan for you to have Bismarck with you for a year as you request. . . . He is welcome at my house to finish at the University now or later on."[93]

And Jim Hogg was still sending his eldest son exhortations to practice frugality:

December 8th, 1898
Dear Will:

Your figures on that horse result very much like the profits on Gilhooley's Goose Ranch. It looks very much like the fellow who trained himself to buy a $50 mantel-piece to put in a $100 house. The point I wish to make is that the horse is a little too fine for a man of my means. In this day of cheap stock you could get an excellent mule or horse—perhaps not so stylish but quite as useful as the Arabian stallion you speak of—at about $12.50 or $18. In speaking of horses, it reminds me of a lesson that I learned when I used to plow at about twenty-five cents a day which was that when the plow ran too deep, the way to remedy it was to set the back-hand back. . . . Perhaps you do not see the point. By way of parenthesis, then, let me say to you, Will, that when you want an Arabian stallion, you must excuse me for not going into partnership with you. That kind of investment would not pay.

All are well, and join in sending much love. Come over Christmas and spend the holidays with us, and we will have a big time.

Affectionately your father,
J. S. Hogg[94]

A few days later Hogg wrote again to Will, repeating his Christmas invitation.

Dec. 18, 1898
Dear Will:

I have talked to Ima and expressed the desire that she make you the visit next Thursday but she pleads against it on the ground that her school will not take a holiday recess until Saturday. She is undergoing, or is to undergo by next Thursday, the quarterly examination and could not leave without serious detriment to her educational progress. As you may know she is making an effort with much hope of success, to graduate from Miss Carrington's School this session so as to enter the University next year. I prefer that she remain in the preparatory school for about two years longer. She wants to get through right away. Probably she's right. At all events it will take about six years I hope for her to graduate from the University! I know you must feel disappointed in not having her with you on the approach of Christmas. But come over next Friday or Saturday and she will take great pains to make your visit during the holidays in all respects very pleasant.

I trust, Will, you shall not neglect to occasionally write to your Grand Father. You know a letter now and then written in a cheerful tone would [do] him much good. Do not neglect him. Explain why on account of the children being in school you cannot take them down there next Christmas, but that you intend to do so next June during their vacation.

We are all well. Don't fail to come over next Friday or Saturday to remain a week or more with us.

Affectionately Your Father,
J. S. Hogg[95]

When Will went back to San Antonio as the new year began, he was planning another career move. For reasons unmentioned in the family letters, his law practice of one year with J. F. Onion was not working out, and Will was planning to open a law office again on his own. His father tried to encourage him:

Jany 19, 1899
Dear Will:—

If I have good success this year I shall cheerfully stand by you in your honorable, economical, effort to succeed, Try a few cases this year and expand a little in professional exercise, even if you should have to do so without pay and furnish fun for the worst of all critics—the "gallery gang"——who usually infest trial courts. Defend a "jail bird" or two, That's a good way to begin. If you'll do so I will pay the usual fee. Now, what do you say?

All well and join in sending much love,

Your Father,
J. S. Hogg[96]

On his birthday, Will wrote to his sister:

Jany 31st 1899
Dear Sister—

Today is my twenty-fourth birthday! We grow old! I duck my head and blush at what I am today—What I am intellectually, in point of scholarship, in point of successful manhood. Manhood I say—yes, for does not or should not twenty-four years given token of the "freshman term" of manhood? Reflecting to my seventeenth year, I find that my ideas of what I should and would be at twenty-four are far removed from the actuality. Still, the dissipation of the illusions of idealistic youth that time has wrought does not fill me with vain regret or soreness of heart. And yet I am young.

I open an office alone tomorrow—Feb'y 1st. I do not want anyone to expect anything of me—I do expect something of myself. Write to
Your
Brother[97]

Will Hogg would eke out a living practicing law on his own in San Antonio for the next three years. No doubt he saw his friend Joe Lee Jameson, who by 1900 had left the insane asylum for a position as a state revenue agent. Jameson now lived at the Menger Hotel. In Austin, Will's father and Judge Robertson had moved their law office to the third floor of a building at 806 Congress Avenue. They were ideally situated, being about halfway between the Capitol and the I&GN railroad depot.[98]

Baylor Hogg, still stationed in Cuba with the First Texas Volunteer Infantry, would soon be home. He and his bride, Josie, were planning to settle in Houston. J. S. Hogg wrote to them on March 23, "You & Josie come and see us on your return home."[99]

Will was growing discouraged with his efforts to practice law in San Antonio, and his father tried to cheer him:

April 3, 1899
Dear Will:

You conclude your letter of the 31st with the following language: "You can rest assured that if I do not honor you and your name I shall not at least disgrace it and you."

This is worth more to me than the amount I have thus far advanced you. So far I must confess, on due reflection you have not only not disgraced me but you have constantly reflected credit upon my name. You have never drawn a draft on me. You have never attempted to run an account against me. You have never been drunk.

You have never gambled. You have never idled away your time on street corners nor at vulgar resorts. You have never forced the blood of shame to my cheeks from a wounded heart by a single disreputable act. For these reasons, contrasted with the condition of most other public men who have "boys," I find myself in good conscience far more indebted to you than the amount of $1334.25 evidenced by your fifteen promissory notes to become due several years hence. I therefore return them all to you settled in full.

My anxiety is for your success. To this end my advice has been constantly aimed. You have already succeeded far greater than most young men of similar environments—you have established the ability to avoid snares which have been set all along young manhood's way to drag them and their good name down to the level of infamy and dishonor. I'll stick to you awhile longer.

Affectionately, with great respect,
Your Father[100]

Jim Hogg also sent words of praise to his daughter, mailing her a letter her cousin Jim McDugald had written to him about her:

I never knew her much until the last fall and I declare that you have one of [the] sweetest girls I have ever met and I'm proud of her as my cousin.

I am not given to flattery one bit but such is most vivid and plain: unassuming modest sweet and pretty Ima is an exceptional girl and with the chances she has had to be despisable and spoiled . . . she has withstood all and as she is just now budding into womanhood a sweeter girl is not to be found.

A note to Ima from her father was appended: "Now don't let this spoil you."[101]

Family matters occupied much of Jim Hogg's time in May: He tried to get Hermilla's husband, Bob Kelso, appointed supervisor of the census for the northern Texas district. He begged his brother John to take a vacation with him: "I am anxious to have you go with me to spend a few weeks at either Hot Springs, Ark., or Marlin, Mineral Wells or Sour Lake, Texas. . . . I know we should both enjoy such a trip. . . . Say the word and we go. . . . The expenses will be light and I will gladly defray them." He wrote to his nephew, Baylor: "I shall cheerfully go as your security for the one hundred dollars you need . . . Now plant yourself and pull ahead."[102]

And there were the younger Hogg boys to see to: Mike was now thirteen and Tom was eleven, and their father decided they needed summer jobs. On May 24, Hogg wrote to John Orr Jr., a friend in Llano, a farming and ranching town about seventy-five miles north of Austin, on the Llano River. Hogg wanted his boys to work on a ranch near there, and Orr arranged for them to work for a rancher named R. H. Moseley. Hogg himself was to deliver the boys to the ranch in July.[103]

Hogg then wrote to Will about Ima's summer visit to her grandparents:

> May 26, 1899
> Dear Will:
> Perhaps within the next few days I will leave on a month's trip to New York on business. Mike and Tom will go to their Grandfather's next Thursday to remain until my return, when I shall take them to a ranch for the remainder of the Summer where they are to work for their wages. Ima desires to spend a week at her Grandfather's, with the "Old Folks" immediately following [the University of Texas] Commencement, about the 17th of June, and I should like, as she especially desires, for you to go with her there and back. Of course I will foot the bills. Now it is very appropriate for these visits to be made down there and I am confident you will heartily enjoy your part of them. Will you go? About July 1st your Auntie and Ima will go to Colorado for the Summer, where later on, I shall probably join them. No news. All well. In haste,
> Your Father,
> J. S. Hogg[104]

Next the busy father wrote to R. H. Moseley, the owner of the ranch where his boys were to work:

> June 1st, 1899
> Dear Sir:—
> I am very much obliged for your consent, communicated through our mutual friend, Mr. Jno. Orr, to send my two boys to your ranch some time in July for the summer. For the next few weeks, they will spend a vacation at their Grand-father's out in East Texas, where they should like to remain all summer, as you know. However, this would teach them idleness and dependence. My purpose is to teach them to labor and to be independent, as well as to give them the advantage of

the bracing mountain atmosphere of your section. Their names are Mike and Tom, aged, respectively, 13 and 11. So far they have been well-trained to do work about home, such as feeding stock, milking the cow, sawing and bringing in wood, and doing errands. While with you I should be glad for it to be understood that they are to get their board and wages at $5 per month. Of course, I will furnish the money to pay their wages through yourself, and shall gladly pay to you their board. Of course, I understand that you are not running a boarding house, but in the indulgence of my whims—if such they be—I do not wish to impose upon you the slightest expense. At the same time, I wish my boys to feel that they are making and earning a living. When I send them to you, I should be glad for you and your good wife to treat them as you would your own children. From the assurances of Mr. Orr, I feel justified in committing this trust to you. I may in person take them out there or shall send them in the care of Mr. Orr. I hope that you will see that they get plenty of exercise such as driving stock, riding horseback, milking your cows, bringing in wood, going [on] errands, etc.

With kindest regards, I am,

Very truly yours,

J. S. Hogg[105]

A few days later he wrote to Will about the family's summer travels:

June 6, 1899
Dear Will:
    When Mike and Tom left on the vacation last Thursday to their Grandfather's it was a spectacle worth seeing and recollecting. You know it was their first trip alone on their own responsibility. "Loaded to the guard" with their guns, and bat and ball, and clothes, and luncheon for six, they walked with a majestic step that made the toads hop, the by-standers gaze and the car quake. And they got to the Old House in good condition for a great time. No doubt they will have it.
    Ima wants you to come by for her at a time of which she will tell you. After staying down there a week she is to go to Decatur from Mineola via Ft. Worth over the T.&.P [Texas and Pacific Railway] to join Sister at John's. Thence they will go to Colorado for the Summer. I should like you to go with her to John's and spend awhile with him. She is a graduate now and is about weaned from me! After Mike and Tom have spent a month at Col. Stinson's they are to go

on Mr. R. H. Moseley's ranch near Llano where I have "hired" them out to work until school opens next fall. They are to get their board and $5 per month. It's a good place for them and the work will keep them from idleness in town and evil thoughts. I expect to leave this P.M. for the North on business to return within a month to take the boys out to the ranch and wind up business affairs for the Summer with the hope of joining Sister and Ima in Colorado. This plan may fail however. If so I shall write to you later about it. Enclosed find check for $100.00 out of which you can defray expenses out to Col. S's and back and also take your allowance.—Of course you will be good to the little ones and gladly make them enjoy their childish frolics without too much restraint. With much love in which Ima and Sister always join.

Affectionately,
Your Father,
J. S. Hogg[106]

Ima had graduated from Miss Carrington's that spring, as she had set out to do, and was planning to enter the University of Texas as a freshman in the fall of 1899. She would be one of many: In the academic year 1898–1899, the university had over eight hundred students, and by 1900–1901 there were over one thousand.[107]

From the Stinsons', Mike and Tom wrote to their father:

June 25 1899
Dear papa,

We have been having lots of fun hunting fishing and going in swimming.

Ben and I can swim about fifty yards and Tom can swim about five feet.

We caught five flying squirrels in one day.

After we had them about three days they got out of the cage the bottom of the cage droped out and the squirrel dropped with it.

I haven't felt a least bit sick only when I ran from the pond home. Write soon.

Your son Mike Hogg.

June 25, 1899
Dear little Pa—

I am fat how are you and I hope you are too. I killed a bird on the 30th shot.

Brother brought me my gun and I hit cinter the second time,
      I have nothing to say.
      Your Son
      Tom Hogg[108]

Soon Aunt Fannie wrote a long letter to Mike and Tom at the
Stinsons'.

Dear Boys:
      Sister and I are very busy this morning getting her ready for our
trip. Sister is now down town for a pattern—lost hers. Papa started
yesterday for New York. The place seems quite deserted. Every whistle I hear I think: "There's Mike and Tom" and I catch myself being
disappointed. Fact is, I'd very much prefer your racket than not to
have you at all. We all have missed you ever so much. Papa looked
lonesome when he came home, and Ima and I feel quite deserted.
      Papa had a letter from Mr. Moor [Moseley], the ranchman, and
he is very pleased to have two boys this summer. He says he is looking forward to your coming with anticipations of much pleasure.
Brother and Sister will be down about the 18th, 19th, or 20th maybe.
I don't know just when, but I want to be in Colorado by the 2nd,
3d or 4th of July. Your Uncle William keeps begging me to "come
on" and there is nothing now to hinder us but the Commencement
and Ima's visit to her Grandparents, a duty and pleasure she must
perform. It is so long since she was there. Sometimes I hear boys
talking outside and I think: "There's Mike and Tom," and listen for
you to "report." Do you report to your grandma? You ought. Let
your grandparents and Aunt Lillie see what good boys you can be.
Now, the best plan to keep from fussing is to shut up your mouth
right tight when the other gets mad and threatens. It is no sign of
bravery for brothers and cousins to contend. Let each one just shut
up right tight when the other gets mad and says: "I'll knock you with
a rock"—or any other threat. Try it one whole day and see how easy
you'll get along. Then try it two days—then a week. You'll see how
nice it is, and your Grandparents will say: "What nice boys. I love
to have such nice, good boys around." Wait until I get to Colorado
to answer this, and be sure to tell me if this plan worked or if you
tried it. Don't just scratch a few lines. Tell me all about everything
good and bad. Will you? Suppose you write a little every day—what
happened that day, where you went, what all you did, and that will
be a kind of diary and make me a good, interesting letter. When you

do, or see, anything you enjoy, first time you are at the house set it down with the date. By the time I get to Colorado you'll have a fine letter. Don't copy after one another, but each write things as they occur, and one send to papa and one to me. That's a good plan—and easy. I must go to work now. Love to all. I send a last handshake and "goodbye" to Tom. Does he remember he didn't tell me goodbye?

Your Aunt[109]

Mike and Tom were prone to fistfights. Ima remembered her brothers' habits: "They loved to test their strength against each other and sometimes the play would end in real fighting. Mike knew how to tease and anger Tom who was by nature, a very sweet and affectionate child, but Mike was witty and a tormenter, so Father's nickname 'the Yellow Kid' [a popular comic strip character] really suited him."[110]

In New York City on July 4, 1899, former governor J. S. Hogg was invited to speak at Tammany Hall, the historic Democratic Party stronghold on Fourteenth Street. He took the occasion to come out strongly for "free silver" (the coinage of silver at a ratio of 16 to 1, a major political issue of the period). He also praised the 1896 Democratic candidate William Jennings Bryan, looking forward to the next presidential race in 1900. Hogg's speech catapulted him once more into national prominence, but Bryan did not win the presidency the second time around, either.

That summer Will took it upon himself to advise Ima about attending the university: He cautioned her not to spend much time on the campus, but to attend classes and go home. (The Nineteenth Street house was only a few blocks from the university.) Otherwise, he feared that she might turn into a frivolous co-ed: "I saw many nice, good, well-meaning girls make ninnies of themselves. . . ."[111]

Will was always stuffy. He also wrote again to Ima about her reading habits:

July 15, 1899
Dear Sister:
    At the same time that I mailed the book I mailed not exactly a letter but a note. I hadn't much to say and I said it. I am very glad that father let you know that he thought of you on Monday [that would have been Ima's seventeenth birthday]. It is almost painful to me to think that you are so near to grown-up womanhood.
    The pronunciation of the name of the little book as near as I can spell it out for you is correctly thus.—Omar Ki-yam. There is much

of the spiritual in the lines of that poem—from time to time, as you read and reread it, the true sense will come to you little by little in keeping with your growth in thought and experience. Make yourself fairly familiar with the scholarly introduction to the poem. And just here let me mention what I consider honest and fruitful advice, never go into the text of any book until you have read carefully the author's preface or the introduction or introductory criticism, which ever there be. Even (if you are ever so vain-glorious as to stultify yourself by reading such rubbish), in reading a cheap common novel begin with the preface or introductory essay. If the book is the result of a purpose on the part of the author and if that purpose be an honest above-board one, in many instances you will find it disclosed or outlined in the preface. . . .

> With love to all—
> Yours
> Will[112]

In July, Mike and Tom, who had spent the month of June enjoying themselves at the Stinsons', moved on to work as young hired hands for the rest of the summer on the Moseley ranch. Their stay did not work out as planned and was cut short by illness: "chills and fever," as Mike called it. In August they returned to Austin, where their father met them, and Aunt Fannie came from Pueblo to help look after them. Once at home, both boys quickly recovered.

On August 18 their father wrote to Mr. Moseley, apologizing for the trouble the boys' illness had caused, and requesting him to send any doctors' bills or medical expenses for reimbursement. With his typical hospitality, Hogg also wrote, "If you and your wife ever come to Austin, I wish it now to be distinctly understood that you are to come directly to my house without further ceremony."[113]

In August, Hogg managed a quick trip to Manitou (now known as Manitou Springs), Colorado, to see Ima. She was apparently having a good time. In a note dated August 9, a young man wrote to her: hoping to "have the pleasure of escorting you to the dance over here tonight. Unfortunately you were out so I left the message with your father.

"For fear that he might forget I write now to know if I may have the aforesaid pleasure. If so I will call for you at eight thirty."[114]

On August 19, a convalescent Mike wrote to Ima, who was still in Colorado.

Dear Sister:

I am very grateful to the Good Lord and to a good doctor for being well of the chills and fever. I am thankful to Aunt Fannie and to Papa for being in the cool shades of home. Here and now I am old Mike again. The pigeons are cooing, the ducks quacking, the hens cackling, the roosters crowing, the sparrows are chirping, the mocking birds are warbling, the ostriches in their guttural voices are snorting, the cow is lowing, Joe and Dainty neighing all in common unison to welcome us home. In all these joyful surroundings we miss you. While the weather is exceedingly warm we are comparatively pleasant out on the big gallery. Alice, Lucy Thornton, Mary Thompson, and Bessy De Lashmutt have called to inquire about you. They are all as sweet and pretty as ever. And you know Sister that I am a good judge of girls. When I get a little larger Papa is going to take me out to see them once in a while. Give my love to all our kin folks and bring them home with you.

Mike[115]

Ima remained in Colorado with her Uncle John, who had been persuaded to go there for his health. Her father wrote to her there on August 22:

Dear Ima:

The enclosed letter from your brother Will shows that you are neglecting him. You should do better by him. He is worth looking after and I trust you shall never leave him to suppose or to suspicion (even if it is so) that you forget him even for a moment in the cool climate of Colorado. Since my return home we have been engaged in an estate case of vast importance in the City of Mexico. It falls to my lot to go there soon. For this reason I cannot return to Manitou. I trust you and John will remain there in Colorado until the last of September. Keep cool. Throw your shoulders back <u>when you happen to think of me</u>. Let buggy rides alone except with Pearl or some of your kin. Observe your accustomed prudence and be happy. By all means bring dear Pearl home with you, Give the agent your ticket and get him to have a stopover privilege allowed. All well.

Lovingly your father.[116]

Hogg, contrary to plan, did return to Colorado before leaving for Mexico. He wrote to Mike and Tom from the Cliff House, a resort in Manitou:

Sept. 8, 1899
Dear Mike and Tom:
I was proud to receive your letters, but gladder still to learn from your Aunt Fannie that you are good boys and have not been guilty of fighting since I left home. When a boy makes a promise and keeps it he is worth knowing; and worthy of love and respect.
I go from here to Denver to-day. Next Tuesday I go to Mexico. Will try to be at home by Oct. the first.

With much love
Your Father.[117]

With Aunt Fannie returning to oversee housekeeping at the Nineteenth Street house, Tom and Mike attended school in Austin and Ima began her freshman year at the university. Her cousin Pearl had come with her from Colorado for a visit. Tom wrote a report of Pearl's stay to Will:

Austin, Texas
Oct 5, 1899

Dear Brother,
Pearl left at 11:50 last night.
Sister and I got home at 25 to 1.
Sister is going to ride Jo and Miss [illegible] is going to break him in for Sister.
What are you going to do.
Mike and I went riding the other day.
Sunday Fred and I went riding in papa's buggy.
Pearl can shoot Mike's gun all right. She hit the bulseye first shot.
Mike is reading to Aunt Fanny. He is reading the Youths Companion.
We have got a good garden and it is coming up all right. Fred planted some oats and they are coming up. The birds are doing well. Mike and I have about 75 pigeons. . . .
You know that book you asked us if we wanted upon the ranch. We would like to have it. Uncle William sent us 17 volumes of histories and they are fine books. Mike and I have about 40 books together.
I will close because I have nothing more to tell. Oh yes I have! Uncle has got a baby. I will close right now.

Your small brother
Tom Hogg[118]

"Uncle" was Jim Stinson, age forty-three, Sallie's brother, and the father of Ben. He had remarried after the death of Ben's mother, and now had a baby girl.[119] "Jo" [Joe] was Jim Hogg's horse. Fred seems to have been the current manservant in the Hogg household.

John Hogg continued in poor health, though family letters do not mention the nature of his illness. After he returned to Decatur that fall, his brother, then back from Mexico, wrote to him:

October 25, 1899
Dear John:—

    I trust that by reason of your ill-health you will not become demoralized and sacrifice your property in and around Decatur, as your letter of the 18th instant would indicate that you intend to do. If you sell during these depressed times, you must do so at a sacrifice. Wait, and you will get a fair value for your property. I am not one of your "I-told-you so" men, but I do wish to remind you that on reflection you are bound to confess that my advice all along as to your physical condition and what you should do to remedy your ills has proven to be good. When I visited you in the Spring, I importuned you to quit taking so much medicine, and urged you to leave Decatur for awhile until you could recuperate. This you failed to do until finally in July you did muster up spirit enough to go to Manitou. Had you stayed there until now, there is not the least doubt that you would have been sound and well, but over my protest you came back into this hot climate, and the surprise now to me is that you are not worse off by reason of the relapse which necessarily followed. I cite to you these instances with the hope of being able to impress you with the value of the advice I now give you. On receipt of this letter, or as soon as you can possibly get off, I want you to come to my house, and there stay until you get well. The mineral waters here, from the artesian wells at the Capitol and three other places in this City are very fine for all stomach complaints. We keep them at the house all the time for domestic use. After staying with me until you get tired, then I want you to go to Sour Lake, where I have heretofore begged you to stay awhile. When you get through there, I have in mind a business engagement or two which you can most likely make, very much to your pecuniary advantage. Bring Eva and either or all of the girls with you. After you have been finally restored to your splendid constitution, I will present you with a sword with

which you can chop off the heads of those pill-slingers who want to
make an apothecary's shop of your stomach.
>With much love,
>Your brother,
>J. S. Hogg[120]

Attending to domestic affairs, Hogg made sure the household
larder would be full that autumn: he ordered "½ dozen hams and
about 50 or 100 pounds of lard" paying ten cents per pound for the
hams and eight cents per pound for the lard, for a total of eighteen
dollars. He also signed a note for eighty dollars to help the struggling
young physician, Baylor, in Houston.[121]

From Austin, Tom wrote a plaintive letter to his eldest brother in
San Antonio:

>Nov. 9, 1899

>Dear Brother,
>We are all well.
>I think it right mean in you not to write to me. Just think how much
>time it would take.
>Any how write a few lines.
>I know you are busy all the time.
>Grandpa wrote 4 pp. to me.
>Well we will leave off letters for awhile.
>I got s in deportment that means B.
>Sister rides every morning on Joe and Mike and I go with her.
>When you see papa tell him to write to me.
>Tell him that Sister goes riding on Joe.
>Pleas write to me.
>Yours truly,
>Tom Hogg[122]

On another trip to New York in November, Jim Hogg was already
thinking about Christmas in Texas. He wrote to James McDugald
in Cleburne, inviting him to spend the Christmas holidays "at our
house," and to bring his half-brother, Bismarck Ferguson, with him.[123]

Back in Austin in December, Hogg wrote to John's daughter Velma
to come for Christmas: "Ima is now hard pressed in the University
with her studies but will then be out for pleasure with Willie to help
her out in giving you all the fun you could want."[124]

Part of the fun included a visit from William Jennings Bryan and a
hunting trip in December, with Hogg and about "100 city sportsmen"

for a "big panther hunt." The panther, a tame one, released especially for the "hunt," was duly captured, to the amusement and satisfaction of all parties.[125]

After a family Christmas in the house on Nineteenth Street, Hogg went back to New York.

With his father traveling and his older siblings apparently not paying him much attention, twelve-year-old Tom, at school in Austin, was lonesome. He wrote to his grandfather Stinson:

Jan. 7, 1900

Dear Grand Pa,

We have all been well and have been in good health.

Why don't you make Ben write to me. He wont write to any body.

I believe you have too much work to do. That is why you don't write to me is it.

Can't Grand Ma write any more.

And can't Aunt Lily. Have they all lost their fingers or tongues.

Tell Uncle Dave to write to me and tell him to tell me what sort he has. And what he does in all times.

Mike and I caught a rabbit. And he aint heart [hurt] at all. But he is as tame as Ben [a pet rabbit]. But Ben aint very tame now. . . .

Tell George I aint forgot the time in the oat patch where de chiggers eat me up.

What has be come of old You know the old hound that we went a hunting wid.

Mike and I and Boyd Wells caught a possem he was as big as Sport.

I went on a panther hunt.

We show enough caught a panther.

Sport [illegible] him to quick. And Texas caught him in the tail joint and hung.

> Your Grand Son
> Tom Hogg
> Write to me quick.
> Your Grand Son
> Tom Hogg[126]

While Tom and Mike amused themselves with dogs and hunting, Ima was enjoying her freshman year at the University of Texas. The campus was only a short walk down the hill from her house. But she also liked to ride horseback, and she was an accomplished horse-woman. A university classmate remembered Ima on horseback in "a black close fitting riding-habit that only a woman of superb physique could carry off to perfection, the shining beaver [hat] with its fluttering veil . . . the gauntlets, the riding-crop, the long sweep of the robe over the feet, the erect and of necessity a bit unnatural carriage in the side saddle. . . . Ima Hogg, unapproachable as she appeared seen atop the gallant steed, was in reality a charming freshman unaffected in manner and a most conscientious student."[127]

As Ima later remembered her college days:

Those were two joyous years. The first year I studied more than I did the second and the professors were either helpful or forbidding . . . . Of course encouragement added zest for study even though the classes were too large in number.

The original main building housed about all the classes. Not until 1900 did the student enrollment reach the exciting One Thousand. It was a day for celebration.

Girls still wore long skirts and the boys coats or rarely sweaters, certainly not slacks. This was not according to any regulation nor was there any off campus control.

There was one dormitory for boys—the Brackenridge Hall, otherwise most of the boys lived in fraternity houses. The Valentine Club, of which I was a member, had applied to the Pi Phi sorority for a chapter. The few out of town girls lived in boarding houses.

Every Saturday night we went to a German*or hop, held usually over one of the fire-stations. The Driskill was reserved for the commencement balls. Sometimes there were hops on weeknights.— Nobody drank alcoholic beverages at a dance—nor did a boy smoke without asking the girl's permission.

The dance halls were crowded and there was competition for a boy to get his name on the dance card, consequently there were more extras signed up for each dance sometimes, breaking in as much as three times.

It was an unwritten law that no one drank at a dance. My escort one night didn't appear at once for his second dance so my extra on the card was entitled to break in. But I preferred to wait a little. When my date did appear I smelled liquor on his breath and I was not allowed to dance with him. I went home with another of his

---

* A "German" was a dance or cotillion with elaborate dance steps, popular in the 1850s and revived at the turn of the century, often organized by a university's German club.

fraternity brothers. The following Sunday afternoon his whole fraternity called with him to apologize.

The second year ended with some five or six balls—fraternity balls—and then the big final ball at the Driskill. There had to be a different dress for each ball. Dancing didn't begin until around ten o'clock p.m. and it lasted until the wee hours. Some dancers even went to a restaurant for breakfast. I usually arrived home near daylight ready for a nap. . . .

Sunday afternoons were usually reception time when the girls awaited the many callers which were sure to appear. Light refreshments were served. It was quite an art to make a good cheese rarebit on the chafing dish.—Actually I did not go out until almost the end of the first year. The boys would walk home with me and carry my books and come as far as the gate. After this went on for some months one of the boys said "I'm tired of not being asked in." So the next Sunday late in the evening he appeared and rang the bell. It was a shock to the family. But Aunt Fannie was on my side. Anyhow the young man took me to church.[128]

When suitors began to call at the Nineteenth Street house in the evenings, Ima's father established a routine: "Promptly at ten o'clock he went up to his bedroom when I was old enough to have young men callers. At ten o'clock a heavy dropping of shoes would be a signal for the caller's departure."[129]

When Ima began to go out with young men, her father was ready with advice. He wrote to her from New York in February 1900:

> When a lady goes with a gentleman she is safe in fact and also against suspicion and criticism. A gentleman is known by his general reputation in the community where he lives or by his acts or language when he is a girl's escort. If his <u>reputation</u> is bad the lady who permits him to accompany her must share it with him. If his reputation is good, yet his language or conduct is bad while an escort or at other times, the woman who finds this out must take notice and avoid his attentions in the future. While alone a couple must act and talk with more circumspection than while in the presence of others.—I do not feel that it is at all necessary to say this much to you, for I have all along known you to be sensible, prudent, and well-poised. It cannot be amiss however to present these general suggestions for your own reflection in the light of the well known axiom that a woman's character is her capital. When it is bad she is poor

indeed. Yours is a fine one. I know you will always prudently guard
it and from that source draw many of the genuine pleasures of life.

I am anxious to get home. The weather is now very cold for the
first time this Winter up here. The snow is thick. Sleigh-riding is the
go. I went yesterday with Mr. Moore of Waco.—William and family
are well and enjoy a fine time.

Your Father[130]

William Davis had contracted tuberculosis sometime during the
previous summer, but the family letters never mention the name of his
disease—the one that had killed his father, William Davis Sr. as well
as Sallie Hogg. But Dr. Davis managed to control his condition, and
in that winter had evidently recovered enough to enjoy an extended
vacation in New York.

William Jennings Bryan was also in New York, and Jim Hogg
wrote to Martha Frances that "he is the most marvelous man I ever
knew. The more I see of him, the closer I feel to him."[131] The former
governor would go on the campaign trail for Bryan's second try at the
presidency later that year.

In March, the business traveler Hogg wrote to Ima about his activities in New York.

March 11 1900
Dear Ima:

Really I have been to a few receptions, but have been too much
engaged to go out much at all. My detention here has been on business, not for pleasure; for I had rather be at home than any place on
earth. No joke. From business considerations alone I am induced to
come here and to remain oftener and longer than my desire from any
other consideration. My sojourn this time in the Metropolis has not
been the financial success that I at first expected it to be, nor has it
been as fruitful as other trips have been here. At times everything is
promising. Again nothing is promising. Of course this is the Financial and Commercial Center of the World. Big transactions occur
here every day. If I could only get in on the ground floor of one of
them. I could then be able to go back home and live much easier. As
you may have observed in times gone by, I am of a sanguine temperament and rarely ever get discouraged. I never suffer much from
disappointment.

Well, I am getting home sick, but I must get through with my business if possible before returning. Go see Mona [House] and give my kindest regards to Mr. House's family. With love to you, Mona, brothers and others.

Your Father,

J. S. Hogg[132]

The Hoggs' friendship with the House family had begun with Mona's mother, Lulie House. She and Sallie Hogg became close friends, and she corresponded with Sallie during those last sad weeks in Colorado. After Sallie's death she took a special interest in Ima. Lulie House's mother had died when she was young, and Ima recalled that

> Motherless girls had her especial attention. . . . She had a charming, gracious personality and was really the one in the family who made the first overture to acquaintance which was followed up by Mr. House. He was innately shy, I thought, but after one knew him he was warm and thoughtful. When I used to go up the hill really to visit Mona, Mr. House who was often at home would call me into the library for a talk—not a searching one, but an interesting one. He often told me about what he was doing and thinking. His big library filled with rich literature was placed at my disposal. And I made good use of it. When Mr. and Mrs. William Jennings Bryan came after his defeat to visit us, Mr. House offered the Bryan family his large stone house for the visit, next to their red stone mansion. This, I believe, was the beginning of Mr. House's interest in national affairs.[133]

Jim Hogg was in New York on business for three months, from January through March. Part of that time he was ill. In April he wrote to a friend in Greenville, Texas, "I am just recovering from a long spell of sickness which held me down sometime in New York before I left there." He was more specific in a letter to his friend Charles Glidden in Lowell, Massachusetts: "I am at last in good condition after recovering from a serious attack of fever at the Waldorf . . . . Of course Mrs. Glidden will at once suspect and perhaps charge that this fever was caused by too much excitement aroused by my long detention at and around 'Peacock Row'. . . ."[134]

Peacock Row was a term for the elegant lobby of the Waldorf-Astoria Hotel, where New York's wealthy socialites liked to be seen.

The Waldorf Hotel, built on the site of what is now the Empire State Building, and the Astor had combined in 1897. Hogg was staying at the largest and most luxurious hotel in the city.

Returning to Austin, the traveler prepared for another campaign, this one devoid of political ambition, but driven by a desire to see the reforms he had worked for as governor written into the Texas Constitution. He launched his tour with a speech in Waco on April 19, ten years to the day since he had opened his campaign for governor. He wanted to amend the state constitution to prevent "insolvent corporations" from conducting business in Texas, to end the "free pass" system on Texas railroads, and to prevent lobbying with corporate funds.[135]

Hogg set out to travel the state at his own expense, making speeches to convince voters to approve his reform amendments. He spoke at Denison on May 4, and announced his aim to campaign around the state until June. Visiting Austin between speaking engagements, he found time to order some of his favorite food: "about 100 pounds of good well cured country hams" from Tyler.[136] He hated the summer heat, but he did not let it stop him from a twenty-three-speech tour for his cherished amendments.

On June 1 he wrote to William Davis, who was still in New York: "If the Leg. does not submit it this time I shall dedicate my life to the cause as an agitator. Probably I'll become a sore head, but alone from patriotism, not from political disappointment. Am to leave again day after tomorrow. . . . Have a good time while not too old like your Uncle . . . ."[137]

Nearing fifty (he turned forty-nine that March) and always overweight, Hogg was feeling his age. Will worried about his father's health, and wrote to Ima that their father was "too fat."[138]

Jim Hogg wrote to Brownlee Ferguson, now a dentist with a "wife and babe," about his plan to stay with them when he spoke at Waxahachie. But in Cleburne he declined an invitation to visit a friend after a speech, excusing himself on the grounds that "the hot weather 'melts my linen' so that I am compelled to hang it out to dry from a hotel back window in my rush to fill my list of appointments, and thus I am compelled to keep away from private homes."[139]

In July the former governor of Texas was off for more politicking, this time to the Democratic Party's national convention in Kansas City. He wrote about it to Ima, who was vacationing with the Lewis Thompsons of Austin and their daughter, Mary, on a ranch in Schleicher County near the town of Eldorado, Texas.

July 9, 1900
Dear Ima:—

My cases at Tyler were continued week before last until next December. So I got home in time to attend the Kansas City Convention, and I have just returned from there. I was very sorry that you were not here to attend it with me. I believe it was the finest convention in all respects that was ever held. The scenes at Chicago Convention in 1896 were marvelous to behold at times, but at all times the Kansas City Convention was one of enthusiasm and excitement from beginning to end. I met many of your friends there who inquired about you, and it took considerable of my time to explain why I did not have you with me. Now that I am at home for the summer, can't you arrange to return and stay with me? It seems that you must have had enough of ranch life by this time. Bring "fat Mary" back with you and I will agree to take you fishing up the River once in a while as a matter of diversion. Your Auntie and the boys are in good health, and I find everything at home in a pleasant, nice condition. Figs are getting ripe and we have plenty of soft peaches for home use. I have bought the Radam place and I want you here to help me fix it up. Tell Mrs. Thompson that her husband was at the Convention and was about the best behaved man there.

With much love and kindest regards to all,

Affectionately your father,

J. S. Hogg[140]

The Radam place was property adjacent to the Nineteenth Street house. A few days later Ima's father wrote to her again. She was still on the ranch and had asked him about buying a pair of horses.

July 13, 1900
Dear Ima:—

We all very much miss you and I think it is about time you were returning home. Had you been here on your last birthday [July 10], we would have given you a great "blow-out." We are all well and Mike and Tom and the two dogs continue to have a fine time this hot weather. Our figs are getting ripe and we are having plenty of fruit. You spoke to me about a pair of horses that have attracted your attention. I should like for you to get Mr. Thompson to pass judgment upon them, and find out what is the least price that will purchase them delivered at Austin. Are they stylish and good matches? About what will they weigh each? How do they hold their heads?

What are their gaits? Do they work single or double? How many times have they run away? What are their ages? How many and what kinds of brands are on them? Have they been scarred, crippled, wind-galled, spavined or stove-up? Have they had the "swiny," fistula or big-shoulder? Are they poor or fat? Have they long or short tails and manes? Have they a pedigree and if so what is it? From your intimation I infer that you would like to have them, and doubtless you will take an interest in them sufficient to find out the answers to these questions and let me know them. I rather inclined to tell you to buy the horses if you want them on your own judgment and that I will pay for them but upon reconsideration I concluded that it would be best for you to first furnish me with the desired information about them, so that I can pass upon the question of purchase myself.

With kindest regards to Mrs. Thompson and the other members of the party as well as to "Fat" Mary I am—
Very truly and affectionately your father,
J. S. Hogg[141]

Four days later he wrote again, begging her to come home:

July 17, 1900
Dear Ima,
For many reasons which I trust are not inconsistent with your happiness I [desire] that you return home. I was offered an improved 860-acre prairie farm for our home place and I should like to have your judgment on the trade. Also I am fixing to improve the Radam garden and desire the benefit of your advice on it. Then again we are all lonesome without you. Mike is sorely afflicted with Poison Oak, and with nail cuts on his feet as well. On receipt of this bundle up and come on. You need not bother Mr. or Mrs. Thompson about it. You can come alone. Do not permit them to become disturbed in the least about your return as they may wish to remain there much longer. . . .
Affectionately, Your father
J. S. Hogg[142]

Ima had spent six weeks at the ranch, and she came home at her father's bidding. She was needed to take over as housekeeper because Aunt Fannie was returning to Pueblo to help her son William and his family. William had been well in New York City that winter, but his tuberculosis had evidently become active again.

In August, former governor Hogg enjoyed something of a triumph: his arduous campaigning around the state on behalf of his constitutional amendments won the reluctant approval of the state Democratic convention in Waco, August 8–10. It was a struggle in a convention filled with acrimony. Hogg's political enemies accused him of relicensing trusts during his governorship, and afterward, when he was out of office, of representing the railroad magnate Collis P. Huntington in cases involving the Southern Pacific Railroad. (Hogg's biographer, Robert C. Cotner, stated that he found no information to support either of these claims, but, according to the *Galveston Daily News* report of the convention, Texas Attorney General Thomas H. Smith condemned Hogg's actions in a speech at the convention, and "the Southern Pacific compromise cases, in which Mr. Hogg appeared as an attorney for Mr. Huntington, were ventilated and the record read.")[143]

When Hogg rose to speak to the convention about his constitutional amendments, hostile members of the audience tried to shout him down. His son Mike attended the convention with him and reported to Ima that "the house was packed at Waco and everyone was armed to the teeth. . . . Men were amazed at his courage."[144] A bystander remembered Hogg's giving as good as he got, calling out, "You white-livered sons of bitches . . . " and roundly cursing the hecklers with "every word in the English language."[145] Hogg refused to be silenced, and after an uproar that lasted nearly half an hour and included a fistfight between two delegates, he began his speech, which lasted over an hour. Other speeches and a vote for the amendments followed, and after a long and exhausting evening, Hogg's amendments were approved at 1:35 a.m. Mike told Ima that "he never saw any man more crushed than Father was after the convention."[146] Ima wrote later that "the strain was very great. It took him sometime to recover. Perhaps he never did physically."[147] He had won a hard-fought victory, but the amendments still had to be submitted to Texas voters.[148]

Afterwards the former governor wrote to Martha Frances, as he always did when he had accomplished something in the political arena: "This is the first movement since I retired from public office in July 1895 that I have felt justifiable in taking part." Now his constitutional amendments would go before the voters. At the convention, "the victory came like a tidal wave . . . . My mail is heavy-loaded with congratulations. My critics have hushed. . . ."[149]

Martha Frances, who had followed the convention in newspapers, was ecstatic:

Aug. 23, 1900
Dear James:

Congratulations! Whenever were congratulations more in order? Victory indeed! Dewey at Manila, Sley [Schley] at Santiago had not a more clean cut victory, nor needed they any more nerve to conquer it. To see you stand there before that mob of henchmen who came organized to down you (and I saw it as I read) was a colossal picture fit for the warrior Gods to see and when they cowered like whipped curs caught red-"mouthed" in their villainy, it was a sight to tickle the fancy of Satan's crew, whose dusky wings hovered around taking notes and spotting their very peculiar friends. I couldn't sleep last night for gladness. And I had to beg William to shut off reading those papers after nearly twelve o'clock. O yes and now they publish, grandiloquently, your Similar Victory over Tammany. Nasty, stinking politics! I do wish, now that you've set things straight, and lashed them into submission you'd not stir up any more strife. You've got glory enough and can rest on your Laurels. You have enough to bind the brow if a "Knight of the Round Table," and should not tempt a dimming of their brightness.

Say, was Mike on hand? It is too bad if he was not. If he was there wouldn't I have enjoyed watching his eyes. I'll wager he wanted a few rocks in his pocket. Well, thank the Lord for his blessings, heartily.

[Portion omitted from typescript.]

Tell Ima not to forget to have the ducks picked. The feathers had best be hung up in the away-up-closet. Does Tom take good care of the ostriches? Are they good boys? both?

There is so much company every evening that I am about busted. . . . I hope the calm after the cyclone will not flatten you out. You've been strung up so long. Keep busy, but let Politics go to thunder. The worry of it is not worth the outlay. Of course I know how it will be, but I do wish you would "rest on your Laurels." . . .

Frank[150]

Hogg answered his sister's query in a hastily written, undated letter. Brackets and dashes indicate material omitted from the typescript.

"Mike," the proud father said, "was by my side from start to finish. He was hardly ever 'out of sight.' I slept but little, and he was often buzzing around till after mid-night. His [illegible] in the hotel lobby was a stray dog. With this he played and listened around the throngs of men. By this he learned more than anyone would suppose. When the climax was reached at about 1 o'clock on that never to be

forgotten morning, this dear boy was by my side <u>drinking</u> in the—
scene and all that occurred. He can tell you all that happened. He's no
sucker but is a [ ] and a politician. We are all well. Willie is spending
a few days with us and is well and happy. Hot weather, no rain. Dust.
[ ] No news. About the last of this month I expect to go to National
headquarters to help out."[151]

Martha Frances also wrote to Will after the tumultuous Waco convention. The letter is undated:

> [Portion omitted from typescript.]
>
> I would glory more in your father's <u>defeat</u> in <u>such</u> a cause than a
> victory for spoliation and the giving over his native State and people
> to chains and ultimate slavery. <u>Say</u> what they will, they know of a
> truth that he is the Soul of honor. Never be a politician Willie, for
> ingratitude is emblazoned in brass upon its banner, and its battle-
> ments builded of lava.
>
> But I'm writing you a silly letter. "From the fullness" &c &c I'm
> not so old but I'd like to be a man in these times. I'd love to enter the
> arena and fight.[152]

It had been a hot summer in Austin as usual, and as usual the
heat was hard on the portly Hogg. The strain of his fight for his constitutional amendments both before and during the state convention
had taken a toll. He wrote to his brother John that he was "partially
recovered from the effects of the long strain" of the struggle for the
amendments but was "yet very tired. . . . My intention is to spend
a week or so at Mineral Wells before I go North to engage in the
National Campaign as requested by Chairman Jones. Get ready to
stay there with me."[153]

When Baylor and Josie asked Jim Hogg to come to Houston that
August to be godfather to their new baby, he asked if they could put
off the christening until "Fall or Winter, say in December? Then I
could make the trip down there specially for that purpose without
too much punishment from the heat. . . . Tell Josie that as soon as the
red gets from the baby's face so that I can kiss it without blushing, she
must either bring it up or I must go down to see it."[154]

John Hogg, true to form, did not come to Mineral Wells. His
brother, undaunted, then invited him to come down to Austin and
visit. Jim Hogg, evidently recovered, was leaving soon for Chicago
for the Democratic Party nominating convention, but he begged his
brother: "<u>Come down right away.</u> If necessary draw on me for the

money to come on. Don't fail."[155] There is no evidence that John came.

On September 8, 1900, a fearsome hurricane hit Galveston. The worst natural disaster in American history, it killed an estimated six to eight thousand people. The numbers were so great that the exact totals were never known. Hogg wrote a letter to comfort his old friend and former secretary, Colonel R. B. Levy, whose son, William F. Levy, was among those missing and presumed dead.[156]

Hogg also found time to assist his nephews that fall. Baylor Hogg, just beginning his medical practice in Houston, had taken out a loan, and his uncle wrote to his creditor about the eighty dollar note: "It is perfectly good, interest and all for I'll pay it myself if necessary. He is struggling and reliable but like most young men is poor." To James McDugald, the fledgling lawyer, to whom he had lent money, Hogg wrote, "As to the amount due on the note, you can take such time as may be suitable to your own convenience."[157]

Hogg left for Chicago on September 22, 1900. He would be away campaigning until after the November 6 election. Despite Hogg's eloquence on behalf of William Jennings Bryan, the Republican incumbent William McKinley was elected to a second term. But Jim Hogg obviously enjoyed himself on the campaign trail, as he wrote to Ima from Olney, Illinois:

Nov. 2, 1900
Dear Ima:

I spoke last night in Mr. Bryan's native county to his old neighbors, school-mates and kin people at Sandoval, and today at Lawrenceville, near the line of Indiana. To-morrow I am to speak here at 9 A.M. and wind up with several speeches in Chicago to-morrow night, several hundred miles from here. This will close my part of the campaign. Everywhere I have had great crowds of enthusiastic auditors. As the election approaches I grow more hopeful of success of our Candidates and cause. The contest is exciting and the result cannot be approximated with reasonable certainty by either side . . . .

If we lose, I'll sneak home. If we win I'll run away—the Lord knows where. I don't.

I am in good health full of hope and in fine spirits, but I am tired of politics.

                                   Love to all.
                                   Affectionately
                                   Your Father
                                   Jym[158]

He was in an extraordinarily good mood: This is one of few letters not signed "J. S. Hogg."

After Bryan's second defeat in the 1900 election, Jim Hogg invited him to Texas for a visit. On November 26, three days before Thanksgiving, he wrote to Bryan: "The Lord permitting we'll take a fine hunt during the holidays."[159] They did.

The holidays came and went. When the Texas legislature met in January 1901, it failed to approve the controversial "Hogg amendments" for submission to Texas voters.

As the new century dawned, J. S. Hogg, politician, was about to become J. S. Hogg, businessman.

PART IV
HIGH HOPES
1901–1906

O N JANUARY 10, 1901, the Spindletop gusher blew an oil boom into Texas and ended an era of happy domesticity in the Hoggs' Nineteenth Street home. By September the house's occupants had all left it for good, and they would never again all live under the same roof. Jim Hogg, building his oil syndicate, shuttled like a great black-coated beetle between Beaumont, Austin, and New York. Ima went off to study music in New York, and Mike and Tom were again sent to boarding school in Texas. Will practiced law in San Antonio until 1903, when he rejoined his father's Austin firm. He would not stay there long.

Hogg's oil syndicate merged profitably with J. S. Cullinan's Texas Fuel Company, and for a time the former governor reveled in his new-found affluence. There were happy times at "the Varner," a Brazoria County plantation he had bought because he believed there was oil under the land. (He was right, but his family would have to wait until 1919 to make its fortune in oil.)

When oil prices dropped precipitously in 1903, Hogg's business interests suffered, and so did his family's finances. There was no festive family Christmas in Texas that year, and Mike and Tom had to spend the holidays at their respective boarding schools. In the fall of 1904, Will left Austin to take a position with a St. Louis bank.

The rest of the family had scattered by 1905: Tom took a job as a ranch hand in Colorado, and Mike prepared to enter the University of Texas. Jim Hogg moved his law office to Houston. Ima divided her time between the social scenes in Austin and Houston.

Early in 1905 an accident changed the Hoggs' family life forever. Jim Hogg was injured in a train collision, and he never fully regained his health. But he was characteristically optimistic, as he wrote to his nephew William Davis: "If I finally recover, as I now believe I will, from the illness which yet afflicts me, I have no fear of the future."[1] But that future was cut short. James Stephen Hogg died of congestive heart failure in Houston on March 3, 1906, three weeks short of his fifty-fifth birthday. He was buried beside Sallie in Austin's Old Oakwood Cemetery.

• • •

At the beginning of 1901, Martha Frances Hogg Davis, "Aunt Fannie," sixty-seven, was again living with the Hoggs in Austin. Her granddaughter Pearl was also visiting them. Martha Frances insisted on keeping house for the family, but she was not in good health, as Jim Hogg wrote to her son William:

January 25th, 1901

Dear William:

I note what you say by favor of the 14th instant, which I have not answered until now on account of a variety of causes which do not involve a lack of respect or appreciation of you or the suggestions you make. Sister has been in feeble health for several months and especially so since she got the impression that you were sick. She has been up most of the time with the exception of a few days from about the 12th to about the 16th of this month. She is growing stronger apparently and says that she will start within a few days to make you a visit. En route she will stop over at Brother John's to spend awhile. I believe that after you see her and administer some of your "magnetic medicines" she will rapidly improve and fatten up again.

The blunder I made in the first instance was in going to house-keeping but I was absolutely miserable away from the children and felt compelled to take this step. Had I left her in some boarding school with them, she would have had less anxiety and been relieved of a heavy encumbrance, which you know she always would assume in house-keeping. I have kept her two servants all of the time and have endeavored to make the burden as light as possible to her. The more servants, the more work she would do. Indeed it looked to me like she felt called upon to help the servants, if not wait on them. You know she has always been a diligent, faithful hard-worker and I have been unable to check her at all in her efforts to do everything on the place. I have often felt distressed at her exertion in going up and down two flights of stairs at home from five to twenty times a day. It was enough to work out any woman. How she stood it has been a wonder to me. There has never been any necessity for her working at all and I have objected to it all along but without success. The attachment of my three children to her is strong, faithful and enduring. They love her with a tenderness that is sublime to me, and she in turn is very fond of them.

Now I want to say this to you: We must indulge her in every way possible. I think, when she gets to your home, it will be well for her to make changes—up to Colorado Springs, to Manitou, to Denver and to other points of interest up there. I shall gladly share equally or all of the expenses wherever she may go. My future plans are to hire a house-keeper until spring or summer. If Sister gets strong enough and wants to return, well and good. In fact this will be exceedingly gratifying to us all. Otherwise I intend to break up house-keeping, sell the place and send my children off to school. There is no other satisfactory alternative left for me. Probably it will be suitable to Sister's convenience to go North in the fall and board with Ima. If so, I can make the arrangement so that she will be entirely relieved from labor and surrounded by enlivening scenes where she can at least pass the time pleasantly.

I am glad that you are taking such good care of yourself. By all means do this. I know your grit, your enduring vitality and staying qualities as well as your intelligence. Take care of yourself and I believe, as you say, that you will live to see scores of the doctors of all kinds who have now prescribed for you, laid in the shade on the other side.

Pearl is getting along happily and is without doubt a magnificent girl. She has made many friends here in all good circles and Ima's attachment to her, as you know, is very strong. We are glad to have her with us. She has spoken several times of returning with Sister, but probably will now remain a little longer as Sister is able to travel by herself.

With love to Fannie and the boy as well as yourself, I am,

Affectionately Your Uncle,

J. S. Hogg[2]

If Martha Frances were no longer able to keep house for them, her brother proposed what must have been for him a drastic measure: to "break up house-keeping" and sell the Austin house. That was partly because Ima wanted to go to New York to study music. She recalled this momentous move in her memoir:

> It was a difficult decision for the whole family as to whether after two years at the University, I should be sent away to continue my piano study. Father was very devoted to music and was very desirous of my developing my talent for the piano. So it must have been a great sacrifice for him when I went [to New York] and the two younger boys entered Carlisle Military Academy.[3]

They did not go until the fall of 1901.

Meanwhile, Ima concentrated on her studies at the University of Texas. Though she and her family did not realize it at the time, that January an event had taken place in Texas that would change their lives in ways they could not have imagined: On January 10, 1901, an oil well came in at a place called Spindletop just outside Beaumont.

The oil well was a gusher, spewing forth more than 75,000 barrels of oil a day. The oil boom was on. Soon producing 100,000 barrels of oil per day, the gusher tripled the nation's oil production and set off a frenzy of oil drilling. Beaumont, a town of about 9,000 in January, turned into a boomtown of 30,000 by March. This development did not go unnoticed by Jim Hogg.

Early in 1901, Hogg did two things: With James W. Swayne, a Fort Worth lawyer friend who had served in the Texas legislature when Hogg was governor and as county judge in Tarrant County until 1900, he formed the Hogg-Swayne Syndicate to invest in land at Spindletop. To enlarge their capital, they invited three other men— Judge Robert Brooks, A. S. Fisher, and William T. Campbell—to join the syndicate. They bought fifteen acres of land at Spindletop, and since prospective buyers were eager to pay thousands of dollars for a fraction of an acre just large enough to drill a well on, the syndicate was soon free of debt and reaping handsome profits.[4]

The second thing that Jim Hogg did that year was to buy an old plantation in Brazoria County. The "Patton Place," as it was known, had a colorful history long before Hogg bought it. Located about fifty miles south of Houston, with lush green fields and magnificent oak trees, it was one of Stephen F. Austin's original land grants to three hundred Texas settlers in 1824. The first owner was Martin Varner, who sold it in 1834 to Columbus Patton, who brought his family and his slaves from Kentucky. The plantation (now Varner-Hogg Plantation Historic Site) declined after the Civil War, and eventually was acquired by the New York and Texas Land Company, from whom Hogg purchased it in 1901. He got a good price: 4,100 acres for $30,000, or about $7 per acre. In today's dollars that would come to more than $783,000.[5]

Spring 1901 was a very busy time for Jim Hogg, who was often in Beaumont tending to his oil interests. When school was out he took Tom and Mike to Beaumont with him. Tom wrote to Ima from the New Crosby Hotel in Beaumont, where his father had established a headquarters. Jim Hogg, who always suffered from the heat in the summertime, was sweltering in Beaumont's humid, subtropical weather (annual rainfall: forty-eight inches) amid swarms of mosquitoes.

June 13, 1901
Dear Sister:
      We are all well. But the mosquitoes sure do raise the skin on you. I went to port Arthur Thursday evening and got back today at

7:30 p.m. it is one of the finest places you ever saw. Papa is out on the verranda sweating to beat 40. I have been going out to the oil fields every day since I got here it makes a person puff if he walks to [two] blocks on a stretch. . . . The town people have an iron factory where they make locomotives. One thing they do is sprinkle the streets with oil four times a day. I saw them this morning about 10 o'clock. Lucas [the Spindletop oil well, named for driller Anthony Lucas] turns loose a gusher every Sunday at 3 oclock a.m. How is Mrs. Smith and your self and mike and Bula and charly and Tex and Dainty and Joe and sport and koney. Tell mike to tell Howard Wells to write to me soon tell him I want to hear from him and all of the home folks oh! yes I forgot newty. Tell Mrs. Smith to write to me. I will write to her tomorrow, Love to all.

> Yours Truly
> Tom Hogg.[6]

Captain Anthony Lucas was the expert who drilled the first gusher at Spindletop in January 1901. It was indeed a gusher, capable of producing 100,000 barrels of oil a day. By 1902, there were 600 oil companies (including the Hogg-Swayne Syndicate) and 285 oil wells.

Tom sent greetings to Mrs. Smith, the Hoggs' housekeeper in Austin, and to various pets, including the aging Shetland pony, Dainty, and Joe, the horse from Tennessee. Howard Wells was a Nineteenth Street neighbor and friend of Tom's. Mike Hogg, who would turn sixteen in October, had his first real job in the Spindletop oil fields, working for a contractor for twenty-three days at two dollars per day.[7]

As her younger brothers were preparing for boarding school that September, Ima was beginning her adventures in New York City. She was no stranger to the city, having visited there with her father in 1894. Since then it had more than doubled in population, with more than 3,500,000 people. On her 1894 visit she had seen the sights—the Brooklyn Bridge (1883), the Statue of Liberty (1886), and the tallest building, Joseph Pulitzer's New York World Building, at twenty stories, completed in 1890. By 1901 a taller landmark, the Flatiron Building, at the intersection of Broadway, Fifth Avenue, and Twenty-Third Street, was under construction. It would be finished in 1902. This triangular architectural oddity, shaped like a flatiron, was twenty-one stories tall.

Ima boarded at Mrs. Greene's School for Young Ladies, just off Riverside Drive at 311 West Eighty-Second Street, but she attended the National Conservatory of Music on East Seventeenth Street, just off Union Square. That was about sixty blocks from Mrs. Greene's, so Ima would most likely have taken a trolley car across Manhattan. With numerous stops, the trip would have taken half an hour or more. New York had no subways until 1904.

The young girl from Texas found Manhattan a place full of exciting things to see and do. Plays and musical comedies and operettas flourished on Broadway (though electric lights on marquees did not make it the "Great White Way" until 1906). Operas and concerts (the Metropolitan Opera had been there since 1883) beckoned. From all accounts, including her own, Ima Hogg, then nineteen, enjoyed herself immensely. As for her studies at the National Conservatory of Music, she recalled:

> My teachers in Austin had greatly exaggerated my talent and status as a performer. I was advised to play for the great master pianist and teacher, Rafael Joseffy [who taught at the conservatory]. . . . When he heard me play he patted me on the back and suggested another preparatory teacher.[8]

Word of Ima's disastrous audition soon spread in Austin, and a friend wrote to say that she had heard of Ima's playing for "Joseffy" and of her "complete failure, improvising, etc., etc., and of his refusing to accept you as a pupil."[9] But all was not lost, as Ima remembered:

> Soon after that I heard Adele Margulies [another pianist who taught at the conservatory] play with her trio and I knew at once she had what I wanted. She was an amazing pedagogue who knew how to impart what she knew to others. . . . Under her I felt transformed and for two or more years with intervals in between for a long time I progressed rapidly.[10]

Meanwhile, Tom was feeling neglected and homesick at his new boarding school in Salado. He wrote to his sister:

> Salado, Texas
> Oct. 3, 1901
> Dear Sis
> Won't you let me have $1.75 to go to show on tenth of Oct, all the boys are going to the show. The School is going to have a holiday. I

am well but home sick. I got a letter from Howard Wells he said the place [the Nineteenth Street house] is alright.

Yours truly
Thomas Hogg.
P.S. Send $1.75[11]

Later in October, Tom's father arranged for him to leave Salado and join Mike at the Carlisle School in Hillsboro. It was a private school run by James M. Carlisle, whom Governor Hogg had appointed as State Superintendent of Public Instruction in 1891. Mike described his new school in a letter to Ima.

Oct. 24, 1901

Dear Sister:—

It is about half past nine o'clock. And I have just came from study hall. We eat breakfast at seven o'clock and at half past eight get ready for school which lasts until half past four. From then on until half past five we drill. Then we get ready for supper which is at six o'clock. At seven we go to the study hall and study until half past nine. Then we go to bed.

I think we have a very fine school of boys. They are not what I expected to find. They are boys from different towns and cities. None of us get to go to town but once a week. And that must be on business.

Brother stopped over the other day and talked to Tom and I about an hour. When he left he gave Tom and I a dollar a piece.

The reason I have not written is because I had not a cent of money. I spent my five dollars on books and nesseceries about the first week and I have been doing with out ever since. I did not want to borrow stamps from Prof. C. because I might for get to pay him back.

My studies are Latin, algebra, grammar, arith., spelling, Civil Gov. and Rhetoric.

Yours truly
Mike Hogg[12]

Although his younger sons were short of spending money at school, Jim Hogg apparently had plenty to buy a place in the country and furnish it with uncharacteristic luxuries that fall. As Ima remembered: "It was at this time that he bought a little farm outside Austin which he called Estrada. It had a nice little house on it which he furnished very nicely. He loved pretty things and I remember with surprise and amazement when he purchased a number of pier mirrors for this cottage and had sent from New York, barrels of china."[13]

However he consoled himself at Estrada, Jim Hogg still missed his children. He wrote to Ima:

> The wild goose, Polly, heard my voice and she came with loud exclamations of goose-joy and unquestioned hilarity to bid me welcome. Her cries attracted the profound attention of other fowls and animals and in silence, and, now and then, with an occasional audible expression, they expressed sentiments of the most cordial welcome to me. As Old Joe, Patsy O, and Dainty [the horses] stood nearby with their heads close together and their eyes set on me, they seemed to ask: "What have you done with Miss Ima?" As Tex, Daisey and Mary [the dogs] pranced around the buggy they stopped suddenly and all looked anxiously at me and seemed to ask: "What have you done with Mike and Tom?" My own silent, conscious, heart's answer was: "I've sent them off from Home!—-to school—to school—to school—Off from Home![14]

When Hogg was in New York again on business, he and Ima enjoyed each other's company. Hogg had met an Englishman named Alfred Suart, who invited Ima to dinner at the Waldorf. "Bring a friend," he told her, and he would send "an automobile" for them.[15] Perhaps it was a 1901 Olds, the first mass-produced automobile in the United States. Whatever it was, it was a novelty. There were only about eight thousand automobiles in the entire nation at the turn of the century.

Ima's father was contemplating a momentous business move, as reported in *The New York Times*: It was said that he aimed to form a company with a capital of $25,000,000 to compete with John D. Rockefeller's Standard Oil in the fuel oil business.[16] Hogg envisioned an oil pipeline from Beaumont to Port Arthur, where Texas oil could then be transported far and wide by rail and ship. For that he needed to interest major investors. He left Austin in May and remained in New York through the fall. Staying at the Waldorf-Astoria, he was cultivating New York contacts and planning a trip to London to seek investors—perhaps on the advice of his new friend Alfred Suart.[17]

Jim Hogg was too caught up in business to visit his family for the Christmas holidays, but he and Ima amused themselves in New York.

As for the Hogg boys, the ever-supportive Aunt Fannie offered to take them for Christmas. Her grateful brother was quick to accept:

December 2, 1901

Dear Sister:

Of course I shall be glad for you to have Mike and Tom for the Christmas holidays. They can get to either Denton or Decatur, within a few hours after leaving Hillsboro any morning by Ft. Worth.

From all accounts I am assured that they are doing very well at School. I first sent Tom to Salado [but] he got so homesick and seemed so lost without Mike I sent him to the Carlisle School so that Mike could look after him. "Old Mike" as they call him is a bundle of dignity and propriety— since he got his uniform on. Probably I shall never encourage their separation again. Nature seems to have fitted them for associates for and during their natural lives.

Ima seems to be doing well with her music. From all indications she has literally captured Mrs. Greene's School.

Willie, after some months' deliberation has about consented to go in as junior member of my firm at Austin. I hope and believe it is now best for him and for me. . . .

[Part of this letter was excised in Ima Hogg's edition of "Family Letters."]

I hope to be able to spend awhile next year in Mexico with William. I hope he will make Monterrey his headquarters.

With love to all,

Your Bro.,

Jym[18]

William Davis's tuberculosis was evidently in remission, and he was about to become a United States consular official in Mexico, where he would remain until 1914.[19] Aunt Fannie took Mike and Tom with her to Decatur for Christmas with their uncle John and his family. Ima and her father stayed in New York. Will may have spent the holiday in San Antonio.

In January Tom wrote to Will, who was now back in Austin at the firm of Hogg & Robertson:

Hillsboro, Texas

Jan. 20, 1902

Mr. W. C. Hogg

Dear brother! how are you? Everything is frozen up now it has

sleeted all day. Give my best regards to the Judge Robertson. I will
close I have to write about five letters tonight.
Your little brother
Tom Hogg[20]

On the same day, Mike wrote to Ima:
Jan. 20, 1902
Dear Sister:—
    I clear forgot to thank you for my Christmas present. I am now
writing with that fountain pen you sent me but not on that paper I
wrote a letter to Aunt Fannie on it and the lines were very crooked
and so I decided not to write to you on it
    We had a very fine time up at Uncle Johns, If I haven't already
told you so in my last letter.
    Papa came through here the other day but did not get off the
train. He said you were very well but pretty fat.
    The papers say that he has struck oil at Columbia.
                                    Your brother
                                    Will C. Nit
                                    M.H[21]

The papers were wrong about the location of the oil strike. In
December, an oil well on the Hogg-Swayne lands at Spindletop—not
Columbia—had begun producing. Jim Hogg now had another selling
point with investors.[22] He returned to Austin from New York in early
January and wrote to Ima:

Jan. 12, 1902
Dear Ima:
    After a three days and nights' uneventful, monotonous, tiresome,
trip, I arrived here last Friday afternoon, and am now quite well
refreshed and rested. At Hillsboro, Friday morning, Mike and Tom,
in their full uniform, came aboard the train and demonstrated—by
hugging and kissing me—to the edification of the curious passengers. They looked well and appeared to be happy. Mike "told me
on" Tom. Poor Tom! Somebody is always "telling on" him. A rule
of the school is that any boy, who prefers to, can, as a choice, chop
wood during Military Drill. Mike says Tom always takes the severe
alternative of chopping wood instead of training to be a soldier! It
seems to cut Mike's dignity, for he looks upon the "Drill" as the

most attractive feature of any school. From this freak in Tom I cherish the hope that one of my boys at least will be a civilian.

Willie is by my side most of the time and is now after me to [let him] room with me. He says he can take care of my clothes and look after me generally if we stay together. You know he was always disposed to pet and spoil me anyway. As I fatten up and get old, this disposition grows in him. So I guess I shall yield to the importunities. We will probably take board at the Driskill, although I am inclined to have the upstairs of my Brush building on the [Congress] Avenue, fitted up for this purpose. What do you think best for us to do? Write candidly on this as you have always done on other matters. You know I respect your opinion more than I do my own—when you give it seriously.

Will and I are to take noon-dinner at Mr. House's to-day. . . . The exceedingly, unprecedented, dry weather for the past six months here has depressed the farmers and cast a gloom over business men generally. Excepting the damage done by the drought, everything at the Estrada looks well. Miles and Lizzie have taken good care of things there. We shall put Joe in the livery stable for use by Will and myself. Then we'll whiz. So far I've seen none of your associates of either sex. The boys will begin to "make inquiries" soon.—Give my undivided love to each of the girls—and keep it all yourself! To Mrs. Greene, husband and daughter present my sincere regards.

Lovingly, Your Father,

J. S. Hogg[23]

Moving on from Austin to Beaumont, he sent a note to Ima in New York:

Citizens National Bank
Beaumont, Texas

Beaumont, Jan'y 21, 1902
Dear Ima:

In all probability I will leave here for England, via the Waldorf-Astoria, within the next day or so. Hope to see you enroute. Have seen many of our friends since I got back, and they all enquire about you. Vivie and Minnie called on me. Nice girls.—Will is well and happy. The boys—Mike and Tom—look forward to our summer outing. Be good. Good bye.

Your Father[24]

While their father traveled, Tom and Mike wrote to their sister from school.

Jan. 23rd, 1902
Dear Sis:
how are you now? you must excuse me for not writing to you sooner than this I have been putting it off for a long time. When are you going home Sis Mr. Carlisle has put some mighty hard rules to the boys down here and the thing I hate about them is that they all have such hard penalties and the penalties have to be acted upon. I tell you Texas pened us down mighty tight. I saw papa about two weeks ago Sis all of my short pants are to tight except one pair. I wear long trousers most all of the time now I thank you for the nice things you sent me Xmas. With love
                    Your little bud
                    Tom Hogg

Sis excuse this rooster scratching I am in a hurry.[25]

Feb. 9, 1902

Dear Sister:—
    I received your letter a day after I had sent mine off I am glad you like those pictures. In the group I look like I was way mad don't I? The pants of my uniform had not been fixed so they would not lag when I had my picture taken.
    I got my first suit of long pants yesterday. There were no short ones in town that would fit me. I look about two feet taller than I did. Tom also got him a suit. But you know he has been wearing long pants ever since we left home. I am half a head taller than Tom.
    We are expecting snow all the time. It snowed and sleeted here for about a week and a half.
    Tom writes to the girls at home nearly every sunday. He got a letter from Eunice today and a couple of other girls. He has a whole trunk full of letters from girls at home.
    What were you doing at West Point?
    Since you have got my picture send me yours.
    How are you getting along in music?
    I guess Papa is in England by now.
                    Your Brother
                    Mike Hogg[26]

What Ima was doing at West Point is best described in her memoir:

> Mrs. Greene, the owner [of Ima's New York boarding school]
> was from Virginia. She was one of those impoverished remnants
> of the Old South Aristocracy. She was hardly fitted to discipline a
> school of girls. Any girl who was a belle or received such attention
> from young men ranked high in her esteem. She encouraged us to
> accept invitations from cadets at West Point. When we went to balls
> . . . our programs were already made out for us by the cadet escort.
> [Among the young men's names Ima remembered on her dance cards
> were Douglas MacArthur and George C. Marshall.] We were invited
> up on Saturday nights. There was one hotel. Bitter cold did not deter
> us from making the train trip. We were always met and escorted to
> the hotel. As many as four or five girls from Mrs. Greene's School
> went periodically to West Point. All the cadets looked handsome in
> their unusual grey blue uniforms with big brass buttons.
>
> When some cadets said they were coming down to New York to
> celebrate Christmas with us, of course we visualized them escorting
> us to the theatre in their uniforms. They appeared in fatigue suits—
> to the girls' dismay. Their glamour was gone.[27]

Ima's social and cultural whirl in New York seemed to leave little
time for her studies, but she managed:

> I really was a hard student of music, in spite of some dissipation.
> A strong constitution made it possible for me to work and attend
> concert after concert, opera after opera, with theater thrown in,
> almost every night. . . .
>
> While I enjoyed social life, it was mostly going to some theater,
> concert, or opera with my escorts—but always with chaperones.[28]

Jim Hogg sailed for England at last, aboard the Cunard liner *Saxo-
nia* on February 8. With him were W. T. Campbell, one of his oil business partners, and Hogg's secretary, Don "Don Alfonso" Aldridge.
Ima's father wrote to her from aboard the ship.

Feby. 11 1902
Dear Ima:
     At this writing 6:30 Tuesday evening, the third day of our voyage,
I am speeding along towards London at the rate of 370 miles a day
in good health and excellent spirits. So far the weather has been as
a Mayday in Texas. No one has up to this hour become sea-sick.

All seem happy and vigorous in health and appetite. Of the seventy cabin passengers there are but a dozen ladies and six children. Reading is my past-time. As I am going to England my necessities lead me to read of her institutions and great men. Following this course I have just finished the life of Oliver Cromwell, by Frederick Harrison, and am now reading William Pitt. Of all the phenomenal freaks in Cromwell, there is one over-shadowing, one that challenges and commands my devout respect for him. In fact this trait or conviction in him is the great veil behind which his courage in war is hidden from my view, it is the well known, unquestioned, conviction in him that God guided his course for the sake of humanity. He believed in God. He saw God through Jesus Christ. His faith in Christ led him to know God to believe in God to pray to God, and to look to God for direction in all his efforts in behalf of human liberty. Probably he was a fanatic. Let this be so. At all events he never went into battle except upon the conviction that he had God's consent, and was directed by Him. <u>And he never lost a battle</u>! While all others at times lost he at no time lost.

Reading this history but refreshes a conviction that has always guided me, and this is none other than the one that there is a God, and that I know him through my Redeemer the Lord Jesus Christ. From the time I could reason on the subject I have had no doubt on it. Never in my life have I undertaken a Herculean task involving the welfare of more than myself—especially of a considerable portion of the people—until I had prayed for God's approval and assistance. Without being subject to self-reproach for self-laudation, I call your attention to the success I've had along these lines. Your dear Mother knew of my religious convictions. I fear that my children misunderstand them. Of course you must have a better impression of me in this respect than the boys. I have talked to Will about it. And so have I spoken to Mike and Tom in a way to lead them to know my feelings on this score. But they are very young for such subjects. They are growing older very fast and I do not want any risk taken with them.

Naturally you are religious. Your Mother taught you religious principles and I do hope the true faith in Christ. To me you have never made any intimation as to how you believe on the subject. Do you not, my dear, think it is time now that you give this all important question serious thought? I hope you will. And I do trust you will now and then tell Will and Mike and Tom that he who lives in the faith of Christ and in the fear of God is a better man in peace or in war, in idleness or in action than any scoffer dead or alive. Without a soul a man is no better than a beast. With a soul unprotected he is worse than a thousand beasts. He cannot protect his soul in defiance of God. Join me now in the fervent prayer that we all shall live in the faith of Jesus Christ in the fear of God, righteously, to the end that we may in due season meet your Angel Mother in Heaven.

Lovingly,
Your Father,
J. S. Hogg[29]

Sailing in February, Hogg did not return home until April 17. The following letters he wrote to Ima record the Texan's adventures in England. He and his two companions had been invited to stay at the London home of Alfred Suart, the wealthy Englishman whom Hogg had met in New York.

29 Great St. Helen's E.C.
London, England
March 1, 1902

Dear Ima:

It is very trying on my patience to not hear from you or any member of my family for so long. Not a line from you since I got here! Can't you take just <u>one minute</u> twice a week to say <u>five</u> words to me? You may probably know, as the truth is, that my circle of acquaintance is very large, and that as I grow older I naturally become more susceptible to social attractions, especially of the <u>feminine gender</u>. There are scores of handsome, <u>winsome</u>, nineteen-year-old girls on this side who are given to making "goo-goo-eyes" at softheaded Americans of my ilk. <u>Look out</u>! You had better be good to me!

"Old London" is a queer place. She stands midst the fog's gloom most all winter. I have seen the sun twice since I came, and then for an hour or so only. There are no street cars in the city, except a horse car line or two out in the remote part. But vehicles of all sizes, shapes and styles abound by the thousands, and passenger fare as a consequence is very cheap. Mr. Suart keeps teams, vehicles, and coachmen at our disposal all the time. He is a fine fellow. He has several Country places and has them all at our disposal. Since our arrival we have dined out nearly every evening. In fact I am worn out by the good treatment of the Englishmen. Were it not for the <u>sauce</u> added by your very unintentional negligence, I should be at a loss to know how to digest so much good things on one trip.

The dinner given to me by Lord and Lady Deerhurst last Tuesday was indeed a notable affair in all respects. The table was decorated with ferns, flowers, and fruits. The courses were elaborate—elegant. Titled men and women surrounded it on all sides and made the circle vibrate with wit and humor. Ambassador Choate was there. Ambassador Metternich, of Germany, was there. So were Bradley Martin and wife, Countess Galloway, Lord Claude Hamilton, . . . &c &c &c. . . . Mrs. Choate, the talented, sweet American lady was by my side.—Yesterday Lord Hamilton "lunched me" and carried me over the Great Eastern RR of which he is the head—Mr. Suart calls me. Carriage ready. Dinner to-night. Every night. Good bye love,

Affectionately, Your Father, J. S. Hogg[30]

London society must have been a heady atmosphere for Jim Hogg, whose roots were in the backwoods of East Texas. He obviously relished his experience, but he drew the line at appearing in court dress at a royal levee:

29 Great St. Helen's E.C.
London, England
March 5, 1902

Dear Ima:

To-morrow, King Edward is to have a levee, and, although I have been invited by Ambassador Choate and also by Lord Deerhurst to go to it, I am compelled to deny myself the pleasure. My rule is to observe the customs of the people wherever I go, aiming at all times to preserve my own self-respect without offense to others. I could not attend this levee and "shake hands" with the King except in "Court dress" as it is called—Knee breeches, Silk stockings low quartered shoes, full-shirt front, low cut vest, "cut-away" coat and plug hat; the coat, pants and vest to be of black velvet. So I have this day called, thanked Ambassador Choate and notified him of my respectful but positive declination. I therefore maintain myself respect as an American gentleman without offending the propriety by violating an ancient custom here. Mr. Choate seemed very much to regret that I had taken this view and followed this course, but it is the only one consistent with my own self respect. Dinner parties are given me every evening and luncheons are waiting for me all the time. No person has ever been treated better than I have been by these people. Many institutions and customs here are entirely foreign to my habits, education and tastes, but I am no critic of them so long as they suit those who must support and endure them no visitor can with propriety condemn them. In official circles the ancient superstitions haunt the pathway of a gentleman as he <u>meanders</u> the red tape lines to pay his respects to officials. In social circles the customs are very much like those of the first class at Austin and in New York.

With love and a knock for your continued dereliction with the pen,

Your Father

J. S. Hogg

"Travel is Vanity"[31]

Hogg claimed he did not want to put on fancy court dress, but the former governor from Texas had other reasons for not wanting to attend the king's levee, as his next letter shows:

Hurlingham Club,

Fulham, S.W.

Thursday, March 6, 1902

Dear Ima:

Well, the King's Levee is over and I am glad I declined to attend the foolish affair. Accounts of it have been given me by a Count who attended it in a <u>brand new</u> Court Suit, which cost him 250.00. He said all <u>he</u> did, or got a chance to do, was to "<u>bow to His Majesty!</u>" No hand shaking. Now you know from observation that I am a great hand-shaker. Had I been there right on <u>this</u> point I should most likely have made a mistake by shaking the King's hand! Then <u>criticisms</u> would have made you blush for me. The severest criticism to be made against Englishmen in their political life is the tenacity with which they hang on to the relics of barbarism and of ancient superstitions that "<u>Kings rule the people by Divine right</u>." . . .

I have been to some places of interest since my arrival, including Parliament. Of these I may tell you when we meet again. Your fondness for history, I do trust, will not abate. A woman who well understands history and political phrases and distinctions finds a welcome place in the centre of the best circles anywhere. For a girl of your age you are exceptionally bright along these lines. Won't you do yourself the credit, and me the honor, to add daily to this good stock you have so well laid in?—In my heart an impulse speaks out at this moment and answering for you says "Papa, <u>I will</u>!" From it I get much comfort. If it is true you will find in it unalloyed happiness.

Courtesies flow in on me unabated in the most generous way

from all sources in London. Indeed I have about worn out at it. This
is the first evening since my arrival that I have been able to leave off
my evening suit. . . .
        Good night.
                            Lovingly, Your Papa, J. S. Hogg[32]

An evening off was rare, indeed. Jim Hogg was proud of his many
invitations, and mailed some samples to his daughter.

                            29, Great St. Helen's E.C.
                            London, England
                            Tuesday, March 11, 1902
Dear Ima:
        I hand you three letters of invitation to show you something of
the style and cordiality of the people here—one from Lord Claud
Hamilton who has given me two luncheons, one from Mr. Caudy
with whom I dined at Mrs. Cooper's, but whose invitation I could
not accept on account of a previous one in conflict, and the other to
Mr. Suart from Lady Calvin with whom we took tea. Many others
of which these are fair sample, have reached me of the same tenor
and effect since my arrival, which strongly testify to the "old time"
hospitality of these people—just such hospitality as characterized the
Old Virginia Homes of Mrs. and Mrs. Green and other good people
over there.—Quite a party lunched with us last Sunday at Mulgrove
Hall—Mr. Suart's "bachelor ranch" where we are yet "quartering."
By the next mail I hope to be able to send you a group picture taken
of the party. By the way, Lady Deerhurst gave me a fine picture of
herself and three children, and in return I sent Peggy, her four-year
old daughter the only standing picture I had of you. The poor little
thing almost had fits over it. I told her she was very much like you
when you were so good to me at her age, and she now can see how
she will look when she gets to be a "big girl.". . .
        Please do me the special favor to keep in touch with our dear
boys, that they may know they are at all times loved and never over-
looked or forgotten.
                            Affectionately Your Father,
                            J. S. Hogg[33]

Ima had been too busy to write to her father while he was in England, as his next letter shows. Besides her music studies in New York,
she was "planning a house," in a scheme that remains a mystery.

29, Great St. Helen's E.C.
London, England
Friday, March 14, 1902

Dear Ima

From your letter of the 1st instant, I derive much pleasure, as it is the only line I have received from you since we parted. Uppermost in your mind seems to be <u>planning a house</u>! This is the only serious thought, I may say, in it, as the remainder of the letter dwells on "<u>Gewgaws and Knee breeches</u>!" which I have not yet worn to see the King or others. When abroad I have no criticism of the manners, customs or institutions of the rulers or the people of the Country in which I sojourn no more than I should offer to those of my host at whose home I accept hospitality. If in entering a Country I should be required to wear its uniform this would be enough to prevent the visit. At no time, under no conditions, should I abandon the customs or costume of a gentleman to go anywhere! For this reason, living by this rule, I did not go to the King's levee. <u>But I made no criticism of the knee breeches requirement</u>! No! To <u>you</u>, however, I must say that any American who would change the <u>dress suit</u> of a <u>gentleman</u> for the <u>Court Suit</u> of a <u>King</u> is a snob whose example at home, if he had influence, would in time raise up in our Country a race of <u>flunkies</u> contemptible among freemen. . . .

By all means, my daughter, keep up interest in politics. Understand well the principles on which your rights are based, and stand by them. In politics, as in all the affairs of man, woman, indirectly or intentionally, certainly wields great influence—<u>when she is posted</u>! Know <u>your lesson</u>—your <u>duty</u>—and you can lead or teach others. . . . And when you go to preside in that <u>house</u> you seem so busily planning, you will be the pleasant, intelligent, autocrat whose sway must be felt far beyond the domestic circle and the culinary department.—<u>What house</u> is that anyway? And why is this your last opera season in NY? When you write again, please tell me if there are any <u>innuendos</u> in these queer expressions! If so, clear them up to me will you? Really I am too obtuse to fully comprehend them.

My "business" here is very slow. Really I get discouraged at the outlook. Of course we <u>hope</u> to get through all right. Mr. Campbell and others believe we will.<u>_ I doubt it</u>! At all events the experiment if it should fail will only retard, but not injure us, Remember me kindly to Mr. and Mrs. Green and family. And kiss all the sweethearts (the <u>girls</u> you know) for me. As some of them "saw me off" on that ship, I have serious doubts now if one of them would shed a tear if the boat should sink and force me to swim out to main land. Wish you would find out on this point and let me know.

Good bye.

Lovingly, Your Father

J. S. Hogg[34]

If Ima answered her father's queries about her activities in New York, her letter has not been found. Jim Hogg's subsequent letters do not mention her plans.

29, Great St. Helen's E.C.

London, England

Tuesday, March 25, 1902

Dear Ima:

Yesterday was a strange day to me. Strange in that it was one of solitude to me in this crowded city of millions of people, among whom I have scores of friends who always welcome me most cordially around their hospitable boards.—I lunched alone. Spent the day by myself. Got supper alone. Went to the theatre alone. Spent the evening alone—all in silent solitude! Wonderful for me! Isn't it? And it was appropriate that I attend the play "Ulysses," drama from one of Homer's greatest poems, the Odyssey. As his long solitude! Wonderful for me! Isn't it? As his long alienage gave him undisturbed time to meditate, so my solitude of yesterday gave me opportunity for reverie.

To add solemnity to thought it was my birthday—the 24th day of March! Over half a century now has passed behind me, and this is the first birthday celebration I ever had! Indeed I enjoyed it. And of all the joyous reflections that illumined my heart on yesterday none was brighter, more lustrous and pleasure breeding than the trickling thoughts that fell from the cataract of my brain, as crystal drops into the Soul, to enliven my convictions and hopes that there is a God, and a better world for those who live a righteous life! Amidst the vicissitudes of a checkered career, from orphanage in boyhood, I know I have, at times, done wrong, but never wantonly, willfully. Looking back I have little to regret. Looking forward I have unshaken hopes that in you and my three boys I shall enjoy much pride and undefiled pleasure in Old Age.—With Constancy of Love,

Your Father,

J. S. Hogg[35]

The discussions of "Texas oil" produced results, as J. S. Hogg reported to Ima in the following letter:

> Confidential
>
> 29, Great St. Helen's E.C.
> London, England
> Tuesday, April 1, 1902
>
> Dear Ima:
>
> Beginning last Friday morning everything has been closed up here until this morning for "Easter holiday." It seems that the "Death Pall" hung over London during the time, as most all the well-to-do citizens had gone to the Country and the others were moping about the Parks. Most of the time I spent on the Sky Scrapers—the high-top Omnibuses that serve as street cars over the City. It looks now as if I shall be able to sail for New York, within the next few days, as our "trade" has about closed. It has taken a long time, but it seems to have been best after all. If it is not finished within 30 days from date we are to get $25,000 cash forfeit which has been put up by check. A company is being formed with $4,500,000 capital stock to take over the Hogg-Swayne Company properties, or most of them. Out of this we are to get $675,000 net cash and $2,000,000 in stock. My part will be $135,000 cash and $400,000 in stock.[36]
>
> If the company succeeds the stock will be very valuable. If it does not the cash will pay me very well for my interest in the property. By this sale we do not part with all our holdings down there, but with five gushers and a lot of land, a pipe line and storage tanks—plenty for a large, lucrative business. So I feel quite safe from the outlook, but must wait longer for returns.
>
> Now, Ima, that dream of yours won't work. I shall not indulge those boys in a "trip to England." I should not do so if I had the wealth of Carnegie. I never saw a "well travelled young man" that was worth kicking out of the back door! My boys must work their way! When they win their expense money they can travel with more pleasure and greater intelligence and benefit. Keep it before them that it is manly in them to succeed; that it is unmanly in them to spend the "Old man's" money except for an education and necessities while going to school, if he should be fool enough to let them have it. Your influence over them will make fine men out of them. Of course I shall be glad to take you anywhere, if I have to make the boys work to defray the expenses. In other words, you shall have carte blanche, as

you have always had and never abused. The enclosed check explains
itself. "Be good." With much love,

Your Father,

J. S. Hogg[37]

On April 7, 1902, while Jim Hogg was about to leave London,
the Texas Company (later Texaco), a merger of J. S. Cullinan's Texas
Fuel Company and the Hogg-Swayne Syndicate, was chartered to do
business in Texas.[38]

On April 17, Hogg arrived in New York aboard the White Star
Line's *Teutonic*, as a *New York Times* article reported: "The Governor was in splendid health, as well as humor, and though he said he
was mighty glad to get back home, he nevertheless took occasion to
say a lot of nice things about the Britons. . . . The big, genial Governor was undoubtedly the most popular of the *Teutonic's* passengers,
especially with the younger women. . . ."[39]

Although he was a great success at sea, Hogg was not yet certain
of his financial success. He wrote to Ima on May 14, "The gushers
gush and oil is yet plentiful," but he worried: "Our trade still hangs
unclosed. For this reason I must continue to mop my brow."[40]

Ima was planning to return to Texas for the summer. What she
meant by telling her father in an earlier letter of March 1 that this
was her last opera season in New York and that she was "planning a
house" is not clear.

When her father returned home, he wrote to Ima from Port Arthur:

Hotel Sabine
Port Arthur, Texas
May 6, 1902
Dear Ima:

At last I am at this fine hotel, having a nice rest, and eating dew-
berries, wearing cape-jessamines, "sniffing" the cool sea breezes,
"yerning" to gallery-loafers and smiling into the mellow-faces of the
fascinating ladies: And all this in Texas, grand young Texas, Democracy's King! I really believe everybody was glad to see me back—for
"they said so." Last Friday morning I reached Austin. Willie "took
up" with me at once, I found everything there in good condition. He
and I spent Friday and Saturday nights and Sunday at the Estrada.

Lizzie had us hot corn bread, country steak, yard eggs, &c. in fine
style. Will looked over my clothes and straightened things up for me.
Sunday night I came to Beaumont. Last night I came here. Enroute

home Hermilla and Velma met me at the Denton depot. They looked as sweet and pretty as ever, and report all well. Velma's girl baby is a fine one and she holds it up high so everyone within a hundred yards shall have a free look at it. Sister was out in the country, and I failed, regretfully, to see her.

At Hillsboro Mike and Tom came aboard the sleeper to see me. In full military uniform they looked nice and dignified. They are in good health, have grown like jointing corn after a June rain, and seem to have very much improved in every way. They appear to me to be fine boys, but you know my partiality to them is so great that I am disqualified as a judge in their cases. After all, regardless of my opinion of them, their life, their character, their destiny, remain more in your hands than in mine. So what I think of them amounts to but little. The influence you wield over them amounts to a great deal. Their attachment to you is indeed strong—almost fanatical,— Tom continues to correspond with Eunice. Mike thinks this is a great piece of foolishness. I do not. The poor fellow is in love. He cannot see her. What is he to do but write! Yes write! Write love letters, just as I used to do at his age. I would give a hundred dollars apiece for those letters, or a few of them, now. That Tom shall not be without such rare specimens of love and literature, I shall save his, or some of them, for him. . . .

I was so rushed at Austin that I got to see none of your sweethearts of either sex. And you know Will could tell me nothing. So I cannot give you any news on those lines, except to say, in a general way, I got the impression that they all are anxious for your early return.—and so am I!

For the next few weeks I shall remain here and at Beaumont— most of the time here—Be good. Be nice. Write often.
With love

> Affectionately Your Father,
> J. S. Hogg[41]

> Beaumont May 29

Dear Ima:

Mike and Tom came home last Friday and remained with me there until Monday evening when they left for a few weeks' outing at Col. Stinson's. They have improved in every way very much. We had a fine time together and expect to renew it when you return home. A telegram to me here telling me when you leave New York will be sufficient. I will see to your proper reception and protection

at Austin. By all means have one of the girls bound for Texas to wait
and accompany you. Otherwise I shall endeavor to come after you.
Let me know about when you expect to leave for home and how
much money you may need. Everything is nice and in good condition at the Estrada and the weather is very cool out there. It is sultry
and hot here.

As to the Episcopal Church: If it is your choice and you so desire
I could have no objections to you joining it. Tom is thinking of joining the Methodist Church. Your mother and her people all belonged
to it. Mine were of the Baptist persuasion. Let your conscience and
better judgment be gratified on this question and I shall be satisfied.
Be good and write to me fully.—I gave Vivie the shawl.*

> Lovingly, Your Father
> J. S. Hogg[42]

Jim Hogg was himself a Baptist, having been baptized around 1860
in the Quitman Baptist Church.[43] Ima considered joining the Episcopal Church in 1902, but she did not make that move until 1910, when
she was living in Houston.

Meanwhile, Ima was enjoying her freedom in New York. It is possible that her reference to "planning a house" and her inclination to
become an Episcopalian had something to do with a romantic attachment she kept secret from her family. In New York she had met a
young man named R. W. Alexander, who wrote to her on June 6,
1902, that he was "delighted . . . that you say 'yes' to my invitation
for a honeymoon trip Monday after dark. . . . Try to be ready about
nine for I will call at about seven forty." Was this merely lighthearted
banter, or were the two considering marriage? No one knows. Ima
came home to Texas a few days later and spent the summer there.
In August, R.W. Alexander wrote to Ima, inviting her to return to
New York for the winter theater season, with stars such as Henry
Irving and Ellen Terry. She would spend another year studying at the
National Conservatory of Music and perhaps seeing R.W. Alexander.
He may have been the "Alec" mentioned in a letter to Ima by her
friend Vivian Breziger.[44]

---

* Vivie was Vivian Breziger, one of Ima's close friends in Austin. *Austin and Travis
County: A Pictorial History* (Encino Press, 1975), 110, has an undated photo of a
parade float with Ima and Vivian driving a flower-bedecked buggy, escorted by Charl-
ton Hall and Will Caswell (Vivian's future husband) two young men on horseback on
horseback.

Jim Hogg was deep in the oil business in the summer of 1902. In June *The New York Times* reported that the company he had formed in England, the Consolidated Oil Company, capitalized at $6,000,000, would take over the Hogg-Swayne Syndicate and begin operating in Texas to build a refinery and oil pipelines. Hogg and four Texas associates would have half the new company's stock and receive $1,200,000 in cash for the rest.[45] But that was not quite the case. It was J. S. Cullinan's Texas Fuel Company, not the English corporation, which had merged with Hogg-Swayne. In 1902, the Texas Fuel Company would complete the pipelines begun by the Hogg-Swayne Syndicate and challenge the domination of Rockefeller's Standard Oil.[46]

Hogg was indeed occupied with "important business engagements," as he wrote to his children:

June 21, 1902
Dear Will, Ima, Mike and Tom:
I wish I could now be with you but important business engagements deny me this pleasure. Be good to each other. Do not quarrel. Deport yourselves so that your Grand Father and Mother will be proud of you and I'll be indeed happy. Have a jolly nice time and let's meet at the Estrada next Saturday the 28th to remain together for awhile. What do you say? If circumstances demand your return earlier let me know in due time.
Give my love to all the family, and at all times know, that, without favoritism you and each of you live in my heart and mind.
Lovingly, Your Father,
J. S. Hogg[47]

On June 24, he wrote to Ima that he was sending her a birthday present (She would be twenty on July 10), a pearl ring he had had made from pearls found in "an Austin river."[48]

Hogg was back in Beaumont in July, but he took time off from business for his first love: politics. He spent three days at the state Democratic convention in Galveston. Ima was now back in Texas and staying in Columbia, at her father's newly acquired Varner plantation. (Columbia, in Brazoria County, is now known as West Columbia.). And so the summer passed.

In the fall, Mike and Tom returned to the Carlisle School and Ima resumed her studies in New York. Over the summer, the headmistress of her boarding school, Mrs. Greene, had developed "distressing heart trouble," and died. As Ima wrote years later, "So I found a school quite different and more convenient, the Comstock School, 20th & W. 40th St." The school, described as a "Family and Day School for Girls" at 32 West 40th Street, was run by Miss Lydia Day, "a delightful and cultured lady." Ima recalled her first weeks there: "One of the older teachers took me under her wing and shocked Miss Day by introducing me to Ibsen, Hauptmann, and Dostoyevsky, etc. The theater was at its height as was the opera."[49] Whether or not Ima attended any performances with the young man named R.W. Alexander, who had written to her about the New York season the previous August, is not known. Later that fall, Ima apparently stayed for a time with Miss Day at Miss Day's apartment on 18 East 40th Street.[50]

Although she was immersed in her music, Ima was still sketching and drawing, as Mike's letter from the Carlisle School indicates:

> November 4, 1902
> Dear Sister:
>   I received your telegram tuesday 28 [October 28, his seventeenth birthday] About ten o'clock. I received the pictures on wednesday the cake and candy on sunday. I think that womans head is a beauty, the rest are fine too. The boys found out that I had the candy and it did not last long. I still have half of the cake. It sure is fine. Mrs. Weeks, a lady here in town gave me a very fine chocolate cake on the day of my birthday. It did not last over ten minutes for I gave every boy in the house a slice. It was the finest cake that I have ever tasted. I am very much obliged for your presents but you failed to send your own picture.
>   We got our reports today. I got ninty two in Eng. history. ninty two in Latin, eighty eight in Geom. eighty two in Rhetoric, ninty seven in spelling and Eighty nine in Algebra. Our teachers sure grade heavy. If you miss three questions in a lesson you get zero and five demerits on your deportment. I haven't had but twenty demerits since school began, that sounds like a whole lot but there weren't but three other boys that got that few. They all averaged from three hundred to fifty. Each boy had to walk a hundred and fifty yards for every three demerits until they were walked off. I will close.
>   Your brother
>   Mike[51]

Besides dealing with his business affairs in Beaumont that fall, Jim Hogg was developing his new country home, the Varner plantation in Columbia: He had hired a manager, planted crops, and managed to get the antebellum house furnished and in good order to entertain his family there. He sent an invitation to Ima:

Sunday, Nov. 16th, 1902

Dear Ima:

I am anxious to have you spend Christmas with our boys. Your influence over them, by reason of their deep love for you, is potent and far-reaching. You have always exercised a fine <u>control</u> over Will. As to Mike and Tom, you know well, how they idolize you, and yield to your will, sometimes, with boyish reluctance, but at all times with <u>manly fortitude</u>, when the issue is made. This is an important period in their young lives. Their characters are being made—molded. My greatest desire now, that you and Will are grown and stand in all respects above reproach in the estimation of all honorable acquaintances, is to raise Mike and Tom to be respectable, self-respecting, honorable men. In this very pleasant task no one can aid me half so well as you.

Your opportunity to influence them could not be greater than on a Christmas outing with them—<u>down on the Old Plantation</u>! Hunting down there is fine for the boys, and it may not be unattractive to you. I have the house comfortably furnished, and plenty of room. With an excellent, large hack and team, and saddle horses and dogs and guns and "plenty to eat" there could be no reason why we shall not have a fine time down there for a week or so. Nothing would please the boys more than this; and you see it would open their young hearts as wide as the Ocean's bosom to receive the good sentiments to be strewn there by you—<u>and me</u>! Of course, if you so desire, you could have some "chum" with you. And probably a "house party" might be allowed also. <u>But</u> as to this, we can talk later. Friends at Houston would like to give you <u>a party</u> before your return to NY. And then, possibly we could find time, before you go back, to attend the Governor's Inaugural Ball early in January. Really I think we can spend a few weeks together very pleasantly. How does this <u>strike</u> you? Write candidly, as usual.

Lovingly, Your Father,

J. S. Hogg[52]

Oil interests were producing income at last, Ima's father wrote again to her on November 24: "I closed up the Adams matter and have 'laid aside' $83,000 of six per cent first mortgage bonds out of it after taking out my money and interest. This is very good. One or two more like this and I can quit, and stay on my farm."

On November 26, the day before Thanksgiving, he wrote again. He had sold his Texas Oil and Fuel Company interest for $35,750.[53] These 1902 dollars would be worth nearly twenty-five times that today. Time for Thanksgiving, indeed.

Will, "taking the waters" for his health at the Hot Sulphur Wells Hotel in San Antonio, wrote to his sister:

Saturday undated [Nov. 29?] 1902
My dearest Sister:
    If I can stick it out I will drink this water and take these baths for two weeks. Need the treatment though I am not quite an invalid. If appearances go for naught you would say that I have the "hypo".*
Not so.
    Prepare to become a comfortably rich woman. Your land at Columbia has healthy prospects of proving gusher territory. Drilling near there, adjoining your estate, is progressing rapidly and James Stephen "would not be surprised to see 'em gush by Christmas." Don't begin to spend money on your prospects, just now.
    We are expecting you at the "Varner" for Christmas week. The boys and I will try to make life tiresome for you. Father has his heart set on your coming, and you know when "Jym" is sot something is bound to give away. You will be permitted to shoot at a duck or two in the company of your three brothers, that is if you be good and proper-like. (Which reminds me to have Miles send your sidesaddle down there. Will write to him now.) Then too your business interests require your presence in the vicinity of the oil fields (to be) and I as your legal adviser and attorney in fact command you to leave at a proper time that you may lead the procession.
    Father invited Vivian to join you there & she may do so.
    The boys complain of no letter from you. You must write to them regularly. With much love and a few kisses
                                    Yours
                                    Will[54]

James Stephen Hogg, newly prosperous from his oil interests, was fulfilling his long-awaited dream of having a big country home.
    Ima recalled that "the Varner" was not an easy place to get to:

* "Hypo," short for "hypochondria," used to mean "morbidly depressed spirits." *Compact Edition of the Oxford English Dictionary* (2 vols., Oxford, UK, Oxford University Press, 1971), 1: 1361.

Transportation was extremely primitive. The old "Tap" Railroad from Houston to East Columbia was antiquated and ran only a few times a week. The railway was on the other side of the Brazos River from East Columbia, and there was no bridge over the river. Many times the roads were impassible, the Brazos River overflowing suddenly without warning. The marshes beyond East Columbia were a jungle into dense woods.[55]

The new master of Varner wasted no time in fitting it with everything his heart desired, and for that first Christmas on the place showering his children with gifts. He invited his brother John and family, who as usual did not come, but his sister Martha Frances did. Aunt Fannie arrived in time for Christmas—and stayed on. She wrote an ecstatic letter to her niece Hermilla—on a special letterhead:

THE VARNER
Joseph Fain, Manager
Columbia, Texas

December 1902
Dear Hermilla:
I don't know how to begin. I've just seen James and the boys off on a short hunt, after birds for my supper; James away ahead in a canter, and Mike and Tom—the happiest boys I ever saw, possessors of a fine new gun, saddle and pony—bringing up the rear with might and main. They are just simply wild. When Tom took it all in he jumped up and said: "Papa, oh, papa, I can't tell you how I thank you!" I think James' eyes filled, as well as Tom's—I know mine did! But I might have been like the drunk man, saw their tears through my own.

I have a fearful cold. Don't know what it may do to me, but am not much bested. I've worked the rabbit's foot [tricked, or deceived, that is, concealed her cold] on the biscuit maker, and he is credulous. There are two of them, good cooks, and a housekeeper, two men and a woman, all black negroes. Then comes the gardener, a Swede—splendid too—and a Dutch boss over all the hands. He carries the trays and dishes out—the finest follow, a bachelor. It sholy do look like old times come back again, and I am a sho nuf child. Oh, the beauty of it all! My room is across a hall, all latticed doors clear across at both ends, and, like the windows, fold back (from James' room)—great Southern home rooms. The house is a massive pile of brick without a crack inside or out, three stories, with the kitchen, dining-room and closets on the first floor of a house that nearly form an "L" but misses about the width of a large room. The upper story of this is used by the gardener and overseer. Is it all furnished? Well, I should say so: just elegantly—parlor and all; wardrobes, beds, dressers—full sets of everything, and even an organ.

. . . Haven't smelt fire since I left your State. But I'm drinking wine—must get some more right now.

It's turning cooler; have ordered a fire and a big back log, not exactly a Yule log, but nearly.

Poor little old Ned [her canary] sang on the train. Since I arrived, he has been trying to make up for lost time. James is just as pleased as he can be with him. Poor James, he took me in his arms and kissed mouth (snuff and all) and both cheeks. He's a dear old boy, big of heart and so pleased that we are so pleased.

Well, of course, I lost all I could; back-comb, umbrella, overshoes and lunch. My gold glasses fell off the net "sacking" and got toated off in the sheets, where I accidentally found them by having the Porter shake them out of the "dirty clothes box."

I write you today because I've got to write William tomorrow. I've just written a postal to Jimmie. By the way, it was a Godsend to have Jimmie [James McDugald] along. (I've just spilt the blood of a gallinipper [mosquito]!) We should all have been lost without him. I should so love to have Baylor [Hermilla's six-year-old son]—what a treat it would be for him! But he couldn't go the gait any more than I can.

Next Tuesday is a big bear hunt. Goodbye.

But it was not "Goodbye." Martha Frances continued her letter:

Oh, I wanted to tell you lots. This house was built fifty years ago, by an aristo-nabob of the old Southland. The moulding was painted on and is perfect yet, and the colorings in the border are fresh as if put on yesterday. Fishy? It is the unvarnished truth! The windows are old style, covering nearly the whole sides of the rooms length and breadth.

Where shall I sign? There are twenty-five negroes at work here and James gives them and their families dinner Christmas also a barn-dance. Look at the crop of vegetables. 140,000 [bushels?] of them which will fill 25 cars when shipped. English peas for Christmas—galore, expect strawberries for Christmas. 250 goats 50 fine cattle, 15 mules, geese, chickens, turkeys, and a horse, saddle and bridle for each member of the family. 4171 acres in the whole place, 1000 in cultivation, and the woodland tangled with blackberries (vines of course.) Good Lord! And all paid for. There is a fine cistern in the yard and about one hundred yards off a flowing artesian well. There are men now at work to develop the <u>oil</u>, two veins of which have been struck—small, but enough to come to the top from a depth of about 350 feet; but they have shut it off to go deeper.

No, James keeps his holdings at Beaumont, and has <u>not</u> been to Galveston at all; notwithstanding the paper stated he was there and said he'd pulled out. He is gone today (Sunday) to meet Ima at twelve tonight in Houston—will, may be, stop over at Baylor's until tomorrow. [Dr. Baylor Hogg and his family lived in Houston, where he practiced medicine.]

I'm pretty well, I thank you; how is your corn? Love to the chaps and a Merry Christmas all round.

Your aunt.[56]

Nearly a month later, Aunt Fannie was still enjoying herself at Varner. Ima spent the holidays there and visited her father's headquarters at Beaumont before departing for New York. But she did not stay for the inaugural ball in Austin, as her father had hoped. She went back to New York. Two letters to her from her Austin friend Vivian Breziger suggest that Ima was romantically involved with a young man there.[57]

Will wrote to Ima, describing the inaugural ball she missed:

January 25, 1903
Dear Sister:

The Inaugural Ball was a great jam—About five thousand perspiring, sorry-we-came, people lined up for the grand march, which opened the still-waltz tableau, in a lock-step crawl for a share in the programs which gave out before the tail of the procession got in earshot of the music. I waited as a looker-on until I saw the ugliest man and homeliest woman in my whole life and then san[g] "Sailor Pull for the Shore"—Thirty minutes there made me glad I was not a fool in every respect.

There were a number of very pretty girls and worlds of spoiled silk-and-lace. Dress-suits from bottom-drawers which made the wearers smile before they got inside—and saw every body had one except me and the door police. Near three before the crowd cleared sufficiently for the dances to begin. I left at 11:30, had to fight my way through the corridors. Of course J. Stephen was there and had more fun than anybody. He was very much perturbed until late in the afternoon for fear that his dress suit was not going to reach him in time. It came, however, and he was glad. Fact is I was in a state of disquietude myself on that account for I really like to see him in dress.

He left last Wednesday night for Beaumont but probably will return in a week. Aunt Frances is at the farm (Columbia). The boys are well but they don't communicate.

Write to me—
Yours
Will[58]

Then, from Beaumont, Jim Hogg sent Ima his own ruminations about the inaugural ball:

Feby. 7th, 1903
Dear Ima:
    I was very much amused at your play on the "Bell of the Ball." You know that Willie had always treated my social pretensions as a joke. Nothing amuses him more than to see me "gear up" in my "Ball Harness." Indeed he is always ready to put it on for me, and will go to more trouble at this than at any other small accommodation for me. Well, I enjoy the "rig" and the joke myself. Some of the family must keep up with the fashions, and I guess you and I will have to do it. Will abhors the past time and I fear now that Mike and Tom will follow his example. So let's agree that no amount of fun made of my shape shall deter us from the past time and the pleasure of dressing fashionably and well at all times wherever we may go. From the time I was a boy, struggling for subsistence I have always kept a dress suit—fashionable and nice—at the "bottom of my trunk."
    Rarely ever have I been anywhere that I could not go into any social circle without attracting attention to my clothes. And the secret of it is that I never wore a dress suit to a corn shucking nor a bob tail coat to a sixteen course dinner. Social life of elegance and graceful simplicity has always been very attractive and pleasant to me. It is true I have indulged in it but little for two reasons: 1. That when I was young, and otherwise equipped for it, I was too busy in

my work for professional and political success to take the time and spare the expense for it. That since I have succeeded politically and professionally and would not mind the time or expense necessary to enjoy it, I find it very awkward for the lack of some one to go with me and by reason of <u>approaching</u> old age, to indulge in the pleasure. But I still keep my dress suit, like the one Will admired so at the Inaugural Ball, and am ready, willing and waiting—for <u>you</u>! Yes, for you to get out of school, and go out with me—<u>at least once in a while</u>; that is, at such times as it may be <u>convenient</u> to you. But thereon hang my "heavy hopes"—on a delicate thread: When <u>convenient</u> to you! I know my rivals to go with you will be much younger, more handsome and—and—well they cannot be more willing, nor at any time prouder of the honor. You have so conducted yourself at all times; been so thoughtful of your brothers; so kind to me and have devoted your time so faithfully and successfully to your music and other studies, that I am proud of you at all times. Yes I shall proudly take you anywhere, everywhere, that you may wish to go. Socially you and I will start out together when you quit school and there yet remains plenty of time for us to get all there is in it.

Lovingly, Your Father,

J. S. Hogg[59]

Aunt Fannie left Varner in February for a visit to Hermilla and Bob Kelso in Denton, and their children: Ethel, fourteen; Lucy, eleven; Mildred, nine, and Baylor, seven. She wrote to Ima, then in New York.

Feb. 16, 1903
Dear Ima:

As the children would say, "Did you get any Valentines?" Lucy got 14, and the other less, according <u>to popularity</u>. I sent Mike & Tom one apiece. I had a letter from Mike on yesterday. He said: "hurry up and get well." I wrote them I'd been sick ever since I got back, which I have, but am much better.

No, I saw no pictures, but found your little brush, button-hook, and brooch-case, the one Willie brought. I put all books in on your papa's mantel. I did so hate to come off and leave things at the mercy of any and everybody: towels, sheets, blankets, and so many things too tedious to mention—with no lock, no nothing. I found napkins and they were nice—and table-cloths scattered all over that empty room next the kitchen, and couldn't help it. I never saw such destruction. But I couldn't do a thing—tried some but to no avail. Mr. Headwell said he meant to open James' eyes if he got a chance. "If de Govnor ask me I tell the troof.". . .

O, yes, and I found your picture in the little frame you gave your papa, on the dresser. I put it in your papa's room—got all I could in my trunk—had it full when I went down. I have the brush, button-hook, brooch-case, in my trunk, the overshoes I use as I lost mine on the way down.

Well, I think it is nice for you girls to build a dress for your-selves. I have perfect confidence in your ability, for a girl couldn't live with me as long as you did and not learn the trick it is done by. I never told you, but many times I would commence an article—dress, shirt waist &c—and get a very severe headache, so you'd have to do it. You never refused, bless your heart, but worked diligently as directed; even to cutting out. You didn't know I was running the rabbit's foot on you, but often it was just that. And I was so proud when you cut, fit and basted your first waist perfectly—even better than I could. I think it a nice accomplishment—let others think as they please. Hermilla says: "Tell Ima I want a picture that I can see." The one I have is so small, you know. It is the only picture I have of you, too, but that's all right. I have very few of anybody now; and I don't need them, as I have a gallery on memory's wall. I have a good one of Mike & Tom in their uniform at the Hillsboro School. It's after one—must eat a snack. Thanks for the thought of sending the little dresden ribbon. O, yes, I've still got the craze. Have your room companion to kiss you for

Your Aunt[60]

In the spring of 1903, Jim Hogg was occupied with his law prac-tice and his oil interests, but not too busy to campaign for reforms he had fought for: He wrote to Ima in March:

March 13, 1903
Dear Daughter:
    Well, I made the anticipated speech mentioned in your Sunday's letter, on last Wednesday night. Although the announcement was made for three days only, people from all over the State were on hand to hear me. It was one of the most flattering demonstrations I ever had shown to me by the people. The great Opera House could not half hold the crowd. The Manager told me that thousands could not get in. By today's mail I send to you several newspaper accounts

and reports of the occasion and of the speech. Everywhere, from all sources in this State, I get flattering congratulations on the effort. I had not the slightest intimation that an effort would be made to invite me to speak in the House of Representatives when the resolution was offered. In view of my openly expressed opposition to the Free Pass System and to Lobbying and to Railway Consolidation I could not have expected or desired to be invited to address a body of men, the majority of whom were not in accord with me in these subjects. So when they voted down the resolution I put out an appointment as a duty to myself and to the public.

About Wednesday noon I got the enclosed invitation to deliver the speech in the House, but it came too late, and rather as a "second thought"; consequently I could not, <u>did not, of course</u>, pay any attention to it. You can keep this resolution as you may some day like to read it. Since your Mother's death, as you know I have always had your criticism of and advice on my public documents and speeches except in this instance. You do not know how much I missed you on this occasion. You cannot appreciate how keenly I felt the loss of your suggestions and criticism of this speech. Under the circumstances I did the best I could on short notice and hope that it will not shock your refined, superior, sensibilities. No man in private or public life can do justice to himself on all occasions when he speaks or writes on public questions, in the absence of women's advice and refining influence. By the time I make another one I do hope to have your assistance in its preparation and presence at its delivery.

The boys are well. Your Aunt Fannie is not well, but is not in bed. She will probably come down here to stay with me at the Avenue Hotel for a while, as I have urged her to do so.—I know but little or no society news as I mingle but little with people since you left me. Oil prospects are fine at Columbia. Land values have recently doubled down there and we expect a boom when the weather dries. The enclosed checks explain themselves—for tuition &c.

Affectionately, Your Father,

J. S. Hogg[61]

When Governor Hogg left office he had vowed to carry on the fight for reforms to keep corruption out of the railroad business, and he did. His next three letters to Ima have him shuttling between Beaumont and Varner and Austin, attending to business and taking a "short rest" at Hot Springs, Arkansas.[62] As his oil prospects looked brighter and brighter, he reveled in spending money on his children.

Hogg, Chilton, Masterson & Swayne
Attorneys-at-Law
Beaumont, Texas
March 20, 1903

Dear Ima:

Your frequent inquiries about the "prospects" of oil at the Columbia Oil Field remind me that you sold Mike an acre of your land there. It is now worth <u>three</u> times the price he paid you for it, and probably much more. So the poor little fellow made a couple of hundred out of you in that trade. A contract was let last Fall for the completion of three wells on the Arnold tract, close to the first one. The weather has been so wretched that but little progress has been made since you were there last January. Recently the first of the new wells got through the Cap Rock and oil was "struck" in apparently fine quantities. No test of it can be made until the weather dries up so as to admit of work. Everyone believes that this well is a good one and "proves the field." As soon as work can be pushed it will be done, and you shall know all the important results.

Now don't get your "sights set" too high, as you may have the trouble of lowering them.—Spindle Top continues to produce lots of oil. Sour Lake is a fine field. Saratoga is a good one. Jennings is excellent. But I have long since been convinced that "The Arnold" is the best. Oil at the wells here sells now at 72 cents per barrel, instead of at 10 cents a barrel this time last year. Much "wildcatting" is being done, and new fields will "come in" to startle the world again this year. Mark my prediction. The business has just got <u>started.</u> When you quit school I trust you will study the land and oil business so that you can profitably employ your fine talents at odd times.

Willie has taken your Aunt Fannie to Austin where she is being treated in the Sanitarium. He reports that she is improving. You know he is a great nurse and of course will take fine care of her. The boys are happy and well. I hope we may spend the first month of vacation at the Varner. Then we can determine whither we will go. Rest easy on this score. I expect to let you <u>help me fix up the programme.</u>

With love,
Your Father,
J. S. Hogg

P.S. Write Vivian and the other girls to go see Sister at the Sanitarium opposite the Morris House.[63]

The Austin Sanitarium, a private hospital at 206–208 West Fourteenth Street, had been there since 1886.[64] Aunt Fannie's ailment was
probably arthritis.

Hogg, Robertson & Hogg
Attorneys and Counsellors at Law
Austin, Texas
Friday, April 9th, 1903
Dear Ima:
    Reports from Columbia are very gratifying. Mr. Underwood
wires that the shallow well, less than 500 feet deep, is bringing 50
barrels of oil a day. Other reports say it is doing better. This <u>proves</u>
the <u>field</u> and makes it very valuable. <u>So "I told you so!"</u> will ring
into ears often when I get to see you, which I hope will be—some o'
these days!—Your Auntie is getting very spry. . . . You know she is
fond of "rolicky" company. Let Dot know this so she can start her to
"going." I expect to be at Dallas to-morrow and hope to have Mike
and Tom dine with me at the Oriental.—Crops are late. Things at the
Varner look well. The Legislature is yet in Session. No news: except
that your bro. Will is "noticing" around the Old Maids at San Antonio again. You had better write to him. Don't go near the Ocean. I'll
get you home in good shape. Here's a hundred dollars.
                              Your Pa,
                              J. S. Hogg[65]

The Arlington
Hot Springs, Ark.
    April 13, 1903
    Dear Ima:
    See, read, study, admire and take to heart, the sentiments of the
enclosed clipping which so graphically portrays the "New York Society Girls with their Sleeves Rolled Up," pie-making, bread-making,
steak-hacking, supper cooking! God bless them! I can taste that
cornbread (<u>without molasses in it</u>!) and can smell that steak as the
gravy soaks and trickles through it, now! Well, on reflection I recall
the time when (you were under ten then) you could "stack up" with
the whole crew as a cook. Have you forgotten how? No! <u>You never</u>
<u>forget anything</u>. Let's have a good time when vacation sets in. What
say you? I wish I had you here with me now. Music three times
a day; the light laughter of gay youngsters; the strained giggles of
the Summer, Sod and Turf Widows; the spry-jerks of the spavined

jointed—"has been"—bachelors, all, all, combined in the hotel hub-
bub of society noise make me long for you.

Mike and Tom met me at Dallas last Saturday and dined with me
at the Oriental. I fitted them out with clothes and everything they
wanted. And gave them a watch and chain each. Now probably you
can imagine how their eyes glowed! But I guess not. I am quite well
but need a short rest. Good by love, good bye for the day.

Jym[66]

Good fortune had come to Jim Hogg at last, and he gloried in it.
However, a few months later, misfortune came to Ima. Visiting at
Varner in July, she accidentally stuck a needle into her knee, and the
cartilage lining became infected. The event made newspaper headlines on July 11, when her father cancelled an important business trip
to rush to Ima's bedside. Ima's worried grandfather Stinson wrote to
her on July 28 that he had read about her "misfortune" in the newspapers.[67]

Besides the pain, Ima was evidently dangerously ill from the infection. In those pre-antibiotic days, wounds such as hers could lead to
sepsis (blood poisoning) and death. She was bedridden and unable to
walk for several weeks. Attended by Aunt Fannie and Mike and Tom,
she convalesced at Varner while her father buzzed about between
Beaumont, Houston, and Austin. Mike and Tom were leaving the
Carlisle School that summer, and were headed for college preparatory
school somewhere in the East. In August, Ima wrote a letter to Arthur
Hadley, the president of Yale University, asking for him to recom-
mend some schools that would prepare her brothers for admission to
Yale. Hadley's secretary sent Ima some catalogs, and a letter telling
her that he "would be very glad to have the sons of Governor Hogg
enrolled at Yale."[68]

In September, Ima, whose knee was still not healed, left Varner for
a stay at the Austin Sanitarium. She was on crutches, but she wrote
to her father that she was "comfortable and happy."[69] She had delegated the needs—from schooling to clothing—of Mike and Tom to
their elder brother. Will was now twenty-eight years old. Mike would
turn eighteen in October, and Tom had marked his sixteenth birthday
that August. Mike was to attend a preparatory school in Annapolis, Maryland, near the U.S. Naval Academy. Tom, who had never
done well in academic pursuits, still needed to find the right niche. He
was ill in early September and joined Ima at the Austin Sanitarium
for a time.

When Tom was well enough, Will took both boys east to outfit them in school clothes and to enroll Mike in the preparatory school in Annapolis. Will reported to Ima from Baltimore:

Hotel Joyce
European Plan
 Dear Sis:
    Tom & I saw Mike off at 6:25 this evening for Ann[apolis], where I yesterday placed him under the care of Prof. Wilmer whom I believe to be the most competent instructor there. We, Tom, Mike & I spent the day buying. I have <u>rigged</u> them out—rain coats, shoes, overshoes, woolen underwear, suit, socks, hats etc. and what a hole the buy made in my pile! But I believe everything is <u>about bought</u>. There is no place suitable for Tom in or about Ann. or Balt.—so far as I can learn. I am going tomorrow to place him (if possible) somewhere in N.J.—to prepare for Princeton & will write—wire when he is <u>located</u>.
    I'll say this much—I think I was more deeply affected when I said "goodbye" to Mike on train awhile ago than either one of the boys.
                                        Yours Affectionately
                                        Will
                                        Address me
                                        Imperial—N.Y.[70]

The "somewhere in N.J." turned out to be the small town of Lawrenceville, near Princeton. Tom would enroll at the Lawrenceville School, a venerable preparatory school founded in 1810. Ima was still in Austin, nursing her knee injury. Tom sent a note to her from Lawrenceville on his school stationery:

                                        Griswold House
                                        Lawrenceville, N.J.
September 29, 1903

Dear Sister:—
I am now in school and settled I am.
I can't write much only to let you know I am contented and well.
Affectionately
Your wee brother
Tom H.[71]

On October 9, Mike wrote to Ima from Annapolis:

Dear Sister:—

I have written you two letters but have not mailed them. You have certainly done four times your share. I am not sick but well.

I have been boating three times since I've been here. The first time I nearly got my neck broke because I did not know how to dodge the sheets.

Annapolis is a very old city there are houses here that are a hundred years old. I mean large stone houses.

I went down to the academy [the U.S. Naval Academy] every day to see boys drill for the first few days I was here. And afterwards found out that I was "spotted." I guess you know what that means. I don't go so often now. The academy is going to play their first game of Ball next saturday and I am going. I will write you the results of the game. I was on our school team for about a week but decided not to play.

I have a very good room mate. He lives in the North though. I met a very fine Texas boy last week from Galveston. His brother went to the university and played on the base ball team. His name is Cannon. There are five boys from Texas in our school one of them is Judge Hendersons nephew. He lives in Bryan.

I will close hoping your knee is fast getting well and that you don't think too hard of me for not writing sooner.

Your brother,
Mike Hogg[72]

Jim Hogg, occupied with business, did not pay much attention to his sons, but he was never too busy for Ima. To amuse her, he wrote a teasing letter from Houston on October 26. She was still in the sanitarium in Austin, and she was concerned about her favorite horse at "the Varner."

Rice Hotel
Houston, Texas
    Oct. 26, 1903
    Dear Ima:

       I returned from the Varner yesterday evening and expect to go to Beaumont to-night.

       Now don't say hard things when I tell you the truth about Napoleon's condition, for it was to be expected under the circumstances.

You know he was raised in Houston where ticks and mosquitoes were rare and his stall was screened against them. Then again he was given candy and sugar regularly which keep his appetite sharpened as they acted as laxatives on him. And again he was rubbed and curried three times a day. And above all he was given regular exercise and handled gently at all times. After we left the plantation he was denied most of these treatments and refining influences. Therefore it could not be expected that he would be otherwise than a bag of bones by this time. If this were all he of course could be refattened by proper attention. No one supposed that he would take the big-jaw or the spavin in this short time to forever disfigure him. Well, Mr. Reynolds is an excellent farmer and a hard worker, but he has necessarily trusted this fine horse to the care of a negro plow hand who knows but little of fine stock and how to treat them. When I got a glimpse of Nap you can imagine my surprise. Tex, the fine squirrel hunter, was dead; Sport was sick and poor; Don has the mange; and the other dogs looked like they were lost and friendless. The mules and cattle and goats and hogs and fowls, even the geese, and ducks looked fine. As I looked on Nap and thought of you I naturally wondered if your surprise could be as great as mine. He looked so taf eh ylriaf delbbow sa eh deklaw! Indeed he looked renif naht I reve was mih! Now quit writing me backwards!

> Lovingly
> Your Father
> J. S. Hogg[73]

Writing backward was a fad among young people at the turn of the century, and Ima's father was getting back at her for writing to him that way. As the last part of the letter indicates, her favorite horse was in fine fettle. She still had him when she moved to Houston in 1906.

By Christmas, Ima was out of the sanitarium and staying at the Driskill Hotel. While there had been a lavish family Christmas at the Varner the year before, Hogg was apparently unable to finance a country holiday for his children in 1903. As a result of the reckless drilling in the Spindletop boom and a glut on the oil market, crude oil prices had dropped dramatically. *The New York Times* reported that "panicky conditions prevail in the Texas oil markets particularly at Beaumont and Sour Lake."[74]

Ima, Will, and their father may have spent Christmas together in Austin, but Mike and Tom did not come home—possibly because their father could not afford their round-trip train fares. They stayed at school, as the following wistful letters show.

Annapolis, Md.

Dec. 11, 1903

Dear Sister: —

You asked me in your last letter would I like a sweater. I would like one very much You can also stick in a cap size 6 5/8. I got myself a nice black suit last saturday. I would not mind if you would stick in a nice tie or two also for since I begin to think about it mine are all old. It is not long before Christmas and I would like for you to look for a pair of cuff buttons for me.

It is or has been raining and snowing ever since I last wrote you.

I don't need latin to enter the academy [Mike was hoping to enter the U.S. Naval Academy]. I expect to get in in June or April.

There is a Fox terrier here in the house which often comes up to my room. He is in here now grabbing at my pants leg. He is pretty smart but not as much as ours.

Not having any more to say, but that I am feeling fine and hope you all are, I will close.

> Your brother
> Mike[75]

Lawrenceville

Sunday

Jan. 4, 1904

Dear Sis:

We received your box and all which was most welcomed. Snow is nearly two ft. deep now and it is still snowing hard and fast.

I sure did miss the dogs and my gun this Xmas.

I saw a play to-day which made me play girl [give way to tears]. It was Under the Southern Skies it was just simply fine in every respect.

Well as I am about to freez will close. The Thermometor is 15 below zero.

Will close.

> Your Wee Little Brother,
> Tom Hogg
> P.S. Am just 5 ft. 9½ and weigh just 170.[76]

9 Jan 1904

Dear Papa:—

Mike and I enjoyed our Xmas very much. But only we were not at home to enjoy it more. So Mike has decided to go into the Naval Academy.

Well as there is no news, close, lovingly your son

Thomas Hogg[77]

Jim Hogg, always busy with business, had little time for his sons that winter. He wrote a note to Ima January 13:

The New Crosby

Beaumont, Texas

Jan. 13, 1904

Dear Ima:

Yes, I am here yet, with but little accomplished towards closing our trades. I spent Saturday and Sunday at the Varner and found everything there very pleasant. Birdie is in charge and is a fine cook. I hope we will be able to spend a while there in the Spring.

So far I have not heard from Mike except through Tom. He writes that Mike has concluded to go into the Naval Academy. Well, this is distressing to me, but it may be best. At all events he has so chosen. I want to get home by Sunday morning, where I hope to see you.

Lovingly,

Your Father[78]

Ima and her brothers kept up their letter writing. They studied diligently, but neither boy did well in school. Mike evidently failed to make the grades to be considered for the U.S. Naval Academy. It was Ima who wrote to console him—and to offer a solution:

January 24, 1904

Dearest "Mickie":

Well, reading between the lines of your letter about Annapolis [the Naval Academy]—I don't think you want any of it. How about it? As far as I'm concerned, I'm glad of it—and I think papa and brother are, too. What do you think of going to Lawrenceville with Tom. There may be no vacancies, so don't get flouried [flurried]. Wouldn't it be dandy?

I finished the copying of that picture you sent. I had nothing to do it in but pencil, am sorry. If you like it, keep it, if not—burn it up.

Yes, I had a grand time in San Antonio, and miss the fun, now. The reception Nellie gave us was one of the prettiest I ever saw. Who told you about it?

At last I walk without crutches, though I limp a good deal at times, and can't walk very far; very little, in fact. You will be surprised when I tell you I danced, while away. And it wasn't any trouble either. Papa was frantic when he heard about it. I really suppose it has put me back some.

Papa went to Houston Thursday night again; and won't be back for some time. So Brother and I are bunking together [at the Driskill]. I have a nice large room with my piano,—fixed so we use it as a sitting room; Brother and Papa have a room connecting. And with a large bath we are very comfortable. Write often & long letters all about yourself. Do you need anything?

Lovingly your Sis, Imie[79]

At age nineteen, Mike Hogg was struggling with his preparatory school courses. As he wrote to Ima on January 21, "I have cut out skating and every other thing and gone to 'boning' [studying] right. I put in six hours outside of school. I don't reely apply myself all that time but I stay up and try to do so. Arithmetic is what gets me. I can do the mechanical part but not problems."[80] Although he did his best, he obviously did not make the grades he needed to enter the Naval Academy.

Mike left the preparatory school in Annapolis in midwinter and joined Tom at the Lawrenceville School, as Ima had suggested. He wrote to his sister in February:

Lawrenceville, N.J.
Feb. 21, 1904

Dear Sister:—

I am at last in Lawrenceville. I got a second letter from brother and the next day I put out for here. Tom & I have rooms together. I am in the third form [roughly equivalent to tenth grade] in everything except Latin & French. I am not far from the bottom in either of these. I certainly left some fine fellows and good friends at Annap.

Snow is about five inches deep.

Princeton and Lawrenceville had a gymnasium contest here last wednesday. It was very fine. You have to go out for some athletic sport here and I think I shall take baseball. Tom is going to take golf. We have bowling alleys here and I bowl once in a while.

You have never sent me that picture that you promised. We need
all we can lay hands on.

I will close hoping you are all well.

Your brother

Mike Hogg[81]

Tom did poorly in his studies at Lawrenceville. Will wrote to him
around mid-term:

March 8th 1904

My dear Tom:

There is a delinquency report received today showing that you
are somewhat behind in your English class. Father has not seen it nor
will he hear of it unless you fail to make up the delinquency. If he
knew it, he probably would suggest that you be assigned to a nearby
kindergarten school.

Now, in the name of the folks at home, I ask you to put your head
to your studies more than you have lately. Why don't you quit the
playing, booby bunch and stay in doors with your books a little of
the time? We don't want any more tutoring, extra tutoring, for you;
if you can't hold up your end of the bargain, say so. The extra tutoring heretofore may have been excusable because your studies were
too advanced but in the present instance, your backwardness is due
to pure negligence on your part. I am writing to Dr. McPherson to
the effect that if you don't come up to the mark with your studies to
degrade you, to put you back to the bottom and then out of school,
if you can't stay at the bottom.

We are glad that you and Mike are rooming side by side. No
doubt you have pleasant and beautiful rooms and you should be
grateful enough to study and make the most of your advantages.
Both of you write oftener than you have been doing. Mike especially
is trifling in this respect.

With much love and best wishes, I am,

Yours affectionately,

Brother Will[82]

It is doubtful that the recipient of this letter felt "much love"
for "Brother Will." Will was trying to do his duty as eldest brother
because his father had little time to be concerned with anything but
business.

On March 17, 1904, Jim Hogg wrote to William Davis, who was
now an honorary consul in Guadalajara, Mexico:

I have intended for some time to write you a newsy family letter, but have not felt much in the humor to do so for various reasons: Most of the past winter I have been engaged in South Texas trying to "round up" my oil interests and get rid of some lawsuits there. I have just closed and won one troublesome suit after several weeks of tedious trial. Others are ahead but I am confident of winning them also. . . . So far I have not been able to sell out, nor quit entirely. I was once told that when a man entered the oil business he never got out until he died out. I am going to be an exception to the rule. The children are all well. Ima at last walks about as well as she ever did without limping. Will is filling out to be a good shape. Mike and Tom are together at Lawrenceville, N.J. at school and I understand are getting along very well.

Two days later J. S. Hogg finally wrote to the boys, telling them that he had two new thoroughbred hounds at Varner, and that "we may expect to have a good pack of them when we hunt down there next winter. . . . I should be glad for you to write me a long interesting letter, but I guess that you are too busy studying your lessons and keeping up with the girls to spare the time for a material exercise of writing letters to the 'old man.'"[83]

The boys did not write often, and their father and sister and older brother scolded them. Mike tried to explain:

May 1, 1904

Dear Sister:

I think you have considerable room to make a kick but brother and father have still more. The fact is there is nothing to write. I wrote a letter to Vivian on the seventeenth but did not get it off.

We are having fine weather up here now and the grass is beginning to turn green, but there is no sign of a leaf on the trees the spring is unusually late this year. We had snow about a week ago.

How is your knee? You never mention it. How is Nap [Ima's horse, Napoleon] and everything and everybody. We would like to have a picture of Nap.

I received letters from friends at Annapolis saying they had passed the exams. School turns out June 14, 04. Lawrence came second in the Penn. Relay races held the other day, and third in Princeton Relay.

Our house team has won five games and lost one. We played ball in the snow the other day. I am going out for the house broad jump.

I have missed so much of this year that I feel simply rotten. I missed about two weeks after I came here on account of my eyes, having pink eye.

I guess father is in Beaumont he usually is.

I will close hoping to hear from you all soon. Brother has not written but one letter since I dont know when.

Your brother

Mike Hogg

P.S.

Tell brother I say send me a written note saying that I can get a suit of clothes. I cannot get one without.[84]

May 10, 1904

Dear Sister:—

Your letter was received to-day. You might as well come on up and be here for Commencement as it will be very nice. Commencement begins about June the 9th or 10th. Be sure and come, but first let me know when or near the date you propose to leave home so I can know just about the time when you come.

As to clothes neither of us have any at all. I am wearring the same clothes as I was before Xmas. Mike is doing the same thing.

Mike and I would be ever so glad to have you come as soon as you can.

I must close. [Tell] All the girls hello for me. As ever, your wee brother

Tom H.[85]

To cheer her brothers, Ima wrote of plans for their summer vacation in New England. And she would come to Lawrenceville for commencement, though neither of the boys was graduating.

At last, J. S. Hogg found time to write a long letter to Mike:

June 3rd, 1904

Dear Mike:

Ima told me last night that I am lazy and you know she is a girl of very fine judgment. Doubtless, you will agree with her for I have written to you so seldom that this is proof evident of her accusation. At no time has my solicitude for or appreciation of either you or Tom in the slightest degree diminished. But as I grow older, with the cares of life daily multiplying, letter writing becomes more burdensome. In my youth I wrote often with much fervor and interest. Should you count letters with me and reply only to those I write to you, our correspondence necessarily would grow lighter year by year until after a while the "old man" would seldom, indeed, hear from his son.

I am trying to shift some of the cares of life to Will and Ima. They take them up honorably and perform them well. Within a few years I hope that you and Tom will be able also to relieve me. Ima will soon join you at Lawrenceville to arrange for suitable quarters through the summer, where I hope that you will be comfortable and happy. Of course, this arrangement will be made at considerable expense with the hope that in all respects you and Tom will be mutually benefited by it, mentally, morally, and physically. I should be glad for you and Tom to take up some special course so that during vacation you may have one or two lessons every day. For instance, you might practice in penmanship and study arithmetic or Latin. In this way you could vastly improve and at the same time enjoy all of the frivolities known to youthful pleasures.

Recently Ima and I spent a month on the plantation. Crops are good down there this year and Mr. Reynolds is making an excellent manager. We have many young calves and pigs and fowls. Everything is very pleasant. The dogs are in good condition, but as you probably know, Tex and Sport died. Bob and Jack are both good hunters and are now mates. Sam is grown and very much like old Sport. Josephine has five fine puppies about three weeks old. We have two new fox terriers, Fino and Margaret; so that with old Grant and Don as the leaders, we are well supplied on the plantation with dogs. Mr. Hart has given me a pup by his famous dog Fox, the son of old Sport, and I shall name him Sport and have him ready for you and Tom when you return from school. Now, this is about all the <u>dog</u> news I can give you.

Now, my son, this should be your red letter year—I mean by that, the one in which you should have spent a part of your vacation at least in laying the foundation of your education which you are now striving for. I am glad indeed that you and Tom have such excellent characters and that you are so fond of each other. People generally watch the conduct of brothers towards each other. When they find them congenial and agreeable they point back to their good raising and agree that they have good stock in them. If they snarl and quarrel or show a disposition to separate, they at once regard them as of bad raising and of no stock. I am proud that you boys get along so well together and are going hand in hand in moulding your characters for substantial manhood now close upon you. You must not fail to look after every want and give every courteous attention to your sister. She is a great girl and her devotion to you boys is simply sublime and admirable in all respects. Now, if you do not forget, while having the good time up East, I should feel grateful for an occasional letter from you. Write at least once a week and tell me what Sunday school you attend and the names of your acquaintances together with a description of the country where you sojourn for the season.[86]

The season's "sojourn" was in South Egremont, a small town in western Massachusetts. Ima and the boys took rooms at the Larkhurst, a resort hotel in the rolling hills of Berkshire County. Their father was planning to spend the summer at Varner.

Jim Hogg's boys might disappoint him, but his daughter could do no wrong: At the beginning of the summer he wrote her a letter of paternal praise: "Your splendid character, your sweet disposition, your charming manners, your fidelity to your younger brothers added to your thoughtfulness of me at all times on all appropriate occasions have so impressed me that it is but natural for me to make you second to no human being. . . . Most girls would have preferred some fashionable watering place where they could smile on other girls' brothers, to a quiet, substantial Summer home surrounded by refinement, where they are compelled to submit to the frowns (now and then) of their own young brothers."[87]

The two Hogg brothers arrived at South Egremont before their sister, and Mike wrote a dutiful description of it to his father:

> South Egremont, Mass.
> June 20 1904

Dear Father:

Tom and I arrived here last thursday morning. This is certainly a great place. We have been bothered more from cold than heat. It is something like Colorado. We are way up in the hills. I played some golf yesterday and walked around the Hills a bit. There is a brook about fifty yards behind the house full of fine trout and perch.

The last time I weighed I weighed one hundred and forty six pounds. Tom weighed 170 and Sister 135. We are both a great deal taller than she.

Miss Houston [one of Ima's New York friends] came yesterday and we expect Sister tomorrow or next day.

I will close hoping you and brother are both well and not suffering from the heat.

Your Son

Mike.[88]

Ima arrived, and reported to her father on June 24:

Dearest Papa:

Only one letter from you, and none from brother. We are almost penniless, too. Mike and Tom have been here nearly two weeks, so their board ought to be paid right off.

South Egremont is beautiful—but since the truth must be told—unexpectedly inconvenient. For instance my knee hurt me—there was but one way of getting to Barrington to find out about X-ray—except in a stable buggy. We are four miles you see. Mike and Tom are very much pleased, notably Thomas, who has an automobile friend, and all the luxuries of life. I am writing you all this in case you may see what I am driving at: Napoleon. What do you think of sending him up?—providing the expense isn't too great. He can be put in the stable on the place. Tom says he & Mike will take care of him.

I have great hopes of Tom. He is courting two girls—sisters—to the extent of his prodigious energy. They play golf and go to church together. We simply see nothing of him. Mike loves to sit about and gas and read with us on the gallery—He is a confirmed old maid—Which reminds me that Betty Greene and I dragged out of him that he is president of his house in Lawrenceville, and captain of his house ball team. Don't be alarmed about this last intelligence—it is only base-ball. Mike isn't such an unsociable youngster after all I suppose.

The kids and all of us send love with many kisses which I hope may blow you a gentle cooling breeze for I know you must be melting—Why not come up? Oh! Please do! And write soon to

Your loving daughter

Ima[89]

She did not write much to Will. In late June, he wrote to his father that he had had "one postal card from sister and not a line from the boys." While Ima and his brothers amused themselves at a New England resort and his father played at being a farmer at Varner, Will was in Austin, living in a rented room above the First National Bank and laboring dutifully at the law firm of Hogg, Robertson & Hogg, two blocks away. Will did his best to keep the family members in touch with each other, and to look after the patriarch. He worried about his father's health in the summer heat at Varner: "Aside from drinking the artesian water, if you will not let the mosquitoes bite you, and if you will not eat quite so much as customary, I am sure you are as safe there as anywhere. But you must watch out for the mosquitoes; there is but one opinion concerning them as vehicles of malarial infection."[90]

Will tried to look after his sister, too. He wrote to his father, "I expect sister wants a little more of a stir socially, so I wrote her to inquire for rates where Miss Day [her New York friend] is going and if the charge is not above her limit for board and lodging, she might take the boys up there later in the season. You received the only letter I have had from her. She had a nice time at the Holyoke house party . . . . Writing her yesterday I enclosed some question blanks for her and the boys to fill out for your and my information and I asked her to send some kodak views of the boys so that I might take them with me to you."[91]

Will and his father had not seen Mike and Tom since September 1903—nearly a year ago. When Will wrote to Ima, he also sent her the money to pay for the New England vacation through the month of August.

At the end of June, J. S. Hogg wrote a long letter to Tom at South Egremont.

The Varner

Columbia, Texas

June 30, 1904

Dear Tom:

For two months (excepting one week spent at Austin) I have been here. Ima spent one month of this time with me. . . . Since my last return, the day she left for Lawrenceville, I have been most of the time solitary—alone—in this big house—at night. During the day I am with the "hands," more or less, and thus pass the time observing them. And also, I am kept amused by the antics and sport-making of the nine little fox terriers. They are great company to me—in the absence of my children. While I am writing Tex and Fox are fighting at the young coon in the cage at the back door. You understand we have four of old Sport's grand pups through Fox, Mr. Hart's famous dog, the son of Sport. Mr. Hart gave me one and I bought the other three. They are about the size of grown house-cats and are very smart and great hunters now. I do not let them go out of the yard, but I have Bob to drag rats when we catch them, about over the yard and hide them. Then I put these pups on the trail and they soon trace them up. Of all the jumping and barking they make the worst I ever heard. One of these little fellows is as much like Old Sport in his marks, shape, spots and ways as it is possible for one dog to be like another.

I have named them Sporty, Fox, Tex and Mary.—The other five are from Josephine by Bob, and are named Rant, Rover, Bravo, Sam and Betsy. They are puny, small but nicely marked pups. Life is made a hard one to them when the four larger ones get after them in play. Like big boys in annoying small ones, these large pups tantalize and worry these little ones,—at times very much to my amusement. Now added to this gang of young dogs we have two hounds—Old Grant and Joe a new one—and Bob, Jack, Fino, Josephine and Margurette, besides Ima's "bird dog," Don Alphonso Aurelius Miles! Several weeks ago Margurette got both her forelegs cut off except the tendons and arteries just about the first joint. So we put her in the hospital and dressed her legs by splintering, bandaging and applying antiseptics to them; and we swung her in the air, so her feet could not touch the ground. Thus we kept her until day before yesterday, when we took off the dressing and let down. Now she lies on her bed in decidedly better condition. In fact she is nearly well. When she was first cut down by the mowing machine the suggestion was made to kill the poor thing to put her out of misery. "No!" said I. "Life is dear to the little animal and she shall have a chance for it." All are glad now that she was spared.

We have a lot of nice calves and our cattle are doing well. Patsy O' has a nice male colt. Somehow he looks very much like Napoleon. Most every one suspicions that it is kin to this great horse. Can you or Mike give any light on the subject?

We have a fine corn crop and everything looks excellent. Pumpkins, peas, potatoes, goobers, cushaws and melons and canteloupes in bountiful quantities. So with all my lonesomeness, without my children, I am having a pretty fair time for an "Old Man"!

Now what else do you want me to write about? Yes! The horses! Well, Hannibal waits for you and Caesar is looking for Mike; while I use Napoleon and Albarac. By the time you and Mike get back I hope to have some new horses for you. And then we'll take a great hunt, won't we?

From what I can hear you and Mike are nice, upright, honorable young gentlemen a credit to our name. Of this I am very proud. It always occurred to me that it was easier in the long run for boys to grow up to be respectable than to become reprobates. So nothing gratifies me more than to know that up to this date there has never been a "black sheep" bearing our name.

Be good to Ima and Mike and to Miss Houston. Write to me the news if you have time. Tell about the country, the people, the pleasures you have, the lessons you take, the reading you do, and how Ima and Mike pass the time. Give me an old-time gossipy letter. And tell me (in confidence if you please) if you have a sweetheart now and how you are getting along with her. And how about Mike's? Is he in love with the widow yet? And do not tell about Ima's. She will do this herself.

Lovingly, Your Father

J. S. Hogg[92]

As for Ima's romantic attachments in the summer of 1904 (and how much she told her father about them), there were at least two young men who wrote ardent letters to her: a Harry Taylor whom she had probably met at the Holyoke house party mentioned earlier, and a young Austin attorney named Wilbur P. Allen. He had a law office at 806 Congress Avenue, as did Hogg, Robertson & Hogg. Allen had been wooing Ima for the past year. He visited her in New York and complained that she gave him "about ten minutes of interrupted talk for my two thousand miles." She apparently kept him at a distance, and he called her "my dear, incorrigible, impossible friend." He called her "my pedestal lady," and wrote, "I want to see you Miss Ima— I've got to see you—. I want to know if I may come to see you then wherever you are."[93]

Meanwhile, Mike and Ima wrote to their father from South Egremont.

July 4, 1904

Dear Papa:—

Tom received your letter today. This being the fourth everybody up here are shooting fire crackers. Tom and I are not participating. We had a golf tournament here today. I came out fourth I came second in one we had last Saturday. I have not played the game over ten times in my life. I am not going crazy over it.

I have just finished the Marble Faun by Scott and am now begin-

ning Waverly by the same author. I am studying algebra for next
year.

Sister got a letter from brother in which he asked every possible
question about Tom and myself. We sent him twelve pictures of sister
Tom & myself. They were never taken at the right time and consequently look foolish.

From your description of the dogs they must be great. As for Pat-
seys colt that is between Caesar & Nap. I think Caesar. You know
he is of fine blood himself. I certainly would like to be down on the
farm myself right now although this country up here is very beautiful.

It has been so cool the last few days that we could not sit on the
porch. You can see the vapor come out of your mouth.

There are a great many wood chucks up here. Their holes are
about the right size for a foxterrier to roll into.

I have written you two letters recently and you don't seem to
have received either. You have the advantage over me for you have a
greater source of material. I will close hoping you are well and will
write me or us another long letter.

Your Son

Mike Hogg[94]

Ima wrote to her father from New York on July 5 about her recur-
rence of knee trouble. She had had to leave South Egremont for treatment in New York. "I have used myself too hard of late," she wrote
matter-of-factly, making light of what must have been a painful epi-
sode. She was having treatments by a Dr. Gibney, which consisted of
applying a "red hot iron—on my knee and spinal column . . . I may
have a light brace."[95] She was staying at the residence of her New
York friend Miss Day at 18 East Fortieth Street. The doctor ordered
Ima to walk as much as she could.

On July 9, the day before her twenty-second birthday, Ima wrote
ruefully to her father that she had spent her last birthday "in bed" on
account of her knee and a year later was "having the same old knee
treated." But she consoled herself by asking for a birthday present: on
one of her walks she had seen a "magnificent necklace" of gold and
opals for eighty dollars in an antique shop. Her father promptly sent
her a check for eighty dollars. On July 10, her birthday, she sent him
a telegram: "All right walked two miles yesterday love to all."[96]

Two days later she went back to South Egremont. Five days after
that, Ima wrote to her father.

July 17, 1904

Dearest Papa:

Today I got a letter from Cousin Jim [McDugald] in which he delicately informs me that he thoughtfully broke the news about my knee to you by telegram! I am certainly relieved to find out who it is that put you into such a state of mind. I knew you couldn't have gotten it from me, for any such thing as a bad set back was far from the truth, so I couldn't have harrowed you. By this time you know I am back in South Egremont on both legs. It will probably please you to know that I have been frantically endeavoring to learn tennis-playing all this afternoon. I can "serve" the balls and hit a few which come my way, but as the boys say, I'm not quite a "shark" yet.—Mike and Tom really are wonderful when it comes to energy and endurance. If nothing else had been done for them by the Lawrenceville School a lot of loginess and weakness has been taken out of them. Tom, this afternoon, rode on a bicycle ten miles and walked to the top of the highest mountain—between dinner and supper! To-night he is as spry and restless as ever. On Saturday, Mike played tennis after breakfast until late and finished the morning with golf, spending the entire afternoon pitching ball for a bum country team. And he was then in for taking Betty and me to one of the hotel dances, down the road.

By the way, Mike is coming around socially until when you see him he may be the beau of the family. Betty has taught him to waltz a little, and at the dance Saturday, he ended his eventful day by bravely launching himself forth as a <u>dancer</u>. He was trembling all over, conscious of every eye in the room being turned on his efforts, and was altogether the most delighted kid and excited I ever saw. He won't as yet dance with any one but Betty and me. You may think this sounds like nothing but athletics—most hated word with you—but we are at the same time endeavoring to cultivate and improve our minds.

Tonight we are afraid to go to bed. Last night we had a horrible storm which we have not gotten over yet. The loudest crash I ever heard came with a bolt of lightning and struck a tree in the yard and as Betty says, everybody in the house thought from the sound that it had come and sat down by their own beds. We find ourselves today—quite the most important household in Egremont—for having had some private excitement. But excuse me please from neighborly interest—I prefer uneventful retirement, and freedom from any such sensational notoriety. They can have our thunder bolts if they will.—It's awfully late, and I must close. Be good and write me soon. Finances are ebbing with breathless speed.

Ever Lovingly,
Ima[97]

This letter from her father must have crossed Ima's in the mail:

July 18, 1904

Dear Ima, Mike and Tom:

No, my children, I shall not take you away from your pleasant environments! You shall stay there until Fall. No man ever had a more dutiful, decent, loving and lovable set of children than I have! Anything I can do to contribute to your education and comfort shall be cheerfully done. When the boys quit school then they will support me, and my "turn" will come—Say, by the way I never had a vacation from the time I was about fourteen until I was over thirty years old! And then I "laid off" to go to the World's fair at N.O. [New Orleans]. We left Ima at her Grand Pa's and took Will with us. He was too big to stay with us so struck out after we got there, by himself. He got lost! We found him about mid-night at the Boat Landing waiting our arrival. He had walked back to the City seven Miles!

Am well and comfortable. No news.
Lovingly, Your Father
J. S. Hogg[98]

In late July, there was more news from Varner and its master:

July 27, 1904

Dear Ima, Mike and Tom:

We tested the young fox terriers the other day in a coon-fight. The coon, trapped the day before, was nearly grown—quite as large as the largest one of the puppies. On taking the nine little fellows in the corn crib we turned his coon-ship amongst them. Such a scampering! Such a scene! Six out of the nine canines hid out between the legs of the standing men. Three of them—Fox, Tex and Sam (Sam is of the youngest set, about the size of a grown rat) made a great fuss, barking and snapping at the varmint. Fox, however, took hold at once made no noise, and fought the coon until he killed it! Then and not until then did the pack (except Sport and Mary) take hold and vigorously fight—the dead animal. Fox took hold and held on and only "changed holds" as he gained decided advantage by it. It was a most remarkable exhibition of courage, tact, and intelligence displayed by this three-month-old dog. From the looks of that coon however it occurred to me that the eight other little dogs showed very great sense in not taking hold of it. Fox now struts around over his victory as if he is ready to whip a bear. So, you see, I am having some sport while my children are having fun playing <u>tennis, golf, hide-and-seek</u> and <u>nursing knees</u> in the cool regions of great old Massachusetts.

I will soon be through with my vacation here, and then regretfully I must "get out." My intention now is to go to Houston next Sunday the 31st and remain there four or five days; thence to Beaumont, Austin and elsewhere about over the State. Write to me care the Rice Hotel.

My dutiful Son William, the patriarch of the family, ever obliging and thoughtful, sent me the Kodak pictures of yourselves. They are very good and I am very much pleased with them. . . .

Lovingly, Your Father,
J. S. Hogg[99]

Will worried about the family's finances and his younger brothers' education. On July 29, he wrote his father at Varner. "We must stir around and make some money soon, so please don't let politics absorb your time and attention. I want the boys to have the best advantages and it takes more money than anything else. . . . Please write me when you leave Columbia."[100]

The next day Will wrote to Grandfather Stinson:

July 30, 1904

My dear Grandfather:

[Portion omitted from typescript.]

Sister and the boys are in South Egremont, Massachusetts, for the summer. The boys have grown quite a good deal and show many signs of improvement. I am sending you by this mail some kodak pictures which Sister took the other day. I have not seen the boys for a year and so I asked Sister to send them to me that I might see what they looked like. Tom weighs less than he did in the winter but is about 5:10½ tall. Mike weighs 146 and is 5:9! Think of that for Mike. Sister is in fine health and is quite pretty at times. She has a beautiful way about her except she seems to be too lazy to write to her brother and father and grandfather. I am afraid she is a little bit spoiled.

We have planned to give the boys the best advantages of colle-
giate education, if they want it. They are both backward somewhat
in their books but are waking up. Soon enough.

Father is at his farm in Brazoria County: Columbia, Texas, is his
address. He has been there almost continuously for three months.

With much love and many kisses to you all, I am,

> Your affectionate Son[sic],
> Will C. Hogg[101]

On August 2, Will wrote to the headmaster at Lawrenceville School
to keep Mike's and Tom's expenses to a minimum in the coming term.
He was especially concerned about Tom's spending habits. Tom was
to have fifty cents a week for pocket money—and only that. "Cut
off all purchases by Tom . . . that are not absolutely necessary to his
welfare."[102]

But vacation time was not yet ended, and summer frolics at
Larkhurst continued. So did the letters.

> August 9, 1904

Dear Ima:

I am glad to have your undated, unpaged, interesting letter, telling me of Mike's debut into social circles. He must inherit this fondness for the fair sex from me, for I always loved the girls—even now.
Now do not encourage him too much on this line, for he may grow
serious. Then the fun will be over. Let both the boys bear in mind
that the "Old Man" is willing for them to marry when they get old
enough and able to support a wife.

Will and I are here together, getting along nicely. He is very popular and is growing daily in more ways than one. Since the boys have
gone so completely into society he and I have despaired of hearing
from them except in very short letters. Vivian has just telephoned me
telling of her great honeymoon &c.* She's going to housekeeping
soon. No news. Give love to the boys. Affectionately,

> Your Father,
> J. S. Hogg[103]

On the same day, Ima sat down to write to her father:

---

* Ima's friend Vivian Breziger had married Will Caswell that summer.

August 9, '04

Dearest Papa

This morning we woke up to find it raining. We can't go on a picnic we had planned to Lake Bull. Yesterday it was quite cold, so this morning feels like a winter's day.

I am getting awfully worried about myself. No amount of dieting seems to keep me from gaining flesh, and as it is I have gained twelve pounds since I left home! I hated to tell you, but am afraid it is better broken to you slowly—the shock won't be so great when you see me! Really I'm at the uncomfortable stage.

Everybody is preparing for a comfy time before the fire. Mike had settled himself before the window for reading but Tom and the other kids of the same age took him off bodily to the hotel to "raise a rough house" with some of the girls from there. It is too good a day to sew, so Betty and I are hard at it. There's only one man, and he's marching up and down like a caged lion. . . .[104]

Ima, like most young women, tried to watch her weight. Mike had written to his father earlier in the summer that "Sister weighs 138 and is now dieting."[105] A photograph of Ima and her brothers at South Egremont suggests that she was exaggerating her plumpness.

Meanwhile, the former governor, who could never stay away from politics for long, was ending his summer idyll at Varner to support the gubernatorial ambitions of his good friend Tom Campbell.[106] (Campbell had lost to the conservative Democrat S. T. Lanham in 1902, would lose to Lanham again in 1904, and at last would be elected in 1906.) At the state Democratic convention in August, Hogg praised the Republican President Theodore Roosevelt's role in securing American control of the Panama Canal. This was a shocking speech for a lifelong Democrat to make, as Ima wrote in her next letter:

South Egremont, Mass.

Tuesday Aug. 16—'04.

Dearest Papa:

Well, I think your bombshell of a speech together with the papers, must have laid you out—How did you happen to do it—and do you feel just a little sorry about it? I read the speech with a good deal of pleasure, for it certainly "be" my sentiments though, they "do be" pretty skittish for a democrat to "out with."

Mike and Tom had no little fun from your letter about their society stunts. By the way, they are off on a hay ride. The young lady who is giving it seems to be a particular friend of Mike's. They went horse-back riding together this morning. Her family live in Sheffield, near here,—and have a great fine place with an ideal farm, which would do your farmer's soul good to see.—Yesterday our whole house went tallyhoing through a new part of the country to me. Oh! the magnificent country places these people do have, with every modern convenience you can imagine.—To-morrow we go on the Lake for a picnic—if it doesn't rain. We planned the same picnic last week, but it rained. I am afraid we will be served the same kind of bad day to-morrow as it looks so much like it.

Write soon, now, and I will forgive you for being bad about neglecting us for the speech. Keep cool above all things—

With love to you and Brother from all,

Ever Your Loving

Imie—[107]

Jim Hogg was never satiated with one taste of politics, and he soon went off again in search of more. It was, after all, an election year in both state and national contests. But his friend and hunting companion William Jennings Bryan did not get the Democratic Party's nomination. That went to a New York judge, Alton B. Parker. Despite his political forays in the East, Jim Hogg did not visit his three children in Massachusetts, and Ima chided him for it.

Aug. 27 '04.

Dearest Papa:

I know you have been wondering what reason I have for not writing—It is wholly because we saw in the papers where you were on your way to Eastern points, and we have been in elated state of expectancy—Almost any day, we would have not been surprised to see you walk in on us! Now, aren't you ashamed of disappointing us thusly!!

Today is winter cold and blowing such a hurricane it is almost death to venture out. Still the sun shines and everything is gloriously green. There are signs of autumn in some of the brilliant colored trees, and I am picturing wonderful days nearing us. Just to think how soon the kids are off to school! You can't imagine how much I've enjoyed having them this way. I only wish you did, too.

Tom is up stairs now, digging at Latin. Mike doesn't seem to care about anything but reading—We are all well and since the mail is soon to go, and I wish this to get to you soon, I will close with stacks of love from

Your Loving Daughter
Ima[108]

In September Aunt Fannie, now living with her son William and his family in Guadalajara, wrote to Ima:

Guadalajara, Mexico
Sept. 15, 1904

Dear Ima:

Good morning—or Buenas dias—as the "yellow peril" say. Yes, I got eased up some time after by the letter of enlightenment you speak of. Had it not come when I did I expect I should have written again. That <u>would</u> have been too bad of me. Well, I'm built that way, and we may not change the leopard's spots, or paint more beautifully the lily, or add tints to the rainbow. See? Poor me!

I would wait an answer to any other letter, but really want to answer your questions.

Your "occupation" is commendable. Yes, boys at their age should have every refining influence folded about them. . . . Hold on to their confidence but steer them over such breakers as best you may. Your head is level, you can find the way. I wouldn't have one of those boys made fools of, and they are so young they might be snapped up by wily, designing, bold girls and never realize the difference until <u>too late</u>, and then have the "might-have-been" ground into their very souls for life—and by girls not so young either, perhaps older, most often older. When they are older men—they will laugh jeeringly at "flip" girls. Write and let me know how the wind blows. Don't get lazy. Will you remain with the boys or do you go home? We've got letters mixed kinder, haven't we?

Aunt

Pearl and Hun are tramping the Exposition grounds [at the 1904 World's Fair in St. Louis, Missouri] about now. Hun has to be back by the 18th to enter school. We don't know what Pearl means to do. The bit's in her mouth. Will you return by way of the St. Louis Exposition? Or do you not mean to go?[109]

Ima and her father did go, but there is nothing about their trip in the family letters. Years later she remarked in an interview that "Father and I went to St Louis for the World's Fair."[110]

Later in September the boys were back at Lawrenceville, and Ima was back in Austin. She left at least one young man in Massachusetts very distraught at her departure. Harry Taylor wrote to her, "If you go back to Austin & I never see you again . . . it will be horrid. Do you care?"[111]

Will made a trip to St. Louis for the exposition, and he was also investigating a position with the St. Louis Mercantile Bank and Trust Company. When he returned to Texas in November, he went first to San Antonio, perhaps to consult with friends there about his St. Louis prospects. His father was not pleased, and sent him a terse telegram from Austin: "Would like for you to come home."[112]

Presumably Will obliged, but by early December he would leave again for St. Louis. He was about to become an attorney for the St. Louis Mercantile Bank and Trust Company, founded in 1850, the largest bank in the fourth largest city in the United States.

For Mike and Tom, the golden summer in South Egremont was a long way from the bleak winter in Lawrenceville. By December, both boys wanted to come home to Texas for Christmas. They had not spent Christmas at home since 1902. Tom wrote a gloomy letter to his sister:

Dec. 8, 1904

My dear Sister:—

Yours was received yesterday.

It is very cold up here and there is some snow on the ground.

For about three or four weeks, I have had a very bad cold and still have it as bad as ever.

This fooling doctor up here could not cure a bruised finger.

Ask Baylor if he can tell me of a sure cold killer.

Now as for what I wish to Xmas, is a hard matter to discuss. As you would naturly expect, I want to come home Xmas. If it is only for about ten days. We could get off before the 21st at any rate, if not later.

If we should stay out here and not come, I am strictly opposed to staying any where near this place. If we come home Xmas I would not care what plans were made then, just so we were at home. It would be a great deal easier to think that thru than it is now.

But if we stay out here in the East, don't make us stay here at school. For it is bad enough being out here so long any how, besides not coming home Xmas or any other time. If we can possibly come home we surely want to; just so it's Texas. What had you been thinking of? If we should come would it be to the ranch or to Austin, ranch for "me." Just so it is home is all I care.

Please give this thing attention at once. Consult Papa and make up your mind as to what course you will take. It is only a short time and delay in this might put us in the same fix as last year. . . .

Well, I must close. Love to all, lovingly,

Your brother
Tom[113]

Tom wrote to Ima again on December 13:

My dear Sister:—

Well what are we going to do Xmas is still the unanswered question.

The snow is about a foot deep up here on the level ground.

Examinations begin on Friday.

We are free on Wednesday the 21st.

Sister if it is avoidable please do not have us stay out here at school. All the boys from Texas are coming home Xmas.

We are well and waiting for your answer, which we hope will soon reach us and decide the thing in some way, the best of course.

Write soon and answer with lots of news.

Lovingly, your brother
Thomas Hogg[114]

Her brothers' holiday plans may not have been uppermost on Ima's mind. After a summer dutifully supervising Tom and Mike in Massachusetts, she was now happily socializing in Houston and San Antonio. In Houston on November 23, Thanksgiving eve, she attended a large and festive ball honoring "King Nottoc" (King Cotton) and his queen. In early December she visited her friend Nellie Paschal in San Antonio and returned to Houston on December 15. The *San Antonio Light* reported that Ima was planning a "house party at 'Columbia' commencing on the 22nd."[115]

But the house party at Varner may not have taken place. As the December days passed, Tom's "very bad cold" turned into pneumonia, and Ima and her father rushed to Tom's bedside. There, as Ima wrote later, "Father took charge with the nurse to follow orders. This treatment was the same as he used when mother had pneumonia each winter while living in the bleak Executive Mansion.—Hot poultices were constantly applied to chest back and sides. All parts were greased with lard & to prevent burning, poultices were made of

cornmeal saturated with kerosene and turpentine put in soft cotton
bags. He sat up all night doing the work, giving orders to the assistant
nurse."[116] That was how the holidays passed in Lawrenceville.

Tom responded quickly to the treatment, and his father left for
New York to attend to business matters. Ima stayed with Tom and
Mike in Lawrenceville. Her father wrote to her from the Waldorf-
Astoria on New Year's Day, "Please assure Tom that he shall return
to Texas with us."[117]

A few days later Ima and a convalescent Tom and their father took
the train to visit Will in St. Louis. Mike stayed behind in Lawrenceville, where a new term's classes were about to begin.[118]

Will, newly settled in St. Louis, had left family concerns behind. In
an undated letter early in 1905, he wrote to Mike in Lawrenceville:
"Keep Father's memory well jogged concerning the many necessities
of your course up there. For the past few years he has left everything
of that kind absolutely to me and now that I am living elsewhere,
and cut away from the family so to speak, he is very negligent in that
respect."[119]

Will was perhaps a bit resentful of having had to shoulder many
family responsibilities, and he was clearly not close to his father. Ima
recalled that when Will came to Austin for a visit after moving to
St. Louis, "Father met him at the door with the customary salute ['a
warm kiss on the cheek'], but Brother Will seemed to shy away as if
he resisted . . . . Father told him he would never be too old to have a
kiss from his Father."[120]

By mid-January Ima and Tom returned to Austin, and their father
went to Houston. He was moving his law practice there, in partnership with two Houston attorneys. He wrote to Ima from the Rice
Hotel, where he boarded: "Have clothes made while you are in
Austin. My luck seems to be with me this year, and before it changes
I want you to fix up nicely—elegantly." He cautioned her to "Keep
Tom under good control, and be with him as much as possible. You
may look for Napoleon next week—as soon as he can get there. Take
rides with Tom often. Get him straight in the back, and make him
know we all love him."[121]

Ima wrote to her father soon after she and Tom arrived in Austin.
They were staying at Burleson House, at 702 Lavaca, a boardinghouse run by Mrs. Mary Dial, much like a private residence.[122]

> Dearest Papa:—
> I am sorry I haven't written you before this. The first day we were

here it was pouring rain, but yesterday morning the sun came up like the old Austin sun. This morning is grand. I am sorry I wasn't sweet about the Austin resort but I am quite sure it is the place for Tom.

He is behaving beautifully, and getting along as well. Mrs. Dial is grand and sees he is tucked in for the night and takes special care of him herself. So, I don't have to nag at him so much myself. Yesterday he was out of doors some in the sun, and today he will be. He is perfectly willing never to go out except on good days and then between the hours of ten in the morning and four in the afternoon. Nobody in the house has much to do—so he has always a way of entertaining himself. Everybody admires Tom's good looks and manners—they tell me so anyway. He has been charming. The girls have been around, of course, and are still the finest ones I ever knew. Cousin Jim [McDugald] is in fine health and spirits.

A good deal of entertaining is going on for Austin—so I shall be going some. Last night went to a dance, this afternoon to receive at a reception and tonight. Next week there will be a good many more receptions besides the Girls' Annual Hop. I wish we had Napoleon.

How are you getting along? Am sorry it is so we can't be together—Tom sends best love to you and to brothers when you see him—as I do with XXXXXXX kisses.

Ever lovingly,
Ima[123]

Besides looking after Tom, Ima was enjoying the festivities that always accompanied the governor's inauguration. Governor Lanham saw to it that her name appeared on many invitation lists.

But in late January a fateful accident took place. On January 26, Jim Hogg, en route by train from Varner to Houston, was involved in a collision. The passenger car in which he was riding rammed into another car, and Hogg was thrown violently to the floor. At first the injuries seemed to be only bruises, and Ima continued her socializing in Austin. She gave a "German" (a ball) on February 3, honoring her visiting San Antonio friends.[124]

Ima's Austin social whirl was halted and the family's life took an unexpected turn two days after Ima's party when she received a telegram that her father was seriously ill in Houston. An abscess had formed at the back of his neck, and he was about to have surgery. "Of course I rushed to him," Ima wrote later.[125]

To reach and treat the abscess, as Hogg later told his physician nephew, William Davis, Houston doctors "had to cut it from five different places in my mouth."[126] These surgical procedures weakened his already strained heart, and Ima became his devoted nurse. He was critically ill and bedridden "for practically eight weeks," as Ima wrote to Mike in Lawrenceville.[127] But by March their father was much improved and able to travel with Ima and Tom to San Antonio for a stay at the Menger Hotel—but not for long.

On March 16, Jim Hogg wrote to Will from the Hill Country resort town of Boerne, near San Antonio:

Reinhardt Ranch
5 ms. from Boerne
March 16, 1905

Dear Will:

On the excuse and for the alleged reason that I "talked too much" at the Menger Ima bundled me up and brought me out here last Monday, without notice or a chance to reform. So I am "in the Mountains" at last as an invalid under rigid surveillance. Tom got a job on [Walter] Schreiner's ranch about 100 ms. North of here and is by this time probably roping cattle—the ambition and joy of his exuberant life. He is a curious boy to me. After we left San Antonio that morning for this place he got acquainted with every cattleman on the train. "Round-ups" soon to come was the theme of their conversations and Tom fell into the fever. He telephones now that he is settled for good and never wants to return. I guess however he will change this tune in due time. Ima is rosy and fine. I am yet very weak but slowly improving. Ima says I have the "hypo." I believe it.

Lovingly your Father
J. S. Hogg[128]

After the stay at the ranch the former governor declared he was strong enough to speak at a banquet honoring President Theodore Roosevelt in Dallas on April 5.[129] He did, but he was not a well man. Years of obesity (all those barrels of lard, all those hams, all those beaten biscuits), in an era when low-fat diets were unheard of, had taken their toll on his heart. It is possible that the "bilious attacks" he had suffered over the years were really small heart attacks.

Aunt Fannie was also failing that spring. In April, William wrote from Mexico that "her memory is growing more uncertain day by day. You can never tell whether she will remember a thing until the next day when you tell her."[130]

On Thursday, April 13, a few days after his Dallas speech, Jim Hogg returned to his desk in Houston for the first time since his January 26 injury. On the following Sunday he reported to Ima, who had gone back to Austin:

April 16, 1905

Dear Ima:

I got here in good condition and started to work next morning, but found I could not "hold out" well. So I took time slowly.—As the church bells chime this bright, cool Sunday morning, as the "humdrum" surging humanity keeps time to passing events, as age stealthily creeps on me to remind me that yesterday is no more and that tomorrow may never come, I think of you—yes, you. My running mate—my Mascot! When do you suppose you will join me without violating outstanding pledges, solemnly made? Everybody most asks me about you—all wanting to know when Miss Ima is coming. Well, now, take your time! If I could have you with me on Sundays I might stand the balance of the week heroically. . . .

Napoleon got here in good condition. While driving him yesterday he attracted great attention.

We have the finest offices in the State and I am very much contented.

With love

Your Pa, J. S. HOGG[131]

One of the first letters Jim Hogg answered when he was able was William Davis's.

He used the letterhead of his new law office in Houston:

Hogg, Watkins & Jones, Lawyers
Rooms 201-2-3-4-5-6-7-8, First National Bank Building.
James S. Hogg, Edward Watkins, Frank C. Jones/W. H. Ward
April 19, 1905.
Dr. W. B. Davis
American Consul
Guadalajara, Mexico

Dear William:—

I was glad to receive your favor of the 14th. It is the only one I have received from you this year, though I may find another yet in my bushel of unanswered mail, which accumulated during my long spell of sickness.

Last Thursday is the first time I have been to my desk since early in January. I got my neck cracked on the railroad on the 26th of January, within about forty miles of this place. The rigors or convulsions followed in quick succession, and in the course of a few days an abscess about the base of my brain or somewhere in my neck set up. From the injury I lost consciousness which continued for something over a month. The torture and misery that I suffered could only be described by some or all of the four doctors who attended me. They could not reach the abscess from the exterior, but finally had to cut it from five different places through my mouth. I am not entirely well, though I am gradually recovering my strength. This explains what would otherwise appear to be negligence in answering the letters which have accumulated. . . .

For the past two years luck seems to have turned against me. Beginning with Ima's affliction, which lasted nearly a year; then came Tom, then Mike [severe measles in Mike's case], so that upon the whole my anxiety of mind and loss of time, as well as expenses, have taken all of the "music" out of me. While these afflictions were on I sustained very heavy losses in many quarters. If I finally recover, as I now believe I will, from the illness which yet afflicts me, I have no fear of the future or of results. The outlook is certainly cheering and cheerful. My children are scattered so that I do not know whether I can ever get them together again.

Will has a fine position with the best prospects of any young man that I know of in St. Louis. He has a fine salary and almost limitless financial backing. He and Ima both stayed with me during my illness here. Of course, Ima is yet my running mate and if it is possible has improved every day. Mike is yet in Lawrenceville, but is not very well on account of a spell of measles which he has not yet recovered from. Tom is out on a cattle ranch seventy miles west of Kerrville. I have moved here and am boarding at the hotel.

I am glad to learn that sister's health continues good and that she is happy in Mexico. I was glad to know that Pearl had married an excellent young man, and I think it would be wise for her to go back to Colorado. I have not seen or heard of Marion lately. The last time I met him at the plantation he had it in his mind to go to the University, which I hope yet he may do.

If at any time you see a chance of promotion and you think I can

help you, let me know it, and I will be glad to make the proper effort
in the right direction.

With love to yourself and mother, I am affectionately

Your uncle,

[unsigned][132]

At the end of April, Hogg was feeling well enough to attend an
"event" honoring Italian Ambassador Baron des Planches. Ima and
her father were among many guests who went on "an automobile
ride" with the ambassador.[133]

When Jim Hogg moved to Houston in 1905, the city's population was approaching 50,000 and growing rapidly. There were eighty
automobiles (though horses still had the right of way), and twenty-six
miles of paved streets. Hogg took up residence at the elegant five-
story Rice Hotel on the corner of Texas and Main. Houston had an
opera house and a library with 14,000 volumes. The Rice Institute
(later Rice University) would open its doors in 1912. By 1913, largely
through the efforts of Ima Hogg, there would be a Houston Symphony Orchestra.[134]

But in the summer of 1905, Ima had other things on her mind:
boarding with her father at the Rice Hotel, she had a serious and
perhaps secret romance. An undated letter written on Rice Hotel stationery and addressed to her at the hotel begins, "Sweetheart." It was
an answer to a note Ima had written to the sender, which, he told
her, brought him "unexpressible joy . . . most heartily do I agree with
you, sweetheart, that Fate could not be so unkind as to keep long
separated two such loving and trusting hearts. Were I to think for
a moment that we were not to be one forever, that moment would
cease to be . . . . I think only that I love you and that you are mine and
that no power on earth can separate us, and none can." The letter is
signed, "Sweetheart."[135] The sender's identity remains a mystery, but
the handwriting and stationery resemble those of an earlier note to
Ima by one Willis B. Reeve. On another occasion he sent a note to her
room after he had escorted her to a "show." He was evidently a guest
at the Rice Hotel, where Ima and her father were staying.

When hot weather came, Ima and her father left the Rice Hotel
for Varner Plantation, where the massive brick walls and high ceilings
of the antebellum house and the breezes from Varner Creek offered
a respite from the heat. One of her Houston friends, W. G. Harris,
wrote to her that he imagined her "in the country" in a white apron
with her sleeves rolled up. Ima entertained him and other houseguests

at Varner that summer. These included Willis B. Reeve, who came for a visit in July.[136]

In August, Ima and her father decided on a vacation in Manitou, Colorado—one of their favorite places. They stayed at the Cliff House, a resort hotel where they had stayed before. When Ima went to Colorado, so did Willis Reeve. When he returned to Houston, his and Ima's mutual friend, W. G. Harris, wrote to Ima, referring to a letter he and Reeve had written to her earlier, saying that they had been "both so overcome & grief stricken over your absence we knew not what we did and are really not responsible for what we said." Harris wrote to Ima at Manitou again that August, telling her how much he missed her and wished her with him.[137]

The presence of Reeve and Harris in Manitou may explain Ima's extraordinary cheeriness in late August when she wrote to Mike. He had left Lawrenceville School without graduating, and now, at age twenty, was back in Austin studying with a private tutor and hoping to finish his education at the University of Texas.[138]

The Cliff House
"At the Foot of Pike's Peak"
E. E. Nichols & Son, Proprietors
Manitou, Colorado
     August 26, 1905
[Ima neglected to put a salutation in her letter to Mike.]
     You poor neglected wretch. Why haven't you written? I should have been awfully worried if we hadn't seen a few people from home who caught sight of you.
     Today after studying over various and sundry reasons why you had been treating your poor old Sis like this I suddenly thought to ask papa if he had sent you any money!
     I am enclosing a check which I hope will serve you in getting enough stationery and stamps to write me all about your studies and—yourself P.D.Q.
     All my fun is over. Have been having a dandy gay time for the last ten days, but—boo hoo—everybody I know left yesterday and before. Had been to a dance every night for ages. There really isn't much to do in the day time but stroll around and talk after you've done all the points of interest. Papa has "sat down upon" my horse back riding and naturally that being the case,—everybody asks me!
     Mr. Reeve was up a few days but went away some where with his sisters. . . .[139]

Meanwhile, there was Wilbur Allen, the Austin attorney who had courted Ima off and on since her University days in Austin. On September 1, he wrote to her at Manitou about their relationship, saying that she had always made him stay "on my own side of the fence" but some day he was going to "hop right on over that fence." He had been to see her in New York the year before, and wrote that he hoped to see her there again when he visited to New York around September 14, 1905.[140]

Ima Hogg kept her affairs of the heart to herself.

She probably wrote to Wilbur Allen around the time she wrote to Mike, early in September.

Sept. 8, 1905
Dear Sister:

I received your letter yesterday. It certainly was newsy.

I have just finished an examination in english which lasted three hours. I don't know whether I passed it or not. If I did I think that I will get in the university without a doubt. If not I don't know. I certainly have been studying. I never stick my head out of this house except on saturdays and that is only in the afternoons. . . .

You haven't any idea how nervous I am. I never wake up in the night that I don't think of those exams and with horror.

Tell papa that I think that he has the pure <u>hippo</u> [hypo], and that he wants to brace up.

Tell Tom to stop his mule riding and climb the mountains on foot.

And when you get this letter I hope you will be in a better humor than when you wrote that thing of yours. Write me P.D.Q. for I just declare I haven't got time to write. My hand is so tired now it can hardly wiggle.

I will close hoping to hear from you as soon and that papa's condition will be much better.

> Your brother,
> Mike Hogg[141]

Mike did well enough on his exams to be admitted to the university. He would enroll that fall. Will, working in his new job in St. Louis, could not resist a long letter of advice to Mike about university life:

Doubtless you will be solicited to join a fraternity. I want you to join some college fraternity; you will find one a source of agreeable

companionship through college and in it you will establish friend-
ships which will endure always. But have a care; know the crowd,
all of them, before you join. Make no promise to any one and tell
whomsoever approaches you on the subject that you are going to
wait until your second year on until the latter half of the first year
anyway. . . . I am a member of the KA frat. Naturally, if the University of Texas chapter should ask you to become a member, you, on
my account, would prefer the KA's and I would like you to join that
frat; but remember, know your crowd and don't let the persistent
solicitation of some one clever fellow fool you into joining some
bunch you do not know all the way through. . . .

   While in college and ever afterwards, I hope you will be able to
wear good-neat, well-made clothes; keep your shoes polished; clean
linen on; hair regularly cut and eider-down off your face . . . one
should dress as well as circumstances will allow, always barring fop-
pishness, of course. . . .

   I want you to know above every thing that I am your friend, first,
last and all the time . . . and your brother afterwards; that no trial
or tribulation which may overcome you, I would not share heartily
and lovingly. Let no fear of what I <u>might</u> think or assume concerning your predicament deter you from being always frank, open and
confiding towards me . . . doubtless you will do some slip-shod thing
which will tend to compromise you in your own estimation . . . let
me know your little college trouble . . . that I may serve you as your
<u>closest</u> friend. Come to me, my boy, not for censure but for loving
assistance. . . .

   Don't be afraid, boy: have more <u>moral</u> courage than brute bravery. . . . Be fearless in your thoughts, actions and speech that they
may be pure. . . . if you are not brave in college and out of it you will
not be worth a damn there or afterwards.

   Keep out of debt at college and try to do so in after life . . . don't
spend any money you have not in hand. . . .

   Confident that you will make a <u>man</u> good and proper first of all
and hoping that you will be a scholar afterwards I am, with constant
love, Yours, Will.

   I never did it but get the habit of going to church every Sunday.
The wisdom and good lessons to be learned at any house of worship
are free and wholesome.[142]

Will could be overly solemn and pompous. Years later Mike dubbed him "Mr. Podsnaps" after a stuffy, self-righteous character in Charles Dickens's 1865 novel, *Our Mutual Friend*.[143]

Meanwhile, in Manitou, Jim Hogg's health was not improving. Despite the cooler weather there, the altitude of 6,500 feet evidently taxed his heart. Later in September his weakened condition worried Ima, and father and daughter took the train back to Texas. They stopped at San Antonio to visit his friend Tom Campbell, and went then on to Mineral Wells for what they hoped would be a recuperative stay.

Jim Hogg was ill, but not too ill to keep up with politics. He had accepted a speaking engagement at a Dallas banquet in November, and he aimed to be there.

Tom, then at Colorado College in Colorado Springs, Colorado, wrote to his father early in October:

My dear Papa:—

I am very glad to learn that you are improving so much. Sister says you were laid over [on the train] again in Kansas. How did it happen again?. . .

. . . I have seen several Texas people in the last few days and they all ask me about you and Sister. The weather is simply perfect out here now.

Well I must close for this time as it is growing late. Love and kisses for yourself and Sister.

I remain

Your loving son

Tom

Monday, Oct 2nd, 1905

Hagerman Hall

Colo Spring Colo[144]

Despite Tom's optimism, his father was not getting better at Mineral Wells. Brownlee Ferguson, now a dentist in Waxahachie, sent some medicine for him to try. From Houston, Dr. Baylor Hogg's wife, Josie, wrote to Ima on October 16 that she was worried about Jim Hogg's refusal to have another operation.[145]

Hogg was anxious to keep his November speaking date in Dallas, in the presence of four candidates for Texas governor. But on the train to Dallas he became too weak to continue and had to stop at

Fort Worth. The resourceful Ima contrived to have her father make an Edison phonograph recording of his speech from his hotel room in Fort Worth. She sent it to Dallas, where an amazed audience listened to Hogg's voice.[146] He and Ima settled in at the Worth Hotel, where they stayed for a month. Hogg remained cheerful about his condition. "By Gatlins," he said a score of times to visitors, "it isn't my time yet to jump into the briar patch." But he did make his will during his stay in Fort Worth.[147]

As soon as he could set foot on a train again, Jim Hogg went to Austin, to his old suite at the Driskill. He held court there, receiving friends, writing letters, and following doctors' orders not to return to his Houston law office until spring.

Ima stayed in Austin with her father, but she found time to socialize. Among the family papers are several dance programs: the "Annual Dance of the University German Club" on November 30 at the Driskill, a dance at Protection Hall on December 7, and a cotillion program December 22 at Concordia Hall. The last two events were evidently debutante balls. Ima's Concordia Hall dance card shows that she danced the first dance with "Renn" (Willis B. Reeve's nickname). She also danced twice more with him, and three times with W. G. Harris.[148]

After recuperating for some weeks in Austin, Jim Hogg returned again to his beloved Varner. Will had come down from St. Louis to visit him. Ima remained in Austin, where her father wrote to her in early December.

THE VARNER
Sunday,
Columbia, Texas
Dec. 3, 1905
My dear Ima,

I am continuing to improve under the skillful treatment of your Brother Will and our servant Richard Davis. The former gives me the medicine and "squirts" my throat, and the latter gives me alternate alcohol and turpentine massage scrubbing and baths before breakfast. Riding, walking and eating constitute my past-time and recreation. We have killed a lot of fat hogs, and you know I have never been willing to stand by and see the spare-ribs, back-bones, sausages, chitlings and sauce, spoil. Will looks as rosy red and saucy as a beer-soaked Dutchman! He is in his element here doctoring the "Old

Man" and riding out among the stock—and writing "back-spelled" postal cards and cheap-material letters. Next in order of importance is your maid, Mary, who is willing as ever. Birdie is the same good cook and is taking good care of the smoke-house, and the chickens and turkeys. Mr. and Mrs. Owens are very nice and agreeable. They occupy the upstairs over the dining room and kitchen. Napoleon is as fine and beautiful as ever. He seemed disappointed when he found you did not come with me. The trap-horses and saddle horses are in excellent condition. The dogs are all in good condition and are ready for the "boys" next Christmas. . . .

We have plenty of hogs, sheep and beef, turkeys, geese and chickens, and milk and butter, and sweet and Irish potatoes, and turnips, radishes, etc., to do during the holidays and all the "boys" must have a big time when you come.

I am proud of the record I heard Mike is making and I hope you may help Tom on to the same point.

With love to everybody,

Affectionately your Pa,
J. S. Hogg[149]

The Varner—Sunday
Columbia, Dec. 9, 1905

Dear Ima:

For more than a week the weather has been frosty, clear and bracing. A stiff, fresh Norther is now blowing. We have killed hogs twice and I have never seen weather better for saving meat. So "you see" I am fixed—just suited. Each day I take plenty of exercise, either walking, talking or horse-back riding. I have "made friends" with Albarac, and go riding nearly every day. He is about as fine as ever. Sometimes I ride Dick, the large, black trap-horse, and he is an excellent saddler; but is too tall—so high that I must mount him from a log or stump, while I can mount Albarac like an eighteen-year-old from the ground. This makes me feel more like a horseman. We are locating the birds, squirrels, ducks and bear for the boys. They shall take you with them hunting and have a gay time. Since arriving here I have steadily improved, until now I begin to feel buoyant and hopeful that my full restoration to my former good health will come some of these days.

I guess, as I hope, you are having a very pleasant time. The attention and kindness shown you everywhere and especially in Austin where you are so well known, shed floods of light-of-pleasure into my heart. And you deserve it all. With your acquaintance and large circle of friends in Texas, won by your own exemplary character and excellent behavior, you have nothing to dread in the future, provided that you do not change radically in your disposition and habits.

With you or away from you I have every reason to be grateful to God for such a girl. One thing I do hope and that is you may go to church a little oftener.

> Affectionately,
> Your father,
> J. S. Hogg[150]

There was a festive family Christmas at Varner, but it would be the last one for J. S. Hogg. Although his health seemed to be improving, Ima and Will convinced him that in the near future he should undergo a thorough medical examination at the Battle Creek Sanitarium in Battle Creek, Michigan, and he agreed.[151] The sanitarium was a famous one known for its holistic approach to medical problems. In 1906 it treated over 7,000 patients. (Dr. John Harvey Kellogg, the sanitarium's founder, and his brother, Will Keith Kellogg, would be better known as makers of whole-grain dry cereals in the early 1900s.)

In March 1906, Jim Hogg, who declared he was feeling much better, set out for Battle Creek. With Ima and Will, he took the train from Columbia to Houston, stopping to spend the night at the home of Frank Jones, his law partner. The Joneses lived in a handsome mansion at 2116 Travis, and the guests spent a pleasant evening on March 2. Hogg was his usual jovial self. He happened to remark that when he died he wanted no monuments at his grave, but a pecan tree and a walnut tree, with the nuts given to the "plain people" of Texas. Ima scolded him for talking of his death, but he assured her that he would be around for "many years."[152]

He died that night. On the morning of March 3, 1906, twenty-one days before his fifty-fifth birthday, James Stephen Hogg was found dead in his bed at the Jones residence. He had died of a heart attack in his sleep. It was Ima who found him. At age thirteen, she had watched her mother die. At age twenty-three, she found her father dead.

As the *Houston Chronicle* reported, Ima was "stricken by the burden of her grief" and was "under the care of a physician."[153] Seldom had the bonds between a father and a daughter been so close.

This collection of letters ends with the death of J. S. Hogg. Larger than life—figuratively and literally—he was the focal point, the fulcrum of an extraordinary family. James Stephen Hogg was buried in Austin's Oakwood Cemetery next to his wife, Sallie.

Will Hogg died in 1930. Mike Hogg died in 1941. Tom Hogg died in 1949. Ima Hogg died in 1975. All are buried in Oakwood Cemetery near their parents.

Abbreviations

AH	Annie Hogg
AMH	Anna McMath Hogg
BH	Baylor Hogg
BCAH	Dolph Briscoe Center for American History, University of Texas at Austin
FL	Family Letters (Ima Hogg, ed.), BCAH
HMRC	Houston Metropolitan Research Center, Houston Public Library, Houston, Texas
HCF	Henry Clay Ferguson
IH	Ima Hogg
IHP	Ima Hogg Papers, BCAH
JM	James McDugald
JAS	James Alexander Stinson
JMF	Julia McDugald Ferguson
JSH	James Stephen Hogg
JWH	John Washington Hogg
MFAH	Museum of Fine Arts, Houston
MFD	Martha Frances Davis
MH	Mike Hogg
RMK	Robert M. Kelso
SH	Sallie Hogg
TH	Tom Hogg
WBD	William Brownlee Davis
WCH	William Clifford Hogg
WRC	Woodson Research Center, Fondren Library, Rice University, Houston, Texas

Notes

INTRODUCTION

[1] WCH to IH, undated letter, quoted in Virginia Bernhard, *Ima Hogg: The Governor's Daughter* (1st ed., Austin: Texas Monthly Press, 1984), 46.

[2] JSH to "Editor *Chicago Record*," Nov. 12, 1896, box 14, letterpress (cited hereafter as LP) 13, pt. II, James Stephen Hogg letter transcriptions and family photographs, MS 008 (Woodson Research Center, Fondren Library, Rice University, Houston, cited hereafter as WRC).

[3] "Those Hogg Stories," *Fort Gibson (Okla.) Post*, Sept. 7, 1899.

[4] Lucille Jones, *History of Mineola: "Gateway to the Pines"* (Quanah, Tex.: Nortex Offset Publications, 1973), 94.

[5] Horace Chilton, "Memoir of JSH printing colleague in Tyler, 1870," 3B116, folder 1, Biographical materials, printed materials, and newspaper clippings, Ima Hogg Papers, cited hereafter as IHP (Briscoe Center for American History, University of Texas at Austin, cited hereafter as BCAH). Governor Hogg appointed Chilton (1853–1932) to fill John H. Reagan's U.S. Senate seat in 1891, and Chilton was later elected as senator, serving from 1895–1901. *The Handbook of Texas Online* <http://www.tshaonline.org/handbook/online/articles/fch30> [Accessed Nov. 12, 2012].

[6] Rose Merriman's recollections are in an article by H. L. Lackey, "Jim Hogg Took Cow to Austin, Ate His Dessert First, Old Friend Says," *Dallas Morning News*, Dec. 10,1933, reprinted in *A Transcript of 1850/1950 Centennial Edition of the* Wood County Democrat, ed. Adele W. Vickery (Mineola, Tex.: Adele W. Vickery, 1974), 192–94.

[7] IH to Robert M. Rennick, a sociology professor at DePauw University, July 14, 1969, Biographical materials, vitae, newspaper clippings, 1908–1975, 3B168, IHP (BCAH).

[8] She gave two copies of the 150-volume set of letters to the University of Texas and one set each to the Texas State Library, Rice University, and Southern Methodist University. Robert C. Cotner edited *Addresses and State Papers of James Stephen Hogg* (Austin: University of Texas Press, 1951). Reviews of Cotner's *James Stephen Hogg: A Biography* (Austin: University of Texas Press, 1959) were not altogether favorable. Historian James Tinsley faulted Cotner for the "partiality and peer reverence with which he treats his subject" in the *Mississippi Valley Historical Review* 46 (December 1959): 537–39. Francis B. Simkins, in *Journal of Southern History* 25 (November 1959): 545–46, noted that Cotner "failed to mention any faults Hogg may have had."

[9] "Texas's Ima Hogg, Philanthropist: Houston Symphony Founder and State Benefactor Dies," *The New York Times*, Aug. 21, 1975; "Services Scheduled for Miss Ima Hogg," *Houston Chronicle*, Aug. 21, 1975.

[10] IH, "Family Reminiscences" (unpaginated typescript, 3B130, General Family Materials, folder 10, IHP (BCAH).

THE LETTER WRITERS

[1] Joe B. Frantz, *Texas: A Bicentennial History* (New York: W. W. Norton, 1976), 154.

[2] "Ex-Gov. Hogg Dies Suddenly in Texas," *The New York Times*, Mar. 4, 1906; *Houston Chronicle*, Mar. 3, 1906; *Houston Post*, Mar. 4, 1906.

[3] Cotner, *James Stephen Hogg*, 45, 67.

[4] Ibid., 68. See also Bernhard, *Ima Hogg*, 23–24.

[5] *Winnsboro* [Tex.] *News*, Oct. 31, 1974.

[6] *Austin Daily Statesman*, Sept. 25, 1895.

[7] "Questions by Dr. Cotner—Answers by Miss Ima Hogg, June 20, 1949," typescript, 31, 3B116, Family Papers: James Stephen Hogg: Biographical Materials, folder 2, IHP (BCAH).

[8] "William C. Hogg, Oil Operator, Dies," *The New York Times*, Sept. 13, 1930; *Houston Chronicle*, Sept. 13, 1906.

[9] Box 4Zg73, Correspondence to Ima Hogg, folder 1, contains letters from various young men to Ima Hogg in 1904 and 1905, IHP (BCAH).

[10] Ima explained her tuberculosis fears to a close friend in Houston many years later. See Marguerite Johnston, *Houston: The Unknown City, 1836–1946* (College Station: Texas A&M University Press, 1991), 135.

[11] IH, 3B153, Personal Papers, Travel Diaries, 1898, 1908, 1912, 1930; TH to IH, Apr. 13, 1908, 3B126, Thomas Elisha Hogg family (son of James Stephen Hogg), 1889–1912, folder 1, IHP (BCAH).

[12] WCH to John Duncan, May 16, 1913, quoted in Bernhard, *Ima Hogg*, 82.

[13] MH to WCH, Feb. 16, 1919, World War I Letters, 1914–1918, Subseries 2.1, Correspondence, Series 2, Hogg Family Personal Papers, MS 21, Hogg Family Papers, Archives (Museum of Fine Arts, Houston, cited hereafter as MFAH).

[14] Wedding announcement, 3B124, Mike Hogg family, folder 3, IHP (BCAH).

[15] "Mike Hogg, Oil Operator and Realtor, Dies," *Houston Chronicle*, Sept. 11, 1941.

[16] JSH to IH, Oct. 31, 1901, 3B111, James Stephen Hogg, 1870–1976, folder Family and general correspondence, IHP (BCAH).

[17] WCH to IH, July 7, 1906, 3B118, William Clifford Hogg, 1888–1974, folder Correspondence, 1900–1906; TH to WCH, Aug. 3, 1907; Marie Hogg to IH, July 10, 1931, 3B126, folder 1, IHP (BCAH).

[18] On Tom's health problems, see WCH to IH, July 10, 1906, and IH to WCH, undated, 1906, 3B118, folder Correspondence, 1900–1906. On Tom's spending, see WCH to Marie Hogg, Mar. 21, 1924; TH to WCH, undated, 1921, 3B126, folder 1, IHP (BCAH).

[19] In 1937 Marie Hogg was living in an apartment in San Antonio. From 1938 to 1941 her name appeared frequently in the *San Antonio Light* at social events. In 1939 she remodeled the mansion she and Tom had once shared, where she entertained lavishly. *San Antonio Light*, Sept. 30, 1937; Dec. 6, 1938; Jan. 24, Aug. 6, Nov. 23, 1939; Jan. 21, Feb. 2, 1940; Mar. 12, May 8, 1941.

[20] MH to IH, Sept. 16, 1936, 3B124, folder 3, IHP, (BCAH). Tom's and Marie's separation and divorce settlements are in *Hogg v. Commissioner*, 13 T.C. 361 (1949), U.S. Tax Court, Sept. 26, 1949, <http://www.leagle.com/xmlResult.aspx?page=4&xmldoc=194937413aytc361_1324.xml&docbase=CSLWAR1-1950-1985&SizeDisp=7> [Accessed Dec. 3, 2012]; TH to IH, Nov. 5, 1941; Margaret Wells to IH, July 22, 1942, 3B126, folder 1, IHP (BCAH).

[21] "Thomas Hogg, 61, Prominent Here, Dies in Arizona," *Houston Chronicle,* Mar. 9, 1949.

[22] Hermilla Hogg, 4Zg89, Hogg Family Letters, folder Biography of Martha Frances Davis, IHP (BCAH).

[23] JSH to Julia Ferguson, Aug. 9, 1888, box 17, LP 40, MS 008 (WRC).

[24] *Galveston Daily News,* Feb. 23, 1896.

[25] "Family Scrapbook compiled by Hermilla Hogg Kelso," 3B130, General family materials, folder 3, IHP (BCAH).

[26] Cliff Cates, *Pioneer History of Wise County* (Decatur, Tex.: Old Settlers Association, 1907), 287.

In addition to the sources cited above, biographical materials were drawn from the U.S. Census records of 1880, 1900, 1910, 1920, and 1930; C. A. Bridges, *History of Denton, Texas from Its Beginning to 1960* (Waco, Tex.: Texian Press, 1978); Vinita Davis (comp.), *Marriage Records Index, Denton County, Texas* (2 vols., Fort Worth: Miran Publishers, 1972); *Denton County, Texas Wills* (Decorah, Ia.: Anundsen Publishing Company, 1994); Lucille Jones, *History of Mineola: "Gateway to the Pines"* (Quanah, Tex.: Nortex Offset Publications, 1973); John Lomax, *Will Hogg, Texan* (Austin: University of Texas Press, 1956); Ida Marie Turner and Adele W. Vickery (comps.), *Cemeteries of Wood County, Texas* (4 vols., Mineola, Tex.: Turner and Vickery, 1971); Adele W. Vickery (ed.), *A Transcript of 1850/1950 Centennial Edition of the* Wood County Democrat (Mineola, Tex.: Adele W. Vickery, 1974); Wise County Historical Committee, *Wise County History: A Link with the Past,* ed., Rosalie Gregg ([n.p]: Nortex Press, 1976), and Booknotes, Hogg Genealogy, 4Zg88, IHP (BCAH).

PART 1

[1] "Some Incidents from the Life of Governor James Stephen Hogg as Related by Mrs. L. Milton Brown, 1941," 3, 3B116, folder 2, IHP (BCAH). Mrs. Brown was the former Annie McCoy, a close family friend in Austin.

[2] David C. Humphrey, *Austin: A History of the Capital City* (Austin: Texas State Historical Association, 1997), 9 (quotation), 25; Mary Starr Barkley, *History of Travis County and Austin, 1839–1899* (Waco, Tex.: Texian Press, 1963), 127, 189.

[3] Austin City Directory,1898–99 (microfilm: Drawer C38 D10, Clayton Library Center for Genealogical Research, Houston, Texas).

[4] *Historic Austin: A Collection of Walking/Driving Tours,* Sharon Greenhill, Karen Glover, et al., comps. (Austin: Heritage Society of Austin, 1981), 2–3, 8–11. As the editor of *The Rolling Stone,* a humorous weekly newspaper in 1894, Porter would make a rotund politician named Hogg the subject of jests and cartoons. Patrick Cox, "Rolling Stone," <http://www.tshaonline.org/handbook/online/articles/RR/eer4.html.> [accessed September 27, 2011].

[5] JSH to WCH, Jan. 29, 1887, box 12, LP 1 A, MS 008 (WRC).

[6] IH, "Reminiscences of Life in the Governor's Mansion" (typescript, dictated in Colorado Springs, Colo., 1944 or 1945; cited hereafter as "Reminiscences") 4, 3B168, folder 4, IHP (BCAH).

[7] JSH to SH, Feb. 17, 1887, box 12, LP 1 A, MS 008 (WRC).

[8] IH, "Family Reminiscences," 3B130, folder 10, IHP, BCAH. Ima Hogg was working on this manuscript in 1973, at age 92. The Willis impeachment case was a complicated one that Attorney General Hogg had inherited from his predecessor. Frank Willis, district judge of the Thirty-First Judicial District in the Texas Panhandle, had been accused of siding with the cattlemen (including the well-known and wealthy

cattle baron Charles Goodnight) in their use of state lands without compensating the state. Judge Willis was acquitted after he made an eloquent speech in his own defense. See Robert C. Cotner, *James Stephen Hogg: A Biography* (Austin, University of Texas Press, 1959), 107–14.

⁹ "Questions by Dr. Cotner—Answers by Miss Ima Hogg, June 20, 1949," 4–5, 3B116, Biographical materials, folder 2, IHP (BCAH).

¹⁰ H. L. Lackey, "Jim Hogg Took Cow to Austin, Ate His Dessert First, Old Friend Says," *Dallas Morning News*, Dec. 10, 1933, reprinted in Adele W. Vickery (ed.), *A Transcript of 1850/1950 Centennial Edition of the* Wood County Democrat (Mineola, Tex.: Adele W. Vickery, 1974), 193.

¹¹ IH, "Reminiscences," 7, 9, 3B168, folder 4, IHP (BCAH).

¹² JSH to BH, Apr. 17, 1887, box 12, LP 1 A, MS 008 (WRC).

¹³ IH, "Reminiscences," 23, 3B168, folder 4, IHP (BCAH).

¹⁴ JSH to JMF, Aug. 9, 1888; JSH to WCH, Aug. 9, 1888, box 17, LP 40, MS 008 (WRC).

¹⁵ WCH to SH, Aug. 12, 1888, 3B130, Family Letters Selected and Compiled by Ima Hogg for Mike and Tom Hogg, Christmas 1935 (cited hereafter as FL), IHP (BCAH). There is also a bound volume of these letters in the Archives, Museum of Fine Arts, Houston.

¹⁶ IH, "Family Reminiscences," 3B130, folder 10, IHP, (BCAH).

¹⁷ C. W. Raines (ed.), *Speeches and Papers of James Stephen Hogg, ex-Governor of Texas, with a sketch of his life* (Austin: The State Printing Company, 1905), 8.

¹⁸ The Supreme Court case was *Asher v. Texas*, which Attorney General Hogg argued before the high court on October 11–12. The case involved the legality of the Texas Drummer Tax, a fee required of out-of-state salesmen, or "drummers," who sold goods in Texas. The attorney general did his best, but on October 30 the Supreme Court ruled that the Texas law was unconstitutional. See Cotner, *James Stephen Hogg,* 148–53.

¹⁹ JSH to MFD, Sept. 16, 1888, box 12, LP 2, MS 008 (WRC).

²⁰ JSH to James B. Bishop, Oct. 23, 1888, ibid.

²¹ IH, "Reminiscences," 8, 3B168, folder 4, IHP (BCAH).

²² MFD to JSH, Sept. 2, 1888, 3B130, FL, IHP (BCAH). This is clearly a reply to Hogg's September 16 letter, and the date, transcribed as "September 2nd," should probably be "September 22."

²³ JSH to WCH, Sept. 27, 1888, box 12, LP 2, MS 008 (WRC).

²⁴ IH, "Reminiscences," 18, 3B168, folder 4, IHP (BCAH).

²⁵ Ibid., 17–18. Colonel Stinson's third wife, the "Grandmother" in Ima's memoirs, was Sarah A. Jones.

²⁶ Ibid., 22–23.

²⁷ JSH to JMF, Nov. 27, 1888, box 12, LP 2, MS 008 (WRC).

²⁸ IH, "Reminiscences," 23, 3B168, folder 4, IHP (BCAH).

²⁹ JSH to Bismarck Ferguson, Dec. 3, 1888, box 12, LP 2, MS 008 (WRC).

³⁰ JSH to AMH, Jan. 3, 1889, ibid.

³¹ JSH to JAS, Jan. 16, 1889, ibid. Attorney General Hogg was preparing for *The State of Texas v. Gulf, Colorado and Santa Fe Railway Company et al.*, the first big lawsuit in his effort to control the mostly unregulated out-of-state railroad corporations operating in Texas. He charged them with creating monopolies and acting against the public interest, and he was about to launch a major crusade against them. He would win this first case and others later on. Meanwhile, he was working behind the scenes on a major legislative achievement, the Texas Antitrust Act of March 1889. See Cotner, *James Stephen Hogg,* 156–67.

[32] IH, "Reminiscences," 17, 3B168, folder 4, IHP (BCAH); IH, untitled, unpaginated typescript (hereafter referred to as "untitled typescript"), 4Zg89, folder Correspondence: Kate Leader, concerning chapter 2, IHP (BCAH)

[33] IH, "Reminiscences," 18–19, 3B168, folder 4, IHP (BCAH).

[34] IH, untitled typescript, 4Zg89, folder Correspondence: Kate Leader, concerning chapter 2, IHP (BCAH).

[35] IH, "Reminiscences," 19, 3B168, folder 4, IHP (BCAH).

[36] IH, untitled typescript, 4Zg89, folder Correspondence: Kate Leader, concerning chapter 2, IHP (BCAH).

[37] IH, "Reminiscences," 18–20, 3B168, folder 4, IHP (BCAH).

[38] JSH to IH, Mar. 7, 1889, box 12, LP 2, MS 008 (WRC).

[39] IH, "Reminiscences," 26, 3B168, folder 4, IHP (BCAH).

[40] IH, ibid., 22.

[41] Ibid.

[42] RMK to JSH, Feb. 18, 1889, box 11, LP vol. 1, MS 008 (WRC).

[43] JSH to Mills & Averill, Apr. 13, 1889, box 12, LP 2, MS 008 (WRC).

[44] He won the case. The "E.L. RR Case" was Hogg's lawsuit to separate the East Line Railroad from the giant Missouri, Kansas and Texas line. It was part of Hogg's ongoing war against what he viewed as illegal combinations and practices of railroads operating in Texas. His stand against the railroads and his effort to create a regulatory Texas Railroad Commission had defined his time as attorney general. Cotner, *James Stephen Hogg*, 186–88.

[45] JSH to MFD, Apr. 24, 1889, 4Zg89, folder l, IHP (BCAH). There is a note in Ima Hogg's handwriting on this letter, stating that Ethel was "burned to death accidentally by lighting a stove with a can of kerosene."

[46] JSH to MFD, June 1, 1889, box 12, LP 2, MS 008 (WRC).

[47] Ibid.

[48] IH, "Reminiscences," 4–5, 3B168, folder 4, IHP (BCAH).

[49] JSH to MFD, June 1, 1889, box 12, LP 2, MS 008 (WRC). Jim Hogg used slang expressions to describe his children: a "buster," one who is amusing or frolicsome; a "duster," one not good at sports, or one who sits on the bench and gathers dust; a "guster," one who is constantly busy; a "whale," one with impressive qualities. See *Compact Edition of the Oxford English Dictionary* (2 vols., Oxford, UK: Oxford University Press, 1971), 1:303 (buster); <http://www.schoolyardpuck.com/2010/04/hockey-slang-term-glossary.html> (duster);<http://www.websters-online-dictionary.org/definition/GUSTER> (guster); <http://www.worldwidewords.org/qa/qa-wha2.htm> (whale). [All websites accessed July 25, 2013].

[50] JSH to SH, June 15, 1889, ibid.

[51] JSH to SH, June 17, 1889, ibid.

[52] JWH to JSH, Aug. 3, 1889, box 11, LP vol. 1; JSH to JWH, Aug 8, 1889, box 12, LP 3, MS 008 (WRC).

[53] *Austin Daily Statesman*, Aug. 10, 1889.

[54] SH to JSH, telegram, 3B127, Sallie Stinson Hogg Correspondence, 1889–1895, IHP (BCAH); JSH to Anna Hogg, Aug. 27, 1889, box 12, LP 4, MS 008 (WRC).

[55] JSH to W. R. McMath, Nov. 9, 1889; JSH to JWH, Nov. 30, 1889, ibid.

[56] JSH to Lillie Stinson, Nov. 30, 1889, ibid.

[57] IH, "Reminiscences." 18, 3B168, folder 4, IHP (BCAH).

[58] IH to JSH, Dec. 5, 1889, 3B130, FL, IHP (BCAH).

[59] JSH to H. G. Robertson, Dec. 18, 1889, quoted in Cotner, *James Stephen Hogg*, 184.

[60] IH, "Reminiscences." 20, 3B168, folder 4, IHP (BCAH).

[61] IH, ibid., 20–21.

[62] JSH to IH, Dec. 8 1889, box 12, LP 4, MS 008 (WRC).

[63] IH, "Family Reminiscences," folder 10, 3B130, IHP (BCAH).

[64] IH to JSH, Feb. 7, 1890, 3B111, James Stephen Hogg: Correspondence: Family 1882–1904, IHP (BCAH).

[65] WCH to JSH and SH, Mar. 14, 1890, FL, 3B130, IHP (BCAH).

[66] JSH to HCF, Mar. 18, 1890, box 12, LP 5, MS 008 (WRC); JSH to JWH. Mar. 14, 1890, FL, 3B130, IHP (BCAH).

[67] JSH to WCH, Mar. 26, 1890, box 12, LP 5, MS 008 (WRC).

[68] The text of Hogg's Rusk speech is in Robert C. Cotner (ed.), *Addresses and State Papers of James Stephen Hogg* (Austin: University of Texas Press, 1951), 63–100.

[69] JWH to JSH, Apr. 21, 1890, box 11, LP 4; JSH to Lucanda Owen, April 28, 1890, box 12, LP 5, MS 008 (WRC).

[70] JSH to AH, Apr. 28, 1890, box 12, LP 5, MS 008 (WRC).

[71] JWH to JSH, May 6, 1890; RMK to JSH, May 25, 1890, box 11, LP 5, MS 008 (WRC).

[72] SH to JSH, May 24, 1890, 3B127, folder 1, IHP (BCAH).

[73] IH to JSH, May 30, 1890, 3B111, James Stephen Hogg, 1870–1976, Correspondence: Family, 1882–1904, IHP (BCAH).

[74] SH to JSH, May 30, 1890, 3B130, FL, IHP (BCAH).

[75] IH, "Reminiscences," 10, 3B168, folder 4, IHP (BCAH).

[76] Ibid., 11.

[77] JSH to SH, July 3, 1890, box 13, LP 7, pt. I, MS 008 (WRC).

[78] JSH to MFD July 8, 1890, ibid.

[79] Cotner, *James Stephen Hogg,* 212.

[80] MFD to JSH, July 16, 1890, 3B130, FL, IHP (BCAH).

[81] For political backgrounds, see Cotner, *James Stephen Hogg.* On Wheeler, 189; Clark, 202; Hall, 201; Matlock, 210–11; McCall, 429n24. Miss Brewster served as "Acting Commissioner of Insurance &c." in 1887. Box 16, LP 38, MS 008 (WRC).

[82] IH to JSH, July 23 and July 26, 1890, 3B111, Correspondence: Family, 1882–1904, IHP (BCAH).

[83] JSH to SH, July 26, 1890, box 13, LP 7, pt. I, MS 008 (WRC).

[84] JSH to SH, Aug. 1, 1890, ibid.

[85] JSH to MFD, Aug. 3, 1890, ibid.

[86] JSH to B. Bryan, Sept. 2, 1890; Sept. 12, 1890, box 13, LP 7, pt. II, MS 008 (WRC).

[87] IH, "Reminiscences," 3B168, 24, folder 4, IHP (BCAH).

[88] JSH to BH, Sept. 18, 1890, box 13, LP 7, pt. II, MS 008 (WRC).

[89] IH to JSH, Oct. 3, 1890, 3B111, folder Family, 1882–1904, IHP (BCAH).

[90] IH to JSH, Oct. 8, 1890, ibid.

[91] JSH to JWH, Oct. 10, 1890, box 13, LP 7, pt. II, MS 008 (WRC).

[92] JSH to JMF, Oct. 10, 1890, ibid.

[93] JSH to WCH, Nov. 12, 1890, box 13, LP 7, pt. II, MS 008 (WRC).

[94] RMK to JSH, Nov. 6, 1890, box 12, LP 8; JSH to RMK, Nov. 12, 1890, box 13, LP 7, pt. II; RMK to JSH, Nov. 14, 1890, box 12, LP 8, MS 008 (WRC).

[95] JSH to HCF Nov 15, 1890, box 13, LP 7, pt. II, MS 008 (WRC).

[96] Article 10, Section 2 of the Texas Constitution amended to provide for the Railroad Commission, stating the "legislature . . . .may provide and establish all requisite means and agencies invested with such powers as may be deemed adequate and advisable (to regulate Railroads)." Adopted at November 4, 1890 election; Proclama-

tion of December 19, 1890. <http://www.rrc.state.tx.us/about/history/chronological/chronhistory01.php> [Accessed April 16, 2013].

[97] JSH to MFD, Dec. 7, 1890, 4Zg89, folder James Stephen Hogg: Letters, 1887–1890, IHP (BCAH).

[98] JSH to Miss Julia E. Hogg, Jan. 2, 1891, box 13, LP 8, MS 008 (WRC).

[99] IH, "Family Reminiscences," folder 10, 3B130, IHP (BCAH).

[100] IH, "Reminiscences," 9, folder 4, 3B168, IHP (BCAH),

[101] Ibid., 10.

[102] Ibid., 2.

[103] Ibid., 1-2.

[104] Ibid., 1–3, 29.

[105] IH, ibid., 24.

[106] IH, "Family Reminiscences," 3B130, folder 10, IHP (BCAH).

[107] Ibid., 16.

[108] IH, "Family Reminiscences," 3B130, folder 10, IHP (BCAH).

[109] Ibid.

[110] "Reminiscences," 17, 3B168, folder 4, IHP (BCAH).

[111] Ibid., 13–14

[112] Ibid., 26–27.

[113] Ibid., 27.

[114] IH, "Trips to Mexico and Hawaii" (unpaginated typescript), AZg89, IHP folder Chapter 6, 1896–1900 (BCAH).

[115] IH, "Reminiscences," 27-29, 3B168, IHP (BCAH).

[116] Ibid., 31–32.

[117] Ibid., 3–4.

[118] Ibid., 5.

[119] IH, "Family Reminiscences," 3B130, folder 10, IHP (BCAH).

[120] IH, "Reminiscences," 4, 5, 6., folder 4, IHP (BCAH)

[121] Ibid., 6–7.

[122] Vickery (ed.), *A Transcript of the 1850/1950 Centennial Edition of the* Wood County Democrat, 190.

[123] IH, "Reminiscences, 12, 3B168, folder 4, IHP (BCAH).

[124] Ibid., 14.

[125] IH, undated note, December 1904, recalling JSH's treatments for pneumonia, 4Zg89, September–December 1904, IHP (BCAH).

[126] IH, "Reminiscences," 10, 3B168, folder 4, IHP (BCAH).

[127] WCH to JSH, May 28, 1891, 4Zg89, folder Copies of Family Letters, IHP (BCAH).

[128] JSH to WCH, June 1, 1891, box 19, LP 1 A, MS 008 (WRC).

[129] JSH to SH, June 1, 1891, ibid.

[130] JSH to HCF Dec. 26, 1891, box 13, LP 9, MS 008 (WRC).

[131] SH to WCH, undated, 1892, FL, 3B130, IHP (BCAH).

[132] SH to WCH, Jan.18, 1892, 4Zg89, folder James Stephen Hogg letters, 1882–1892, IHP (BCAH).

[133] SH to WCH, Jan. 25, 1892, Ibid.

[134] SH to WCH, Feb. 15, 1892, FL, 3B130, IHP (BCAH).

[135] SH to WCH, Mar. 6, 1892, ibid. On Brock Robertson, see Cotner, *James Stephen Hogg*, 143–45.

[136] The Supreme Court case is discussed in Cotner, *James Stephen Hogg*, 372–77.

[137] JSH to WCH, April 19, 1892, box 13, LP 10, pt. I, MS 008 (WRC).

[138] SH to JSH, May 6, 1892, 3B127, folder 1, IHP (BCAH).

[139] IH, "Reminiscences," 33, 3B168, folder 4, IHP (BCAH).

[140] As a lobbying practice in the 1880s, many railroads issued free passes allowing certain persons to travel free of charge. See William G. Thomas, *Lawyering for the Railroad: Business, Law, and Politics in the New South* (Baton Rouge: Louisiana State University Press, 1999), 178–80.

[141] Quoted in C. A. Bridges, *History of Denton, Texas from Its Beginning to 1960* (Waco, Tex.: Texian Press, 1978), 246.

[142] IH, "Reminiscences," 33–34, 3B168, folder 4, IHP (BCAH).

[143] *The Atchison (Kans.) Daily Globe*, May 19, 1891.

[144] Ed Kilman, "Texas Heartbeat," *Houston Post*, Nov. 11, 1946.

[145] Owens to JSH, Dec. 23, 1892, box 5, LP 33, MS 008 (WRC).

[146] JSH to HCF, July 9, 1892, box 13, LP 10, pt. 2, MS 008 (WRC).

[147] IH, "Reminiscences," 23, 3B168, folder 4, IHP (BCAH).

[148] On this campaign, see Bernhard, *Ima Hogg*, 33–39.

PART 2

[1] *The New York Times*, June 24, 1904.

[2] JSH to M. M. Crane, Sept. 7, 1892, box 14, LP 10, pt. 2, MS 008 (WRC).

[3] JSH to JM, Sept. 6, 1892, ibid.

[4] SH to WCH, Sept. 8, 1892, 3B130, FL, IHP (BCAH).

[5] IH, "Reminiscences," 10, 3B168, folder 4, IHP (BCAH).

[6] JSH to WCH, Sept. 16, 1892, box 14, LP 10, pt. 2, MS 008 (WRC).

[7] IH, "Reminiscences," 24–25, 3B168, folder 4, IHP (BCAH).

[8] SH to WCH, Oct. 2, 1892, 3B127, folder 1, IHP (BCAH).

[9] SH to WCH, Nov. 2, 1892, 4Zg89, folder James Stephen Hogg letters, 1882–1892, IHP (BCAH).

[10] The final election results gave Hogg 43 percent of the vote, with Clark receiving 30 percent and Nugent coming in third with 25 percent. *Houston Daily Post*, Nov. 10, 1892.

[11] JWH to JSH, Nov. 25, 1892, box 5, LP 22, pt. 1, MS 008 (WRC).

[12] Kiam Clothiers to SH, Dec. 15, 1892, ibid.

[13] IH, "Family Reminiscences," 3B130, folder 10, IHP (BCAH).

[14] IH, "Reminiscences," 15, 3B168, folder 4, IHP (BCAH).

[15] IH, "Family Reminiscences," 3B130, folder 10, IHP (BCAH).

[16] IH, "Reminiscences," 15, 3B168, folder 4, IHP (BCAH).

[17] Ibid., 25.

[18] JWH to JSH, Dec. 27, 1892, box 5, LP 22, pt. 2, MS 008 (WRC).

[19] JWH to JSH, Mar. 15, 1893, box 6, LP 25; JWH to JSH, Apr. 29, 1893, box 6, LP 26, MS 008 (WRC).

[20] IH to JSH, Apr. 14, 1893, 3B111, folder Correspondence: Family, 1882–1904, IHP (BCAH).

[21] JSH to SH, Apr. 19, 1893, box 14, LP 11, MS 008 (WRC).

[22] IH to JSH, Apr. 21, 1893, 3B111, folder Correspondence: Family, 1882–1904, IHP (BCAH).

[23] JSH to RMK, May 17, 1893, box 14, LP 11, MS 008 (WRC).

[24] IH, "Reminiscences," 31, folder 4, 3B168, IHP (BCAH).

[25] SH to JSH, June 20, 1893, 3B127, folder 1, IHP (BCAH).

[26] IH to JSH, June 16, and June 17, 1893, 3B111, folder Correspondence: Family, 1882–1904, IHP (BCAH).

[27] IH, "Reminiscences," 27–28, 3B168, folder 4, IHP (BCAH).

[28] JSH to IH, June 3, 1893, box 14, LP 11, MS 008 (WRC).

[29] IH, "Reminiscences," 21, 3B168, folder 4, IHP (BCAH).

[30] IH to JSH, June 6, 1893, 3B111, folder Correspondence: Family, 1882–1904, IHP (BCAH).

[31] JSH to SH, June 23, 1893, 3B130, FL, IHP (BCAH).

[32] IH to JSH, June 23, 1893, 3B111, folder Correspondence: Family, 1882–1904, IHP (BCAH).

[33] JSH to IH, June 26, 1893, box 14, LP 11, MS 008 (WRC).

[34] IH to JSH, June 30, 1893, 3B111, folder Correspondence: Family 1882–1904, IHP (BCAH).

[35] JSH to SH, June 20, 1893, box 14, LP 11, MS 008 (WRC).

[36] JSH to SH, July 8, 1893, 3B130, FL, IHP (BCAH).

[37] IH to JSH, July 10, 1893, 3B111, folder Correspondence: Family, 1882–1904, IHP (BCAH).

[38] "Miss Lillie Stinson Burkett, Winnsboro, TX, May 27, 1946" (interview in "Questions by Dr. Cotner—Answers by Miss Ima Hogg, June 20, 1949"), 3B116, folder 2, IHP (BCAH).

[39] JSH to BH, Aug. 12, 1893, box 14, LP 11, MS 008 (WRC).

[40] JSH to JM, Aug. 23, 1893, ibid.

[41] IH to JSH, Sept. 6, 1893, 3B 111, folder Correspondence: Family, 1882–1904, IHP (BCAH).

[42] *The New York Times,* June 24, 1894; Cotner, *James Stephen Hogg,* 42.

[43] IH, "Reminiscences," 34, 3B130, IHP (BCAH).

[44] Ibid., 35.

[45] IH to SH, June 24, 1894, AZg89, folder 1894, IHP (BCAH).

[46] *The New York Times,* June 24, 1894, reported the Texas group as a "notable theatre party." DeFrece is listed in Moses King, *Notable New Yorkers of 1896–1899* (New York: Orr Press: 1899), 578. See also Cotner, *James Stephen Hogg,* 484.

[47] "Questions by Dr. Cotner—Answers by Miss Ima Hogg, June 20, 1949," 11–12, 3B116, folder 2, IHP (BCAH).

[48] IH to SH, June 26, 1894, 3B127, folder 1, IHP (BCAH).

[49] JSH to SH, June 29, 1894, 3B130, FL, IHP (BCAH).

[50] SH to JSH, July 7, 1894, 3B127, folder l, IHP (BCAH).

[51] WCH to JSH, July 9, 1894, 3B130, FL, IHP (BCAH).

[52] IH, "Reminiscences," 13, folder 4, 3B130, IHP (BCAH). Adjutant General W. H. Mabry had organized the first Encampment in 1891 at Hyde Park in Austin, where forty-eight companies of the Texas Volunteer Guard (after 1904, the Texas National Guard) met to drill and parade. In 1892, Mabry raised funds for the purchase and installation of a permanent campground, and Camp Mabry in Austin was named in his honor by vote of the companies. Barkley, *History of Travis County,* 131.

[53] WCH to JSH, July 11, 1894, 3B118, William Clifford Hogg, 1888–1974, folder Correspondence: 1888–1899, IHP (BCAH).

[54] Cotner, *James Stephen Hogg,* 384.

[55] Cotner, *Addresses and State Papers,* 376–400.

[56] JSH to SH, Oct. 5, 1894, 3B130, FL, IHP (BCAH). See Hogg's speech of October 1, 1894, at Rockdale, Texas, in Cotner, *Addresses and State Papers,* 400–442.

[57] JSH to SH, Oct. 21, 1894, 3B130, FL, IHP (BCAH).

[58] Barkley, *History of Travis County,* 307.

[59] JSH to MFD, Dec. 20, 1894, 3B130, FL, IHP (BCAH).

[60] MFD to WCH, undated letter, 1894, ibid.

61 JSH to JMF, Feb. 15, 1895, box 14, LP 12, pt. 1, MS 008 (WRC).

62 Hogg had a plan to buy the Link Line, "extend it a few miles and make a pile of money by selling it for nuisance value to a major trunk line." Quoted in James Tinsley's review of Cotner's biography of Hogg, *Mississippi Valley Historical Review* 46 (December 1959), 537–539 (quotation, 538). His plan failed to attract eastern investors.

63 Cotner, *James Stephen Hogg,* 455.

64 JSH to SH, Mar. 28, 1895, 3B130, FL, IHP (BCAH).

65 JSH to IH, Apr. 6, 1895, ibid.

66 JSH to SH, Apr. 13, 1895, ibid.

67 MFD to JSH, Apr. 14, 1895, ibid.

68 MH and TH to SH, Apr. 17, 1895, ibid.

69 JSH to SH, Apr. 18, 1895, 4Zg89, folder James Stephen Hogg Letters, 1895, IHP (BCAH).

70 JSH to IH, Apr. 19, 1895, ibid.

71 "Gov. Hogg at Fire Island," *The New York Times,* Apr. 22, 1895.

72 JSH to SH, Apr. 22, 1895, 4Zg89, folder James Stephen Hogg letters 1895, IHP (BCAH).

73 JSH to IH, Apr. 29, 1895, 3B130, FL IHP (BCAH).

74 JSH to SH, May 1, 1895, 4Zg89, folder James Stephen Hogg Letters, 1895, IHP (BCAH).

75 JSH to IH, May 4, 1895, 3B130, FL, IHP (BCAH).

76 SH to JSH, May 8, 1895, quoted in Cotner, *James Stephen Hogg,* 437–438.

77 "Questions by Dr. Cotner—Answers by Miss Ima Hogg, June 20, 1949," 45–46, 3B116, folder 2, IHP (BCAH).

78 Cotner, *James Stephen Hogg,* 458–59; Bernhard, *Ima Hogg,* 29.

79 WCH to SH, May 10, 1895, 4Zg89, folder James Stephen Hogg Letters, 1895, IHP (BCAH).

80 Years later Annie McCoy Brown contributed "Some Incidents from the Life of Governor James Stephen Hogg as Related by Mrs. L. Milton Brown, 1941," 3B116; IHP (BCAH); SH to JSH, May 17, 1895, 4Zg89, folder James Stephen Hogg Letters, 1895, IHP (BCAH).

81 SH to WCH, May 17, 1895, 3B127, folder 1, IHP (BCAH).

82 WCH to SH, May 21, 1895, 3B130, FL, IHP (BCAH).

83 MH to JSH, May 24, 1895, ibid.

84 JSH to SH, May 27, 1895, ibid.

85 SH to WCH, June 26, 1895, 3B127, folder 1, IHP (BCAH).

86 JSH to IH, June 13, 1895, quoted in Cotner, *James Stephen Hogg,* 459.

87 JSH to SH, June 14, 1895, box 14, LP 12, pt. 2, MS 008 (WRC).

88 JSH to SH, June 17, 1895, ibid.

89 SH to WCH, June 26, June 18, 1895, 3B127, folder 1, IHP (BCAH).

90 Minnie Carrington to SH, June 18, 1895, 4Zg89, folder 1, IHP (BCAH).

91 JSH to IH, June 19, 1895, box 14, LP 12, pt. 2, MS 008 (WRC).

92 JSH to SH, June 28, 1895, 3B130, FL, IHP (BCAH).

93 JSH to SH, June 26, 1895, 4Zg89, folder Copies of Family Letters, IHP (BCAH).

94 JSH to SH, July 7, 1895, 3B130, FL, IHP (BCAH).

95 SH to WCH, July 8, 1895, 3B127, folder 1, IHP (BCAH).

96 JSH to IH, July 10, 1895, box 14, LP 12, pt. 2, MS 008 (WRC).

97 JSH to WBD, July 11, 1895, ibid.

98 JSH to SH, July 11, 1895, ibid.

[99] JSH to SH, July 20, 1895, 3B130, FL, IHP (BCAH).

[100] JSH to Marion Davis, July 22, 1895, box 14, LP 12, pt. 2 MS 008 (WRC).

[101] IH to JSH, July 25, 1895, 3B 111, folder Correspondence: Family, 1882–1904, IHP (BCAH).

[102] WBD to JSH, July 26, 1895, 3B111, ibid.

[103] JSH to SH, July 27, 1895, 3B130, FL, IHP (BCAH).

[104] JSH to SH, July 31, 1895, ibid.

[105] JSH to JM, Aug. 2, 1895, box 14, LP 12, pt. 2, MS 008 (WRC).

[106] JAS to JSH, Aug. 21, 1895, 2J 214, "Family Letters Received: Original material," James Stephen Hogg Papers 1836-1969 (BCAH).

[107] WCH to Mrs. Marsh, Sept. 6, 1895, 3B118, William Clifford Hogg, 1888–1974, folder Family Papers: Correspondence, 1888–1899, IHP (BCAH).

PART 3

[1] Inscription on cover of bound volume of letters and telegrams about Sallie Hogg's death, compiled by Ima Hogg, 3B127, folder 4, IHP (BCAH). The official date of death was September 21, 1895.

[2] IH, "Reminiscences," 11, 3B168, folder 4, IHP (BCAH).

[3] *Austin Daily Statesman*, Sept. 25, 1895.

[4] JSH to J. W. Blake, Oct. 8, 1895, box 14, LP 12, pt. 2, MS 008 (WRC).

[5] JSH to JMF, Oct. 14, 1895, ibid.

[6] IH, "Reminiscences," 35–36, 3B168, folder 4, IHP (BCAH).

[7] Ibid., 25.

[8] Ibid. 11, 25, ibid; Herschel C. Walling (comp.), *History of Coronal Institute: Early Private School, 1866–1918* (San Marcos, Tex.: Hays County Historical and Genealogical Society, 1991), 1, 2, 39.

[9] IH, "Family Reminiscences," 3B130, folder 10, IHP (BCAH).

[10] JSH to MFD, Nov. 8. 1895, box 14, LP 12, pt. 2, MS 008 (WRC).

[11] WCH to IH, Dec. 17, 1895, 3B111, folder Family Papers: William Clifford Hogg Correspondence, 1888–1899, IHP (BCAH).

[12] JSH to MFD, Feb. 20, 1896, box 14, LP 17, pt. 1, MS 008 (WRC).

[13] IHP, Manuscript Collection No. 21, Series No. 6, folder 2 (MFAH).

[14] *Galveston Daily News*, Feb. 23, 1896; *Houston Daily Post,* Feb. 23, 1896; *Fort Worth Gazette*, Feb. 23, 1896.

[15] JSH to MFD, Feb. 29, 1896, box 17, LP 12, pt. 1, MS 008 (WRC).

[16] JSH to AH, Mar. 3, 1896, ibid.

[17] JSH to RMK, Mar. 3, 1896; JHS to Alvin Owsley, Mar. 13, 1896, ibid.

[18] JSH to MFD, Mar. 6, 1896, ibid.

[19] JSH to MFD, Mar. 20, 1896, ibid.

[20] JSH to JAS, Apr. 7, 1896, box 14, LP 12, pt. 2, MS 008 (WRC).

[21] JSH to JWH, Apr. 2, 1896; Apr. 8, 1896 ibid.

[22] JSH to AH, Apr. 25, 1896, ibid.

[23] JSH to AH, May, 26 1896, box 14, LP 13, pt. 1, MS 008 (WRC).

[24] IH, memoir draft (untitled, unpaginated typescript) 3B111, folder 3, James Stephen Hogg correspondence, 1870–1901, IHP (BCAH).

[25] George M. Bailey "Biography of James Stephen Hogg, 1940," 4Zg85, III, 807, IHP (BCAH).

[26] JSH to WBD, May 28, 1896, box 14, LP 13, pt.1, MS 008 (WRC).

[27] JSH to JWH, June 1, 1896, ibid.

[28] JSH to R. B. Levy, June 1, 1896, ibid.
[29] IH, "Family Reminiscences," 3B130, folder 10, IHP (BCAH).
[30] IH, memoir draft, 3B111, folder 3, James Stephen Hogg correspondence, 1870–1901, IHP (BCAH).
[31] Ibid.
[32] IH, "Reminiscences," 36–37, 3B168, folder 4, IHP (BCAH).
[33] Ibid., 11 (house on Nineteenth Street), 30 (gardens, pets at Nineteenth Street house), 3B168, folder 4, IHP (BCAH).
[34] JSH to George Wilson, June 3, 1899, box 16, LP 15, pt. III, MS 008 (WRC); IH, "Mansion—Austin," typescript, 4Zg89, folder Chapter 6, IHP (BCAH).
[35] IH, "Reminiscences," 30, 3B168, folder 4, IHP (BCAH).
[36] IH, memoir draft, 3B111, folder 3, James Stephen Hogg correspondence, 1870–1901, IHP (BCAH).
[37] IH, "Reminiscences," 32, 3B168, folder 4, IHP (BCAH).
[38] Ibid.
[39] Ibid., 25.
[40] IH, "Family Reminiscences," 3B130, folder 10, IHP (BCAH).
[41] Ibid.
[42] JSH to R. Kelso, June 6, 1896, box 14, LP 13, pt. II, MS 008 (WRC).
[43] Cotner (ed.), *Acts and State Papers,* 25.
[44] JSH to AH, July 31, 1896, box 14, LP 13, pt. I, MS 008 (WRC).
[45] JSH to AH, Aug. 4, 1896, ibid.
[46] JSH to MH and TH, Aug. 26, 1896, FL, 3B130, IHP (BCAH).
[47] JSH to JWH, Dec. 9, 1896; Dec. 16, 1896, box 14, LP 13, pt. II, MS 008 (WRC).
[48] JSH to JWH, Mar. 8, 1897, box 15, LP 13 A, pt. I, MS 008 (WRC).
[49] JSH to IH, Mar. 13, 1897, ibid.
[50] JSH to IH, Mar. 20, 1897, ibid.
[51] JSH to JWH, Mar. 24, 1897, ibid.
[52] JSH to IH, Mar. 29, 1897, ibid.
[53] JSH to JM, Apr. 17, 1897, ibid.
[54] JSH to AH, Apr, 17, 1897, ibid.
[55] JSH to WBD, May 24, 1897, box 15, LP 13 A, pt. II, MS 008 (WRC).
[56] JSH to RMK, June 29, 1897, ibid.
[57] JSH to BH, Oct, 16, 1897, ibid.
[58] JSH to JWH, Oct. 21, 1897, ibid.
[59] J. H. Robertson to J. S. Davis, Nov. 16, 1898, box 15, LP 18, MS 008 (WRC).
[60] JSH to WCH, Nov. 21, 1897, box 15, LP 14, pt. I, MS 008 (WRC).
[61] Ibid.
[62] WCH to IH, Nov. 27, 1897, FL, 3B130, IHP (BCAH).
[63] JSH to IH, Dec. 3, 1897, ibid.
[64] JSH to JWH, Dec. 8, 1897, 3B111, folder 3, IHP, BCAH.
[65] WCH to IH, Dec. 11, 1897, FL, 3B130, IHP (BCAH).
[66] WCH to IH, Dec. 31, 1897, ibid.
[67] WCH to IH, 1897 and 1898, ibid.
[68] IH, "Reminiscences," 25, 3B168, folder 4, IHP (BCAH); Composition book inscribed by Ima Hogg, undated, IHP, folder 2, Series No. 6, Manuscript Collection No. 21 (MFAH).
[69] JSH to WCH, Jan. 11, 1898, box 15, LP 14, pt. I, MS 008 (WRC); "Recollections of John Wesley Spivey," typescript, 3B116, folder 1, IHP (BCAH).
[70] JSH to WCH, Feb. 18, 1898, box 15, LP 14, pt. 1, MS 008 (WRC). By 1901, J. F. Onion had taken another partner into his practice. "Onion & Henry" were listed

in the Kampmann Building, where Will Hogg also had his office. San Antonio City Directory, 1901–1902 (microfilm: Drawer C38 D11, Clayton Library Center for Genealogical Research, Houston, Texas).

[71] JSH to J. D. Moody, Feb. 16, 1898; JSH to WCH, Feb. 18, 1898; JSH to JAS, Feb. 18, 1898, box 15, LP 14, pt. 1, MS 008 (WRC).

[72] IH, "Trips to Mexico and Hawaii," AZg89, folder Chapter 6, 1896–1900, IHP (BCAH).

[73] JSH to Charles Culberson, Apr. 23, 1898, box 15, LP 14, pt. I, MS 008 (WRC).

[74] JSH to J. E. Banks, June 7, 1898, box 15, LP 14, pt. II, MS 008 (WRC).

[75] He was still in the military in April 1899, stationed in Galveston. JSH to BH, Apr. 17, 1899, box 16, LP 15, pt. III, MS 008 (WRC).

[76] JSH to BH, Apr. 7, 1898, box 15, LP 14, pt. I, MS 008 (WRC).

[77] J. H. Robertson to JSH, May 6, 1898; May 27, 1898, box 15, LP 18, MS 008 (WRC).

[78] JSH to IH, May 25, 1898, 3B111, folder 3, IHP (BCAH).

[79] Austin City Directory, 1898 (microfilm: Drawer C38 D10, Clayton Library Center for Genealogical Research Houston, Texas); <http://en.wikipedia.org/wiki/Beach_Hotel_(Galveston)#cite_note-sinclairbib-2> (accessed May 3, 2013).

[80] JSH to JWH, June 25, 1898, box 15, LP 14, pt. II, MS 008 (WRC).

[81] JSH to BH, July 1, 1898; JSH to Brownlee Ferguson, July 1, 1898, ibid.

[82] JSH to Marion Davis, July 6, 1898, ibid.

[83] JSH to J. F. Leslie, July 26, 1898, ibid.

[84] JSH to WCH, [July 2?] 1898, ibid.

[85] MFD to MH and TH, undated, 1898, FL, B130, IHP (BCAH).

[86] JSH to WCH, July 26, 1898, box 15, LP 14, pt. II, MS 008 (WRC).

[87] IH, "My Freak Book," 1898, 3B153, Diaries 1898, 1908, 1912, 1930, folder travel diary, 1898, IHP (BCAH).

[88] IH, "Trips to Mexico and Hawaii," 4Zg89, folder Chapter 6, 1876-1900, IHP (BCAH).

[89] Bernhard, *Ima Hogg: The Governor's Daughter*, 43.

[90] JSH to AH, Oct. 23, 1898, box 15, LP 14, pt. II, MS 008 (WRC).

[91] If Annie was pregnant when she married in the summer of 1896, the infant did not survive. She gave birth to a son in November 1897. Annie herself died in 1900. The census of 1900 shows her husband, listed as "widower," and two-year-old Edward Jr., residing in Mississippi. United States Twelfth United States Census (1900; Clayton Library Center for Genealogical Research, Houston, Texas.)

[92] JSH to BH, Oct 26, 1898, box 15, LP 14, pt. II; JSH to BH, Nov. 12, 1898, box 15, LP 15, pt. I, MS 008 (WRC).

[93] JSH to JM, Nov. 3, 1898, box 15, LP 15, pt. I, MS 008 (WRC).

[94] JSH to WCH, Dec. 8, 1898, ibid.

[95] JSH to WCH, Dec. 18, 1898, ibid.

[96] JSH to WCH, Jan 19, 1899, box 16, LP 15, pt. II, MS 008 (WRC).

[97] WCH to IH, Jan 31, 1899, B130, FL, IHP (BCAH).

[98] San Antonio City Directory, 1899–1900, 1901–1902, microfilm, Drawer C38 D11; Austin City Directory, 1898, microfilm, Drawer C38, D10 (Clayton Library Center for Genealogical Research, Houston, Texas).

[99] JSH to BH, Mar. 23, 1899, box 16, LP 15, pt. III, MS 008 (WRC).

[100] JSH to WCH, Apr. 3, 1899, ibid.

[101] JM to JSH, undated, 1899, 3B111, folder James Stephen Hogg Correspondence: transcriptions, IHP (BCAH).

[102] JSH to RMK, May 11, 1899; JSH to JWH, May 26, 1899; JSH to BH, May 22, 1899, box 16, LP 15, pt. III, MS 008 (WRC).

[103] JSH to John Orr, Jr., May 24, 1899, ibid.

[104] JSH to WCH, May 26, 1899, ibid.

[105] JSH to R. H. Moseley, June 1, 1899, ibid.

[106] JSH to WCH, June 6, 1899, ibid.

[107] Barkley, *History of Travis County*, 194, 198.

[108] MH and TH to JSH, June 22, 1899, B130, FL, IHP (BCAH).

[109] MFD to MH and TH, June, undated, 1899, ibid.

[110] IH, "Reminiscences," 23–24, 3B168, folder 4, IHP (BCAH).

[111] WCH to IH, Jan. 18, 1899, 4Zg89, folder James Stephen Hogg Letters, 1896–1900, IHP (BCAH).

[112] WCH to IH, July 15, 1899, 3B130, FL, IHP (BCAH).

[113] JSH to R. H. Moseley, Aug. 18, 1899, box 16, LP 15, pt. III, MS 008 (WRC).

[114] B. Gross [Grock, Grose, Groce?] to IH, Aug. 9, 1899, 4Zg78, folder Correspondence, 1899–1904, IHP (BCAH).

[115] MH to IH, Aug. 19, 1899, B130, FL, IHP (BCAH).

[116] JSH to IH, Aug. 22, 1899, box 16, LP 15, pt. III, MS 008 (WRC).

[117] JSH to MH and TH, Sept. 8, 1899, B130, FL, IHP (BCAH).

[118] TH to WCH, Oct. 5, 1899, 3B126, folder Correspondence, 1899–1970, IHP (BCAH).

[119] "Miss Lillie Stinson Burkett, March 27, 1946," 3B116, folder 2, IHP (BCAH).

[120] JSH to JWH, Oct. 25, 1899, box 16, LP 16, pt. I MS 008 (WRC).

[121] Potatoes ordered, Oct. 13, 1899; ham and lard ordered, Oct 25, 1899; JSH to BH, Oct. 24, 1899, ibid.

[122] TH to WCH, Nov. 9, 1899, 3B126, folder Thomas Elisha Hogg: Correspondence, 1899–1970, IHP (BCAH).

[123] JSH to JM, Nov. 20, 1899, box 16, LP 16, pt. I, MS 008 (WRC).

[124] JSH to Velma Hogg, Dec. 21, 1899, ibid.

[125] "The Big Panther Hunt," *Austin Statesman*, Dec. 28, 1899.

[126] TH to JAS, Jan. 7, 1900, 3B126, folder Thomas Elisha Hogg: Correspondence, 1899–1970, IHP (BCAH).

[127] IH, "Reminiscences," 29, 3B168, folder 4, IHP (BCAH); University of Texas alumni magazine, *Alcalde* (November 1923): 363.

[128] IH, "Trips to Mexico and Hawaii," AZg89, folder Chapter 6, IHP (BCAH).

[129] IH, "Family Reminiscences," 3B130, folder 10, IHP (BCAH).

[130] JSH to IH, Feb. 18, 1900, FL, 3B130, IHP (BCAH).

[131] JSH to MFD, Jan. 27, 1900, 4Zg89, folder James Stephen Hogg Letters, 1896–1900, IHP (BCAH).

[132] JSH to IH, Mar. 11, 1900, B130, FL, IHP (BCAH).

[133] IH, "Family Reminiscences," 3B130, folder 10, IHP (BCAH).

[134] JSH to John Craddock, April 9, 1900; JSH to Charles Glidden, May 24, 1900, box 16, LP 16, pt. I, MS 008 (WRC); Rupert Hughes, *The Real New York* (New York: Smart Set Publishing Company, 1904), 52.

[135] Cotner (ed.), *Acts and Speeches*, 452–54.

[136] JSH ordered 100 pounds of hams on Apr. 9, 1900, box 16, LP 16, pt. I, MS 008 (WRC).

[137] JSH to WBD, June 1 1900, box 16, LP 16, pt. II, MS 008 (WRC).

[138] WCH to IH, May 28, 1900, 3B118, folder Correspondence, 1900–1906, IHP (BCAH).

[139] JSH to Brownlee Ferguson, June 1, 1900; JSH to S. M. Cunningham, June 1, 1900, box 16, LP 16, pt. II, MS 008 (WRC).

[140] JSH to IH, July 9, 1900, ibid.

[141] JSH to IH, July 13, 1900, ibid.

[142] JSH to IH, July 17, 1900, ibid.

[143] *Galveston Daily News*, Aug. 10, 1900; Cotner, *James Stephen Hogg*, 507–508. On the conflict at the Democratic convention, see 503–511.

[144] "Questions by Dr. Cotner—Answers by Miss Ima Hogg, June 20, 1949," 38, 3B116, folder 2, IHP (BCAH).

[145] Edward Crane to John Lomax, Mar. 23, 1939, Lomax Papers (BCAH); *Houston Daily Post*, Aug. 10, 1900.

[146] "Questions by Dr. Cotner—Answers by Miss Ima Hogg, June 20, 1949," 29, 3B116, folder 2, IHP (BCAH).

[147] Note in IH's handwriting on copy of MFD's letter to JSH, Aug. 23, 1900, 3B130, FL, IHP (BCAH).

[148] Hogg's reform amendments did not become law until his friend Thomas A. Campbell's first term as governor in 1907. Worth Robert Miller, in "Building a Progressive Coalition in Texas: The Populist-Reform Democrat Rapprochement, 1900–1907," *Journal of Southern History* 52, No. 2 (May 1986): 163–82, called Hogg "a patriarch of Texas progressivism" (163); see also 181, n45.

[149] JSH to MFD, Aug. 13, 1900, box 16, LP 16, pt. II, MS 008 (WRC). On the page following this August 13 letter in LP 16 there is a typewritten note: "Pages 467 to 472 of Letter Press No. 16 torn from book." The missing pages may have contained material about Hogg's critics and what they said about him. Someone, most likely Ima Hogg, removed the pages.

[150] MFD to JSH, Aug. 23, 1900, B130, FL, IHP (BCAH).

[151] JSH to MFD, Aug. 1900, undated, box 16, LP 16, pt. III, MS 008 (WRC).

[152] MFD to WCH, Aug. 1900, undated, 3B130, FL, IHP (BCAH).

[153] JSH to JWH, Aug. 1900, undated, box 16, LP 16, pt. III, MS 008 (WRC).

[154] JSH to BH, Aug. 19, 1900, ibid.

[155] JSH to JWH, undated; JSH to JWH, Sept. 7, 1900, ibid.

[156] JSH to R. B. Levy, Sept. 14, 1900, ibid.

[157] JSH to T. W. House, Sept. 12, 1900; JSH to James McDugald, Nov. 13, 1900, ibid.

[158] JSH to IH, Nov. 2, 1900, 3B130, FL, IHP (BCAH).

[159] JSH to W. J. Bryan, Nov. 26, 1900, box 16, LP 16, pt. III, MS 008 (WRC).

PART 4

[1] JSH to WBD, Apr. 19, 1905, 4Zg89, folder 1905, IHP (BCAH).

[2] JSH to WBD, Jan. 25, 1901, box 16, LP 16, pt. III, MS 008 (WRC).

[3] IH, "Reminiscences," 25–26, B168, folder 4, IHP (BCAH).

[4] W. T. Campbell was a banker from Lampasas, and, according to Ima Hogg, "a very handsome young man. "Questions by Dr. Cotner—Answers by Miss Ima Hogg, June 20, 1949," 29, 3B116, folder 2, IHP (BCAH). According to Robert C. Cotner, the records of the Hogg-Swayne Syndicate's history have been lost. Cotner, *James Stephen Hogg*, 518–558.

[5] Cotner, *James Stephen Hogg*, 524.

[6] TH to IH, June 13 190l, 3B130, FL, IHP (BCAH).

[7] John O'Neil & Co. to MH, Sept. 7, 1901, ibid.

[8] IH, "Family Reminiscences," 3B130, folder 10, IHP (BCAH).

[9] Bertie Lucy to IH, Dec. 1901, 4Zg78, folder Correspondence: 1899–1904, IHP (BCAH).

[10] IH, "Family Reminiscences," 3B130, folder 10, IHP (BCAH). The National Conservatory was declining in prestige when Ima went there. As a music scholar noted in a 1990 article about the conservatory, "Around the turn of the century, the institution began a pathetic descent into obscurity." Emanuel Rubin, "Jeanette Meyers Thurber and the National Conservatory of Music," *American Music* 8 (Autumn 1990): 294–325.

[11] TH to IH, Oct. 3, 1901, 3B126, folder Thomas Elisha Hogg Correspondence, 1899–1970, IHP (BCAH).

[12] MH to IH, Oct. 24, 1901, 4Zg89, folder 1901, IHP (BCAH).

[13] JSH to IH, May 29, 1902, FL, 3B130; IH, "Reminiscences," 26, 3B168, folder 4, IHP (BCAH).

[14] JSH to IH, Oct. 31, 1901, 3B111, folder James Stephen Hogg, IHP (BCAH).

[15] Alfred Suart to IH, Nov. 21, 1901, 3B111, folder 3, IHP (BCAH).

[16] "Oil for Smelting Purposes," *The New York Times*, May 8, 1901; "Standard Oil's New Rival," *The New York Times*, Sept. 5, 1901.

[17] During Hogg's stay at the Waldorf-Astoria his gold watch, valued at $1,000, was stolen from his room on October 20 and later recovered from a thief in Philadelphia. "Stole Ex-Gov. Hogg's Watch," *New York Times*, Oct. 25, 1901. This expensive timepiece may have been the one presented to Hogg at the Austin encampment in 1894.

[18] JSH to MFD, Dec. 2, 1901, 3B130, FL, IHP (BCAH).

[19] Hermilla Kelso, "Biography of Martha Frances Davis," 4Zg89, folder Biography of Martha Frances Davis, IHP (BCAH).

[20] TH to WCH, Jan. 20, 1902, 3B126, folder Thomas Elisha Hogg Correspondence, 1899–1970, IHP (BCAH).

[21] MH to IH, Jan. 20, 1902, 3B130, FL, IHP (BCAH).

[22] Hogg was reported as selling part of the Hogg-Swayne holdings to Standard Oil, which would operate in Texas under a new name. But J. W. Swayne, in an interview at the Waldorf-Astoria in New York, claimed to have "no knowledge of any such transaction." "Report of Big Oil Deal by Hogg-Swayne Combine," *The New York Times*, Jan. 6, 1902.

[23] JSH to IH, Jan. 12, 1902, 3B111, folder James Stephen Hogg: Correspondence: General: Transcriptions, 1902–1906, IHP (BCAH).

[24] JSH to IH, Jan. 21, 1902, 3B130, FL, IHP (BCAH).

[25] TH to IH, Jan. 23, 1902; ibid.

[26] MH to IH, Feb. 9, 1902, ibid.

[27] Ima Hogg, "Family Reminiscences," 3B130, folder 10, IHP (BCAH).

[28] Ibid.

[29] JSH to IH, Feb. 11 1902, 3B130, FL, IHP (BCAH).

[30] JSH to IH, Mar. 1, 1902, Vertical file, Hogg Family Personal Papers: Correspondence, 1888–1909 (MFAH).

[31] JSH to IH, Mar. 5, 1902, 3B130, FL, IHP (BCAH). The ex-governor's refusal to wear formal court dress made the papers back home: "Balked at Knee Breeches," *The New York Times*, Mar. 2, 1902.

[32] JSH to IH, Mar. 6, 1902, Vertical file, Hogg Family Personal Papers: Correspondence, 1888–1909 (MFAH).

[33] JSH to IH, Mar. 11, 1902, 3B130, FL, IHP (BCAH).

[34] JSH to IH, Mar. 14, 1902, Vertical file, Hogg Family Personal Papers: Correspondence, 1888–1909 (MFAH).

[35] JSH to IH, Mar. 25, 1902, ibid.

[36] According to *The New York Times,* the English connection resulted in the Consolidated Texas Oil Company, with a capital stock of $6,000, to take over the Hogg-Swayne holdings, with Hogg and his retaining half of the stock in the new company, with a cash payment to them of $1,200,000 for the other half. "Consolidated Oil Company," *The New York Times,* June 10, 1902.

[37] JSH to IH, April 1, 1902, Vertical file, Hogg Family Personal Papers: Correspondence, 1888–1909 (MFAH).

[38] According to Hogg's biographer, the "English option" was not used. Cotner, *James Stephen Hogg,* 544. See also, 545–551. But "Texas Oil Merger: Hogg-Swayne Syndicate Amalgamates with Texas Oilfield Company of England," *The New York Times,* Aug. 13, 1902, reported otherwise. Hogg also put part of his holdings into the Export Oil and Pipe Line Company, headed by former senator Charles A. Towne. *The New York Times,* Aug. 31, 1902.

[39] "Ex-Gov. Hogg Home Again," *The New York Times,* Apr. 18, 1902.

[40] JSH to IH, May 14, 1894, 3B111, folder James Stephen Hogg Letters, 1902–1906, IHP (BCAH).

[41] JSH to IH, May 6, 1902, 3B111, James Stephen Hogg, folder Correspondence: General: Transcriptions, 1902–1906, IHP (BCAH).

[42] JSH to IH, May 29, 1902, 3B130, FL, IHP (BCAH).

[43] Mollie Lehnis, whose father was a merchant in Quitman, remembered that Hogg was baptized at a church there in 1860 at the same time she was. Vickery, *Wood County Democrat,* 63.

[44] Letters from R.W. Alexander to IH, June 6, 1902; Aug. 4, 1902, and one undated from Nov. 1902, are in 4Zg78, folder Correspondence, 1899–1904, IHP (BCAH). On February 6, 1903, Vivian Breziger wrote to Ima, about "poor Alec!" . . . Sure and you are driving him distracted with your foolishness— . . ." 3B 131, folder Personal Papers: Correspondence: General, 1895–1903, IHP (BCAH).

[45] "Consolidated Oil Company," *The New York Times,* June 10, 1902.

[46] Arthur M. Johnson, "The Early Texas Oil Industry: Pipelines and the Birth of an Integrated Oil Industry, 1901–1911," *Journal of Southern History* 32 (November 1966): 516–528.

[47] JSH to WCH, IH, MH, and TH, June 21 1902, 3B130, FL, IHP (BCAH).

[48] JSH to IH, June 24, 1902, 3B111, folder James Stephen Hogg letters, 1902–1906: transcriptions, IHP (BCAH).

[49] IH, "Family Reminiscences," 3B130, folder 10, IHP (BCAH).

[50] Ima's father wrote to her at Miss Day's address in October. JSH to IH, Oct. 7, 1902, B3111, James Stephen Hogg letters, 1902–1906: transcriptions, IHP (BCAH).

[51] MH to IH, Nov 4, 1902, 3B130, FL, IHP (BCAH).

[52] JSH to IH, Nov. 16, 1902, ibid.

[53] JSH to IH, Nov. 24, 1902; Nov. 26, 1902, 3B111, James Stephen Hogg letters, 1902–1906: transcriptions, IHP (BCAH).

[54] WCH to IH, Nov. (undated) 1902, 3B130, FL, IHP (BCAH).

[55] IH, "Family Reminiscences," 3B130, folder 10, IHP (BCAH).

[56] MFD to Hermilla Hogg Kelso, Dec. (undated) 1902, 3B130, FL, IHP (BCAH).

[57] Vivian's two letters may refer to R. W. Alexander. Vivian Breziger to IH, Jan. 23, 1903 and Feb. 6, 1903, 3B131, folder Correspondence: General, 1895–1903, IHP (BCAH).

[58] WCH to IH, Jan. 25, 1903, 3B130, FL, IHP (BCAH).

[59] JSH to IH, Feb. 7, 1903, ibid.

[60] MFD to IH, Feb. 16, 1903, ibid.

[61] JSH to IH, Mar. 13, 1903, ibid.

[62] JSH to IH, Mar. 20, Apr. 9, Apr. 13, 1903, ibid.

[63] JSH to IH, Mar. 20, 1903, ibid.

[64] Barkley, *History of Travis County and Austin*, 244.

[65] JSH to IH, Apr. 9, 1903, 3B130, FL, IHP (BCAH).

[66] JSH to IH, Apr. 13, 1903, ibid.

[67] "Miss Ima Hogg Sick," *Galveston Daily News*, July 11, 1903; JAS to IH, July 28, 1903, 3B130, folder 4, IHP (BCAH).

[68] IH to Anson Phelps Jr., Aug. 22, 1903, 3B131, folder: Correspondence: General, 1895–1903.

[69] JSH to IH, Sept. 1, 1903, 4Zg89, folder Hogg Family Letters, January–September, 1903, IHP (BCAH).

[70] WCH to IH, Sept. 25, 1903, 3B130, FL, IHP (BCAH).

[71] TH to IH, Sept. 29, 1903, 3B126, Correspondence, 1899–1970, IHP (BCAH).

[72] MH to IH, Oct. 9 1903, 3B130, FL, IHP (BCAH).

[73] JSH to IH, Oct. 26, 1903, ibid.

[74] *The New York Times*, Mar. 12, 1904.

[75] MH to IH, Dec.11, 1903; 3B130, FL, IHP (BCAH).

[76] TH to IH, Jan. 4, 1904, ibid.

[77] TH to JSH, Jan. 9, 1904, 3B126, folder Correspondence, 1899–1970, IHP (BCAH).

[78] JSH to IH, Jan. 13, 1904, 3B130, FL, IHP (BCAH).

[79] IH to MH, Jan. 24, 1904, 4Zg89, folder January–June 1904, IHP (BCAH). This letter of Ima's to Mike does not appear in her edition of "Family Letters". In her later reminiscences, she had another version of Mike's move to the Lawrenceville School: "Mickie had gotten a commission with the help of Father to go to Annapolis, and he prepared for this and passed the examination, then we all got cold feet regarding the navy so we persuaded him to join Tom at Lawrenceville." "Questions by Dr. Cotner—Answers by Miss Ima Hogg, June 20, 1949," 31, 3B116, folder 2, IHP (BCAH).

[80] MH to IH, Jan. 31, 1904, 3B130, FL, IHP (BCAH).

[81] MH to IH, Feb. 21, 1904, ibid.

[82] WCH to TH, Mar. 8, 1904, 4Zg89, folder January–June 1904, IHP (BCAH).

[83] JSH to WBD, Mar 17, 1904; JSH to MH and TH, Mar. 19, 1904, box 16, LP 23, MS 008 (WRC).

[84] MH to IH, May 1, 1904, 3B130, FL, IHP (BCAH).

[85] TH to IH, May 10, 1904, 3B126, folder Correspondence, 1899–1970, IHP (BCAH).

[86] JSH to MH, June 3, 1904, box 16, LP 23, MS 008 (WRC).

[87] JSH to IH, June 12, 1904, 4Zg89, folder January–June, 1904, IHP (BCAH).

[88] MH to JSH, June 20, 1904, 3B130, FL, IHP (BCAH).

[89] IH to JSH, June 24 1904, ibid.

[90] WCH to JSH, June 29, 1904, box 9, LP 35, MS 008 (WRC).

[91] WCH to JSH, June 26, June 27, 1904, ibid.

[92] JSH to TH, June 30, 1904, 3B130, FL, IHP (BCAH).

[93] Letters from Harry Taylor to IH, 1904, are misfiled in 4Zg78, folder Family: Alice and Mike Hogg, Marie, 1930–1940, IHP (BCAH); Wilbur Allen's letters to IH, Apr. 7, 1904; Nov. 28, 1904; Feb. 19, 1905; Mar. 26, 1905; and Sept. 1, 1905 are in 4Zg73, folder 1, IHP (BCAH).

[94] MH to JSH, July 4, 1904, 3B130, FL, IHP (BCAH).

[95] IH to JSH July 5, 1904, 4Zg89, folder July–August 1904, IHP (BCAH).

[96] IH to JSH, July 9, 10, and 12, 1904, ibid.

[97] IH to JSH, July 17, 1904, 3B130, FL IHP (BCAH).

[98] JSH to IH, MH, TH, July 18, 1904, ibid.

[99] JSH to IH, MH, TH, July 27, 1904, ibid.

[100] WCH to JSH, July 29, 1904, box 9, LP 35, MS 008 (WRC).

[101] WCH to JAS, July 30, 1904, 4Zg89, folder 1, IHP (BCAH).

[102] WCH to Lawrenceville School, Aug. 8, 1904, 4Zg89, folder 1, IHP (BCAH).

[103] JSH to IH, Aug. 9, 1904, box 16, LP 23, MS 008 (WRC).

[104] IH to JSH, Aug. 9 1904, B3111, folder James Stephen Hogg: Correspondence: Family, 1882–1904, IHP (BCAH).

[105] MH to WCH, June 28, 1904, 4Zg89, folder Copies of Family Letters, IHP (BCAH).

[106] Miller, "Building a Progressive Coalition in Texas," 163.

[107] IH to JSH, Aug. 16, 1904, 3B130, FL, IHP (BCAH).

[108] IH to JSH, Aug. 27, 1904, ibid.

[109] MFD to IH, Sept. 15, 1904, ibid.

[110] "Questions by Dr. Cotner—Answers by Miss Ima Hogg, June 20, 1949," 19, 3B116, folder 2, IHP (BCAH).

[111] Harry K. Taylor to IH, Sept. 10, 1904, 4Zg78, folder Correspondence, 1930–1940, IHP (BCAH).

[112] The telegram was sent in care of Jack Locke, who was probably a San Antonio friend of Will's. JSH to WCH, Nov. 7, 1904, box 16, LP 23, MS 008 (WRC).

[113] TH to IH, Dec. 8, 1904; 3B126, folder Correspondence, IHP (BCAH).

[114] TH to IH, Dec. 13, 1904, ibid.

[115] *Galveston Daily News*, Nov. 27, 1904; *San Antonio Light*, Dec. 15, 1904.

[116] IH, undated note, 4Zg89, folder Sept.-Dec. 1904, IHP (BCAH).

[117] JSH to IH, Jan. 1, 1905, 3B130, folder 3, IHP (BCAH).

[118] IH wrote to MH from St. Louis on Jan. 9, 1905, 4Zg89, folder l, IHP (BCAH).

[119] WCH to MH, undated letter, 4Zg89, folder James Stephen Hogg Letters, 1882–1892, IHP (BCAH).

[120] IH, "Family Reminiscences, 3B130, folder 10, IHP (BCAH).

[121] JSH to IH, Jan. 13, 1905, 3B130, folder 3, IHP (BCAH).

[122] IH, untitled typescript, 4Zg89, folder Correspondence . . . concerning chapter two, IHP (BCAH).

[123] IH to JSH, Jan. 14, 1905, 3B130, folder 3, IHP (BCAH).

[124] *San Antonio Light,* Feb. 1, 1905.

[125] *San Antonio Light*, Feb. 5, 1905, reported that Ima had left for Houston that day. Ima's handwritten note, undated, is in 4Zg89, folder Letters 1905, IHP (BCAH).

[126] JSH to WBD, Apr. 19, 1905, 4Zg89, folder 1905, IHP (BCAH).

[127] IH to MH, Mar, 7, 1905, 4Zg89, folder 1, IHP (BCAH).

[128] JSH to WCH, Mar. 16, 1905, 4Zg89, folder 1905, IHP (BCAH).

[129] Cotner (ed.), *Acts and State Papers*, 26.

[130] WBD to JSH, Apr. 14, 1905, box 10, LP 36, MS 008 (WRC). Martha Frances Hogg Davis was now in her seventy-first year. She died in 1920 at age eighty-five.

[131] JSH to IH Apr. 16, 1905, 3B130, folder 3, IHP (BCAH).

[132] JSH to WD, Apr. 19, 1905, 4Zg89, folder 1905, IHP (BCAH).

[133] Among the guests was Houston attorney James A. Baker, who helped to found the Rice Institute (now Rice University) in 1912. *Galveston Daily News*, Apr. 30, 1905.

134 On early Houston, see David G. McComb, *Houston: A History* (Austin: University of Texas Press, 1981); Marguerite Johnston, *Houston: The Unknown City, 1836–1946* (College Station: Texas A&M University Press, 1991).

135 From the handwriting and the stationery of other notes to Ima Hogg in 1905, the author of this letter was very likely Willis B. Reeve. Undated letter to IH, 4Zg73, folder Correspondence to Ima Hogg, 1905–1907, IHP (BCAH).

136 W. B. Reeve to IH, June 13, 1905, 4Zg73, folder l, IHP (BCAH).

137 W. G. Harris to IH, Aug. 12, 1905; Aug. 24, 1905, ibid.

138 Kirkland, *The Hogg Family and Houston*, 279, n126.

139 IH to MH, Aug. 26, 1905, 4Zg89, Copies of Hogg Family letters, IHP (BCAH); W. B. Reeve to IH, undated, 4Zg73, folder Correspondence to Ima Hogg, 1905–1907, IHP (BCAH).

140 Wilbur Allen to IH, Sept. 1, 1905, 4Zg73, folder Correspondence to Ima Hogg, 1905–1907, IHP (BCAH).

141 MH to IH, Sept. 8, 1905, 4Zg89, folder Copies of Family Letters, IHP (BCAH).

142 WCH to MH, Aug. 10, 1905, 4Zg89, folder 1905, IHP (BCAH).

143 MH to IH, Apr. 8, 1917, manuscript Collection No. 21, Series No. 6, folder 3, IHP (MFAH).

144 TH to JSH, Oct. 2, 1905, 3B126, folder Correspondence, IHP (BCAH).

145 Brownlee Ferguson to IH, Oct. 10, 1905; Josie Hogg to IH, Oct. 16, 1905, 4Zg73, folder 8, IHP (BCAH).

146 Jack Maguire, "The People Who Lived in the Mansion," *The Governor's Mansion of Texas: A Historic Tour* (Austin: Friends of the Governor's Mansion, 1985), 114.

147 Quoted in Hogg's obituary, *San Antonio Gazette*, Mar. 3, 1906 Hogg's will is in Box 2J215, James Stephen Hogg Papers 1836–1969, James Stephen Hogg Collection, BCAH.

148 Dance cards and programs are in 4Zg73, folder Correspondence and Ball Programs, IHP (BCAH).

149 JSH to IH, Dec. 3, 1905, 4Zg89, folder 1905, IHP (BCAH).

150 JSH to IH, Dec. 9, 1905, ibid.

151 WCH to IH, Feb. 23, 1906, 3B118, folder 2, IHP (BCAH).

152 Quoted in Cotner, *James Stephen Hogg*, 577.

153 *Houston Chronicle*, Mar. 3, 1906; *Houston Post*, Mar. 4, 1906.

Index